	DATE DUE		

W

Th
fa
p
re

B

NO NEED FOR TENCHI!

Volume 12: No Need for Endings
VIZ Media Edition

STORY AND ART BY HITOSHI OKUDA

English Adaptation/Fred Burke
Translation/Shuko Shikata
Transcription for Reformat Edition/Alison King
Touch-up Art & Lettering/Primary Graphix: John Hunt
Design/Sam Elzway
Editor/Shaenon K. Garrity

Editor in Chief, Books/Alvin Lu
Editor in Chief, Magazines/Marc Weidenbaum
VP of Publishing Licensing/Rika Inouye
VP of Sales/Gonzalo Ferreyra
Sr. VP of Marketing/Liza Coppola
Publisher/Hyoe Narita

Published by VIZ Media, LLC
P.O. Box 77010
San Francisco, CA 94107

10 9 8 7 6 5 4 3 2 1
First printing, February 2008

www.viz.com
store.viz.com

VIZ MANGA

No Need for Tenchi!

Volume 12:
No Need for Endings

STORY AND ART BY
HITOSHI OKUDA

CONTENTS

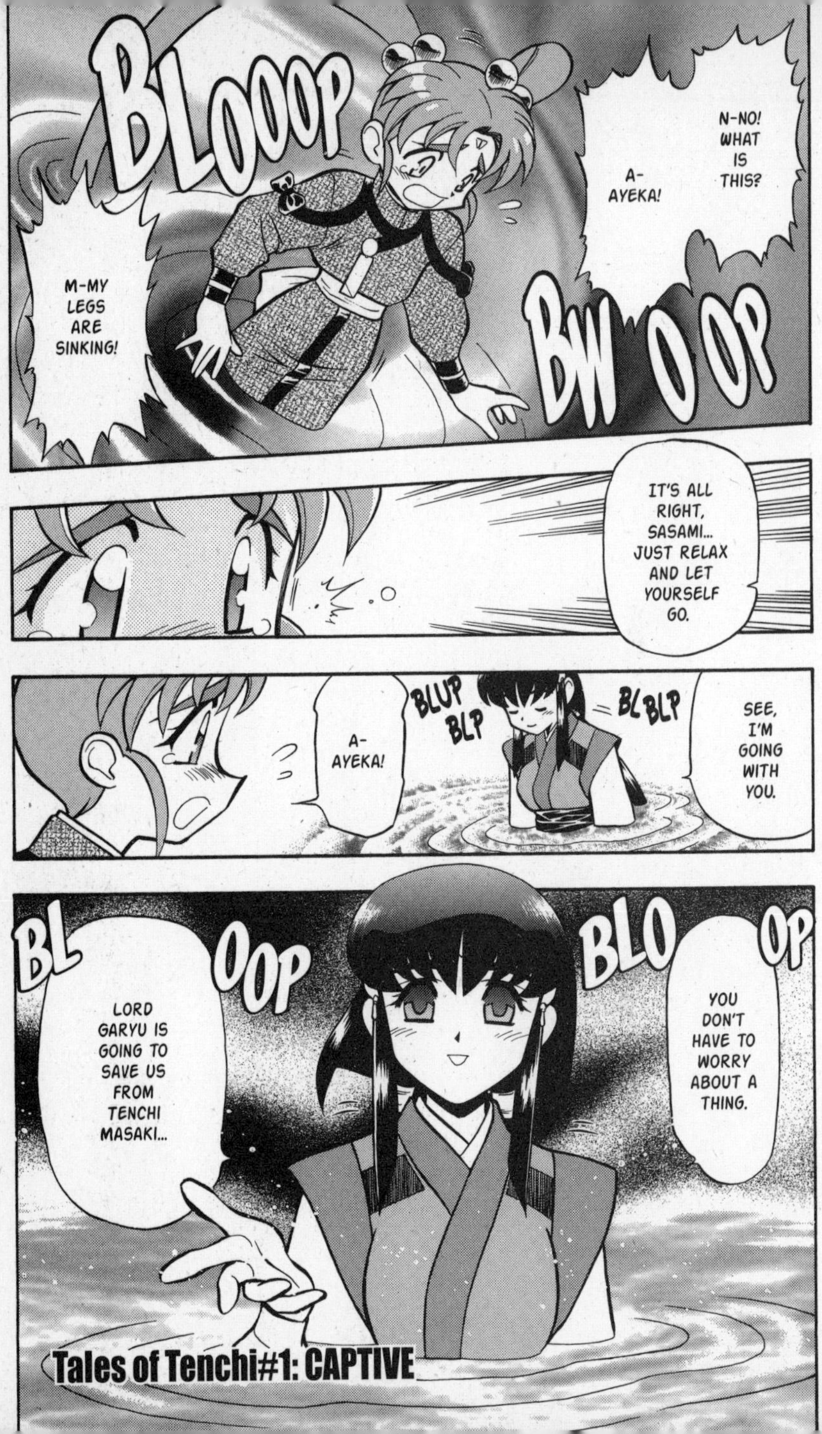
N-NO! WHAT IS THIS?
A- AYEKA!
BLOOOP
BW O OP
M-MY LEGS ARE SINKING!
IT'S ALL RIGHT, SASAMI... JUST RELAX AND LET YOURSELF GO.
SEE, I'M GOING WITH YOU.
BL BLP
BLUP BLP
A- AYEKA!
BLO OP
YOU DON'T HAVE TO WORRY ABOUT A THING.
BL OOP
LORD GARYU IS GOING TO SAVE US FROM TENCHI MASAKI...

Tales of Tenchi#1: CAPTIVE

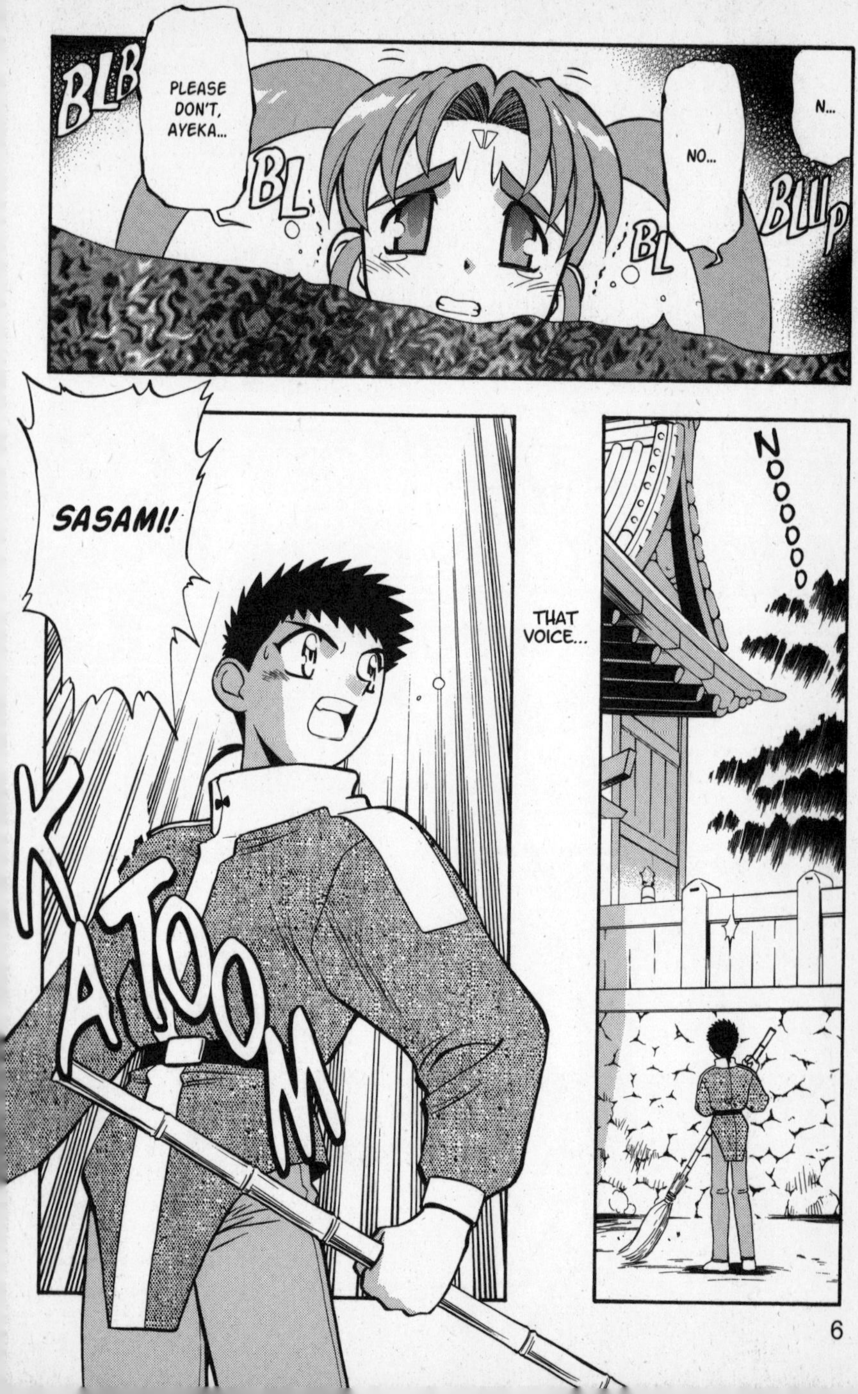
N...
NO...
BLUP
BL
BL
PLEASE DON'T, AYEKA...
BLB
NOOOOOOO
THAT VOICE...
SASAMI!
KATOOM

Tales of Tenchi#1: CAPTIVE

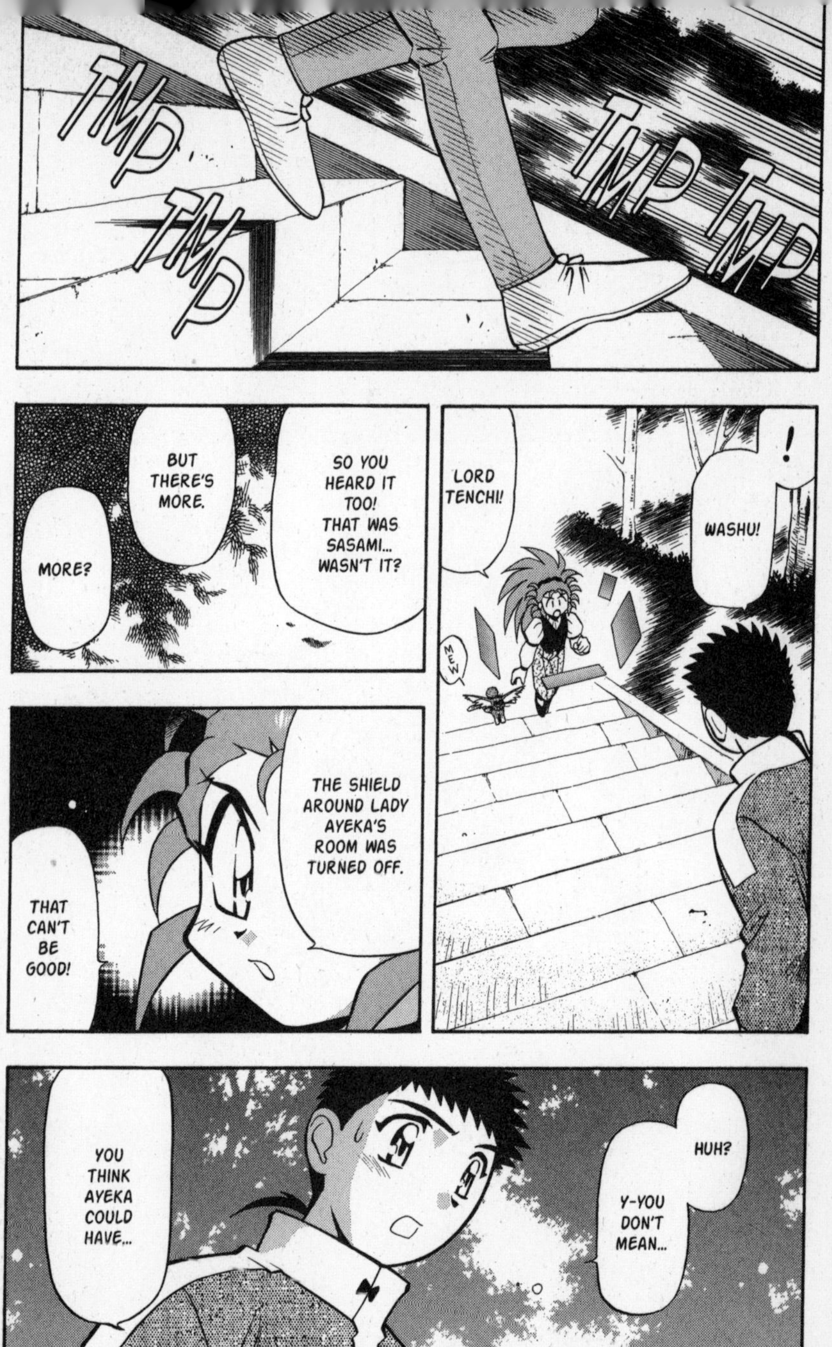
TMP TMP
TMP
TMP
!
WASHU!
LORD TENCHI!
MEW
SO YOU HEARD IT TOO! THAT WAS SASAMI... WASN'T IT?
BUT THERE'S MORE.
MORE?
THE SHIELD AROUND LADY AYEKA'S ROOM WAS TURNED OFF.
THAT CAN'T BE GOOD!
HUH?
Y-YOU DON'T MEAN...
YOU THINK AYEKA COULD HAVE...

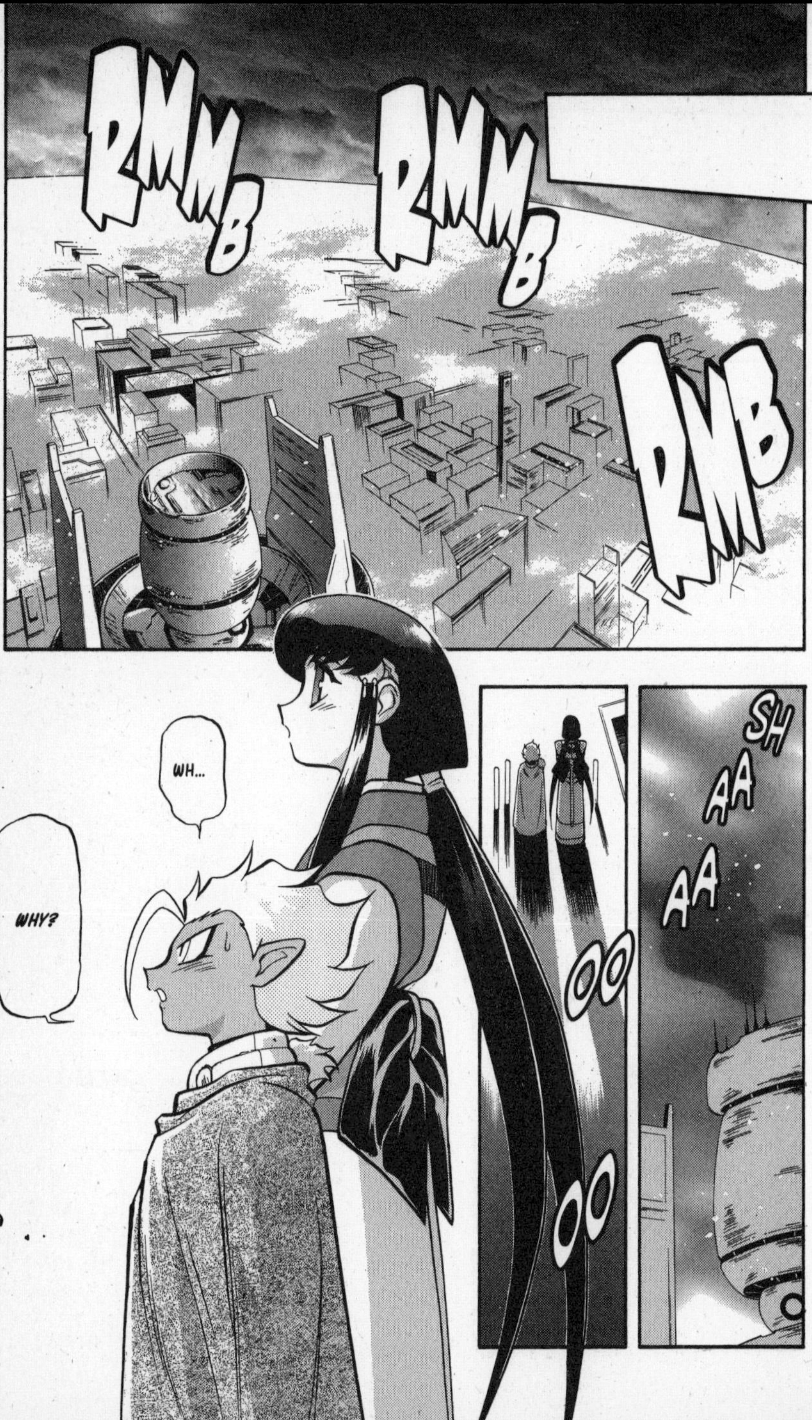
RMMB
RMMB
RMB
SHAAAAA
OOOO
WH...
WHY?

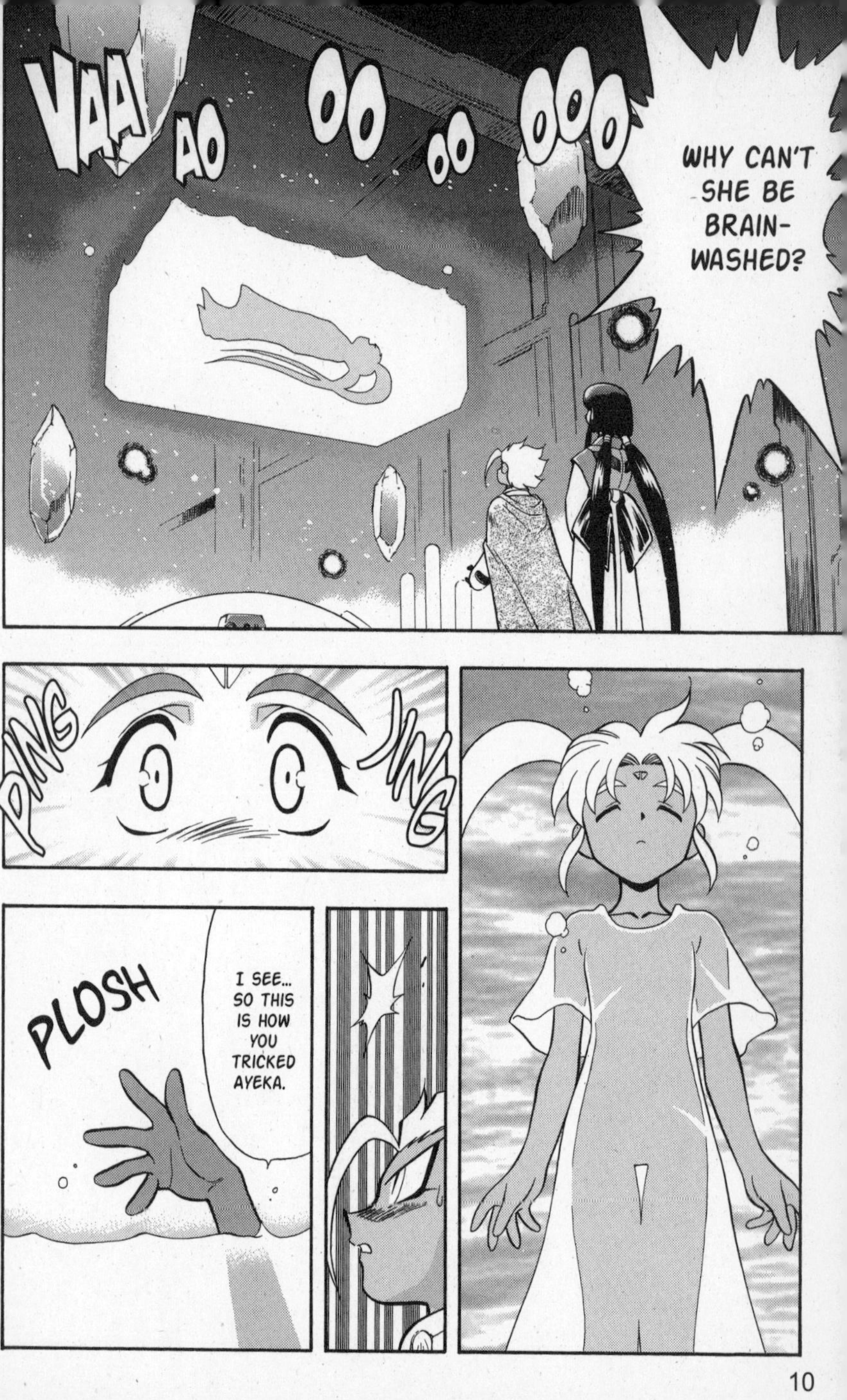
VAAAOOOOOOOO
WHY CAN'T SHE BE BRAIN-WASHED?
PING JING
I SEE... SO THIS IS HOW YOU TRICKED AYEKA.
PLOSH

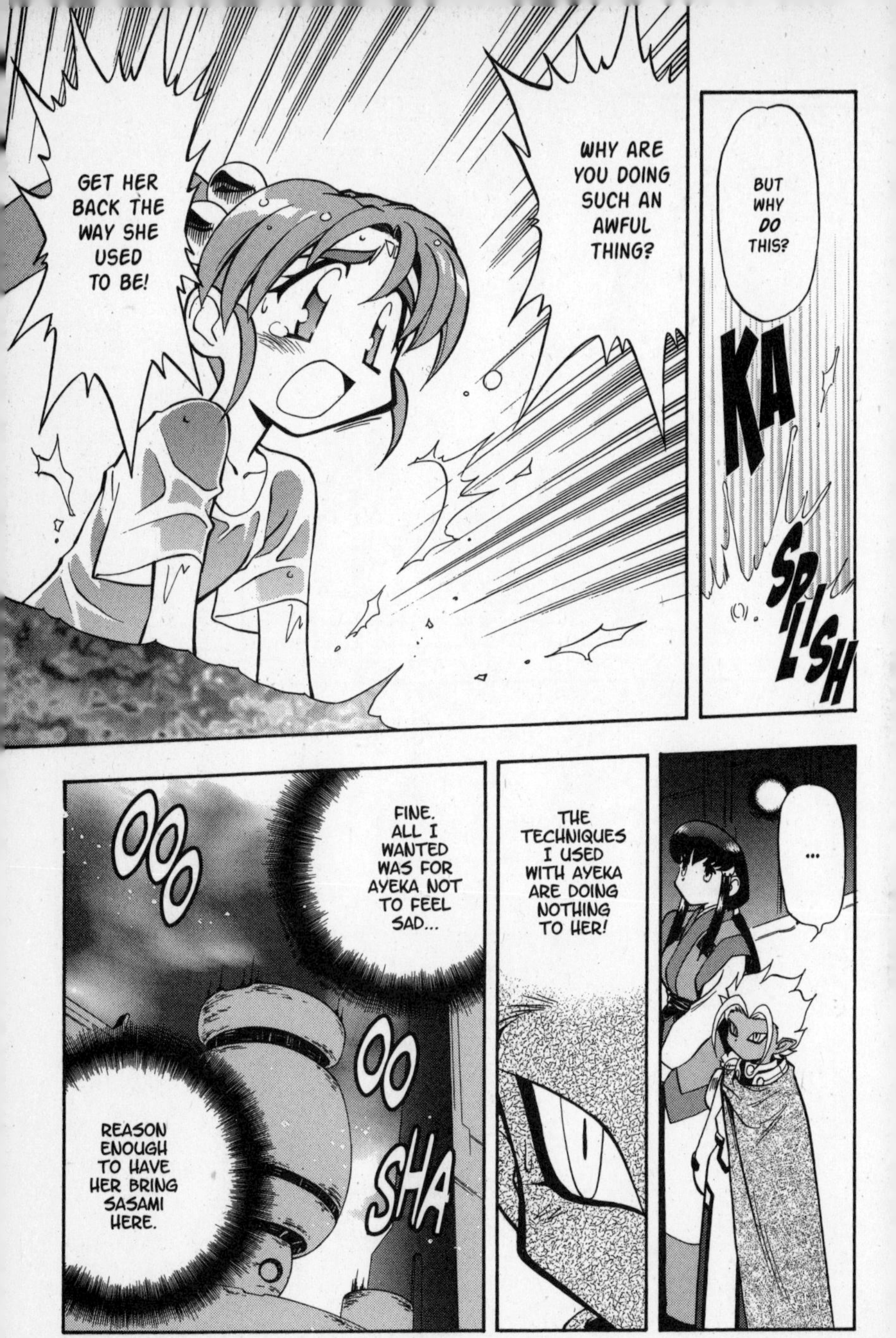
BUT WHY *DO* THIS?
KA
SPLISH
WHY ARE YOU DOING SUCH AN AWFUL THING?
GET HER BACK THE WAY SHE USED TO BE!
...
THE TECHNIQUES I USED WITH AYEKA ARE DOING NOTHING TO HER!
FINE. ALL I WANTED WAS FOR AYEKA NOT TO FEEL SAD...
OOO
OO
SHA
REASON ENOUGH TO HAVE HER BRING SASAMI HERE.

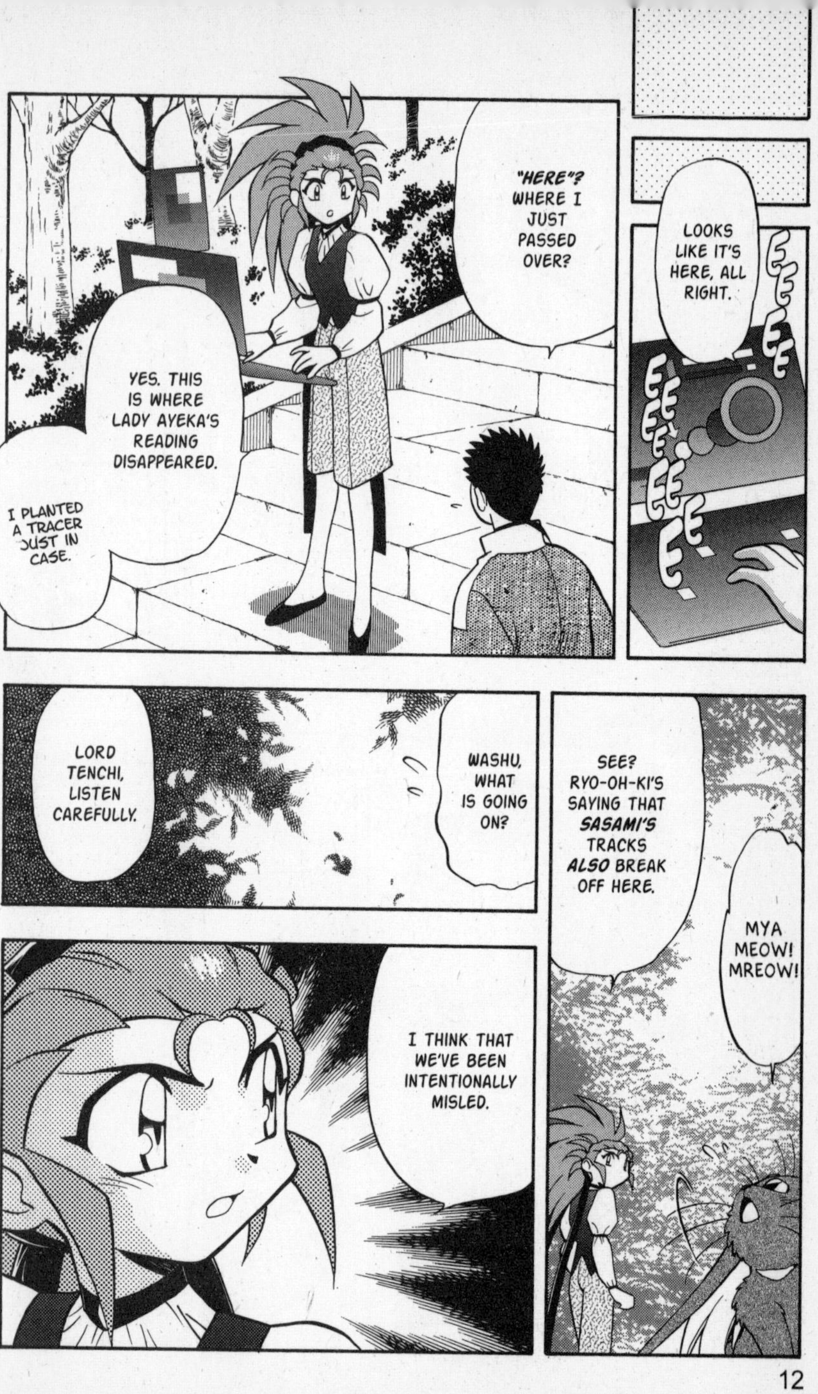
LOOKS LIKE IT'S HERE, ALL RIGHT.
EEEE
"HERE"? WHERE I JUST PASSED OVER?
YES. THIS IS WHERE LADY AYEKA'S READING DISAPPEARED.
I PLANTED A TRACER JUST IN CASE.
SEE? RYO-OH-KI'S SAYING THAT ***SASAMI'S*** TRACKS ***ALSO*** BREAK OFF HERE.
MYA MEOW! MREOW!
WASHU, WHAT IS GOING ON?
LORD TENCHI, LISTEN CAREFULLY.
I THINK THAT WE'VE BEEN INTENTIONALLY MISLED.

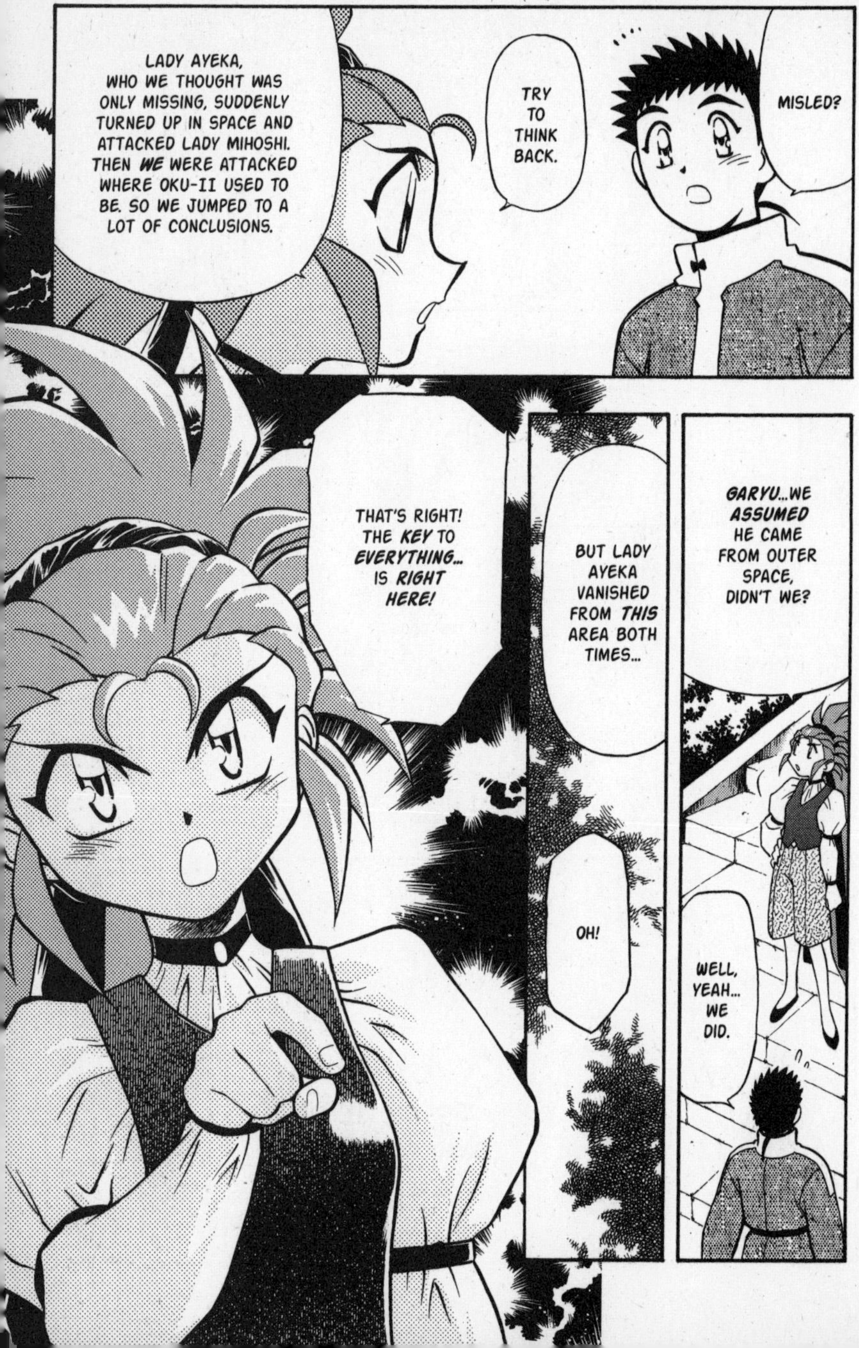
MISLED?
TRY TO THINK BACK.
LADY AYEKA, WHO WE THOUGHT WAS ONLY MISSING, SUDDENLY TURNED UP IN SPACE AND ATTACKED LADY MIHOSHI. THEN *WE* WERE ATTACKED WHERE OKU-II USED TO BE. SO WE JUMPED TO A LOT OF CONCLUSIONS.
GARYU...WE *ASSUMED* HE CAME FROM OUTER SPACE, DIDN'T WE?
WELL, YEAH... WE DID.
BUT LADY AYEKA VANISHED FROM *THIS* AREA BOTH TIMES...
OH!
THAT'S RIGHT! THE *KEY* TO *EVERYTHING*... IS *RIGHT HERE!*

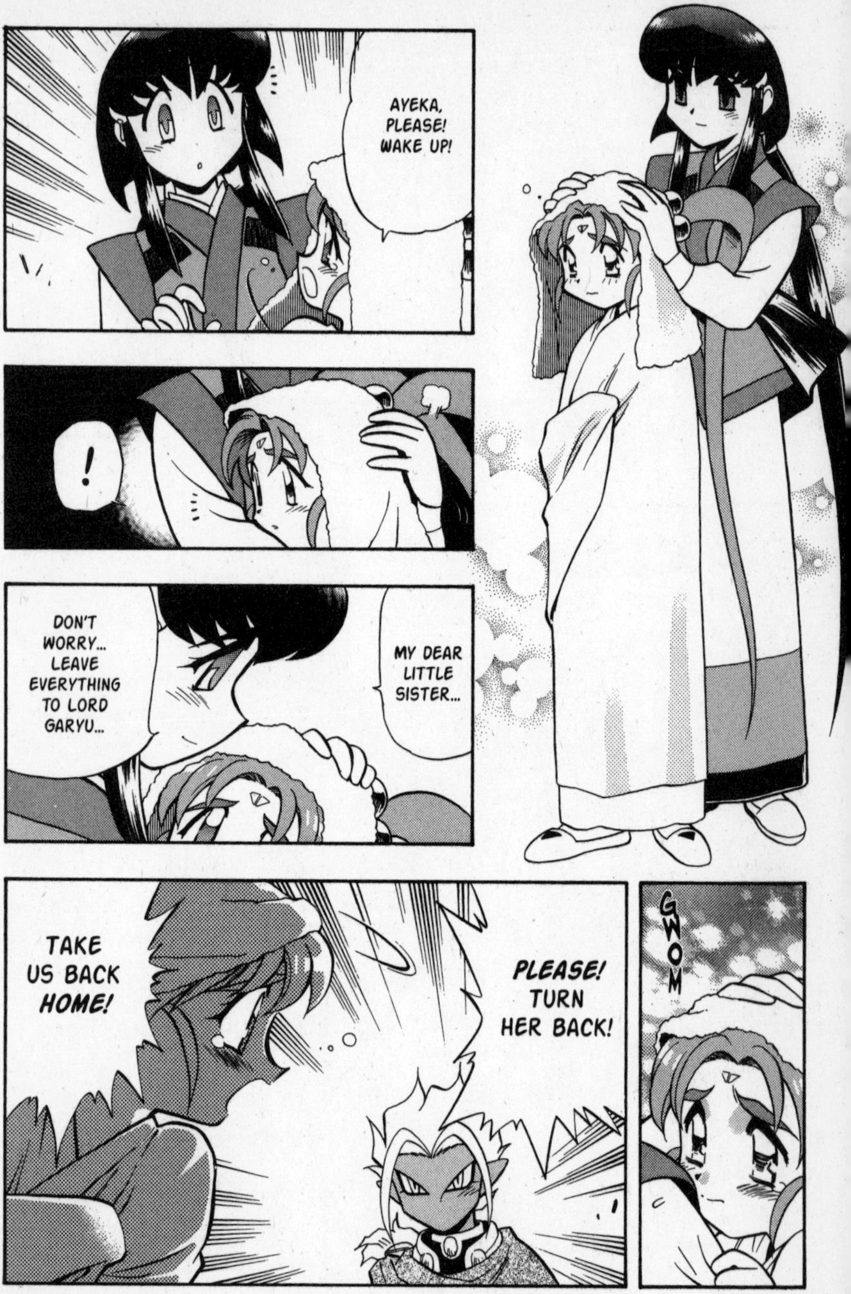
AYEKA, PLEASE! WAKE UP!
!
MY DEAR LITTLE SISTER...
DON'T WORRY... LEAVE EVERYTHING TO LORD GARYU...
GWOM
PLEASE! TURN HER BACK!
TAKE US BACK HOME!

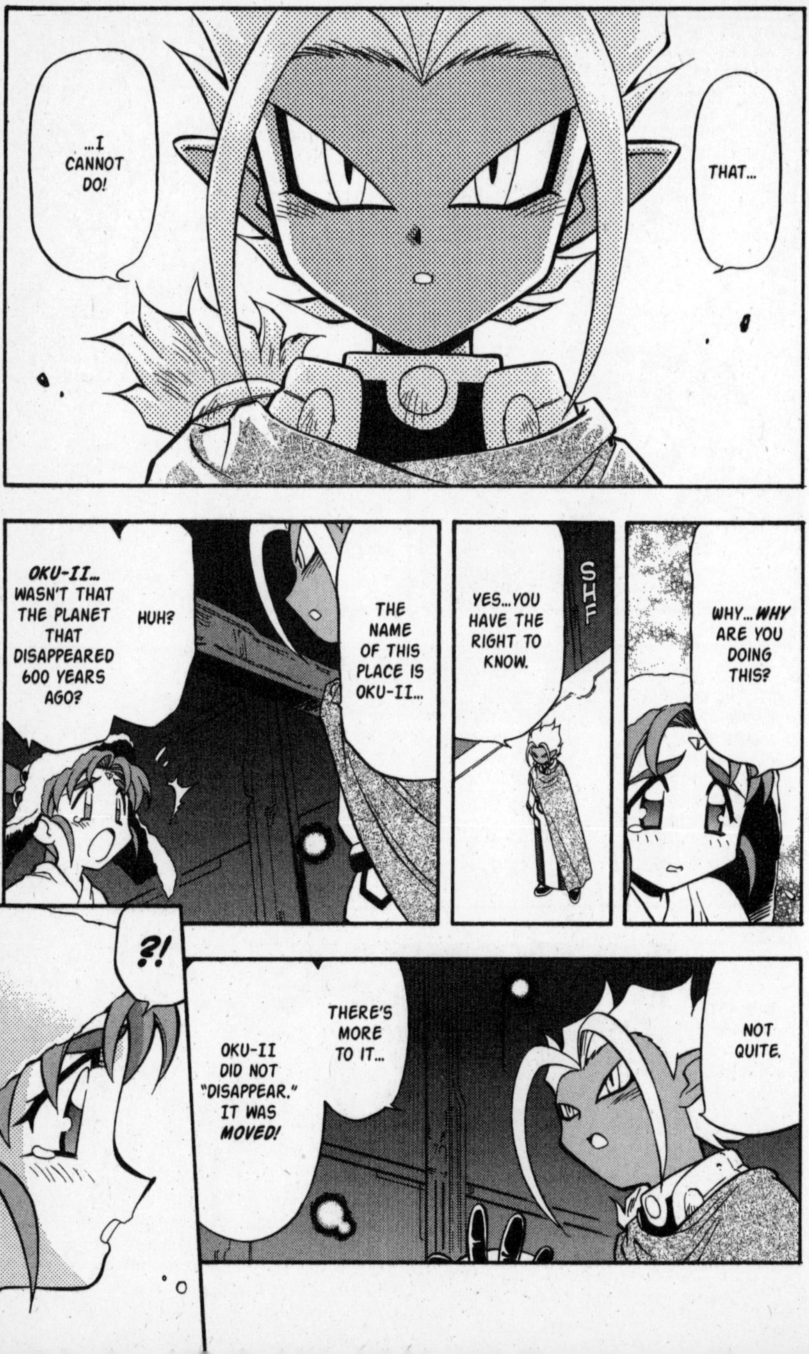
THAT...
...I CANNOT DO!
WHY... *WHY* ARE YOU DOING THIS?
SHF
YES...YOU HAVE THE RIGHT TO KNOW.
THE NAME OF THIS PLACE IS OKU-II...
HUH?
OKU-II... WASN'T THAT THE PLANET THAT DISAPPEARED 600 YEARS AGO?
NOT QUITE.
THERE'S MORE TO IT...
OKU-II DID NOT "DISAPPEAR." IT WAS *MOVED!*
?!

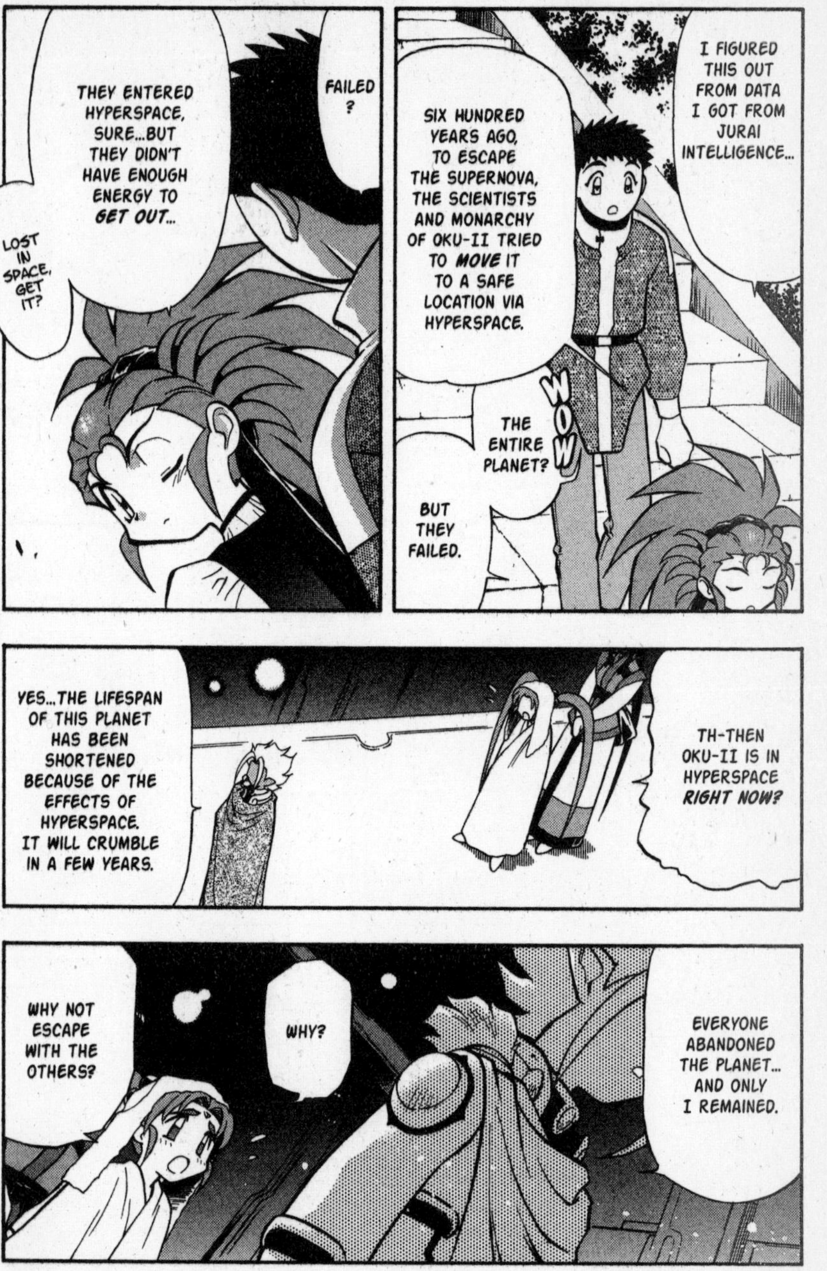
I FIGURED THIS OUT FROM DATA I GOT FROM JURAI INTELLIGENCE...
SIX HUNDRED YEARS AGO, TO ESCAPE THE SUPERNOVA, THE SCIENTISTS AND MONARCHY OF OKU-II TRIED TO MOVE IT TO A SAFE LOCATION VIA HYPERSPACE.
WOW
THE ENTIRE PLANET?
BUT THEY FAILED.
FAILED?
THEY ENTERED HYPERSPACE, SURE...BUT THEY DIDN'T HAVE ENOUGH ENERGY TO GET OUT...
LOST IN SPACE, GET IT?
TH-THEN OKU-II IS IN HYPERSPACE RIGHT NOW?
YES...THE LIFESPAN OF THIS PLANET HAS BEEN SHORTENED BECAUSE OF THE EFFECTS OF HYPERSPACE. IT WILL CRUMBLE IN A FEW YEARS.
EVERYONE ABANDONED THE PLANET... AND ONLY I REMAINED.
WHY?
WHY NOT ESCAPE WITH THE OTHERS?

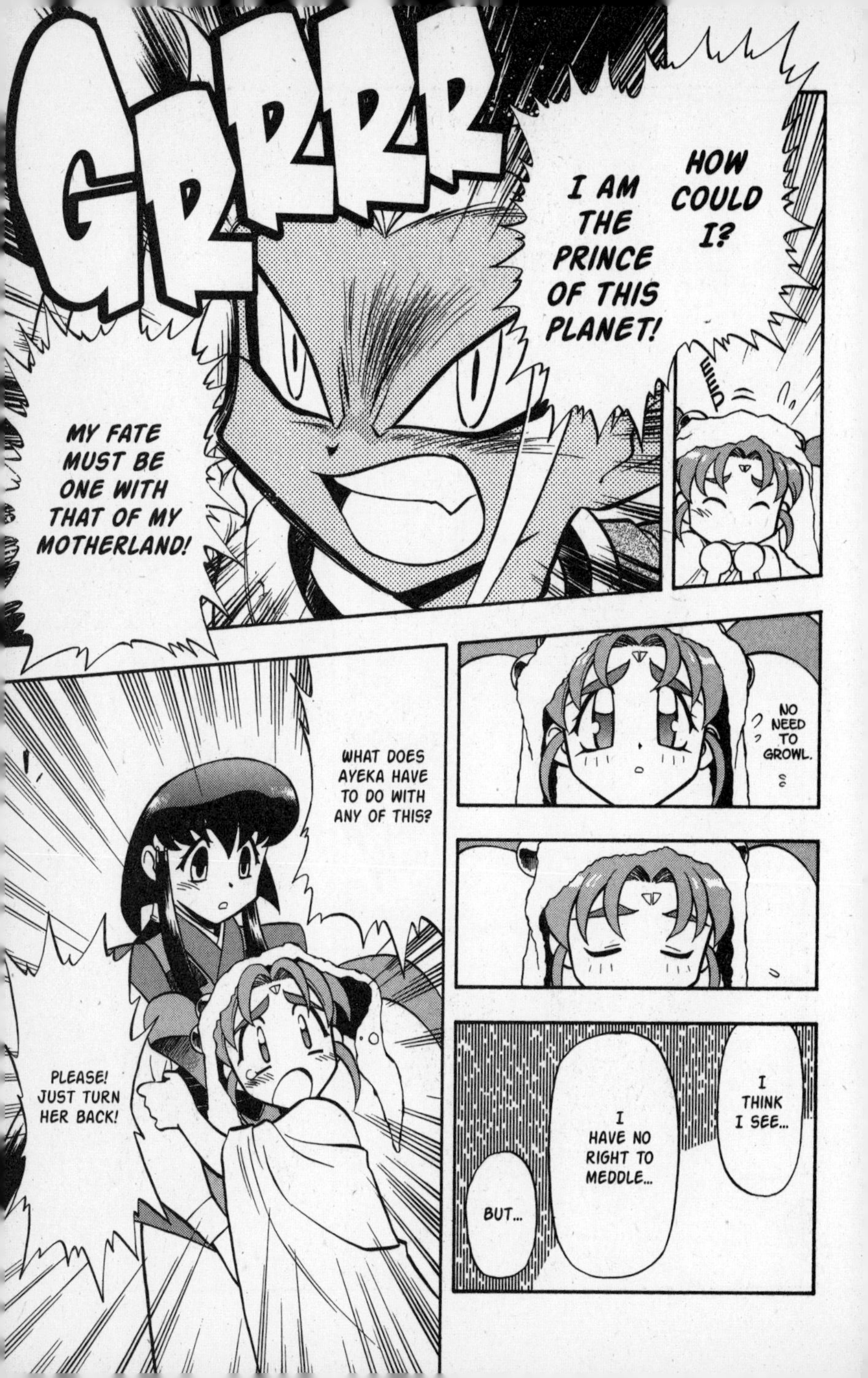
GRRRR
HOW COULD I?
I AM THE PRINCE OF THIS PLANET!
MY FATE MUST BE ONE WITH THAT OF MY MOTHERLAND!
NO NEED TO GROWL.
I THINK I SEE...
I HAVE NO RIGHT TO MEDDLE...
BUT...
WHAT DOES AYEKA HAVE TO DO WITH ANY OF THIS?
PLEASE! JUST TURN HER BACK!

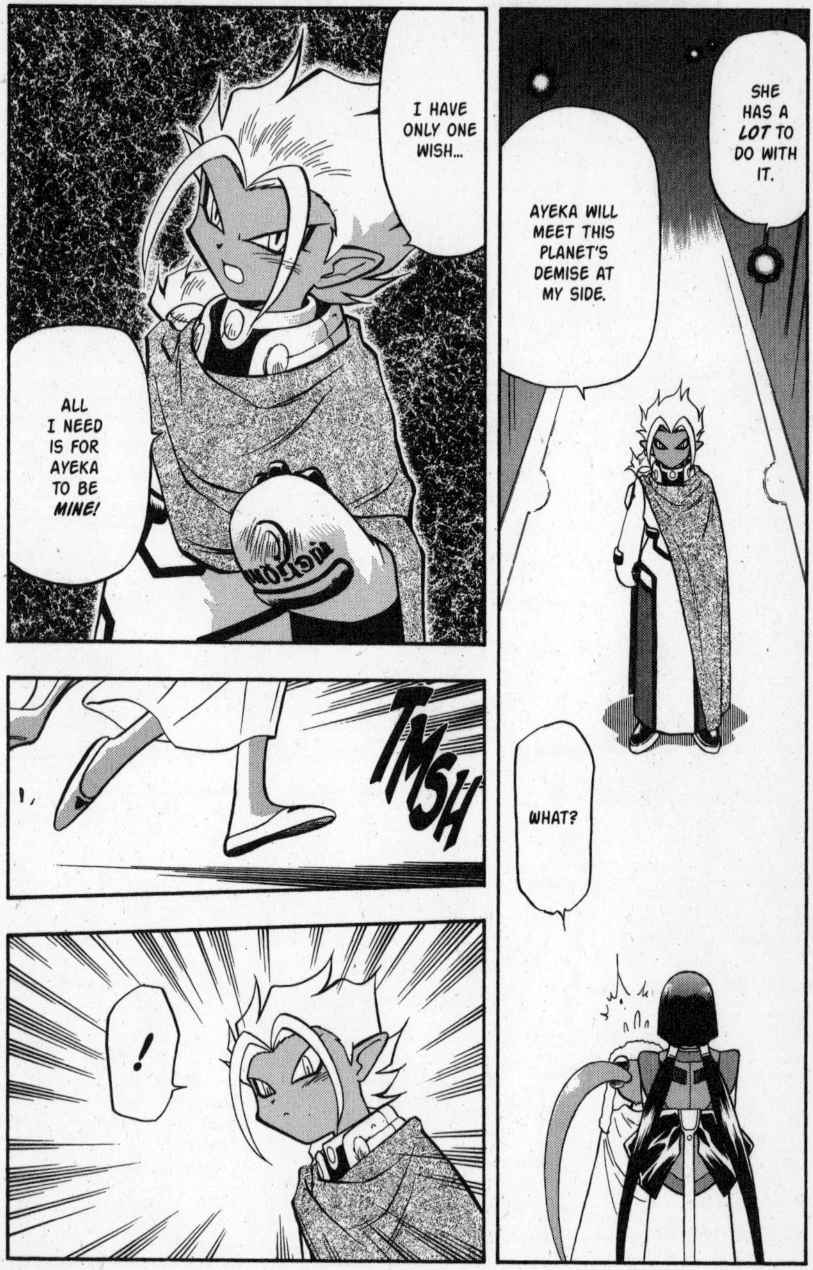
SHE HAS A LOT TO DO WITH IT.
AYEKA WILL MEET THIS PLANET'S DEMISE AT MY SIDE.
WHAT?
I HAVE ONLY ONE WISH...
ALL I NEED IS FOR AYEKA TO BE MINE!
TMSH
!

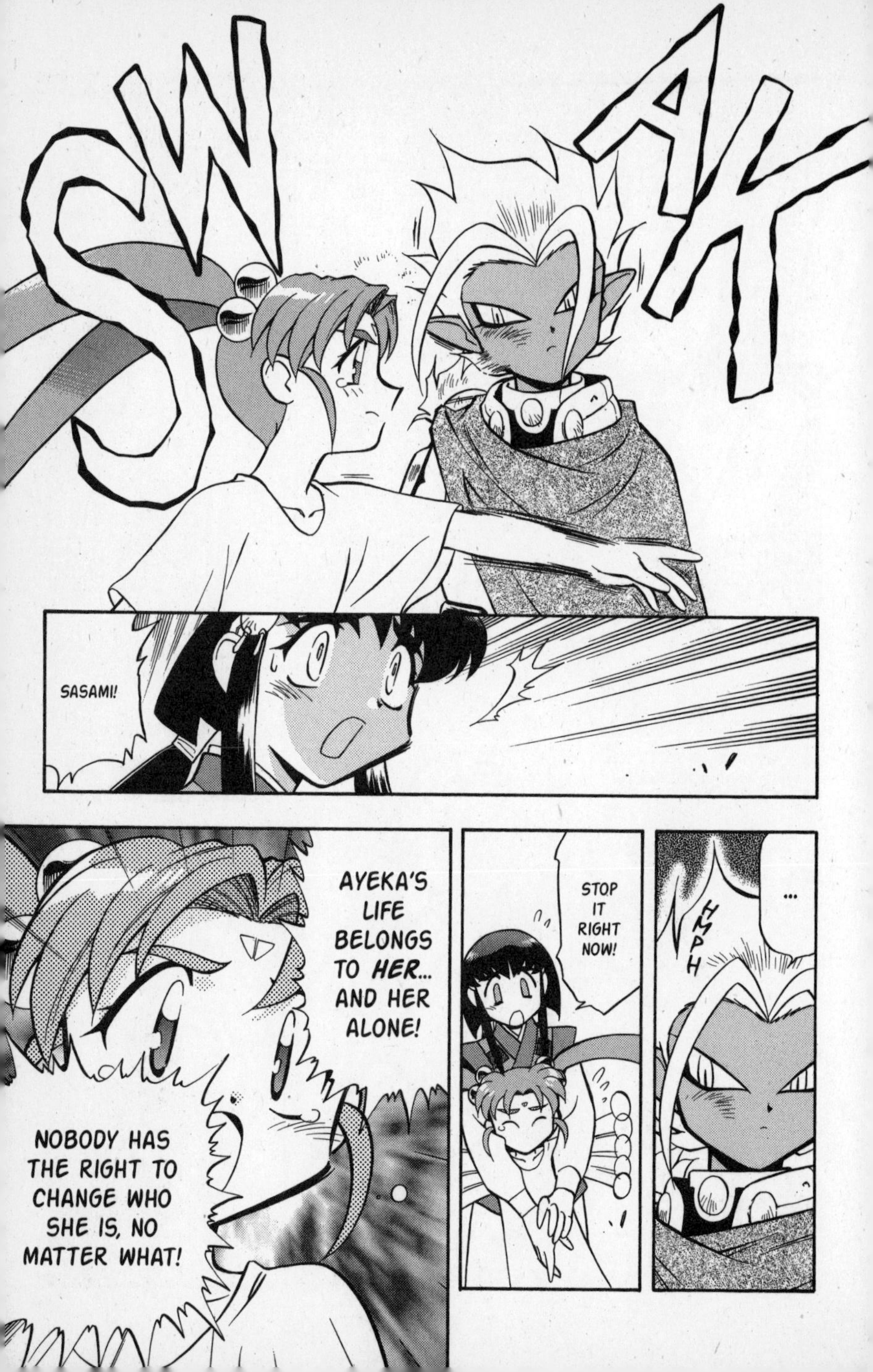
SWAK
SASAMI!
...
HMPH
STOP IT RIGHT NOW!
AYEKA'S LIFE BELONGS TO *HER*... AND HER ALONE!
NOBODY HAS THE RIGHT TO CHANGE WHO SHE IS, NO MATTER WHAT!

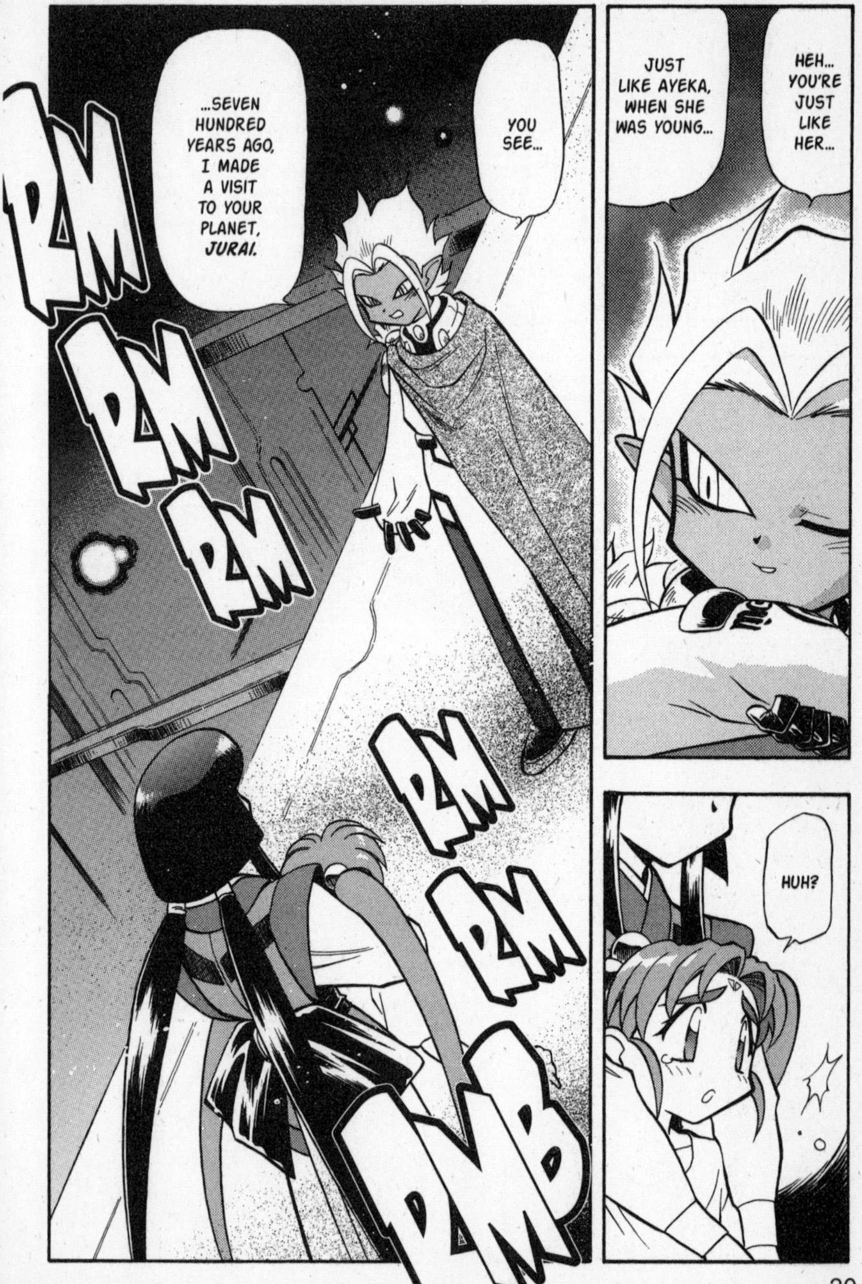
HEH... YOU'RE JUST LIKE HER...
JUST LIKE AYEKA, WHEN SHE WAS YOUNG...
HUH?
YOU SEE...
...SEVEN HUNDRED YEARS AGO, I MADE A VISIT TO YOUR PLANET, JURAI.
RM RM RM RM RM
RM RM RMB

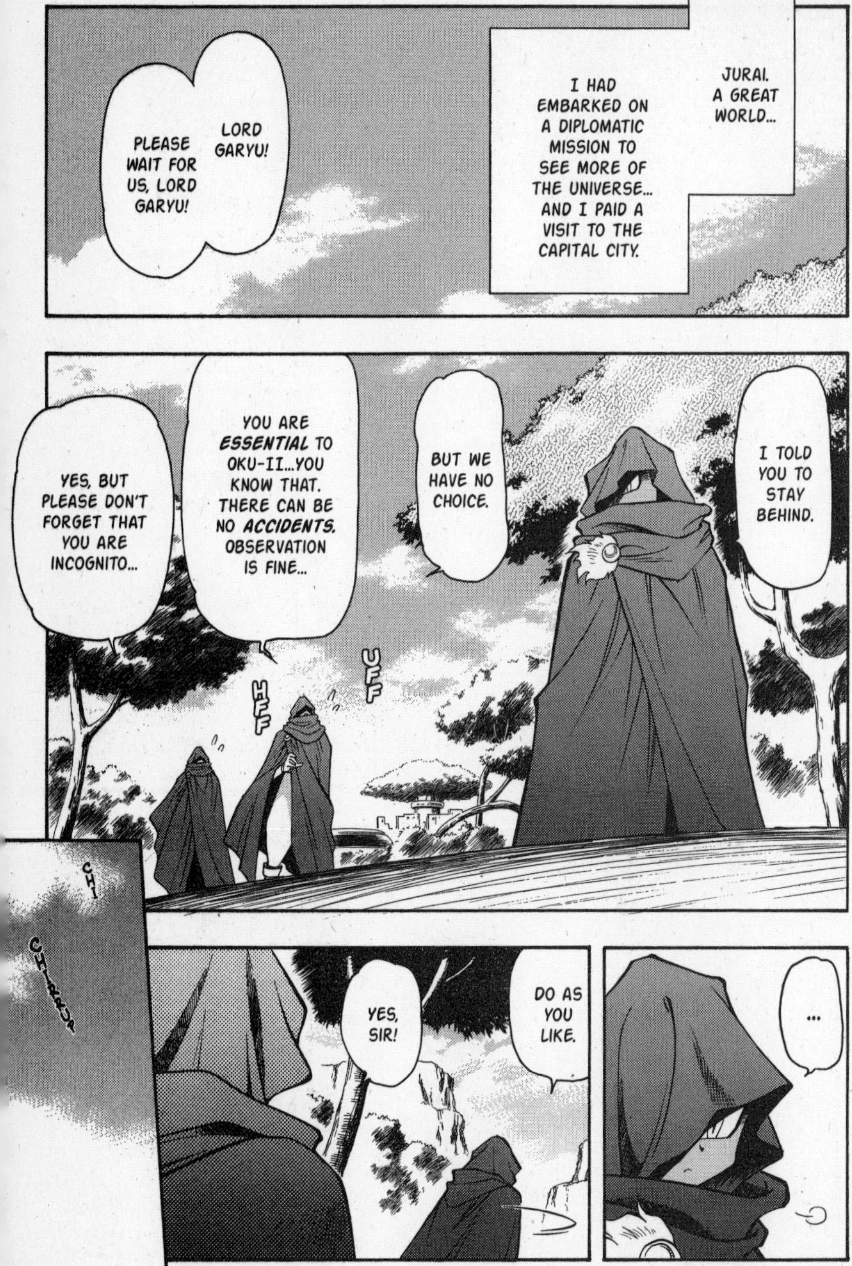
JURAI. A GREAT WORLD...
I HAD EMBARKED ON A DIPLOMATIC MISSION TO SEE MORE OF THE UNIVERSE... AND I PAID A VISIT TO THE CAPITAL CITY.
LORD GARYU!
PLEASE WAIT FOR US, LORD GARYU!
I TOLD YOU TO STAY BEHIND.
BUT WE HAVE NO CHOICE.
YOU ARE ESSENTIAL TO OKU-II...YOU KNOW THAT. THERE CAN BE NO ACCIDENTS. OBSERVATION IS FINE...
YES, BUT PLEASE DON'T FORGET THAT YOU ARE INCOGNITO...
UFF
HFF
...
DO AS YOU LIKE.
YES, SIR!
CHI
CHIRRRUP

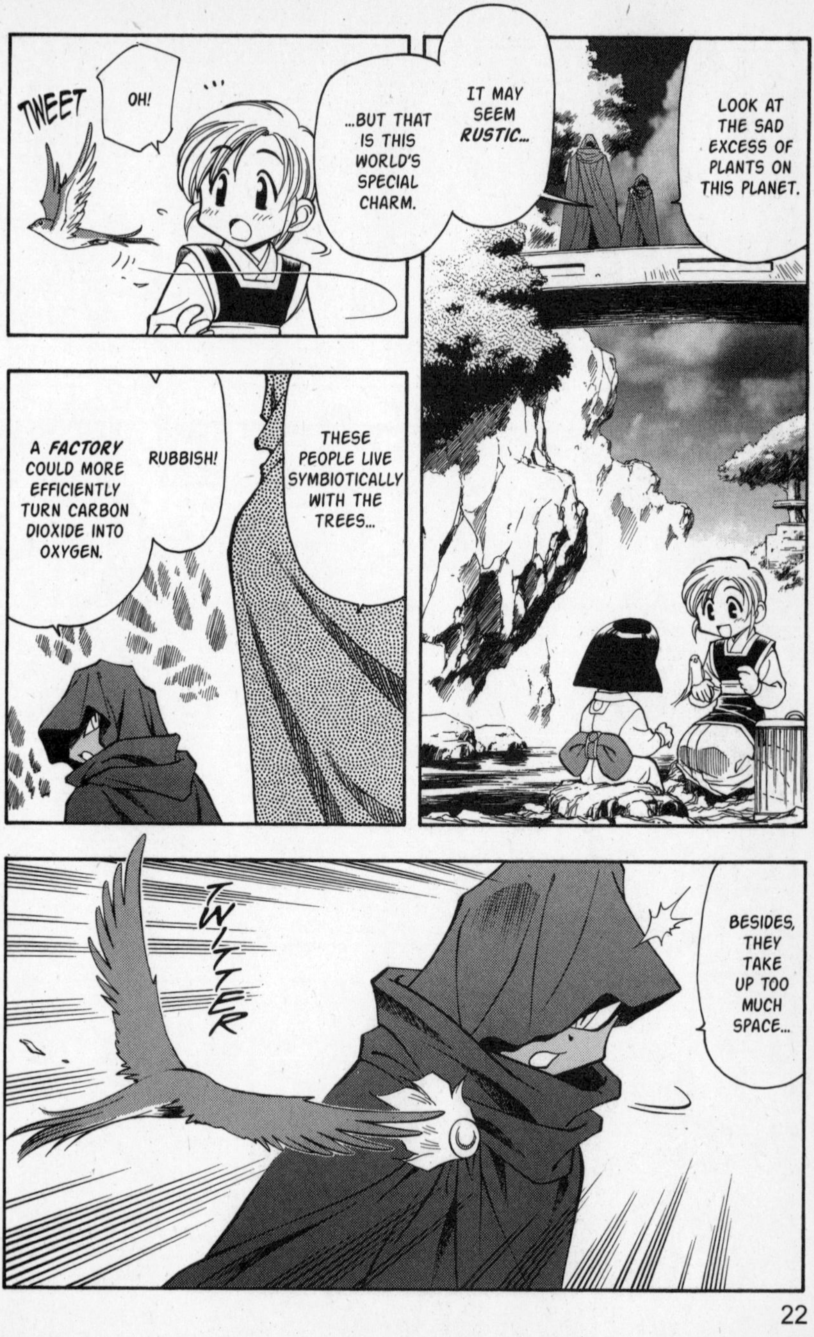
LOOK AT THE SAD EXCESS OF PLANTS ON THIS PLANET.
IT MAY SEEM *RUSTIC*...
...BUT THAT IS THIS WORLD'S SPECIAL CHARM.
TWEET
OH!
...
THESE PEOPLE LIVE SYMBIOTICALLY WITH THE TREES...
RUBBISH!
A *FACTORY* COULD MORE EFFICIENTLY TURN CARBON DIOXIDE INTO OXYGEN.
BESIDES, THEY TAKE UP TOO MUCH SPACE...
TWITTER

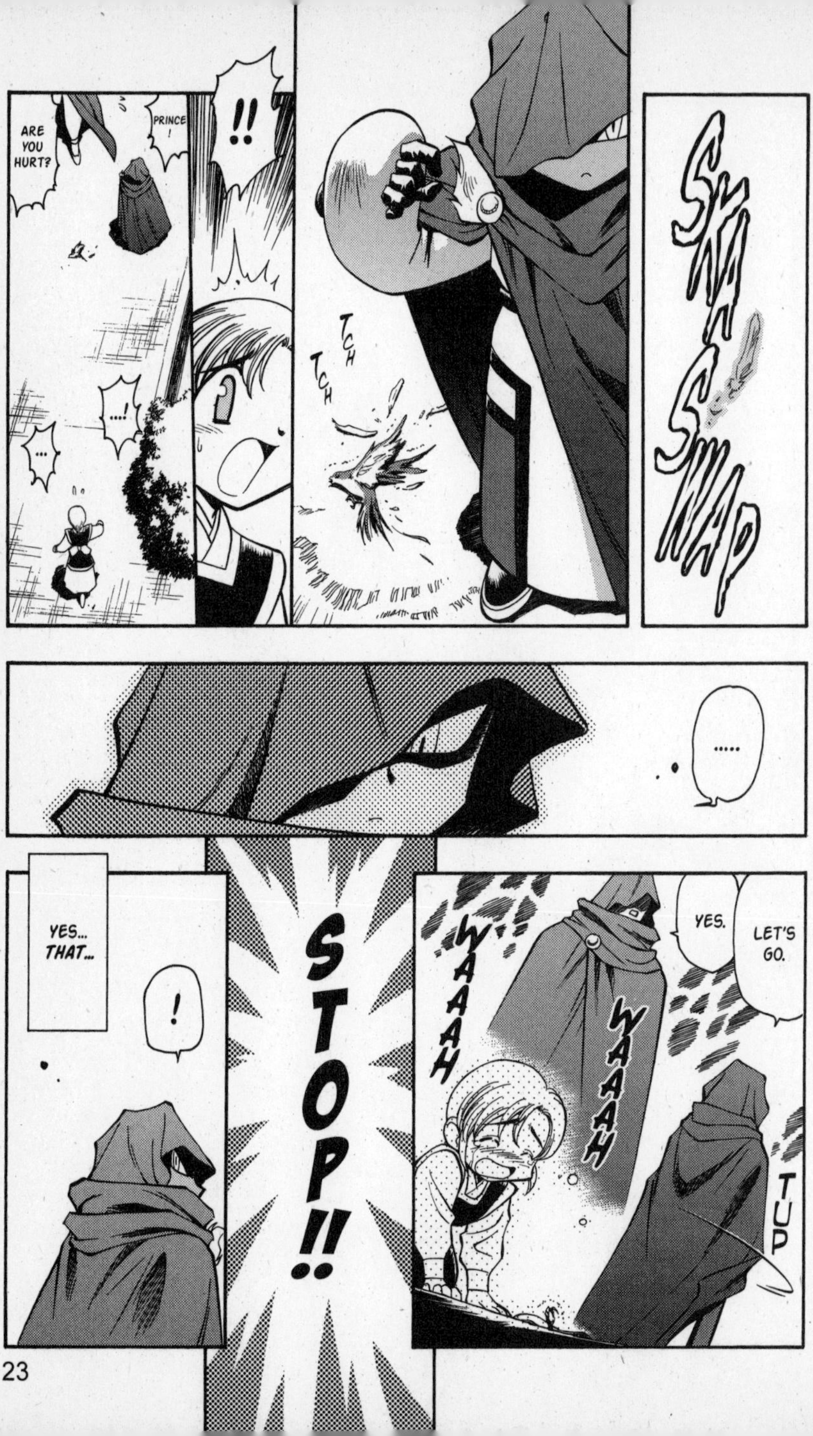
SNA SNAP
TCH TCH
!!
PRINCE!
ARE YOU HURT?
...!
...
.....
YES.
LET'S GO.
WAAAAH
WAAAAH
TUP
STOP!!
YES... THAT...
!

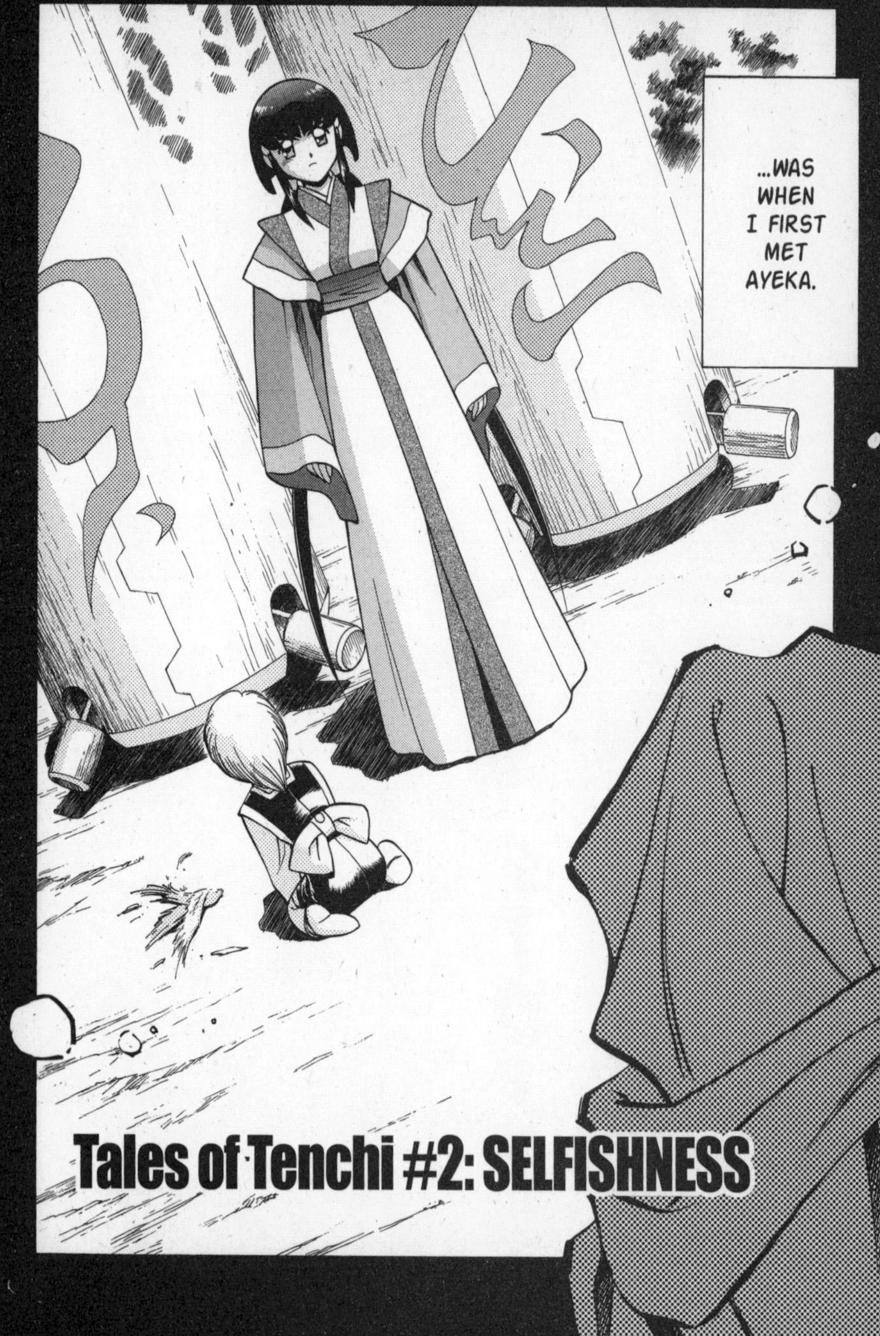
...WAS WHEN I FIRST MET AYEKA.
Tales of Tenchi #2: SELFISHNESS

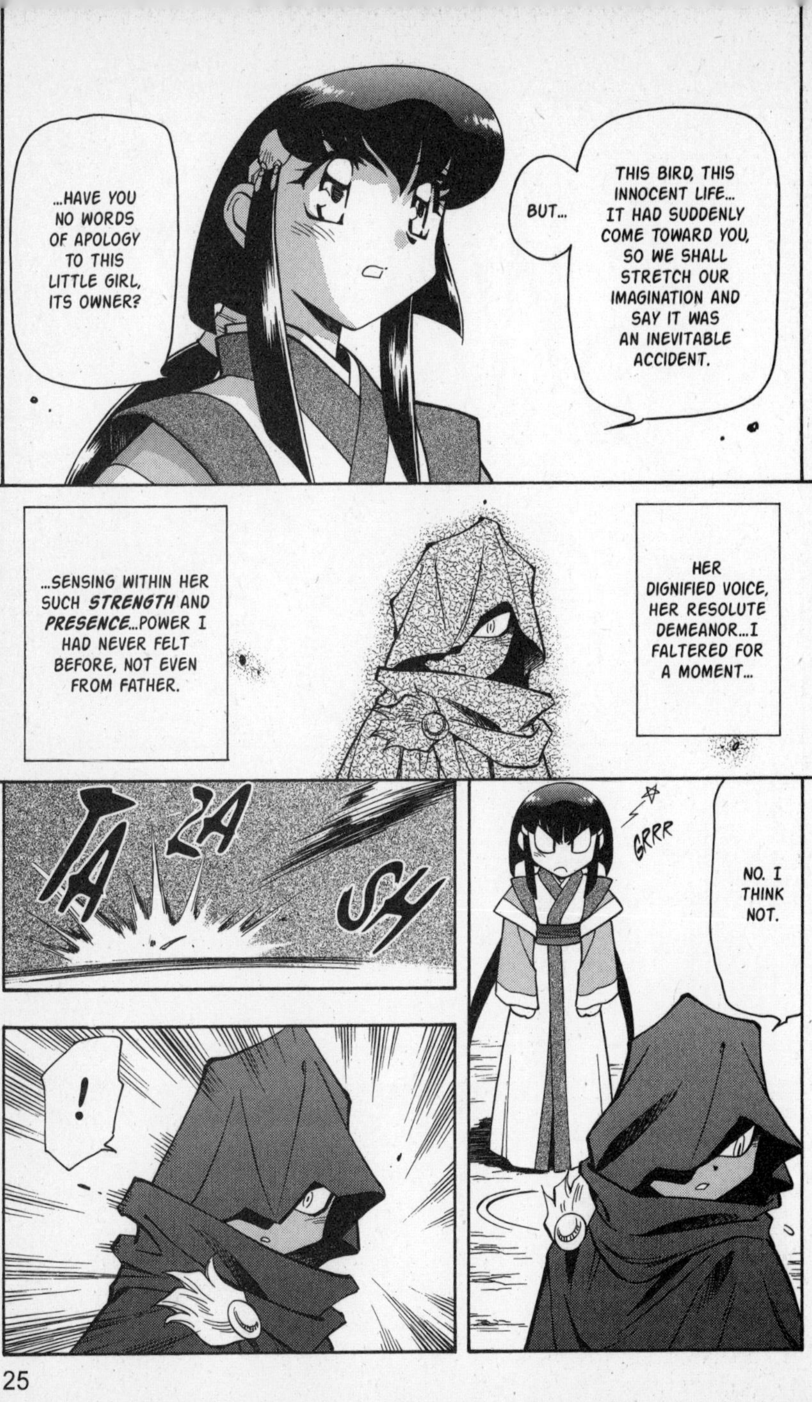
BUT...
THIS BIRD, THIS INNOCENT LIFE... IT HAD SUDDENLY COME TOWARD YOU, SO WE SHALL STRETCH OUR IMAGINATION AND SAY IT WAS AN INEVITABLE ACCIDENT.
...HAVE YOU NO WORDS OF APOLOGY TO THIS LITTLE GIRL, ITS OWNER?
HER DIGNIFIED VOICE, HER RESOLUTE DEMEANOR...I FALTERED FOR A MOMENT...
...SENSING WITHIN HER SUCH *STRENGTH* AND *PRESENCE*...POWER I HAD NEVER FELT BEFORE, NOT EVEN FROM FATHER.
GRRR
NO. I THINK NOT.
TAZASH
!

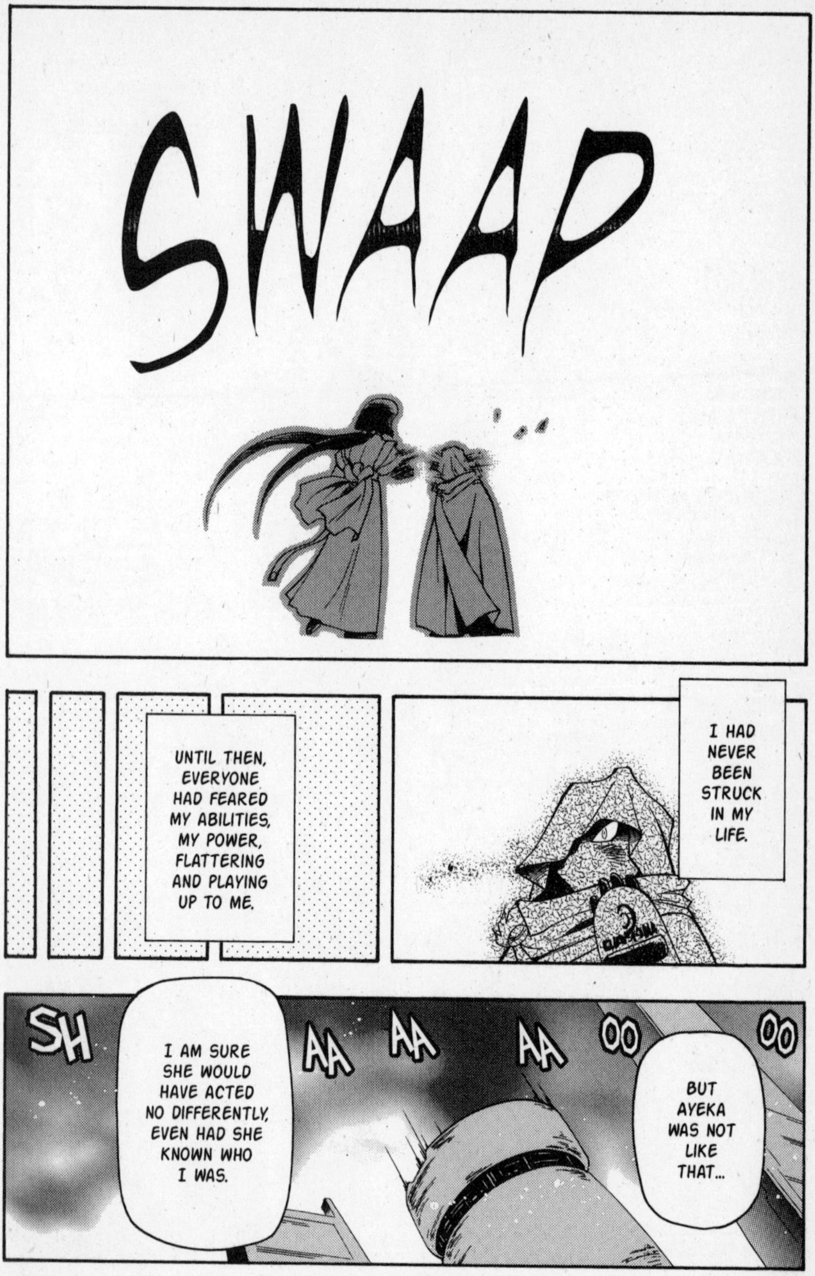
SWAAP
I HAD NEVER BEEN STRUCK IN MY LIFE.
UNTIL THEN, EVERYONE HAD FEARED MY ABILITIES, MY POWER, FLATTERING AND PLAYING UP TO ME.
SHAAAAAAOOOO
BUT AYEKA WAS NOT LIKE THAT...
I AM SURE SHE WOULD HAVE ACTED NO DIFFERENTLY, EVEN HAD SHE KNOWN WHO I WAS.

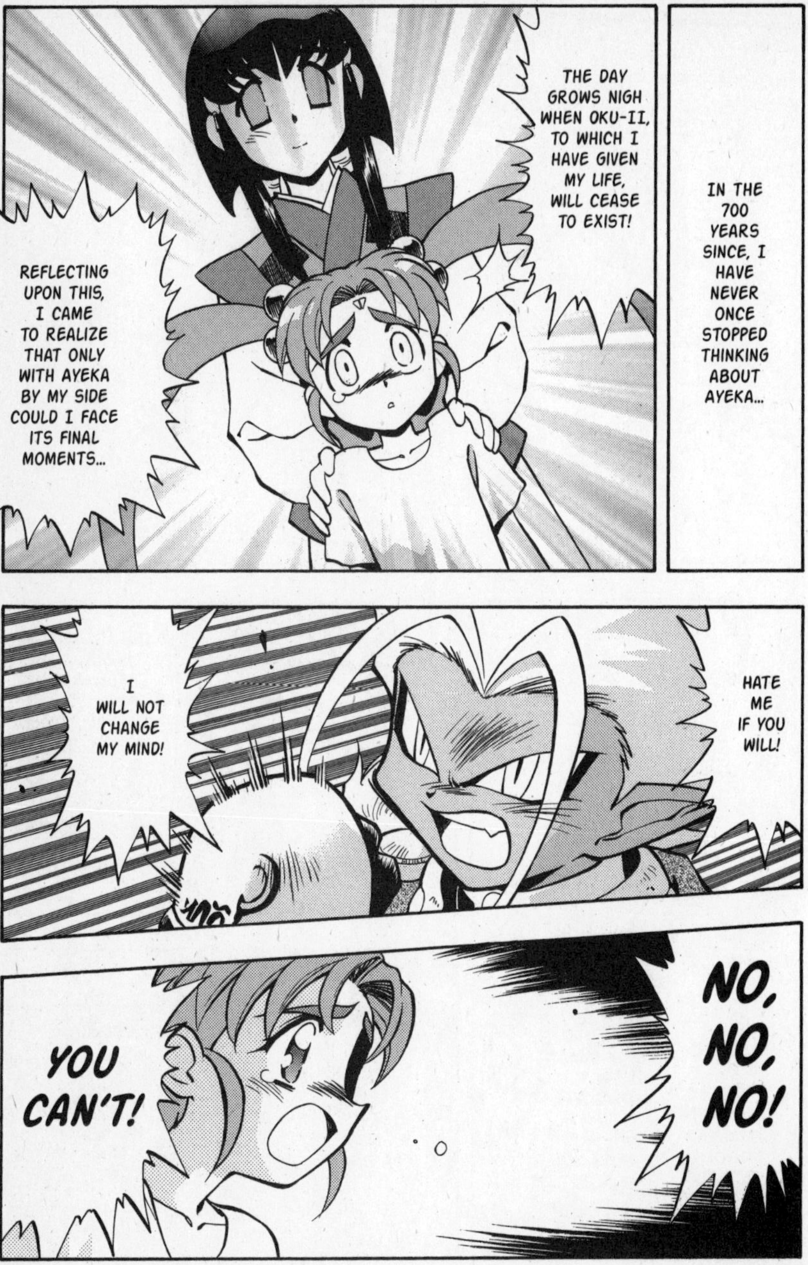
IN THE 700 YEARS SINCE, I HAVE NEVER ONCE STOPPED THINKING ABOUT AYEKA...
THE DAY GROWS NIGH WHEN OKU-II, TO WHICH I HAVE GIVEN MY LIFE, WILL CEASE TO EXIST!
REFLECTING UPON THIS, I CAME TO REALIZE THAT ONLY WITH AYEKA BY MY SIDE COULD I FACE ITS FINAL MOMENTS...
HATE ME IF YOU WILL!
I WILL NOT CHANGE MY MIND!
NO, NO, NO!
YOU CAN'T!

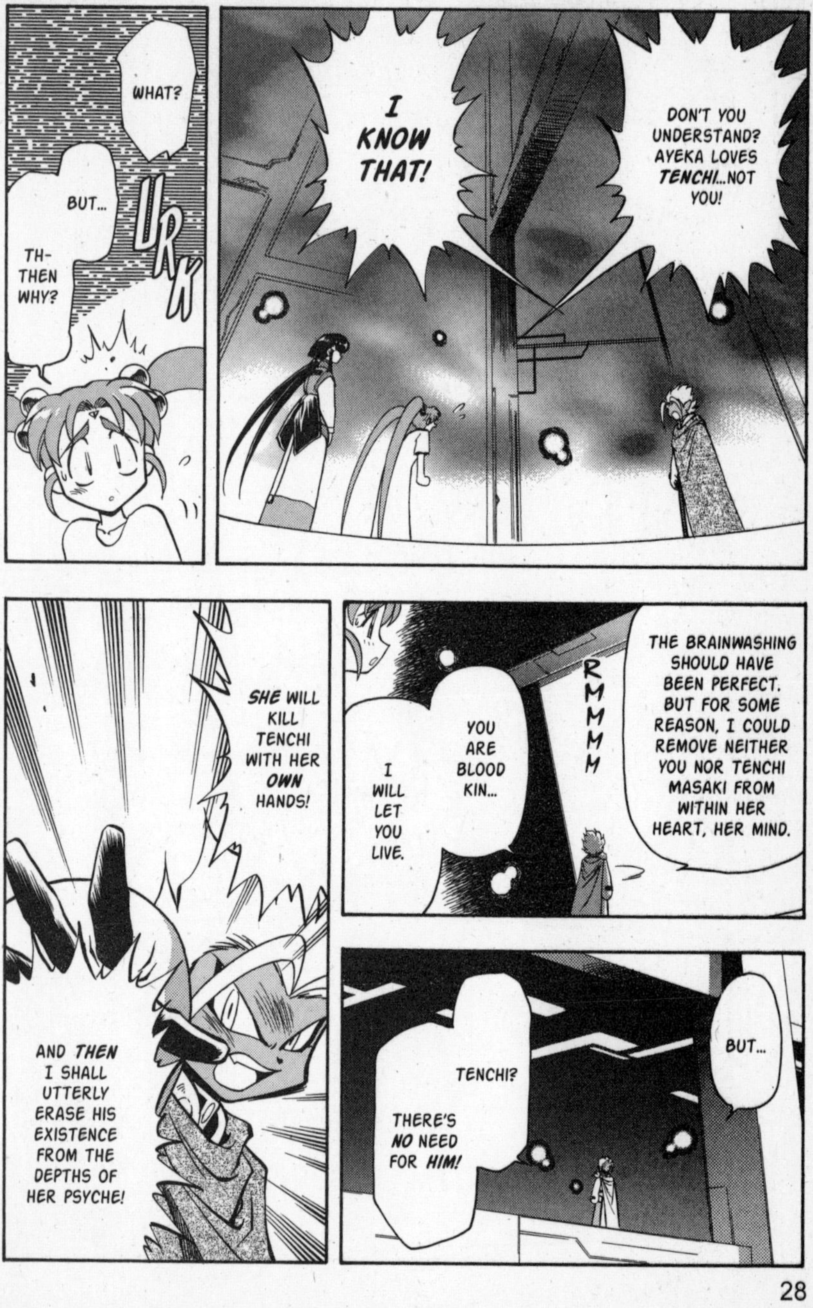
DON'T YOU UNDERSTAND? AYEKA LOVES TENCHI...NOT YOU!
I KNOW THAT!
WHAT?
URK
BUT...
TH-THEN WHY?
THE BRAINWASHING SHOULD HAVE BEEN PERFECT. BUT FOR SOME REASON, I COULD REMOVE NEITHER YOU NOR TENCHI MASAKI FROM WITHIN HER HEART, HER MIND.
RMMMM
YOU ARE BLOOD KIN...
I WILL LET YOU LIVE.
BUT...
TENCHI?
THERE'S NO NEED FOR HIM!
SHE WILL KILL TENCHI WITH HER OWN HANDS!
AND THEN I SHALL UTTERLY ERASE HIS EXISTENCE FROM THE DEPTHS OF HER PSYCHE!

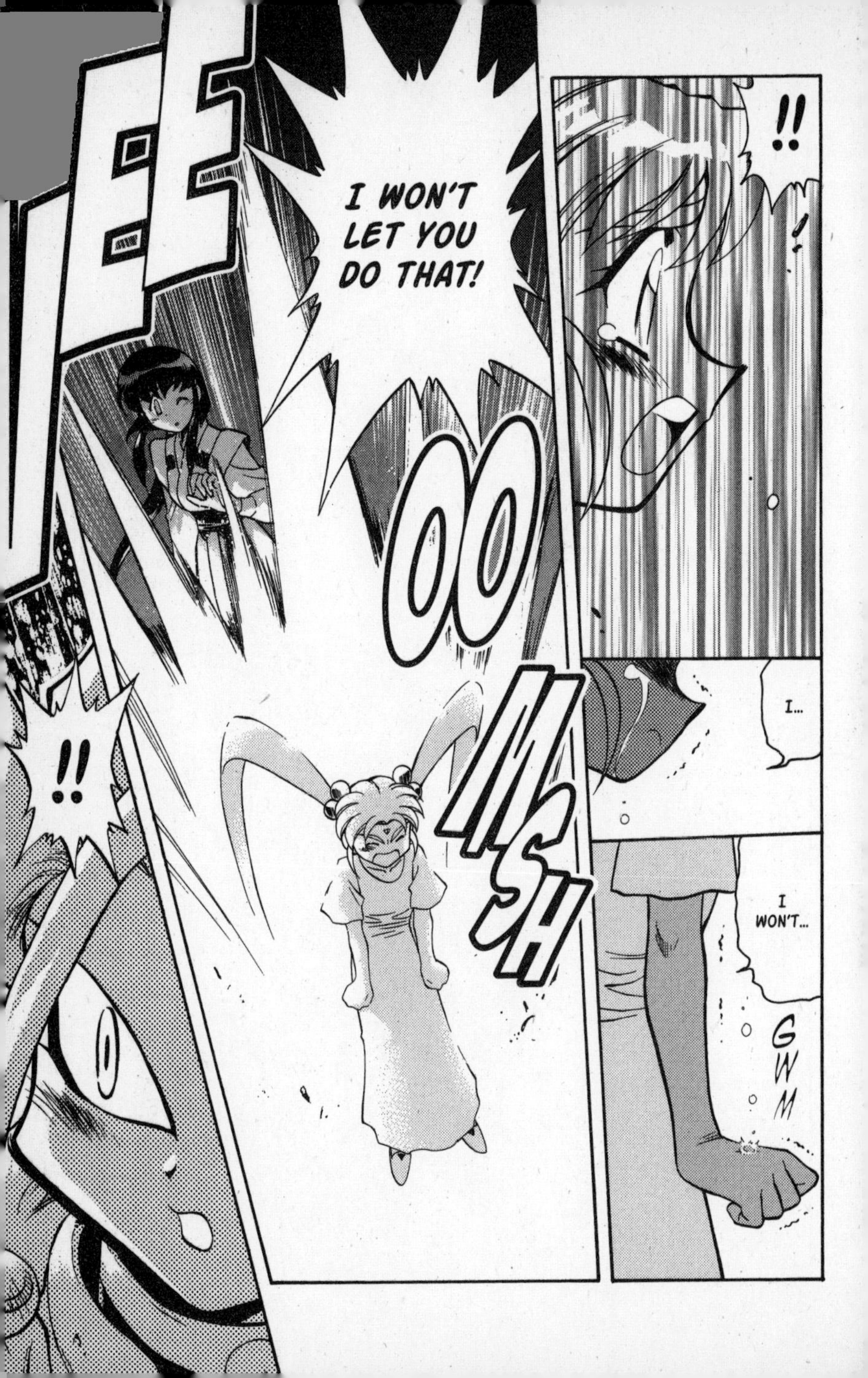
!!
I...
I WON'T...
GWM
I WON'T LET YOU DO THAT!
OOMSH
!!

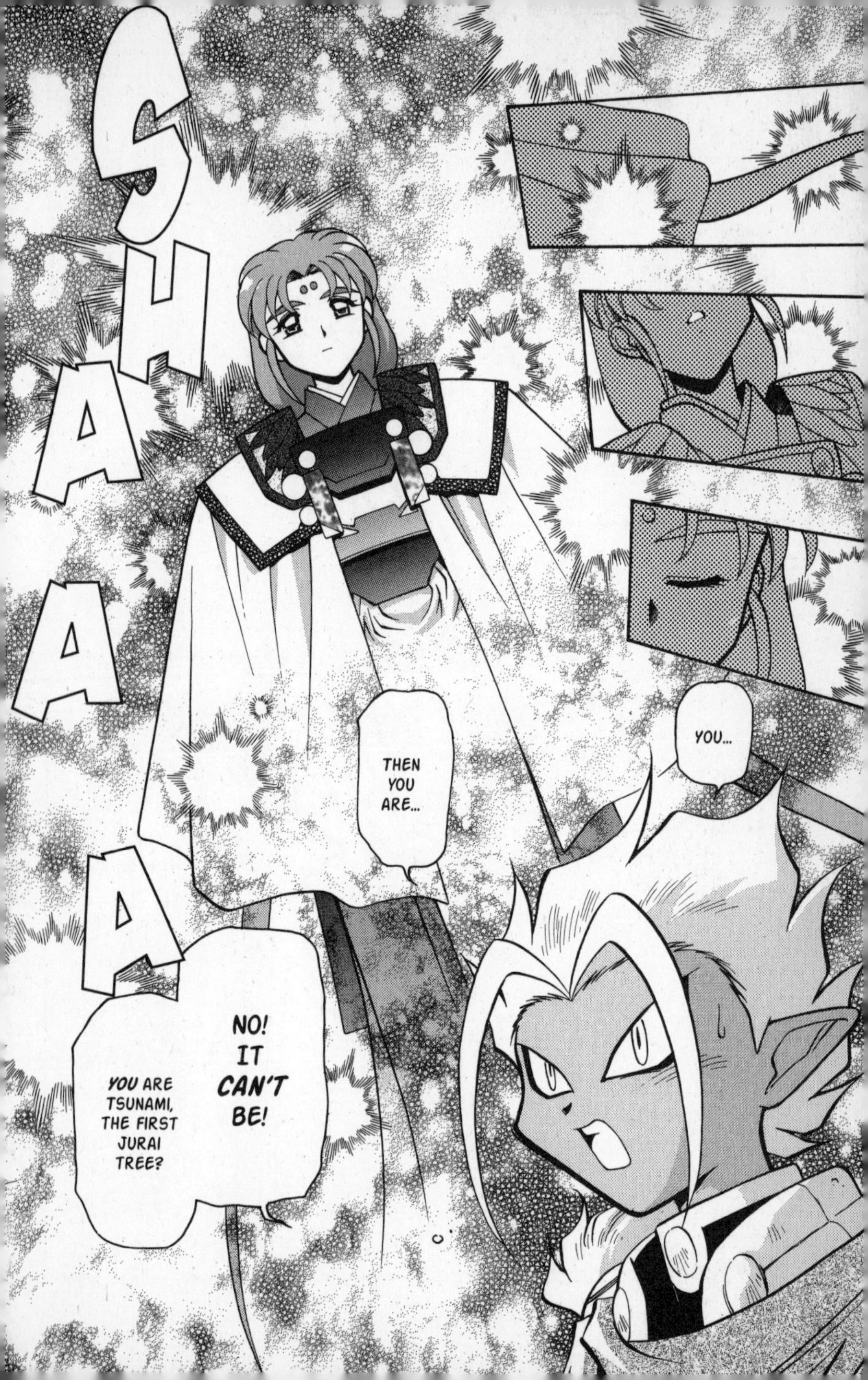
SHAAAA
YOU...
THEN YOU ARE...
NO! IT CAN'T BE!
YOU ARE TSUNAMI, THE FIRST JURAI TREE?

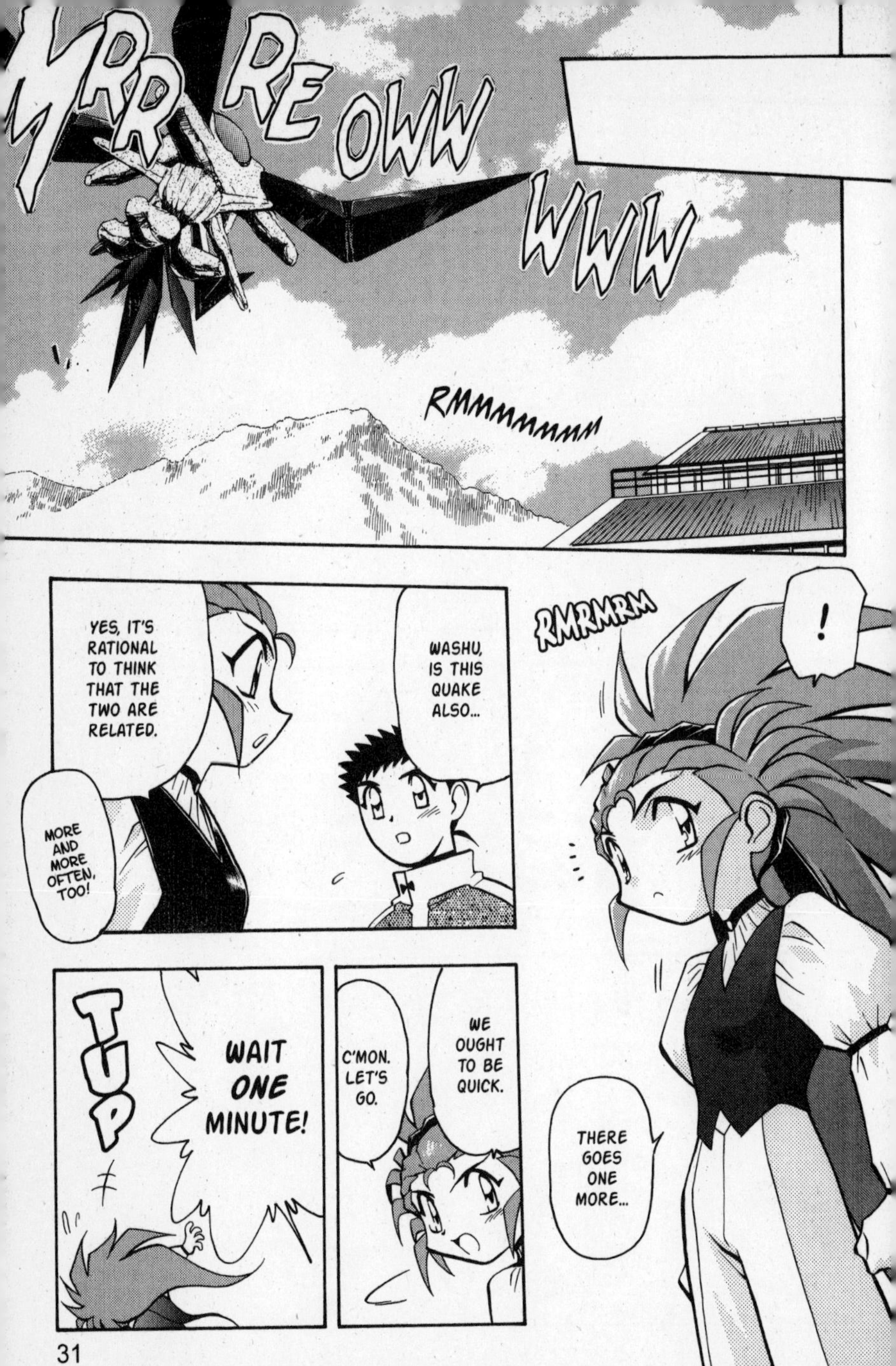
YRR REOWW WWW
RMMMMMMMMM
RMRMRM
!
THERE GOES ONE MORE...
WASHU, IS THIS QUAKE ALSO...
YES, IT'S RATIONAL TO THINK THAT THE TWO ARE RELATED.
MORE AND MORE OFTEN, TOO!
WE OUGHT TO BE QUICK.
C'MON. LET'S GO.
WAIT ONE MINUTE!
TUP

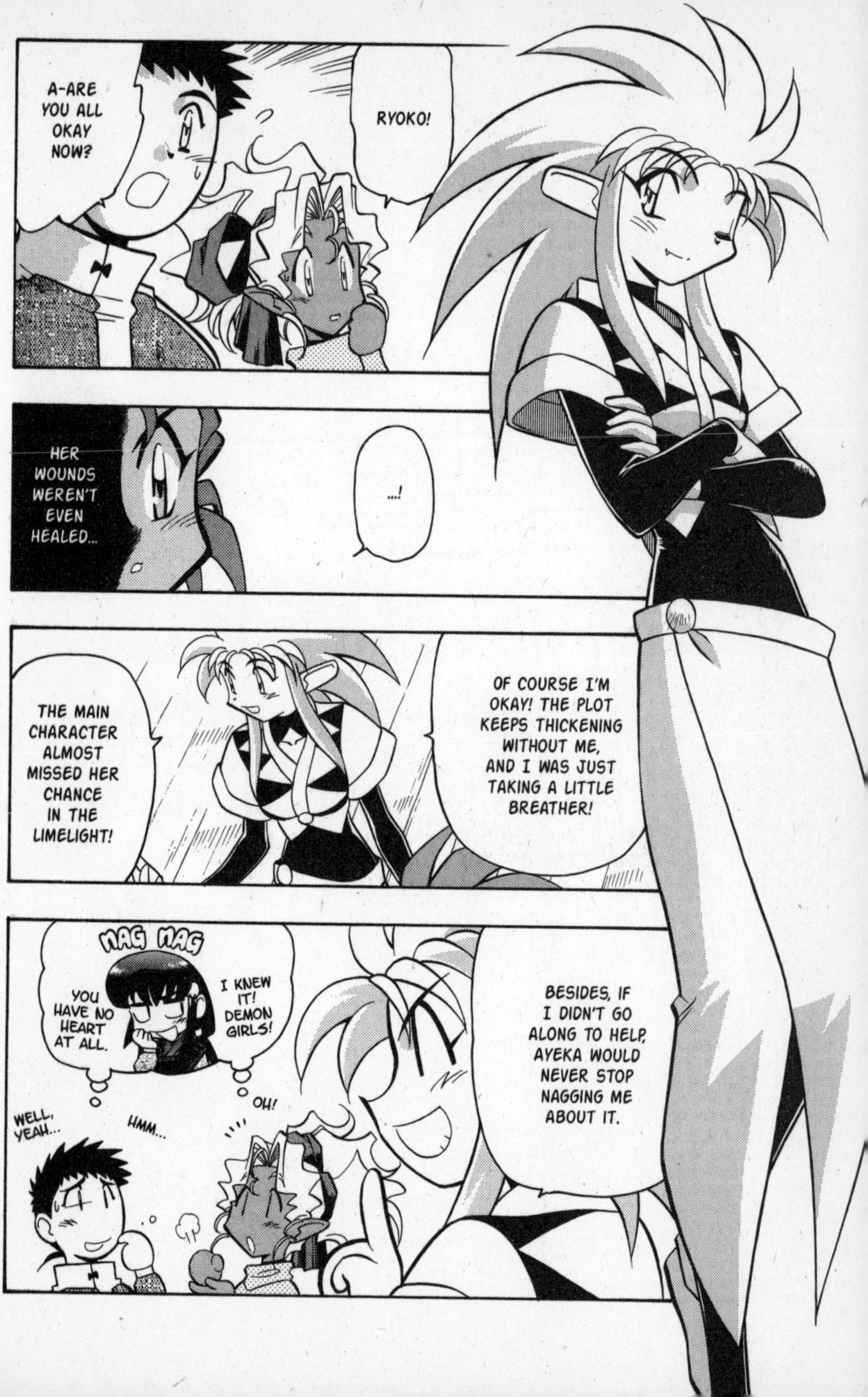

RYOKO!
A-ARE YOU ALL OKAY NOW?
...!
HER WOUNDS WEREN'T EVEN HEALED...
OF COURSE I'M OKAY! THE PLOT KEEPS THICKENING WITHOUT ME, AND I WAS JUST TAKING A LITTLE BREATHER!
THE MAIN CHARACTER ALMOST MISSED HER CHANCE IN THE LIMELIGHT!
BESIDES, IF I DIDN'T GO ALONG TO HELP, AYEKA WOULD NEVER STOP NAGGING ME ABOUT IT.
NAG NAG
I KNEW IT! DEMON GIRLS!
YOU HAVE NO HEART AT ALL.
OH!
HMM...
WELL, YEAH...

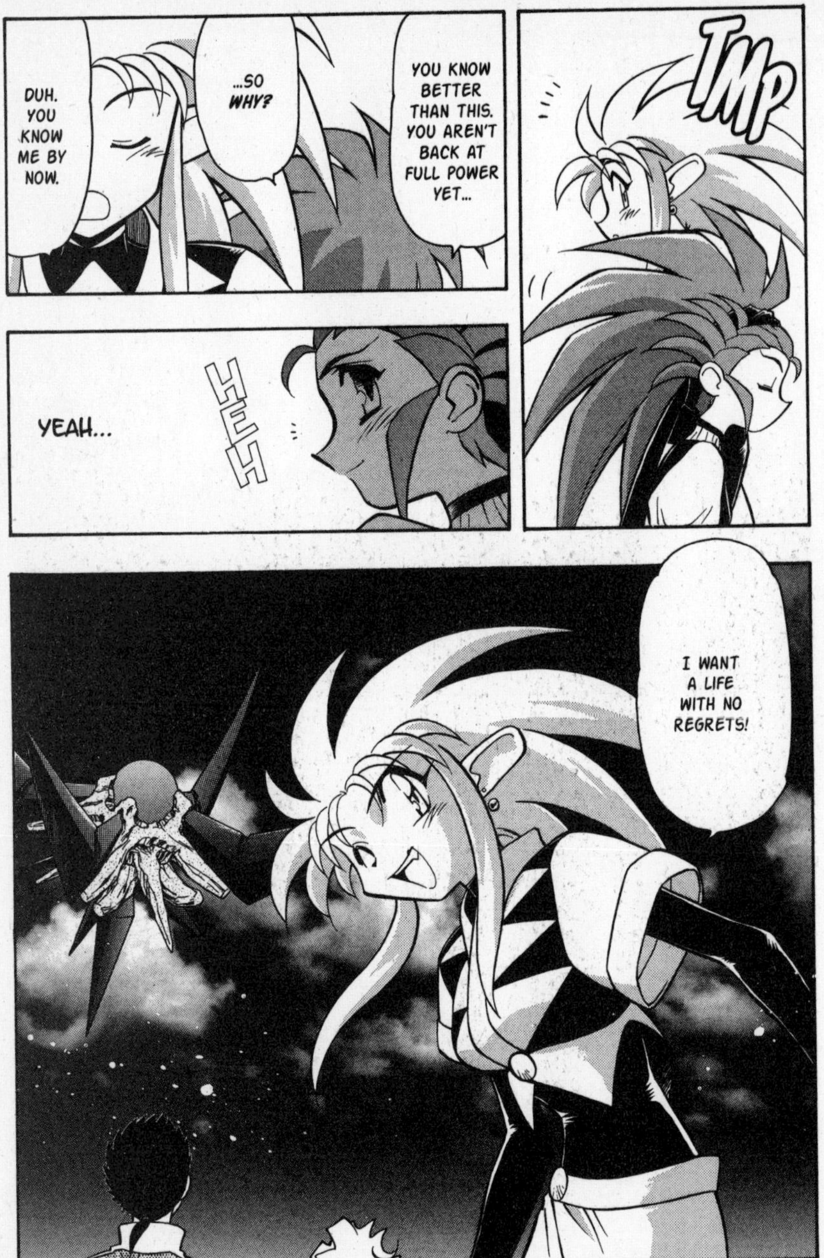
TMP
YOU KNOW BETTER THAN THIS. YOU AREN'T BACK AT FULL POWER YET...
...SO WHY?
DUH. YOU KNOW ME BY NOW.
HEH
YEAH...
I WANT A LIFE WITH NO REGRETS!

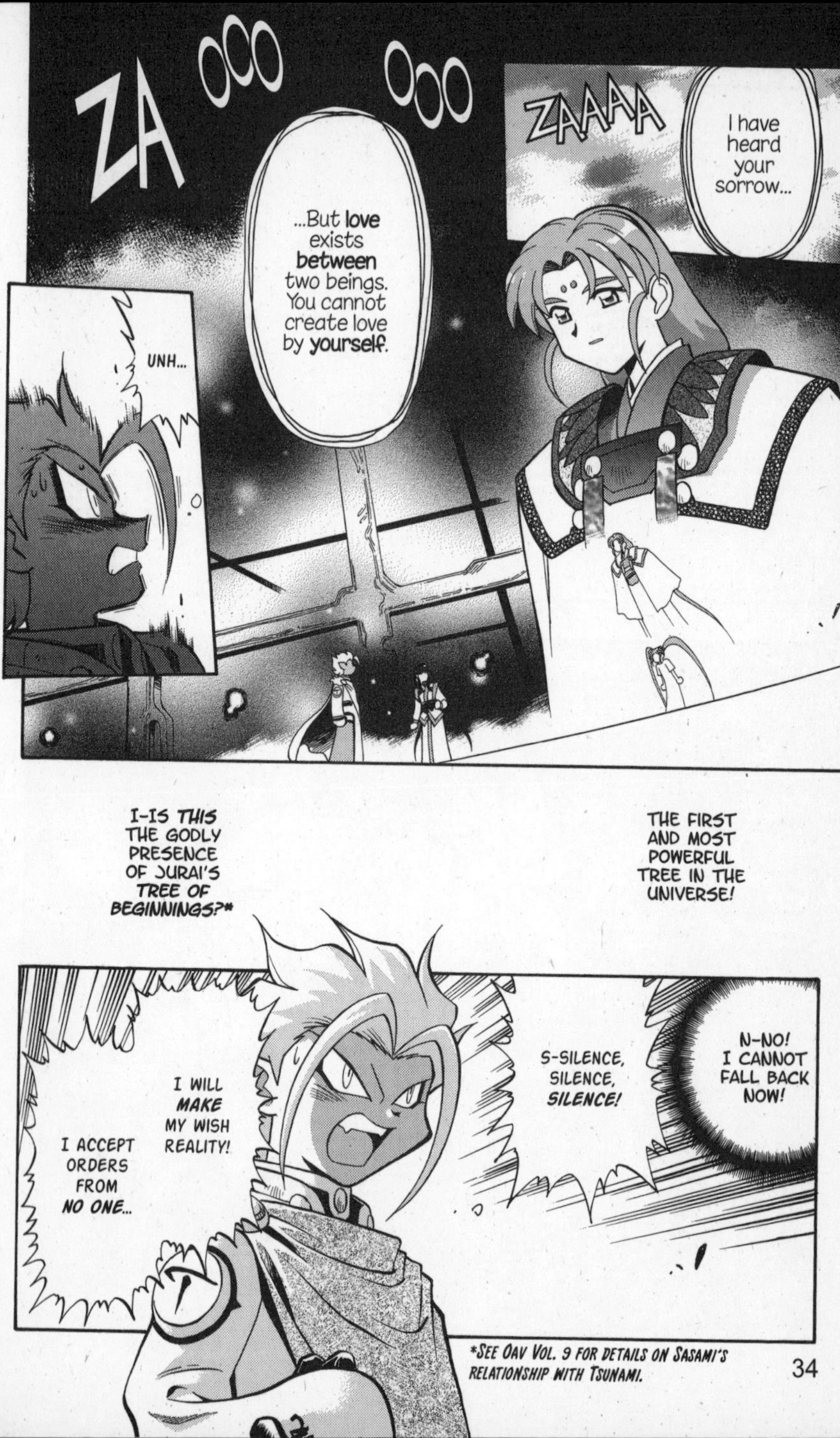
ZAAAA
I have heard your sorrow...
ZA OOO OOO
...But **love** exists **between** two beings. You cannot create love by **yourself**.
UNH...
THE FIRST AND MOST POWERFUL TREE IN THE UNIVERSE!
I-IS *THIS* THE GODLY PRESENCE OF JURAI'S *TREE OF BEGINNINGS?**
N-NO! I CANNOT FALL BACK NOW!
S-SILENCE, SILENCE, *SILENCE!*
I WILL *MAKE* MY WISH REALITY!
I ACCEPT ORDERS FROM *NO ONE*...

**SEE OAV VOL. 9 FOR DETAILS ON SASAMI'S RELATIONSHIP WITH TSUNAMI.*

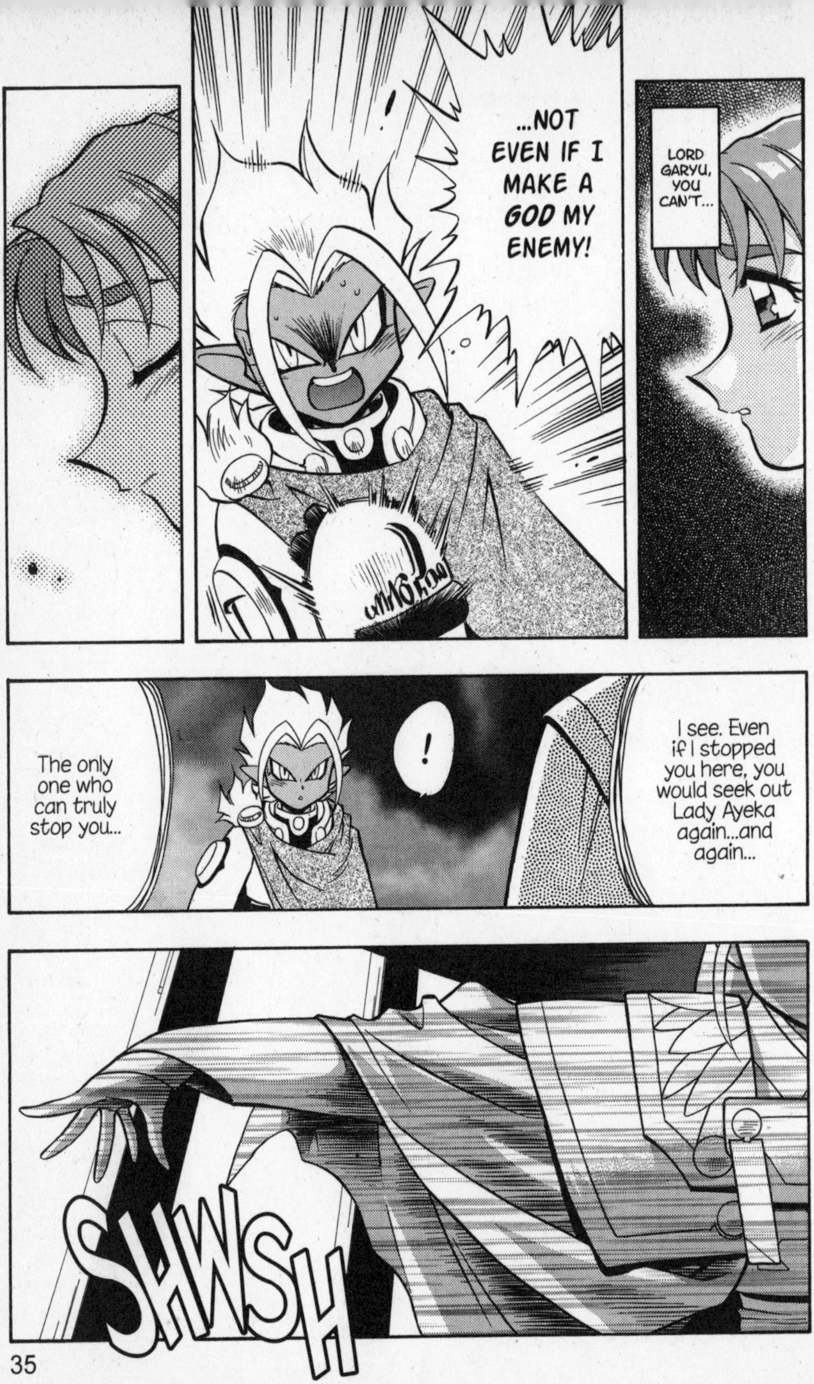
LORD GARYU, YOU CAN'T...
...NOT EVEN IF I MAKE A GOD MY ENEMY!
I see. Even if I stopped you here, you would seek out Lady Ayeka again...and again...
!
The only one who can truly stop you...
SHWSH

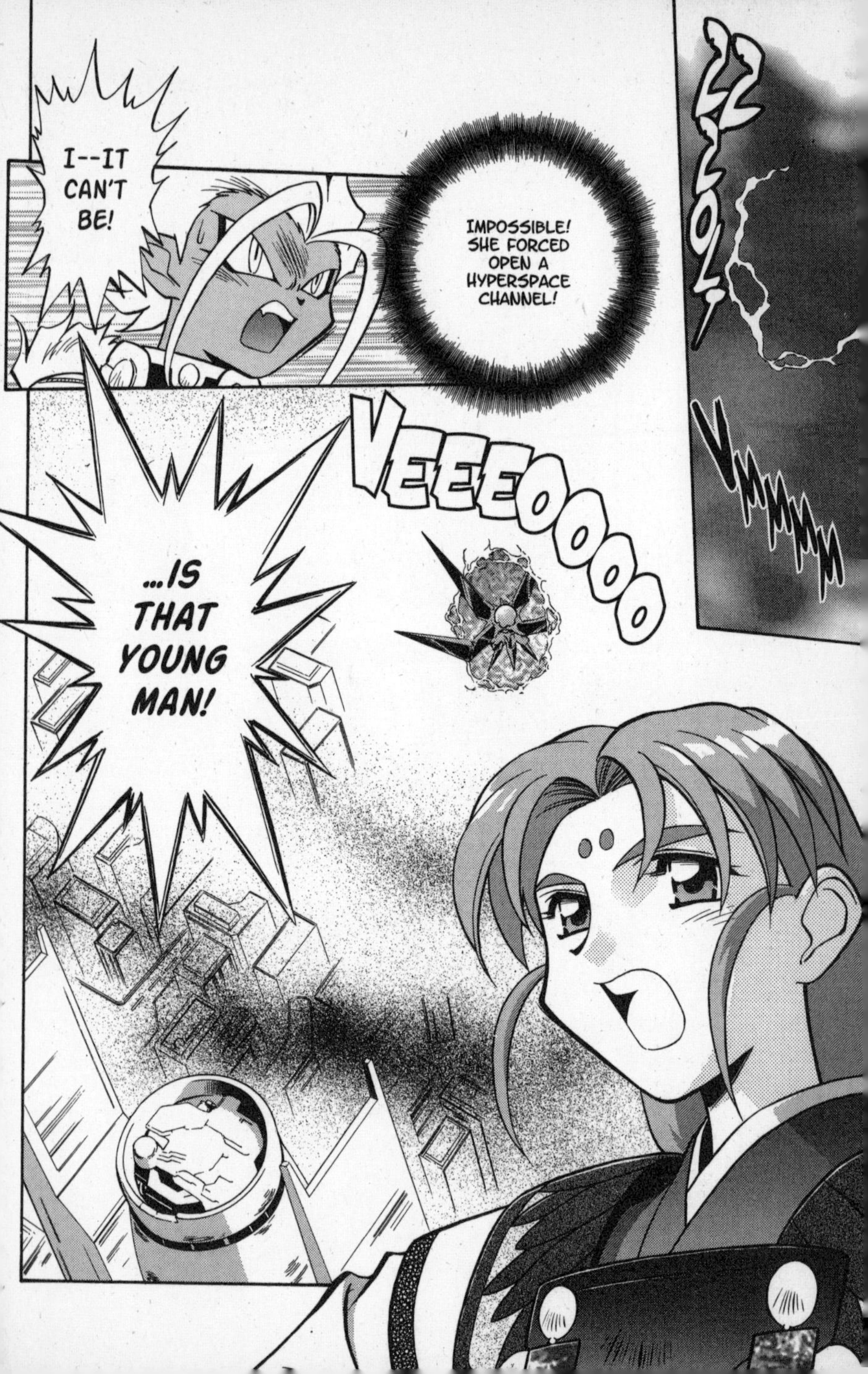
VMMMMM
IMPOSSIBLE! SHE FORCED OPEN A HYPERSPACE CHANNEL!
I--IT CAN'T BE!
VEEEOOOOO
...IS THAT YOUNG MAN!

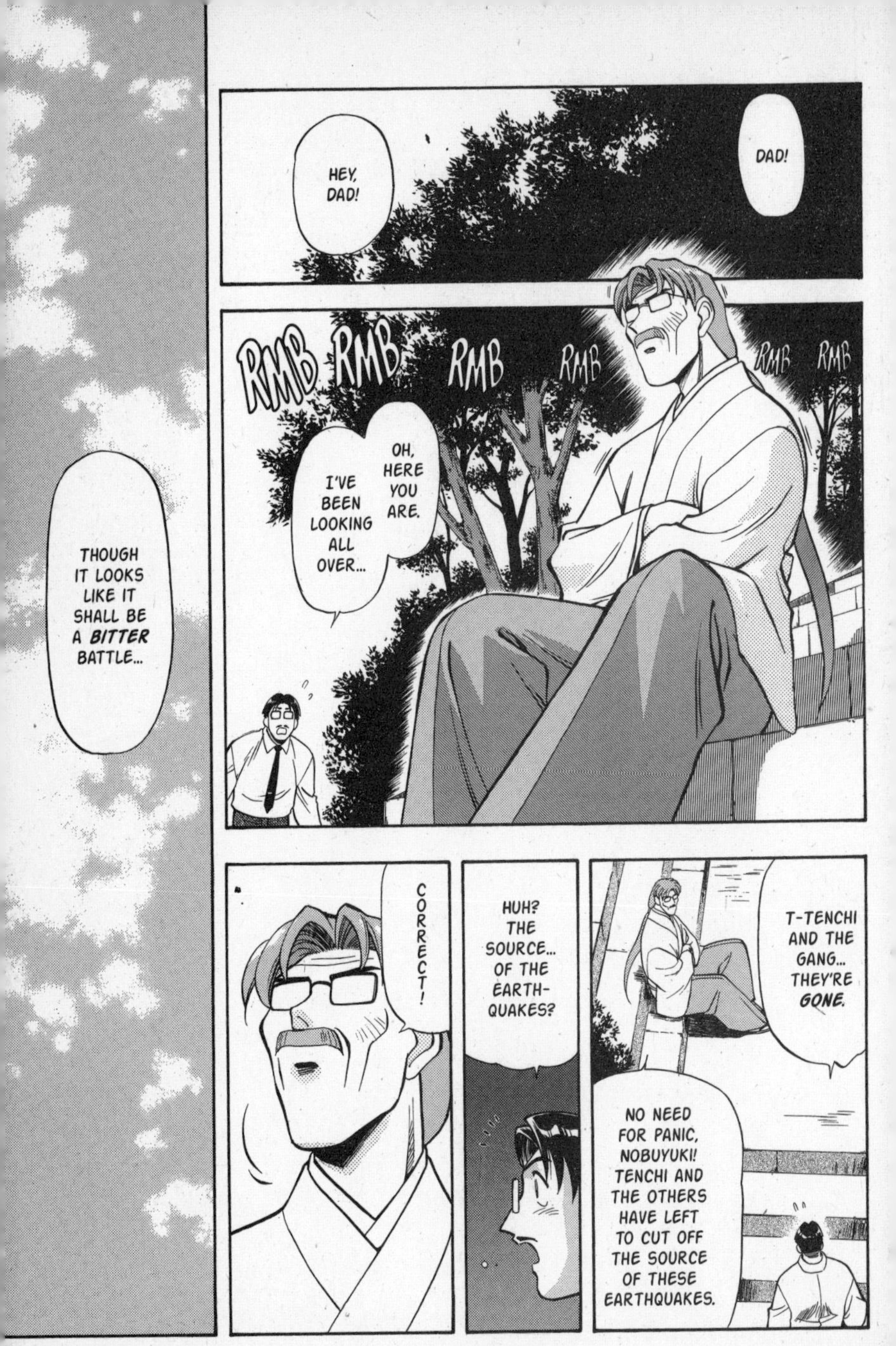
DAD!
HEY, DAD!
RMB RMB RMB RMB RMB RMB
OH, HERE YOU ARE.
I'VE BEEN LOOKING ALL OVER...
T-TENCHI AND THE GANG... THEY'RE GONE.
NO NEED FOR PANIC, NOBUYUKI! TENCHI AND THE OTHERS HAVE LEFT TO CUT OFF THE SOURCE OF THESE EARTHQUAKES.
HUH? THE SOURCE... OF THE EARTHQUAKES?
CORRECT!
THOUGH IT LOOKS LIKE IT SHALL BE A BITTER BATTLE...

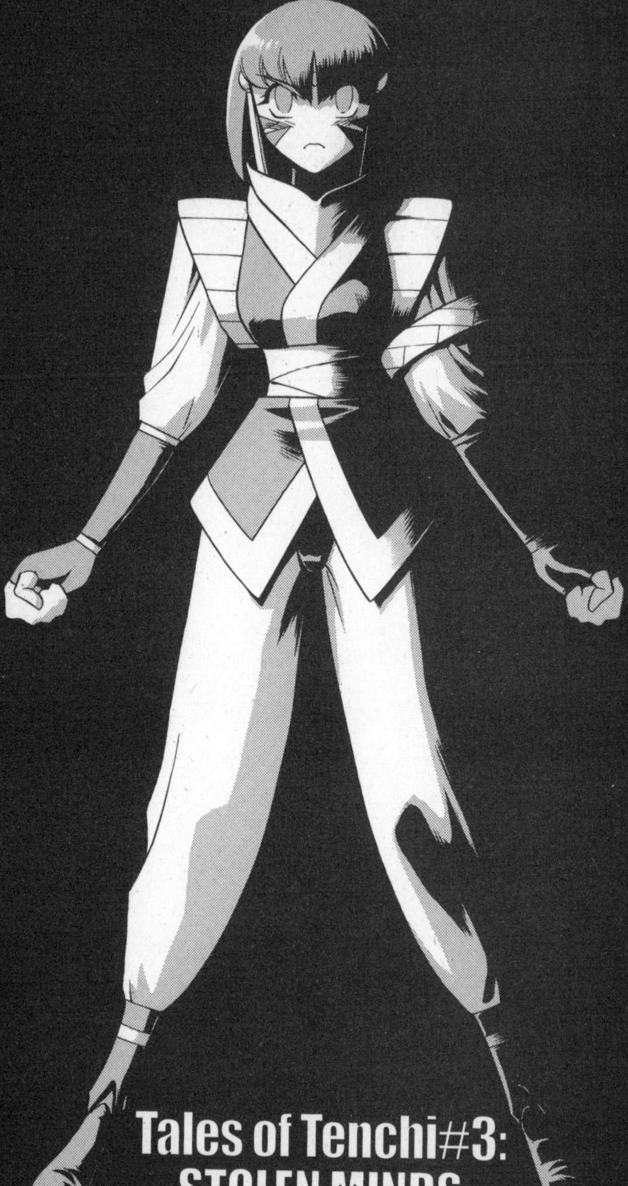

Tales of Tenchi#3: STOLEN MINDS

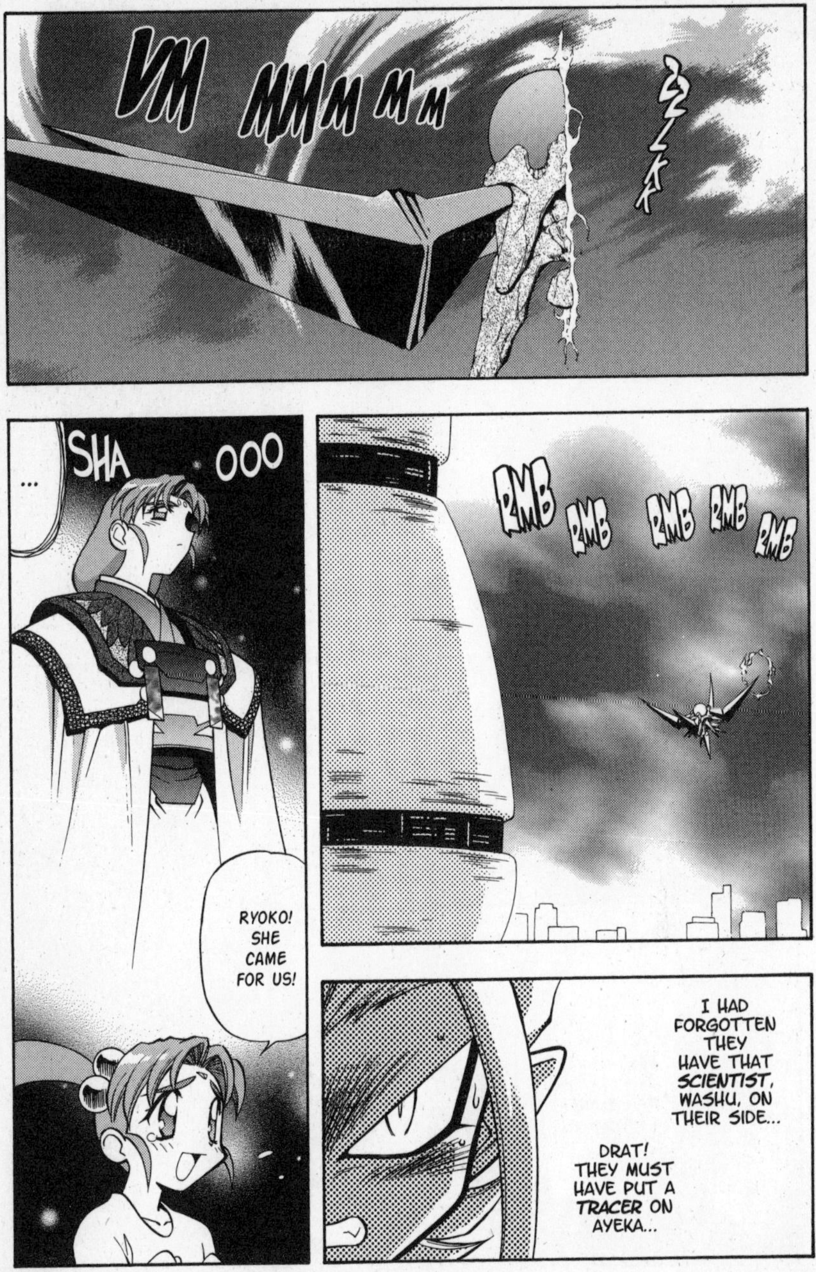
VM MMMM MM
ZZLKK
RMB RMB RMB RMB RMB
I HAD FORGOTTEN THEY HAVE THAT SCIENTIST, WASHU, ON THEIR SIDE...
DRAT! THEY MUST HAVE PUT A TRACER ON AYEKA...
SHA OOO
...
RYOKO! SHE CAME FOR US!

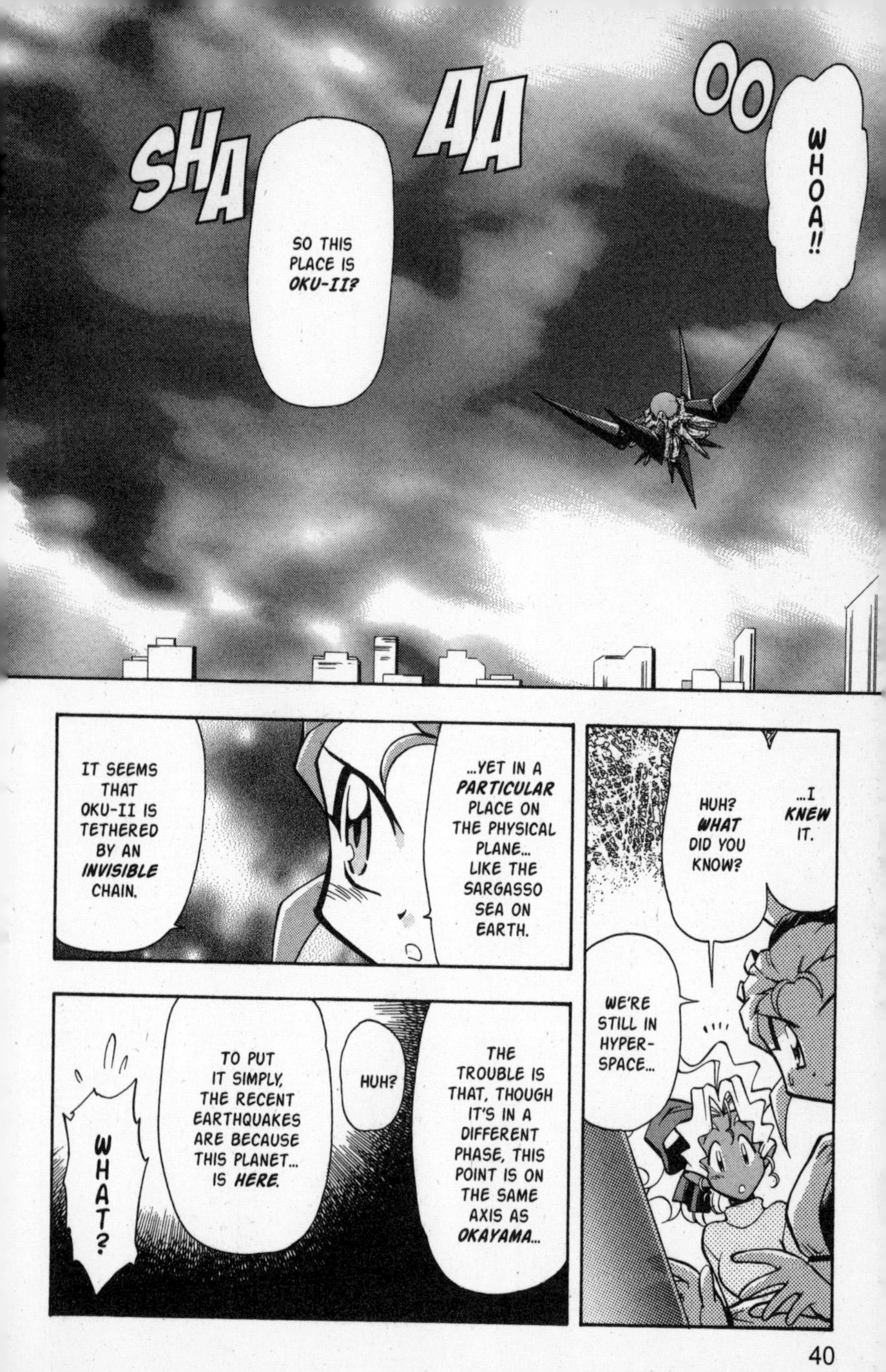
WHOA!!
SHA AA OO
SO THIS PLACE IS OKU-II?
...I KNEW IT.
HUH? WHAT DID YOU KNOW?
WE'RE STILL IN HYPER-SPACE...
...YET IN A PARTICULAR PLACE ON THE PHYSICAL PLANE... LIKE THE SARGASSO SEA ON EARTH.
IT SEEMS THAT OKU-II IS TETHERED BY AN INVISIBLE CHAIN.
THE TROUBLE IS THAT, THOUGH IT'S IN A DIFFERENT PHASE, THIS POINT IS ON THE SAME AXIS AS OKAYAMA...
HUH?
TO PUT IT SIMPLY, THE RECENT EARTHQUAKES ARE BECAUSE THIS PLANET... IS HERE.
WHAT?

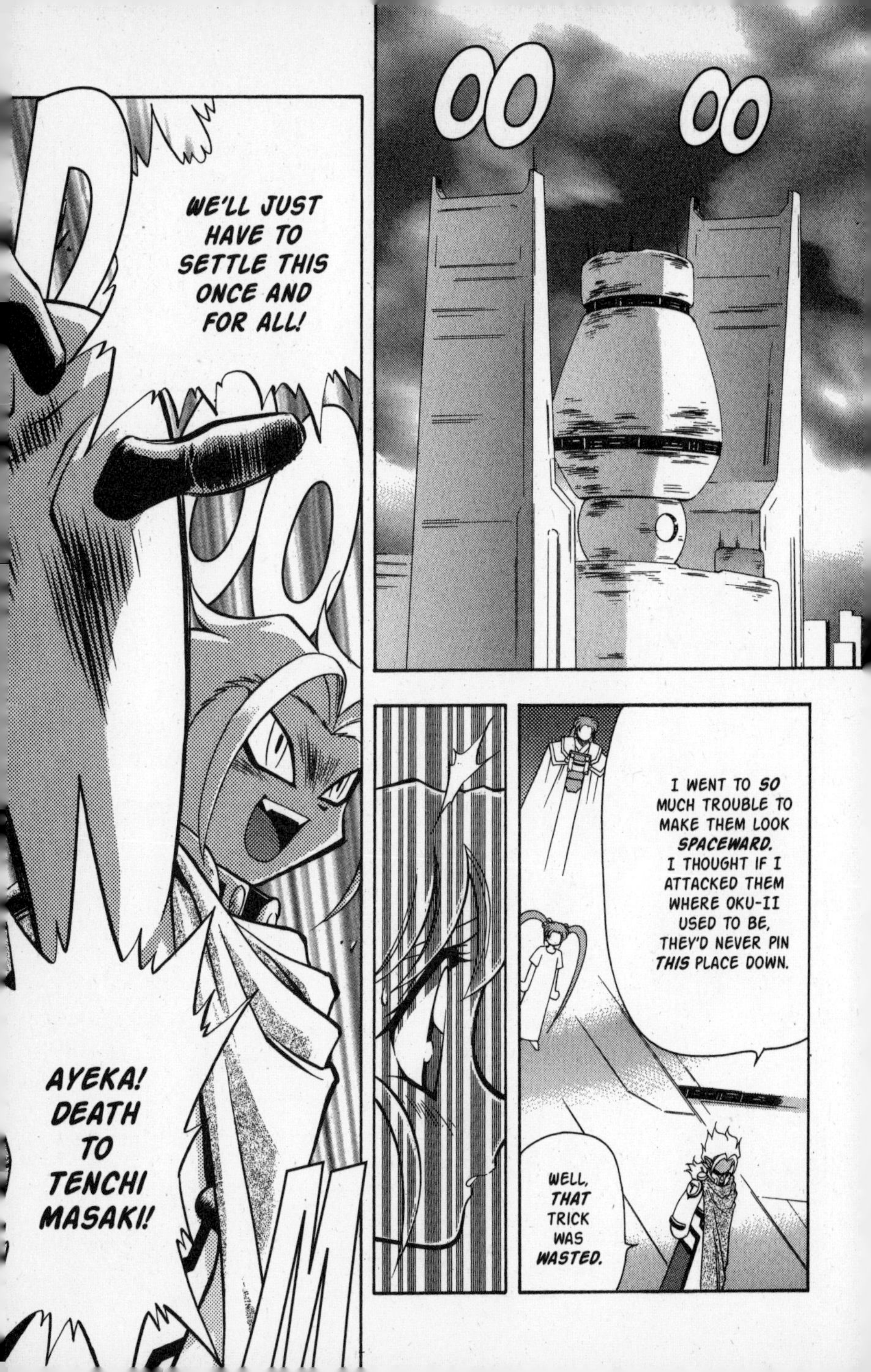
OO OO
I WENT TO SO MUCH TROUBLE TO MAKE THEM LOOK SPACEWARD. I THOUGHT IF I ATTACKED THEM WHERE OKU-II USED TO BE, THEY'D NEVER PIN THIS PLACE DOWN.
WELL, THAT TRICK WAS WASTED.
WE'LL JUST HAVE TO SETTLE THIS ONCE AND FOR ALL!
AYEKA! DEATH TO TENCHI MASAKI!

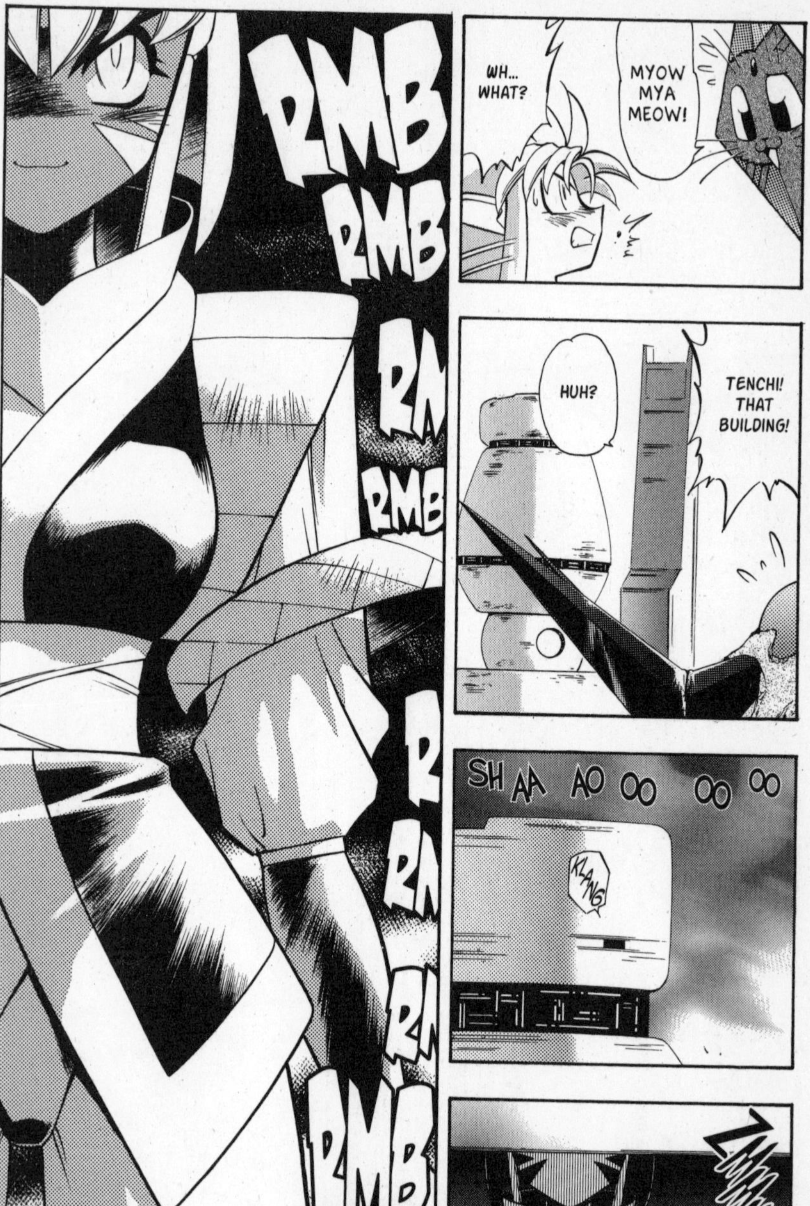
MYOW MYA MEOW!
WH... WHAT?
TENCHI! THAT BUILDING!
HUH?
SH AA AO OO OO OO
KLANG
RMB
RMB
RMB
RMB

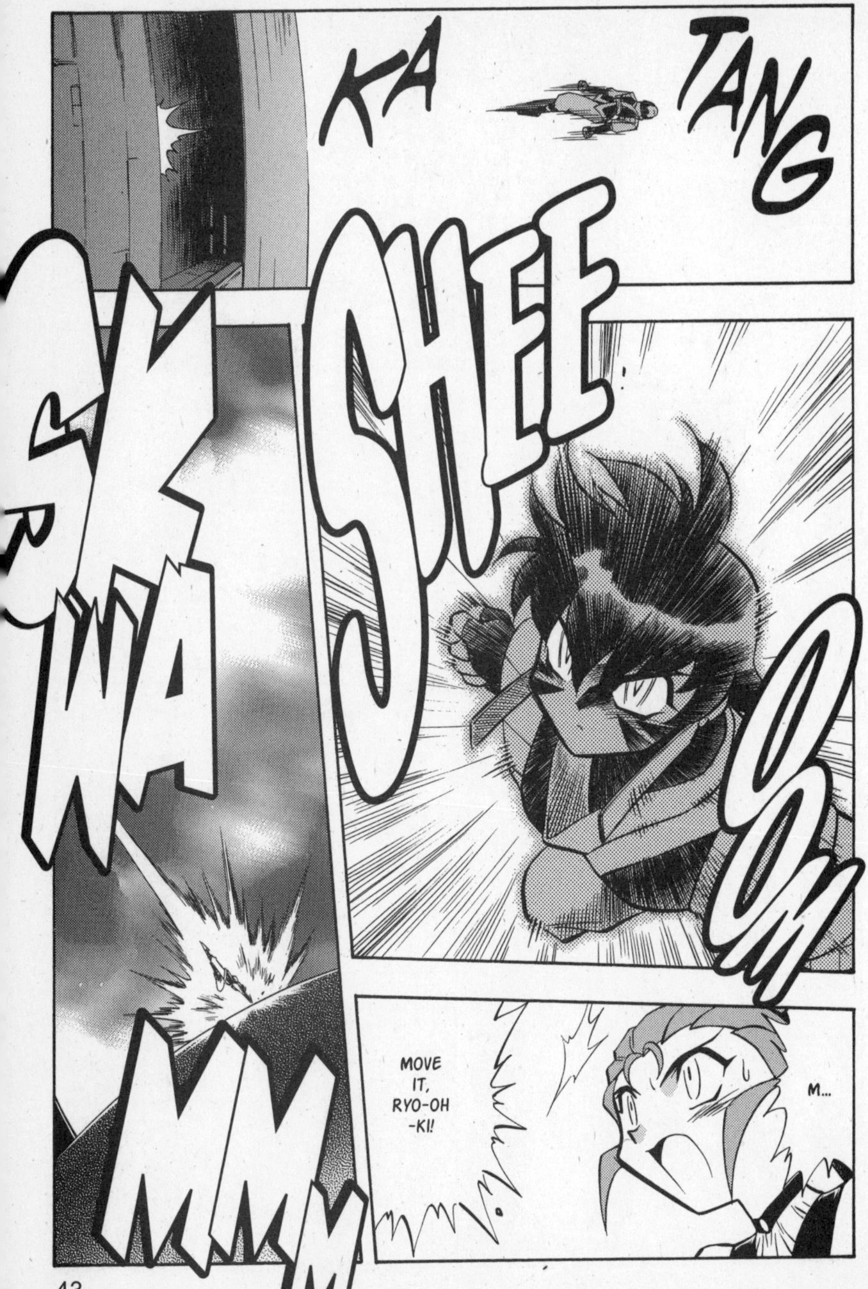
KA TANG
SHEE
SOOM
SKRWAMMM
M...
MOVE IT, RYO-OH-KI!

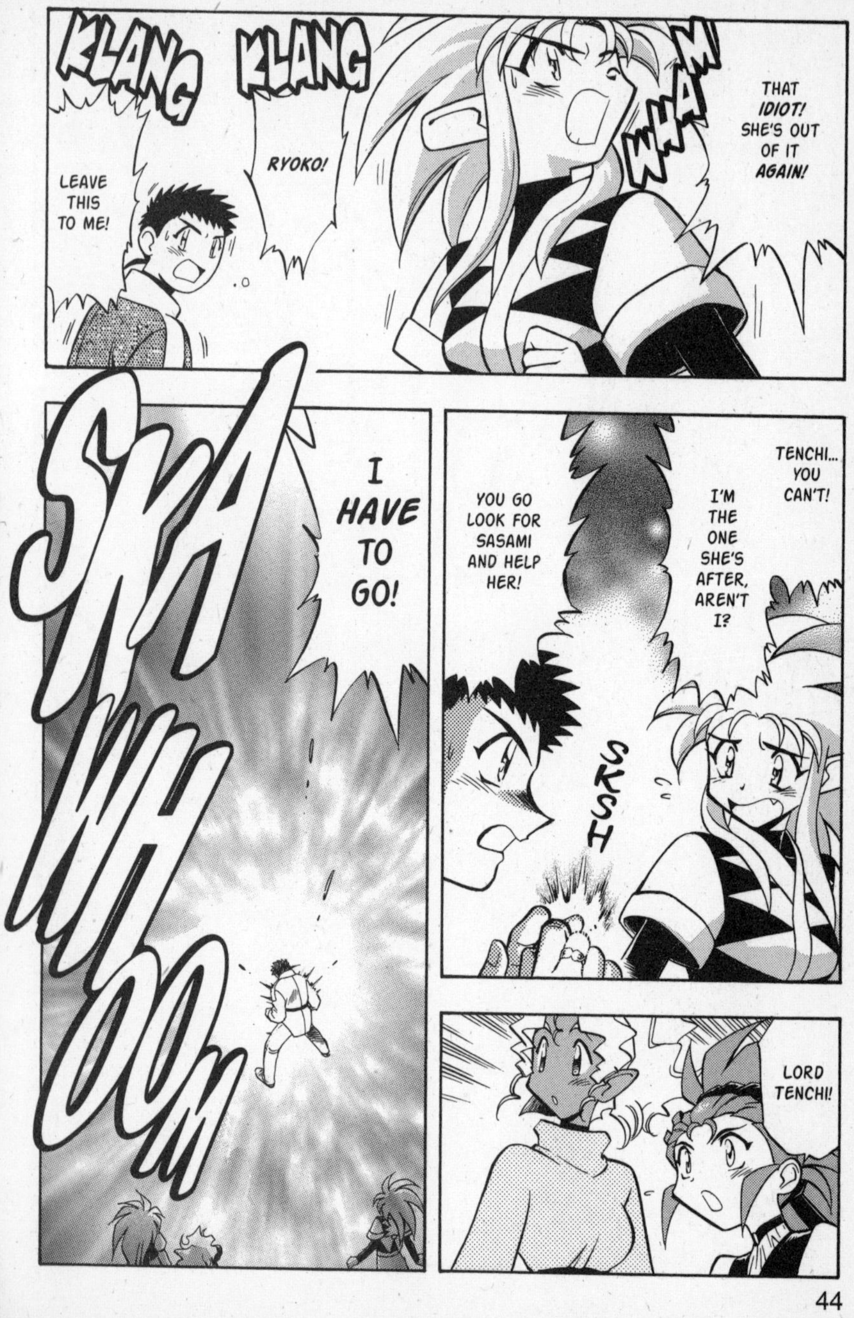
THAT IDIOT! SHE'S OUT OF IT AGAIN!
WHAM
KLANG KLANG
RYOKO!
LEAVE THIS TO ME!
TENCHI... YOU CAN'T!
I'M THE ONE SHE'S AFTER, AREN'T I?
YOU GO LOOK FOR SASAMI AND HELP HER!
SKSH
LORD TENCHI!
I HAVE TO GO!

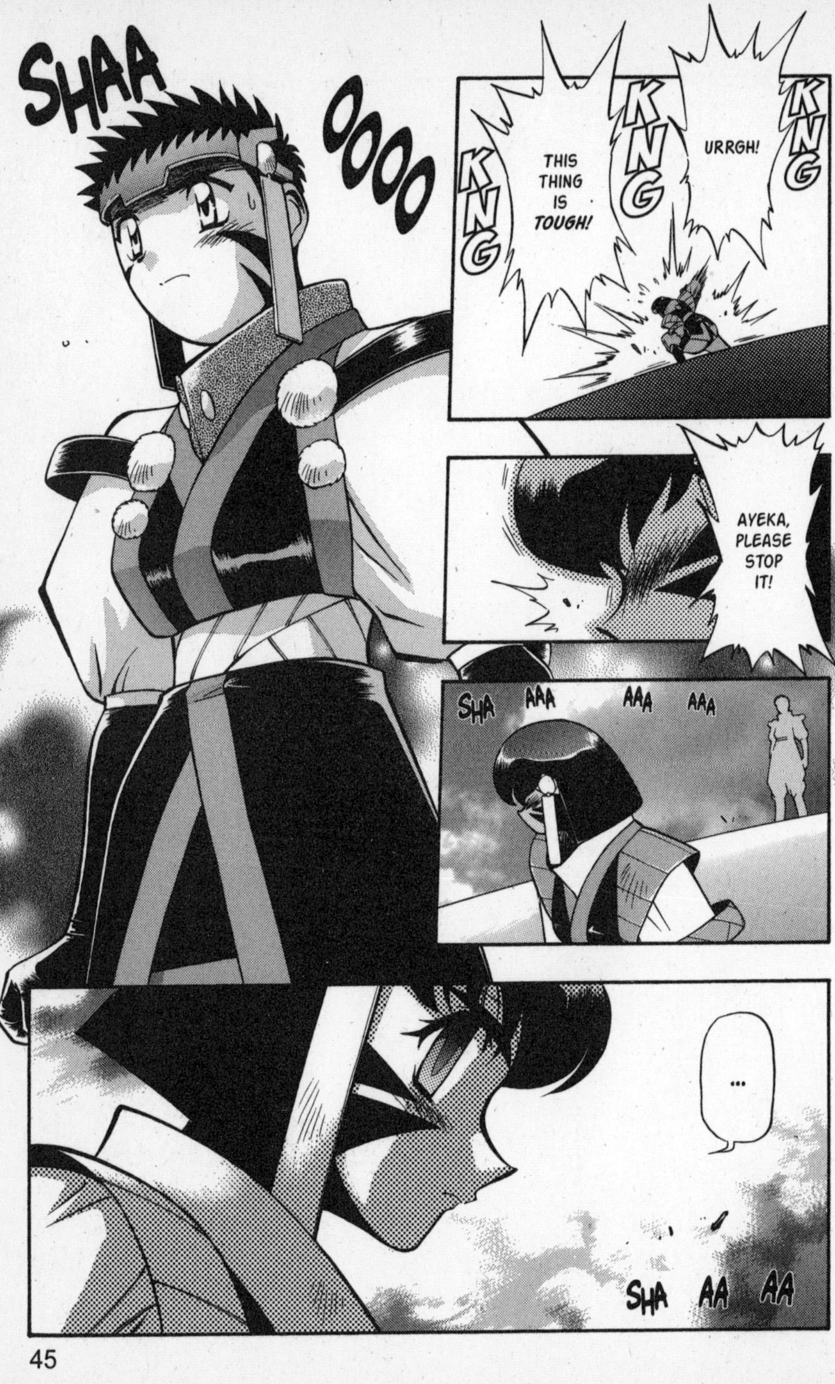
KNG
URRGH!
KNG
THIS THING IS TOUGH!
KNG
AYEKA, PLEASE STOP IT!
SHA AAA AAA AAA
SHAA OOOO
...
SHA AA AA

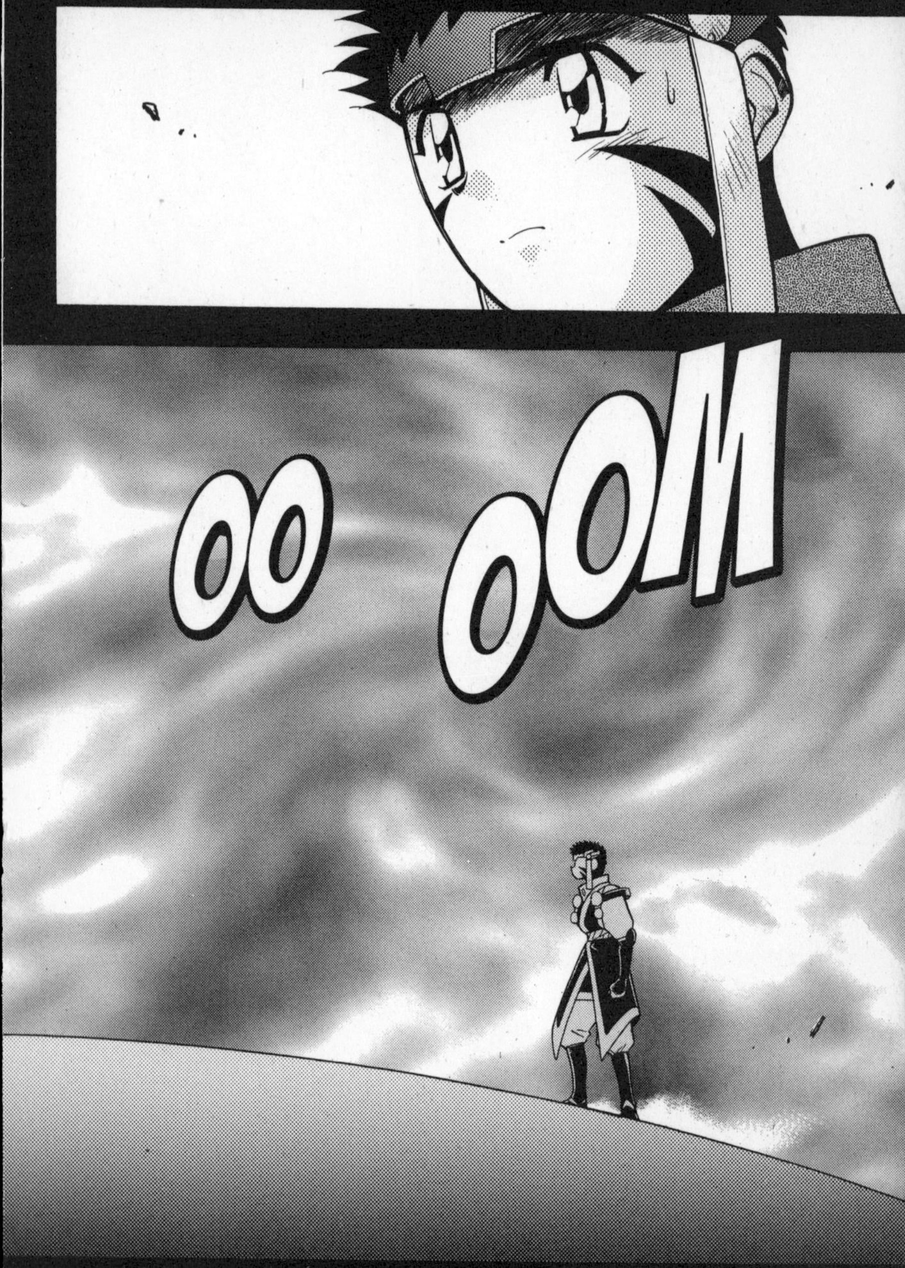
OO OOM

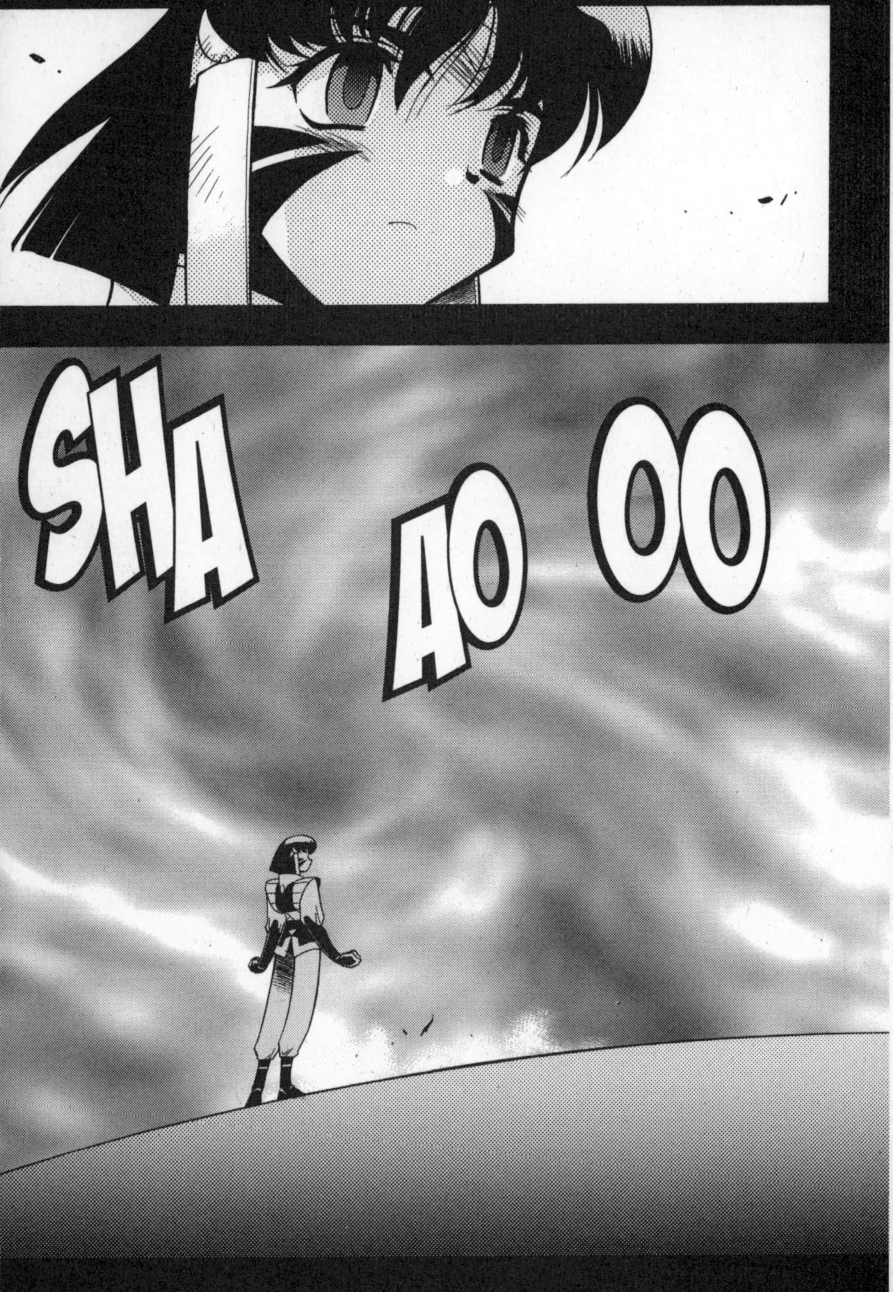
SHA
AO
OO

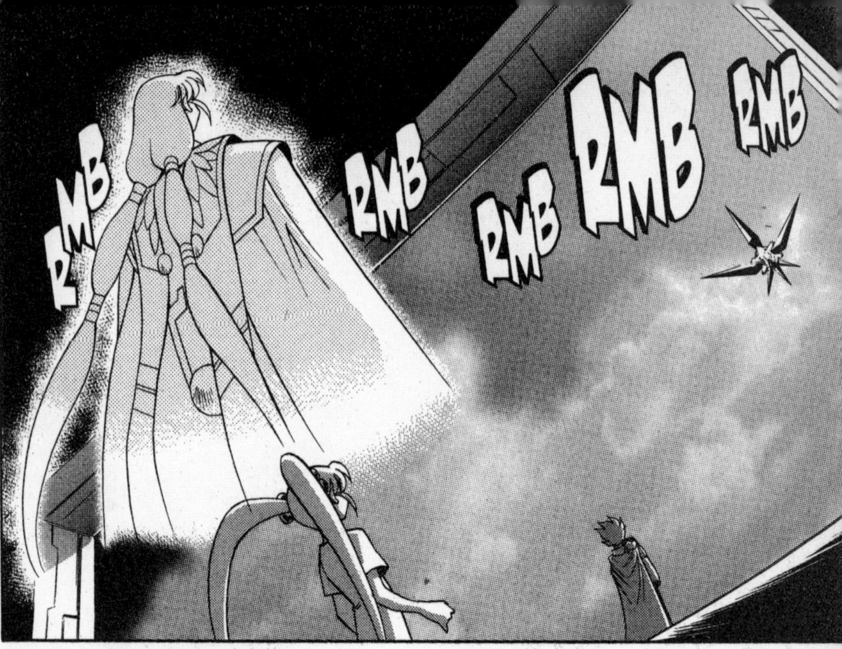
RMB
RMB
RMB
RMB
RMB

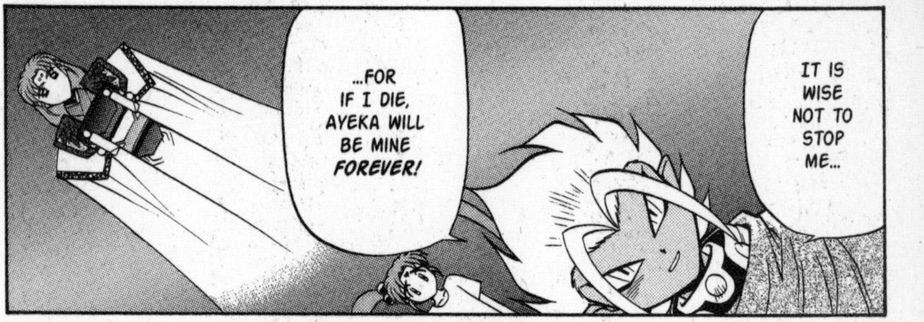
IT IS WISE NOT TO STOP ME...
...FOR IF I DIE, AYEKA WILL BE MINE *FOREVER!*

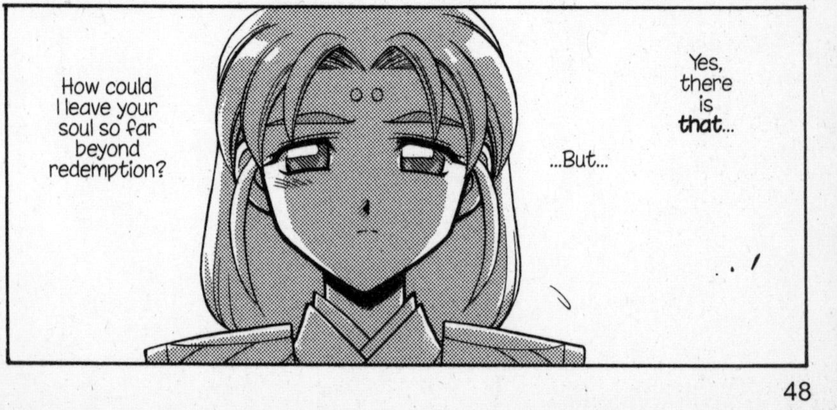
Yes, there is **that**...
...But...
How could I leave your soul so far beyond redemption?

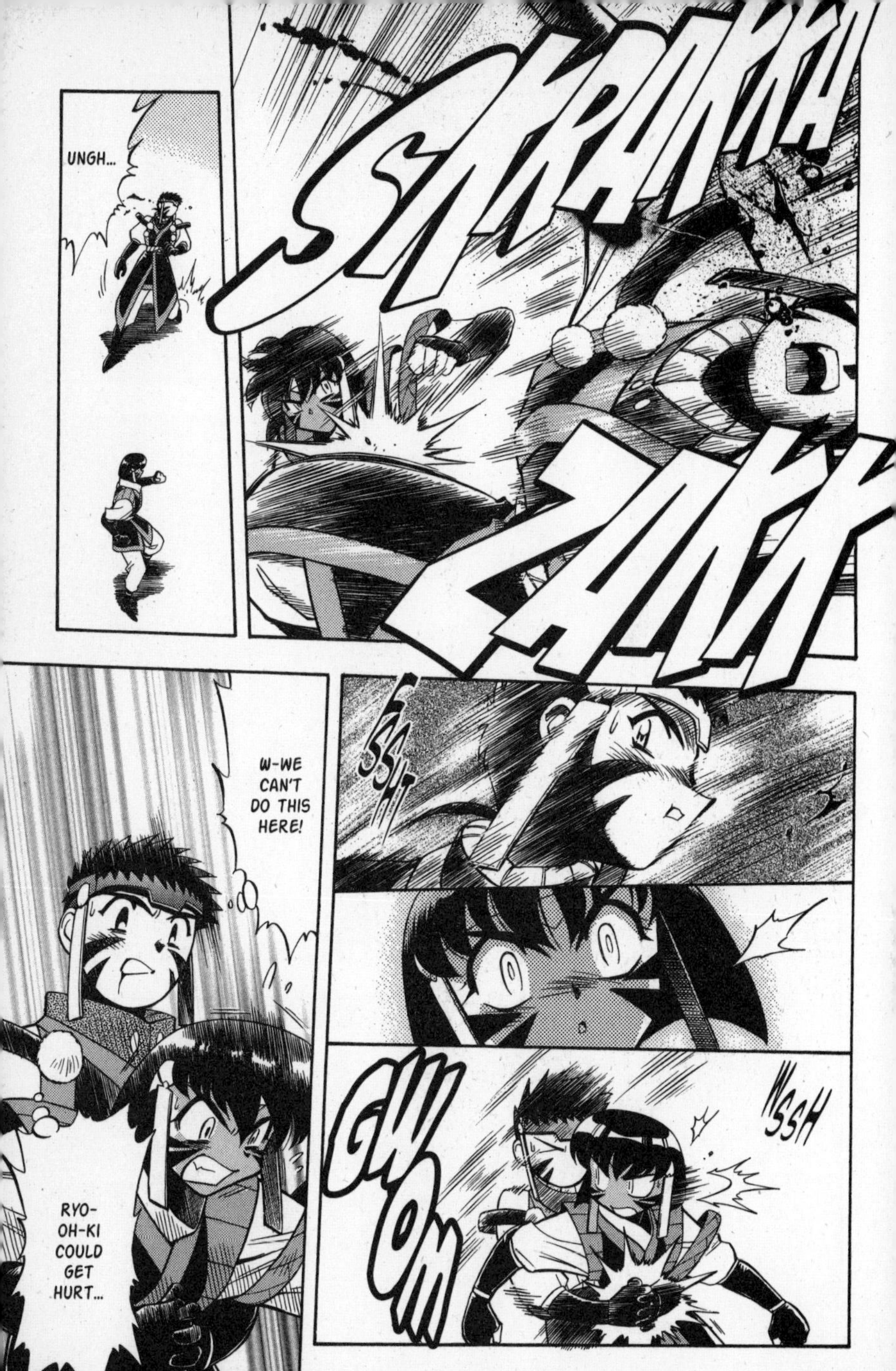
SHRAKKA
ZAKK
UNGH...
FSSHT
W-WE CAN'T DO THIS HERE!
WSSH
GWOM
RYO-OH-KI COULD GET HURT...

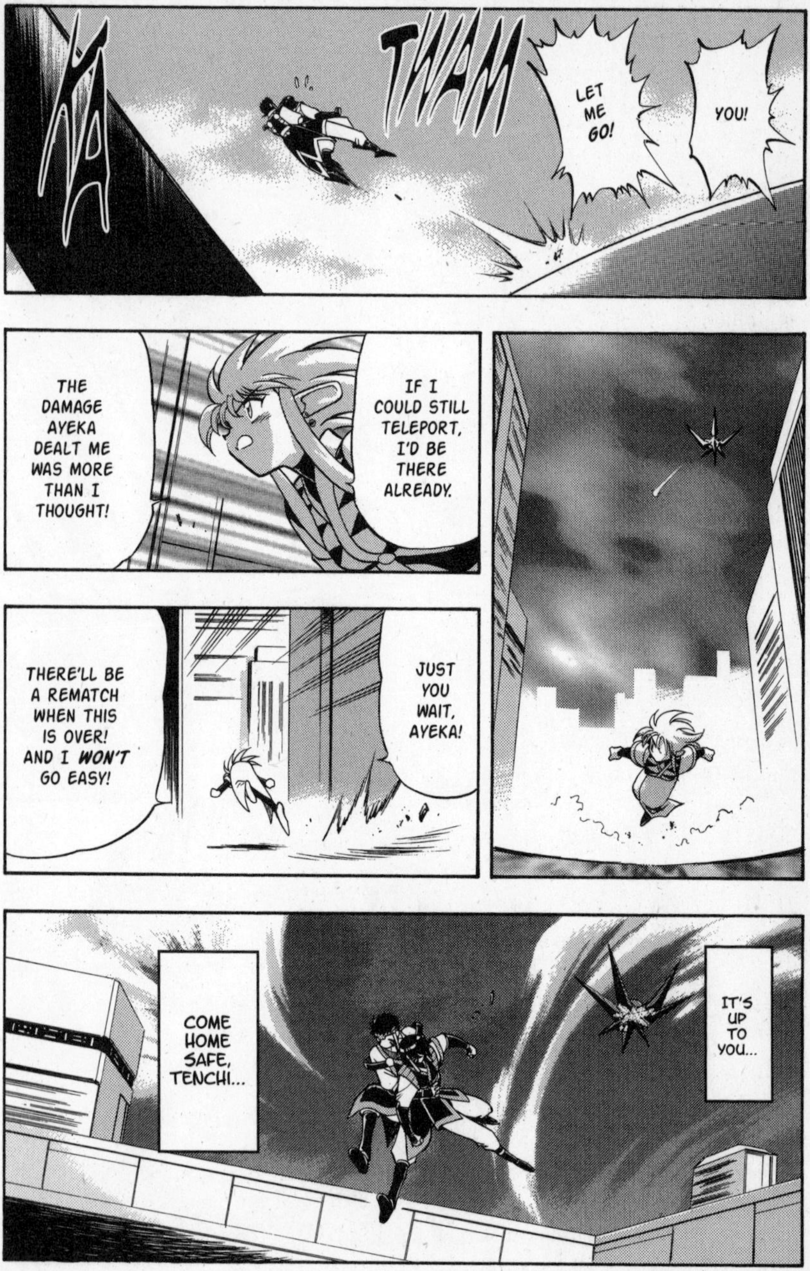
YOU!
LET ME GO!
THAM
KA
IF I COULD STILL TELEPORT, I'D BE THERE ALREADY.
THE DAMAGE AYEKA DEALT ME WAS MORE THAN I THOUGHT!
JUST YOU WAIT, AYEKA!
THERE'LL BE A REMATCH WHEN THIS IS OVER! AND I *WON'T* GO EASY!
IT'S UP TO YOU...
COME HOME SAFE, TENCHI...

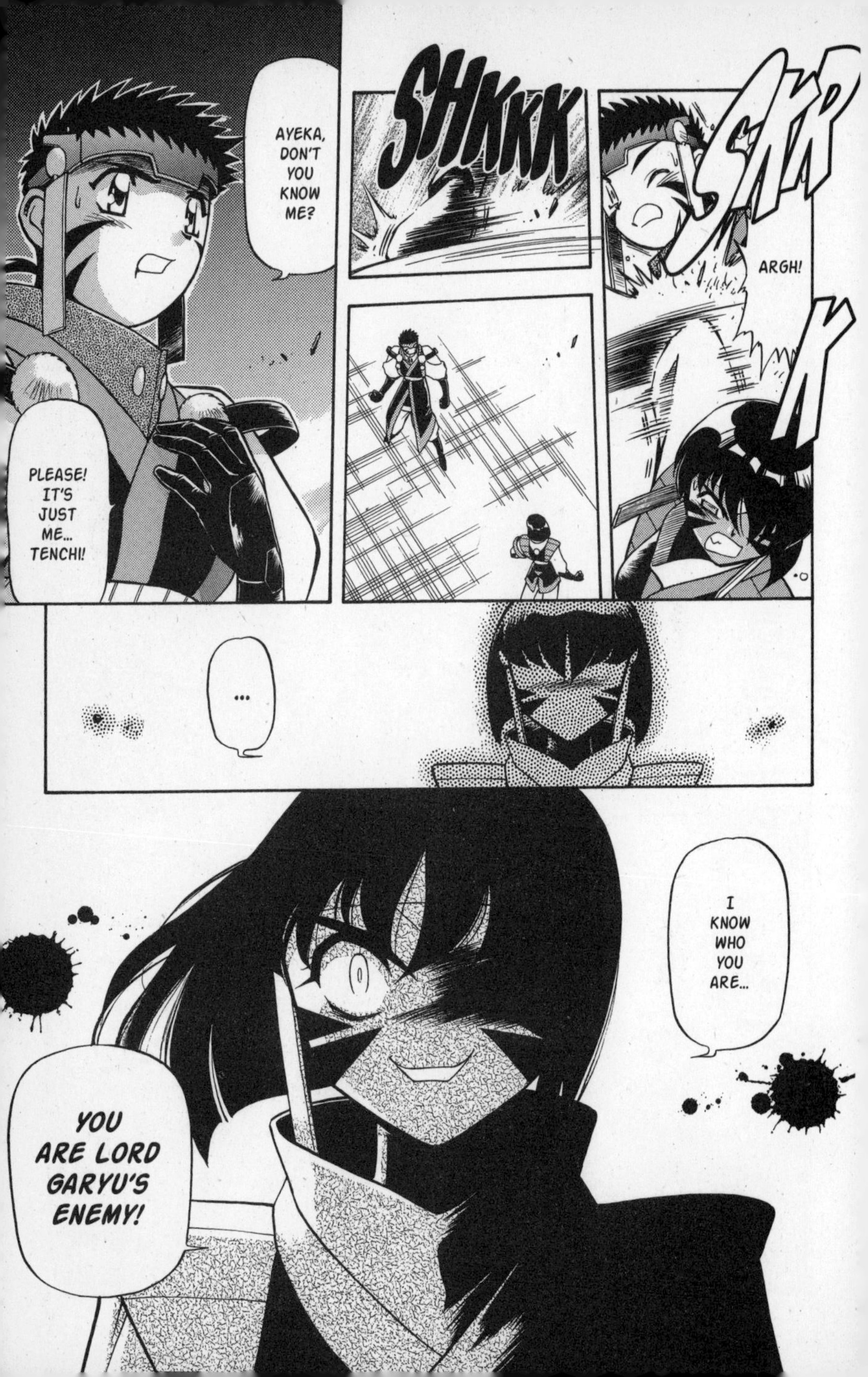
SKRAK
ARGH!
SHKKK
AYEKA, DON'T YOU KNOW ME?
PLEASE! IT'S JUST ME... TENCHI!
...
I KNOW WHO YOU ARE...
YOU ARE LORD GARYU'S ENEMY!

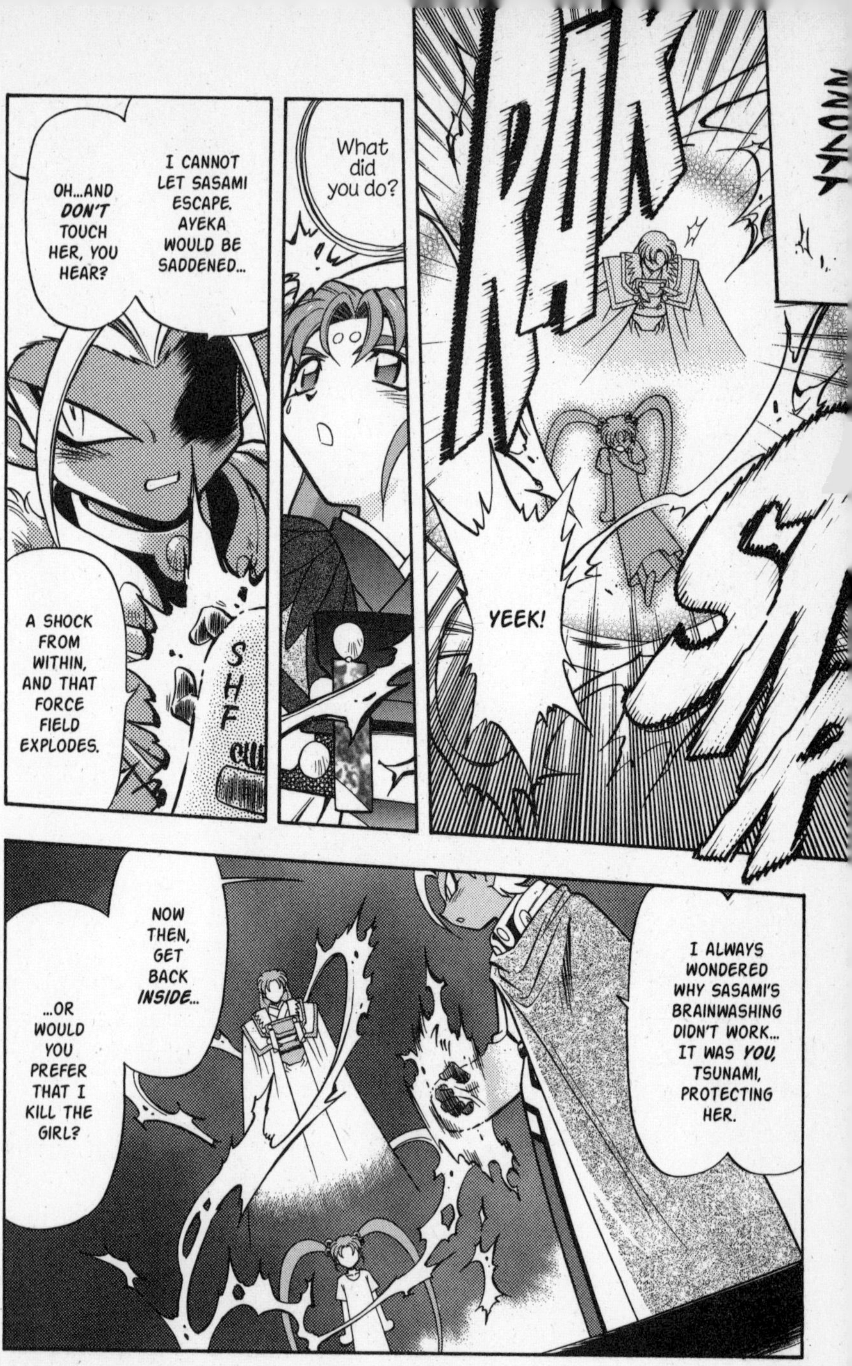

YEEK!
What did you do?
I CANNOT LET SASAMI ESCAPE. AYEKA WOULD BE SADDENED...
OH...AND *DON'T* TOUCH HER, YOU HEAR?
A SHOCK FROM WITHIN, AND THAT FORCE FIELD EXPLODES.
SHF
I ALWAYS WONDERED WHY SASAMI'S BRAINWASHING DIDN'T WORK... IT WAS *YOU,* TSUNAMI, PROTECTING HER.
NOW THEN, GET BACK *INSIDE*...
...OR WOULD YOU PREFER THAT I KILL THE GIRL?

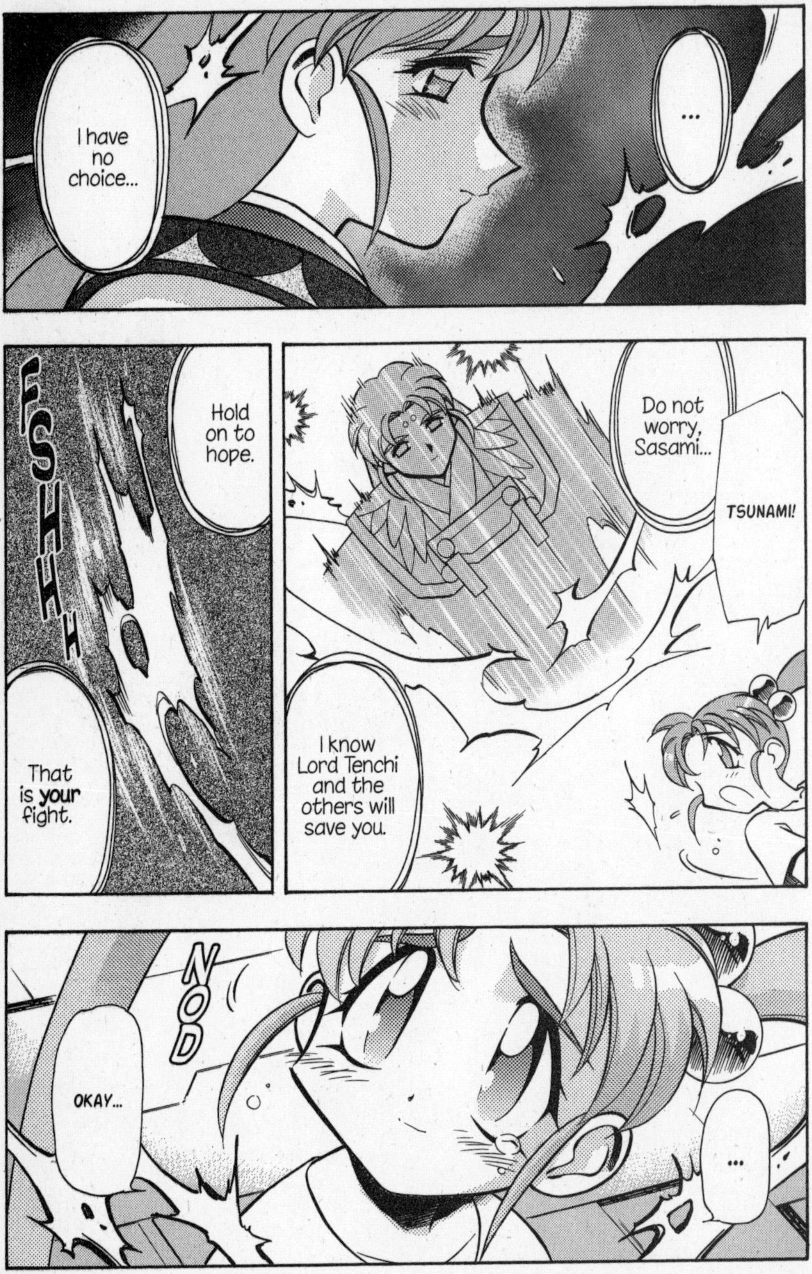
...
I have no choice...
TSUNAMI!
Do not worry, Sasami...
I know Lord Tenchi and the others will save you.
FSHHHH
Hold on to hope.
That is **your** fight.
...
NOD
OKAY...

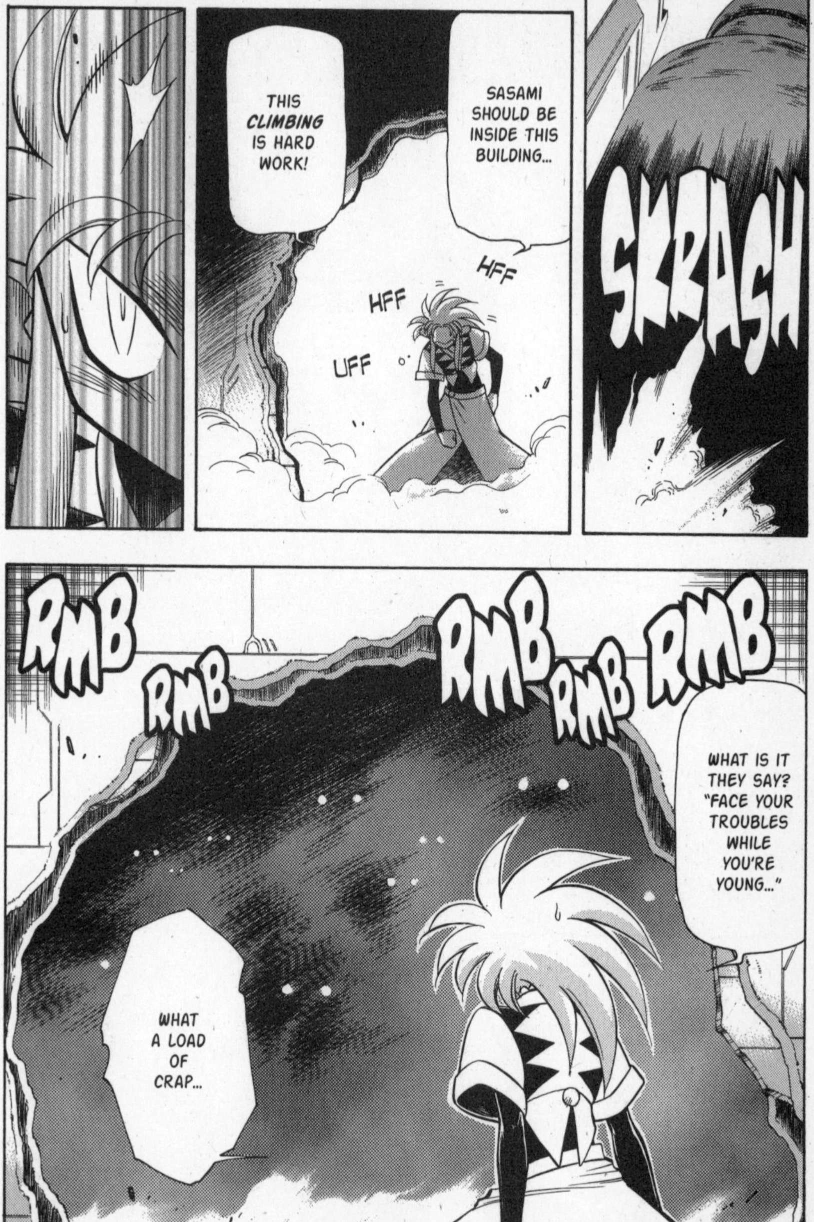
SKRASH
SASAMI SHOULD BE INSIDE THIS BUILDING...
THIS *CLIMBING* IS HARD WORK!
HFF
HFF
UFF
RMB
RMB
RMB
RMB
RMB
WHAT IS IT THEY SAY? "FACE YOUR TROUBLES WHILE YOU'RE YOUNG..."
WHAT A LOAD OF CRAP...

Tales of Tenchi #4: FALLING

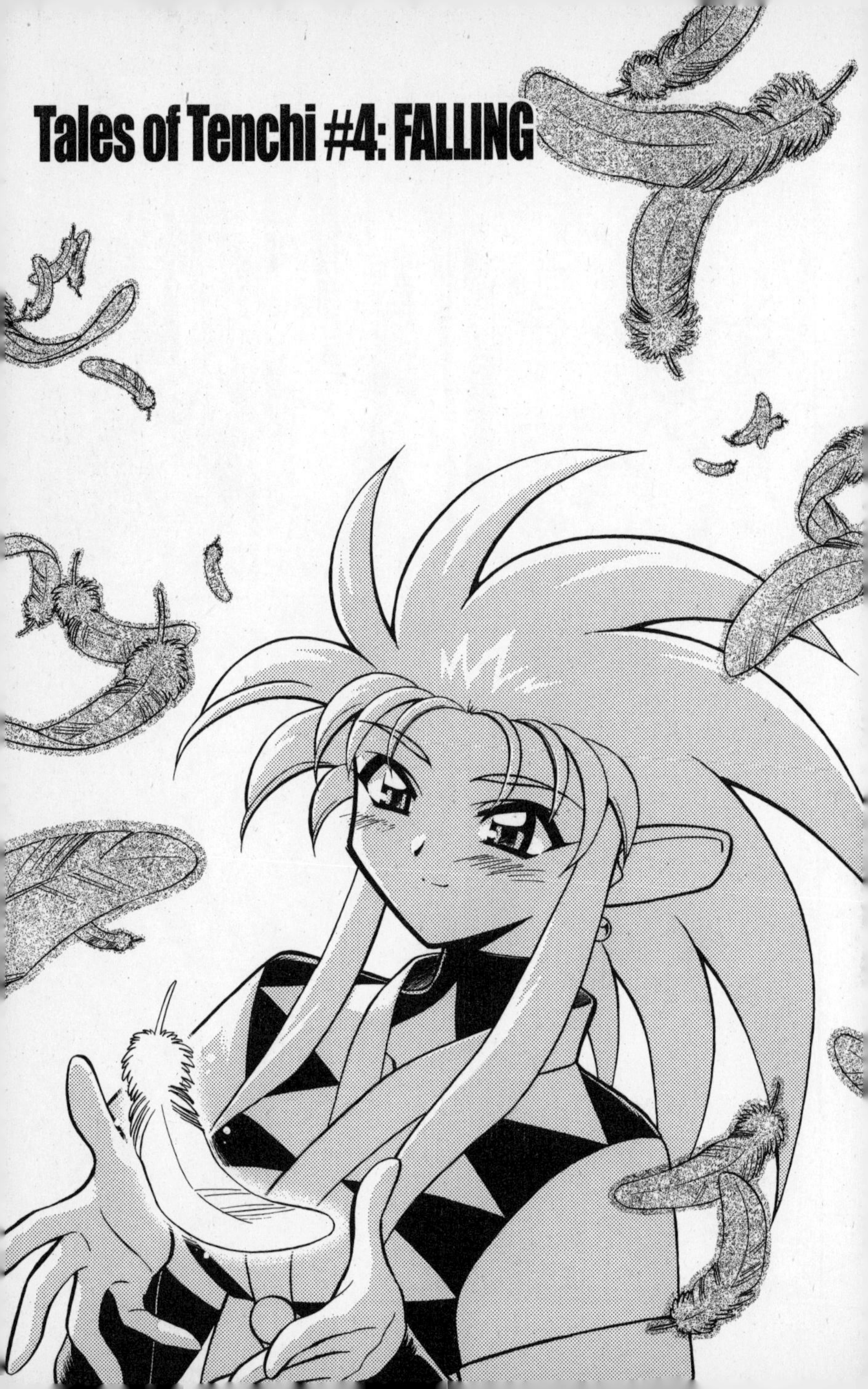

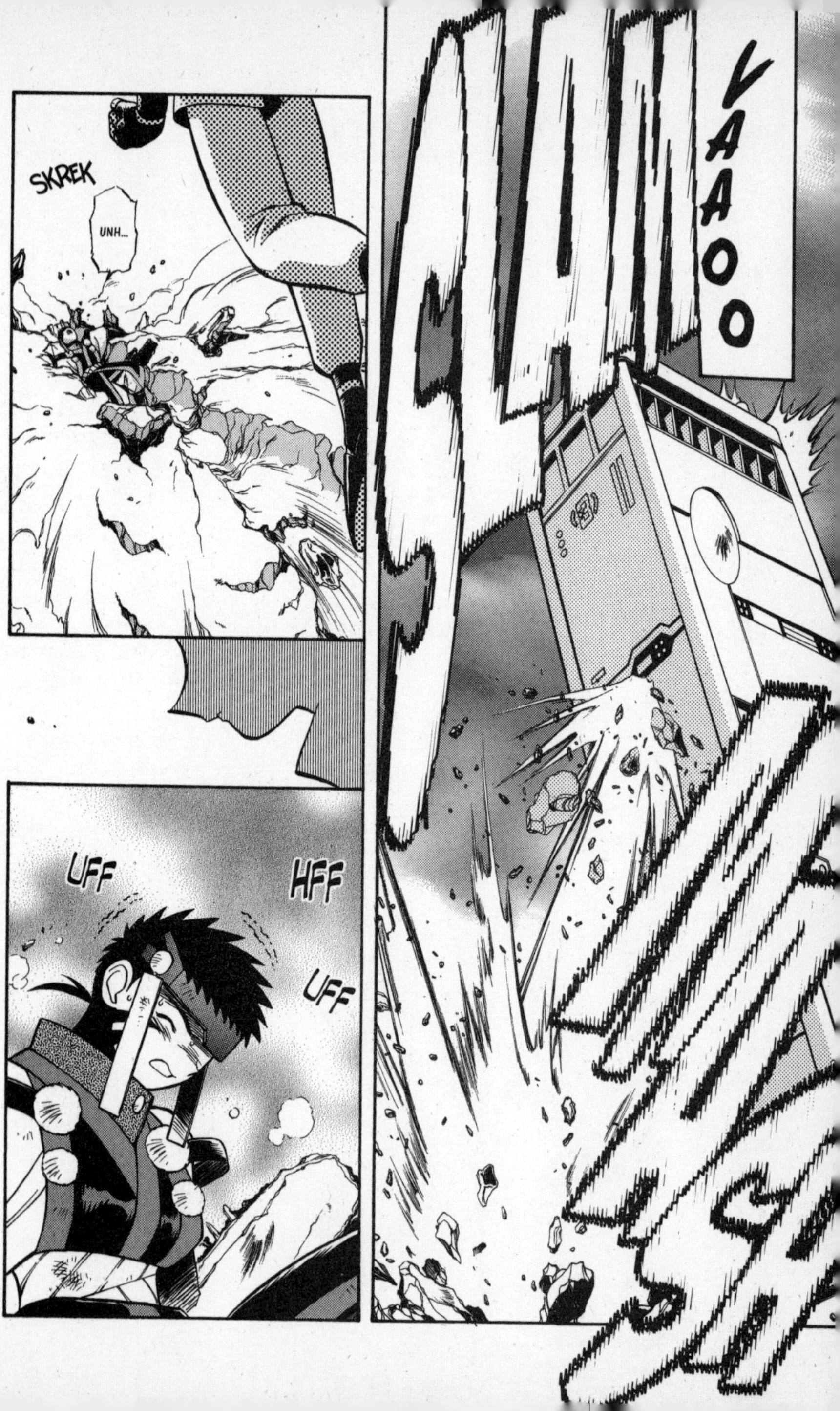
VAAOO
SKREK
UNH...
UFF
HFF
UFF

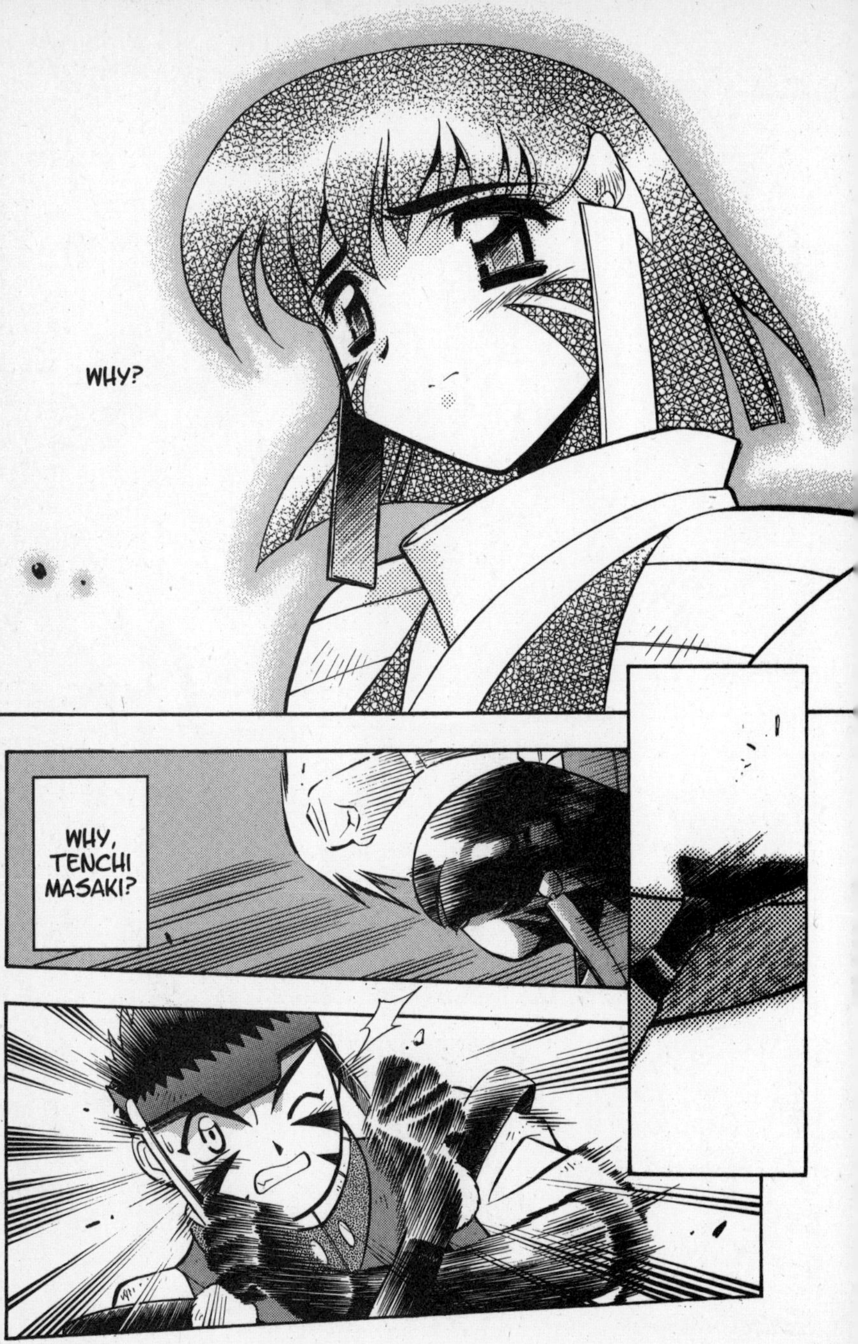
WHY?
WHY, TENCHI MASAKI?

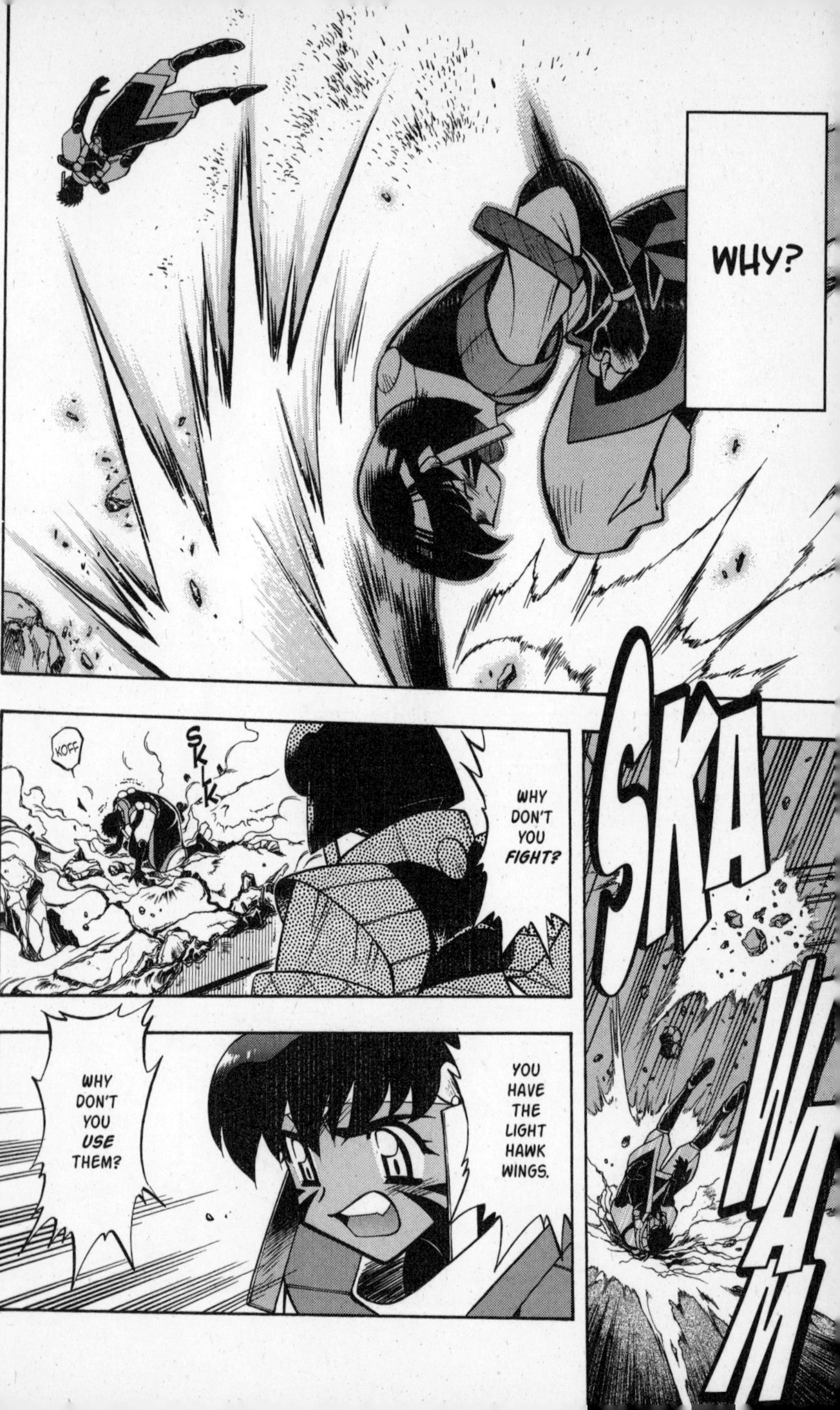
WHY?
SKA
KOFF
WHY DON'T YOU *FIGHT?*
YOU HAVE THE LIGHT HAWK WINGS.
WHY DON'T YOU *USE* THEM?

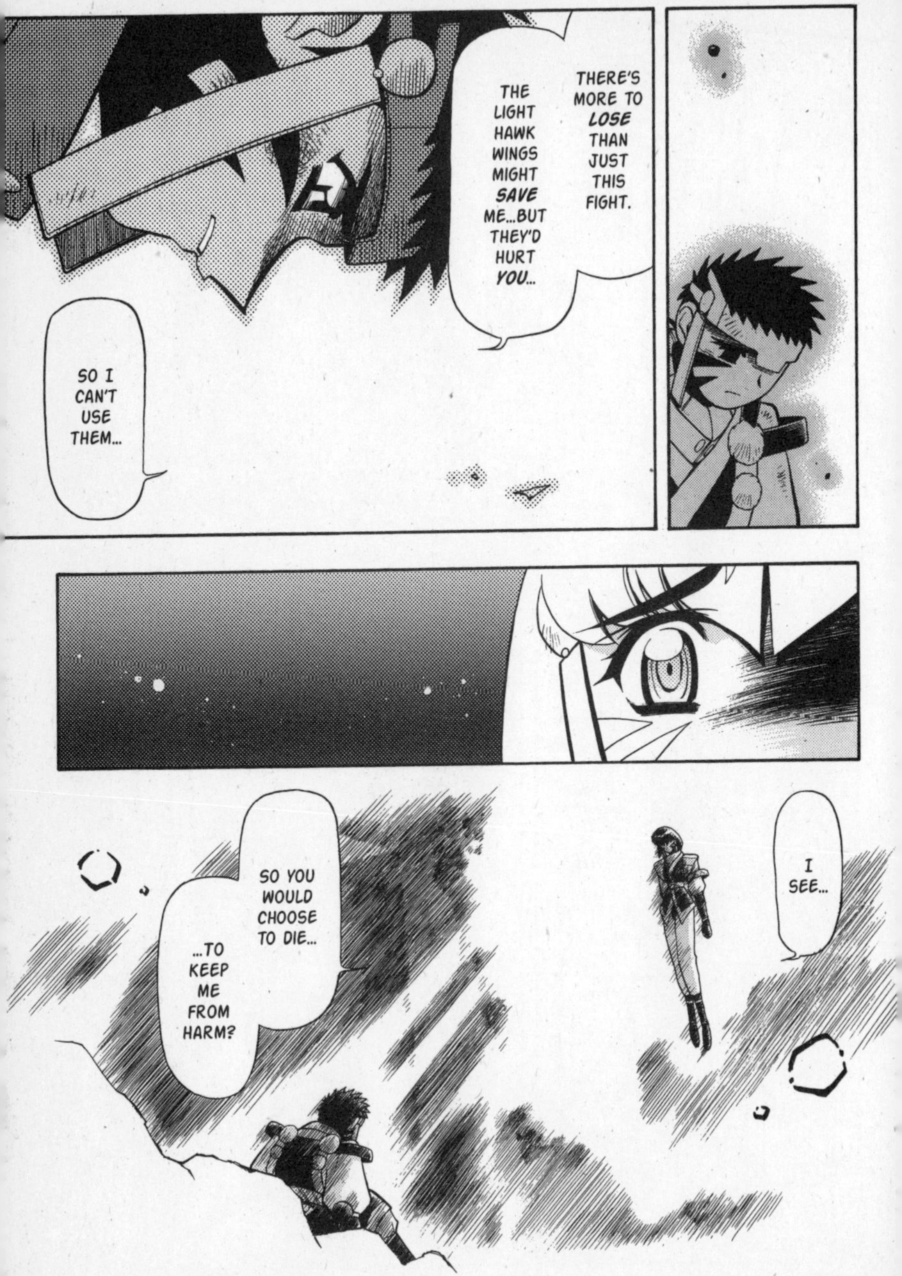
THERE'S MORE TO LOSE THAN JUST THIS FIGHT.
THE LIGHT HAWK WINGS MIGHT SAVE ME...BUT THEY'D HURT YOU...
SO I CAN'T USE THEM...
I SEE...
SO YOU WOULD CHOOSE TO DIE...
...TO KEEP ME FROM HARM?

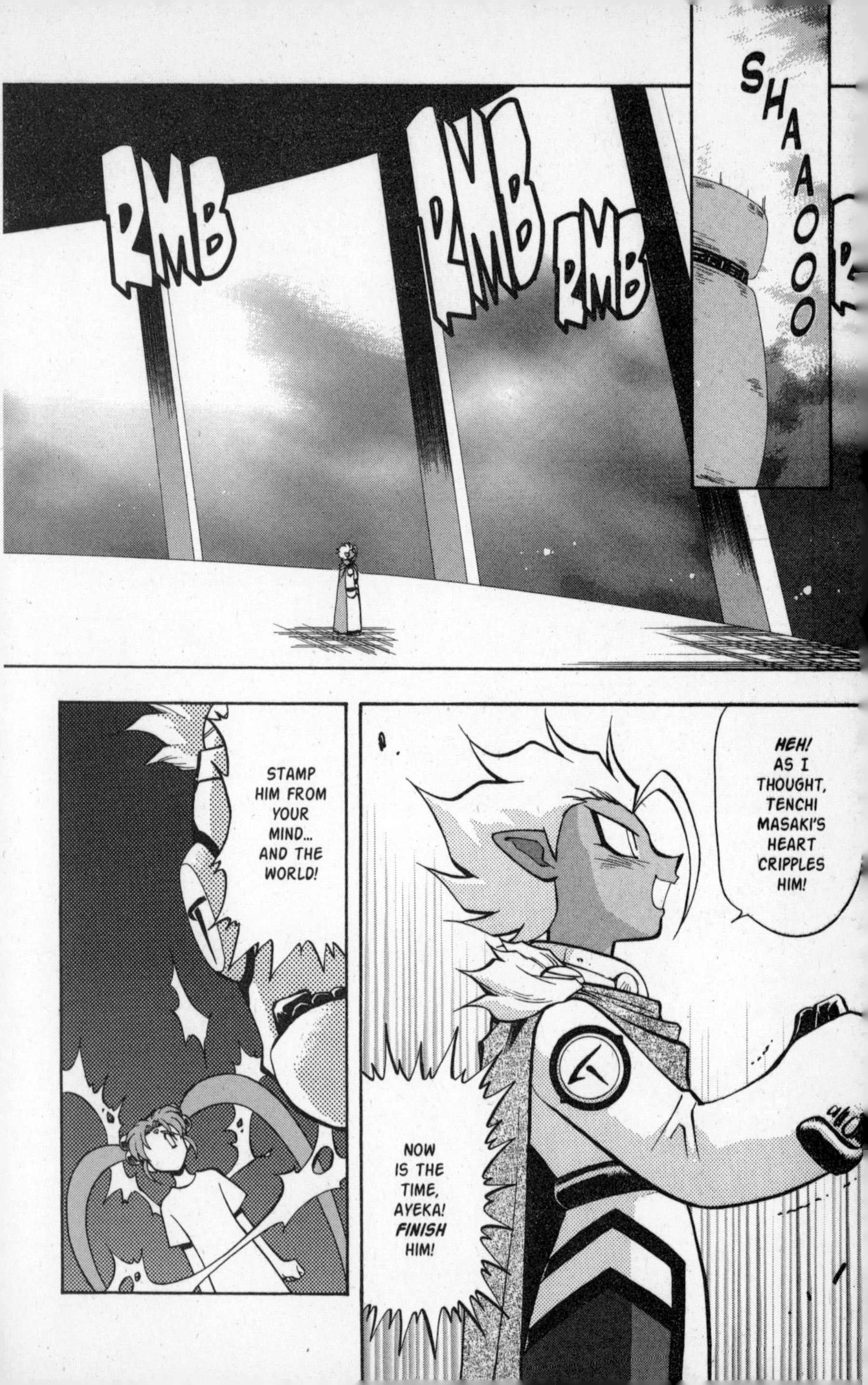
SHAAOOO
RMB
RMB
RMB
HEH! AS I THOUGHT, TENCHI MASAKI'S HEART CRIPPLES HIM!
NOW IS THE TIME, AYEKA! FINISH HIM!
STAMP HIM FROM YOUR MIND... AND THE WORLD!

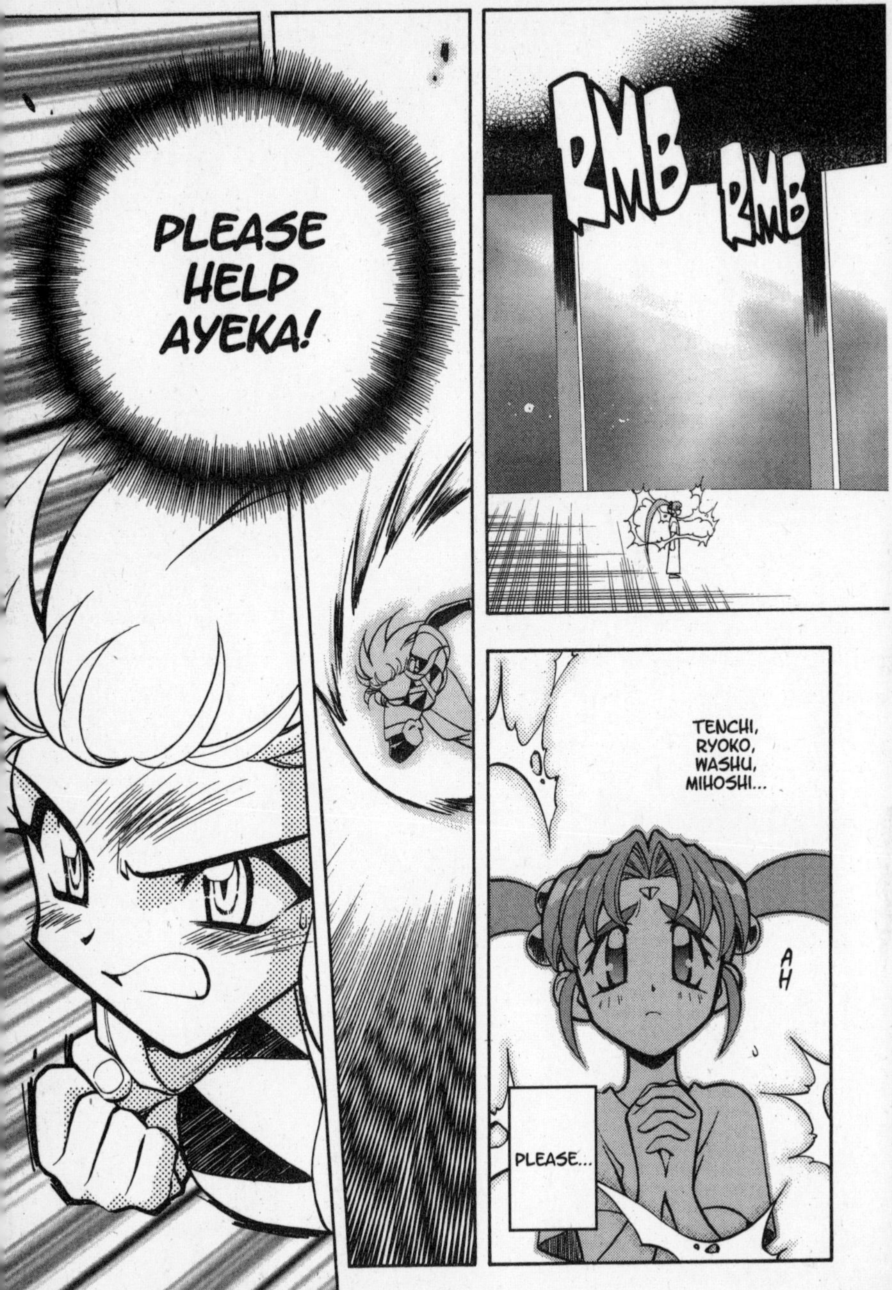
RMB
RMB
TENCHI, RYOKO, WASHU, MIHOSHI...
AH
PLEASE...
PLEASE HELP AYEKA!

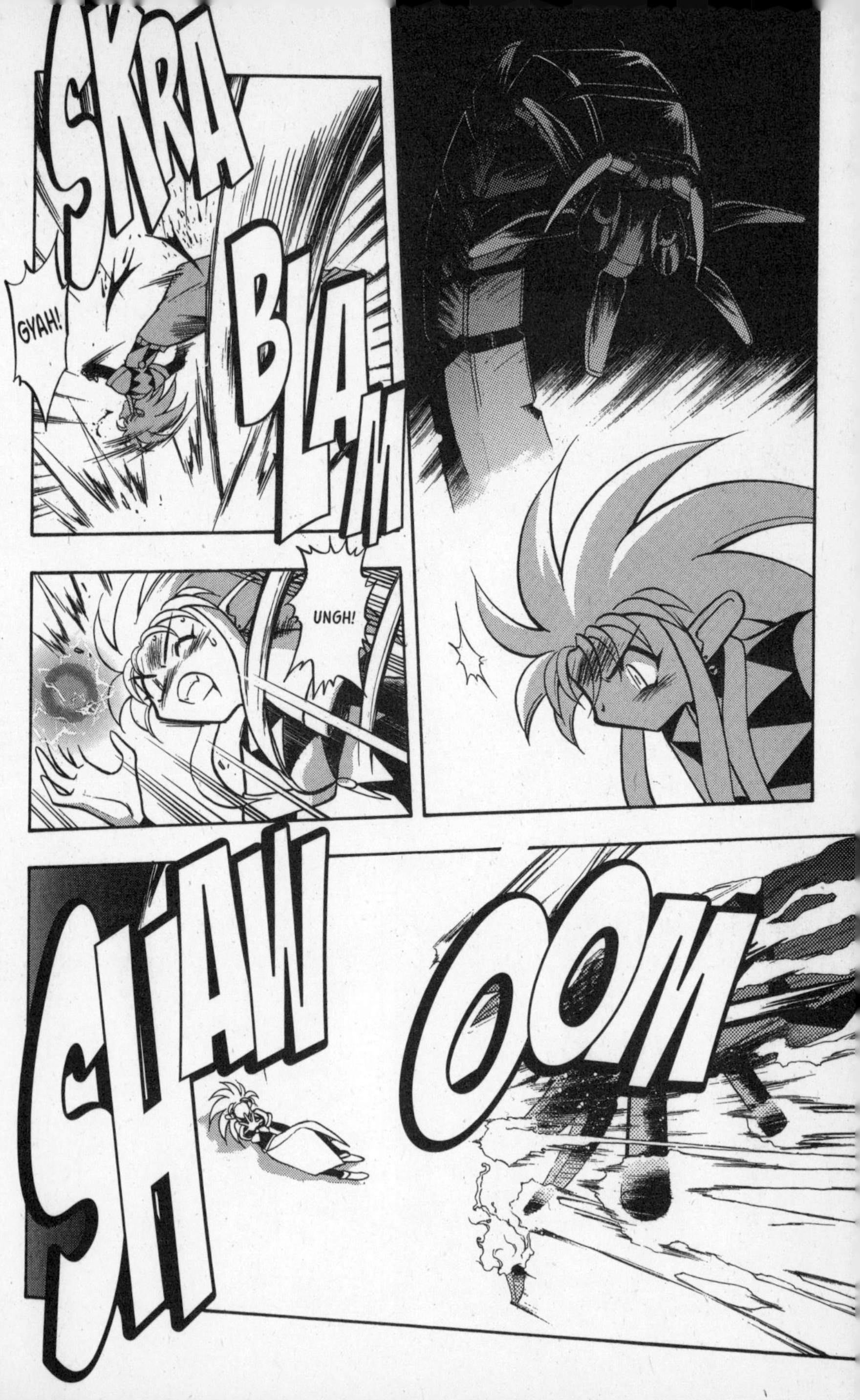
SKRA BLAM
GYAH!
UNGH!
SHAWOOM

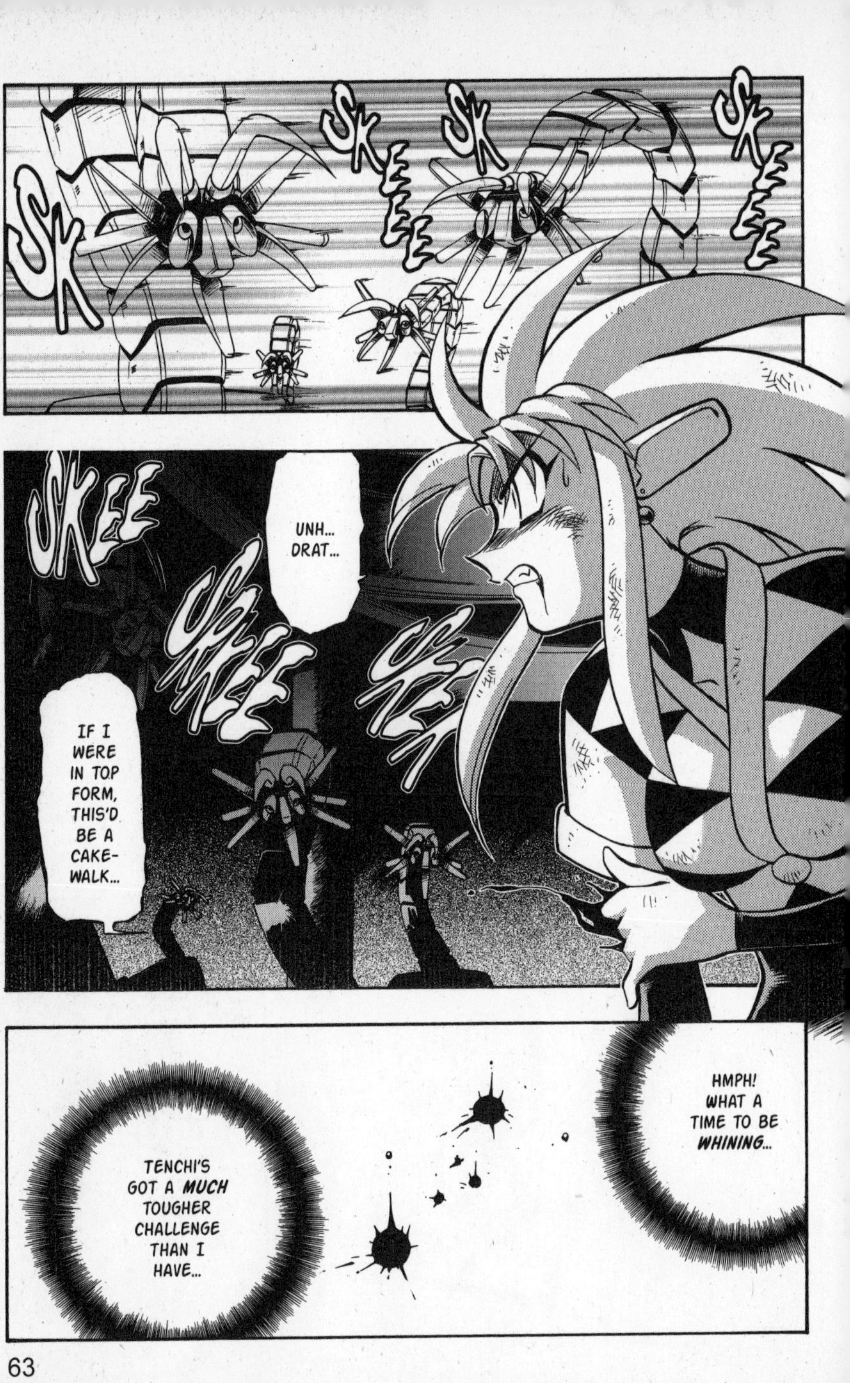
SKEEEE
SKEE
SK
SK
UNH... DRAT...
SKEE
SKEE
SKEE
IF I WERE IN TOP FORM, THIS'D BE A CAKE-WALK...
HMPH! WHAT A TIME TO BE *WHINING*...
TENCHI'S GOT A *MUCH* TOUGHER CHALLENGE THAN I HAVE...

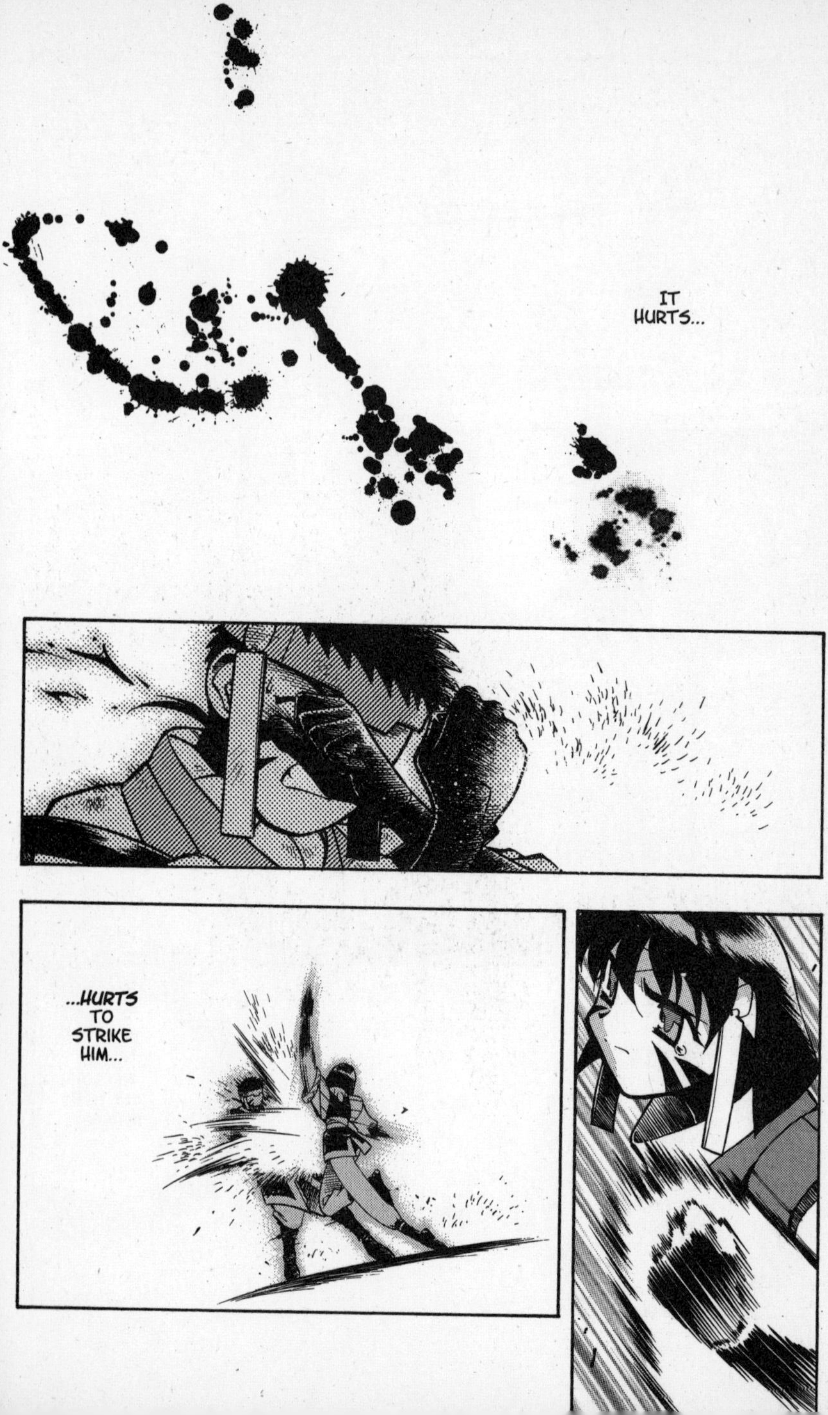
IT HURTS...
...HURTS TO STRIKE HIM...

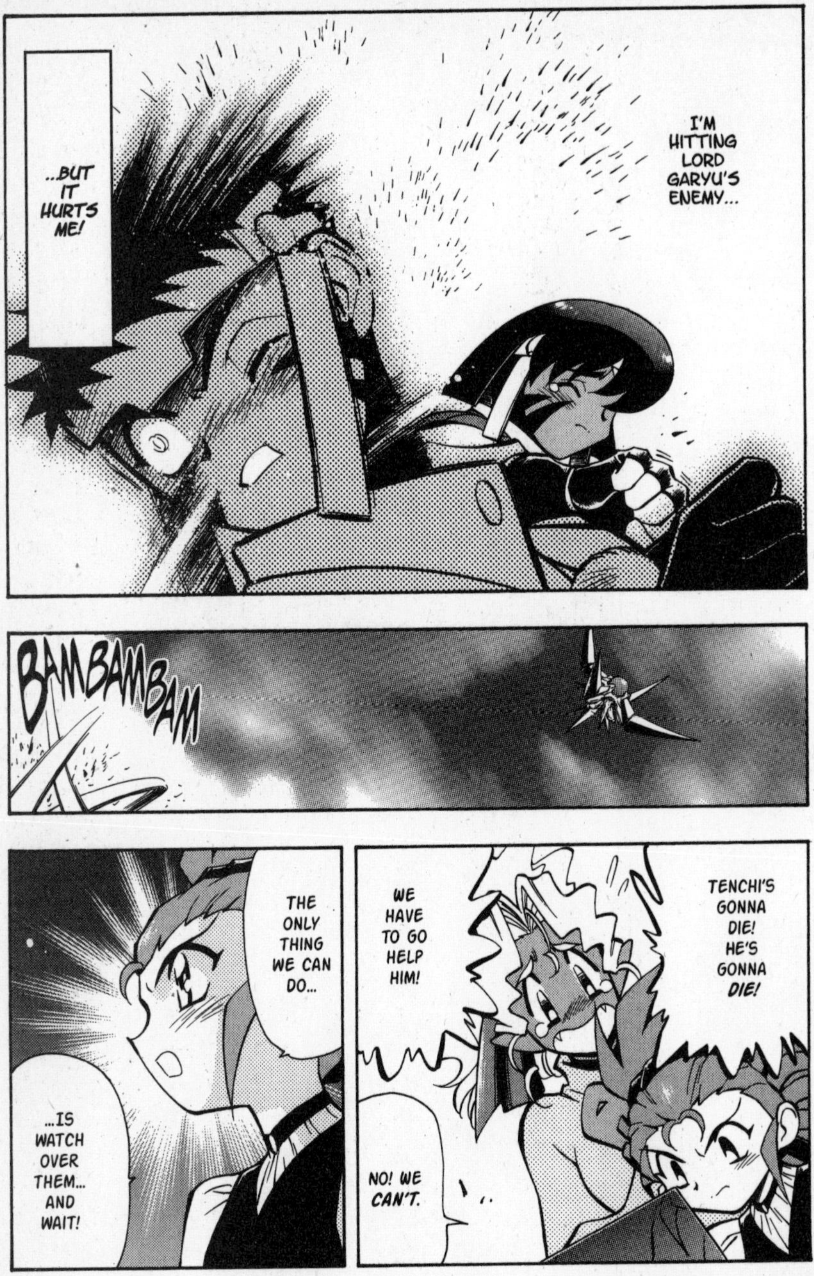
I'M HITTING LORD GARYU'S ENEMY...
...BUT IT HURTS ME!
BAMBAMBAM
TENCHI'S GONNA DIE! HE'S GONNA *DIE!*
WE HAVE TO GO HELP HIM!
NO! WE *CAN'T.*
THE ONLY THING WE CAN DO...
...IS WATCH OVER THEM... AND WAIT!

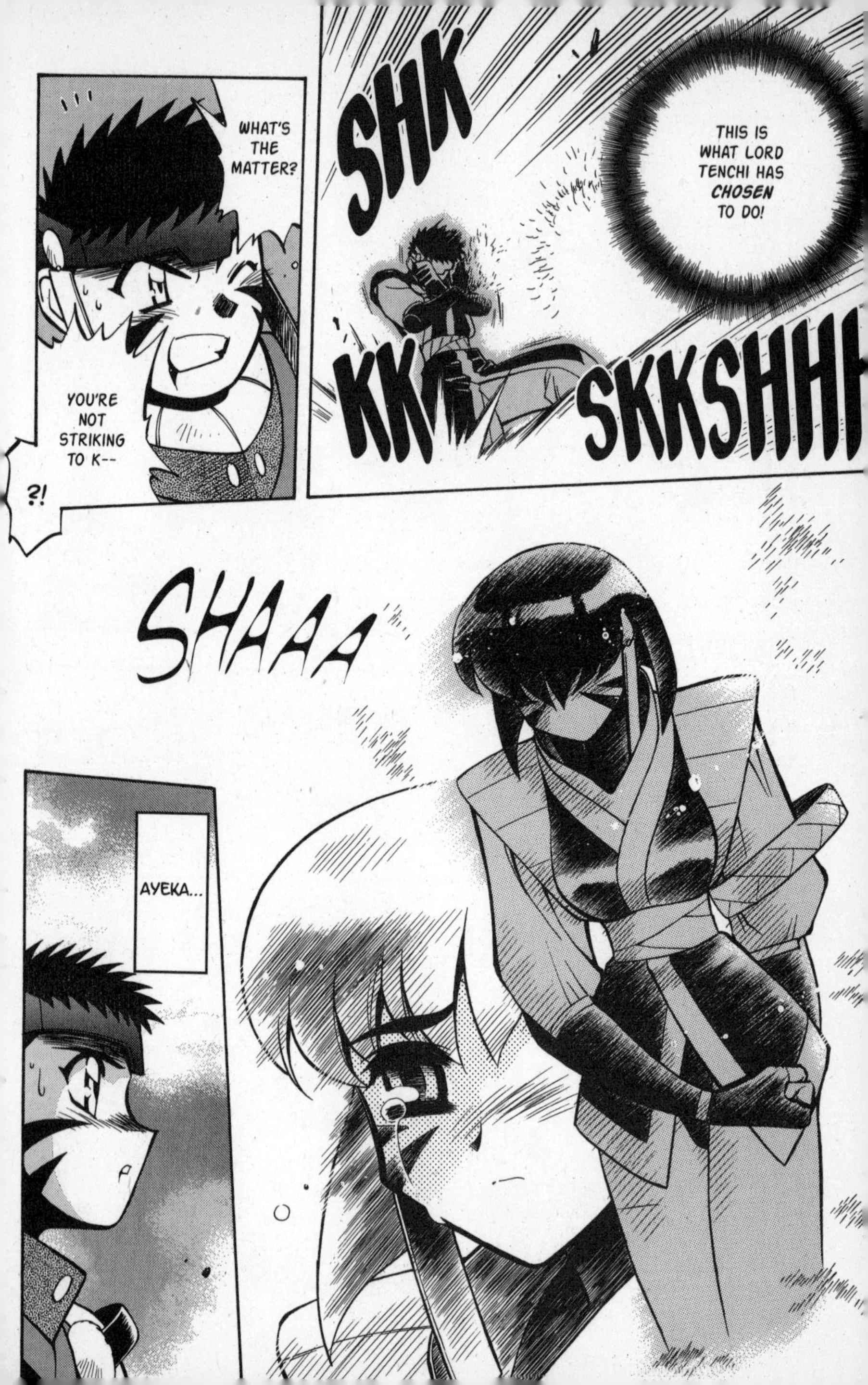
THIS IS WHAT LORD TENCHI HAS CHOSEN TO DO!
SHK
SKKSHHH
KK
WHAT'S THE MATTER?
YOU'RE NOT STRIKING TO K--
?!
SHAAA
AYEKA...

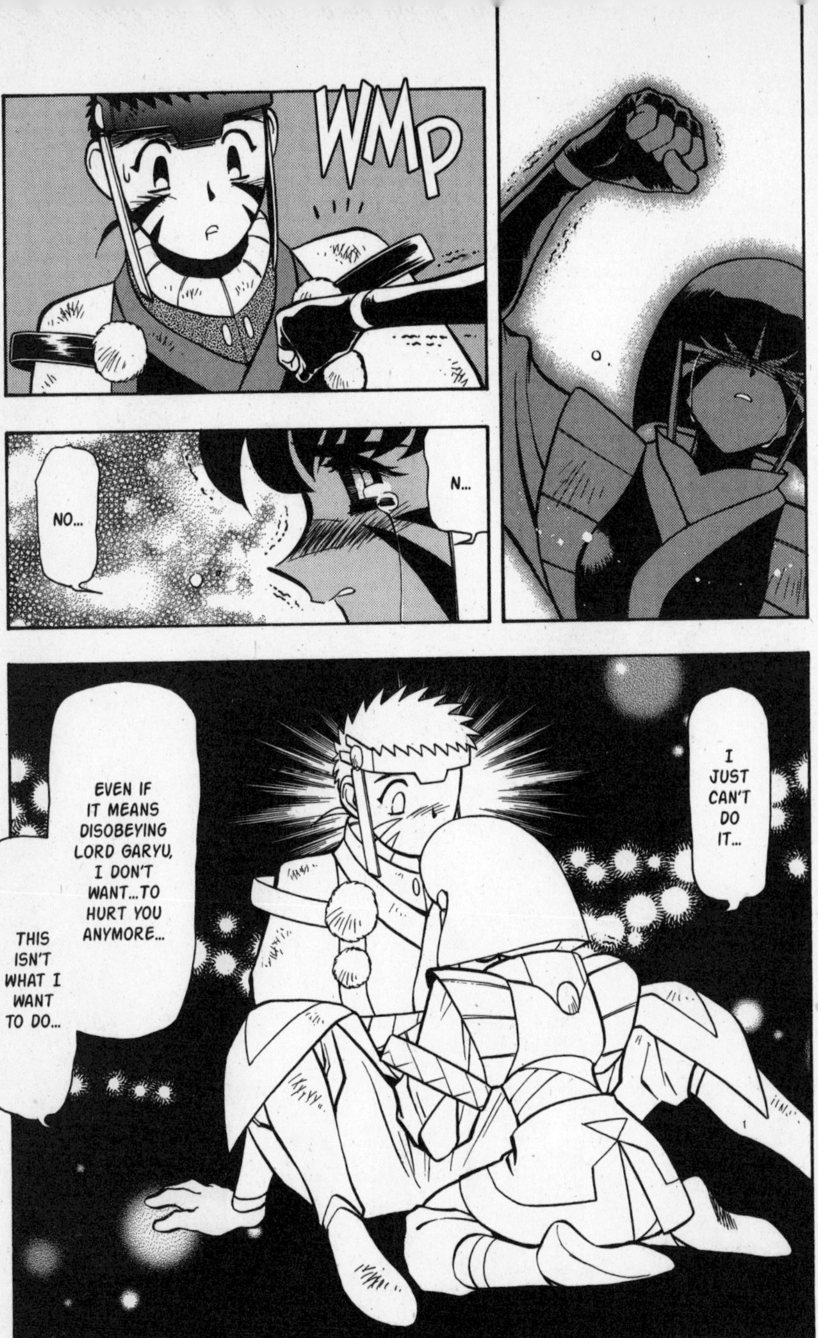
WMP
N...
NO...
I JUST CAN'T DO IT...
EVEN IF IT MEANS DISOBEYING LORD GARYU, I DON'T WANT...TO HURT YOU ANYMORE...
THIS ISN'T WHAT I WANT TO DO...

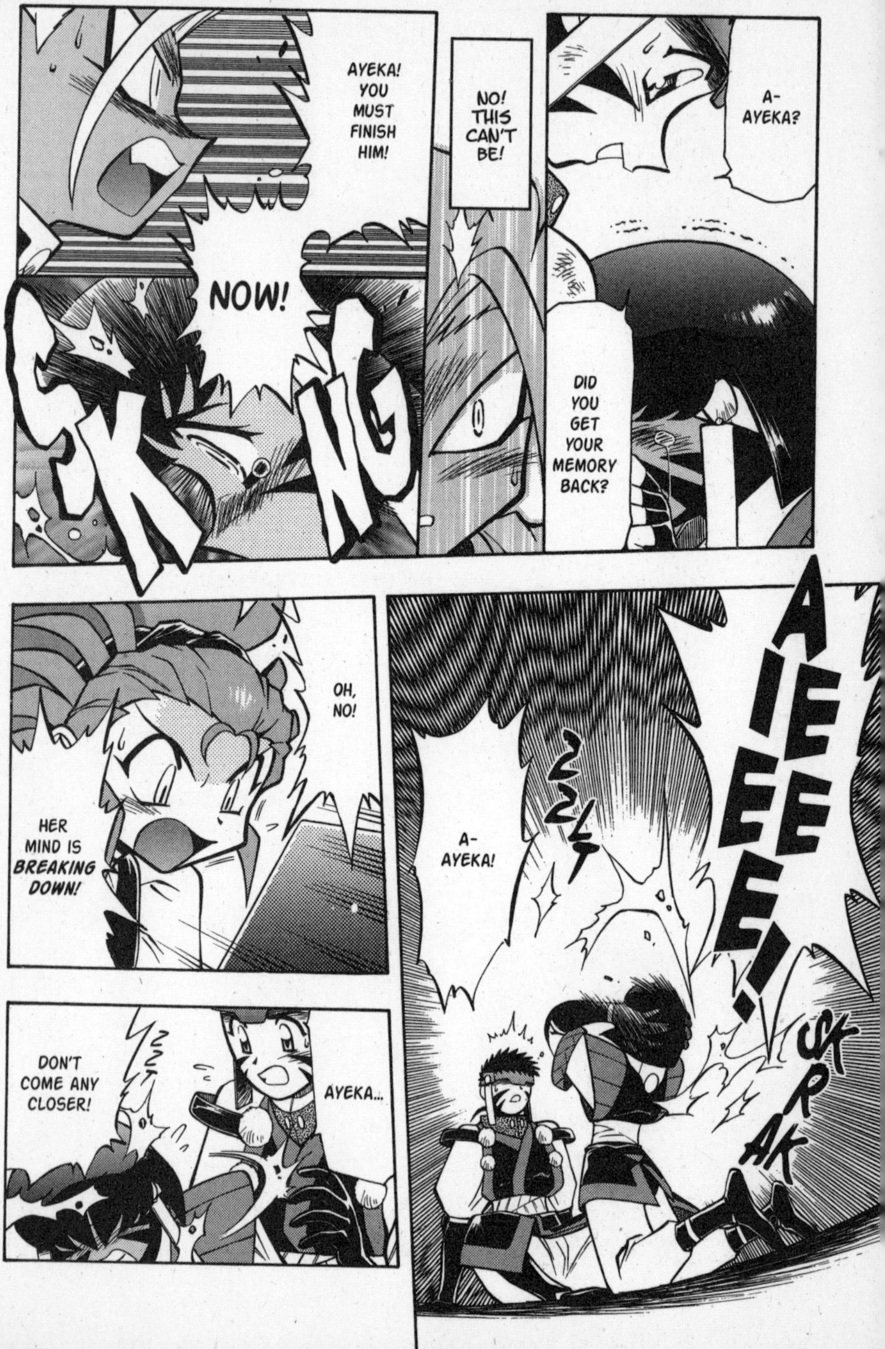
A- AYEKA?
DID YOU GET YOUR MEMORY BACK?
NO! THIS CAN'T BE!
AYEKA! YOU MUST FINISH HIM!
NOW!
AIEEEEE!!
A- AYEKA!
SKRAK
OH, NO!
HER MIND IS BREAKING DOWN!
AYEKA...
DON'T COME ANY CLOSER!

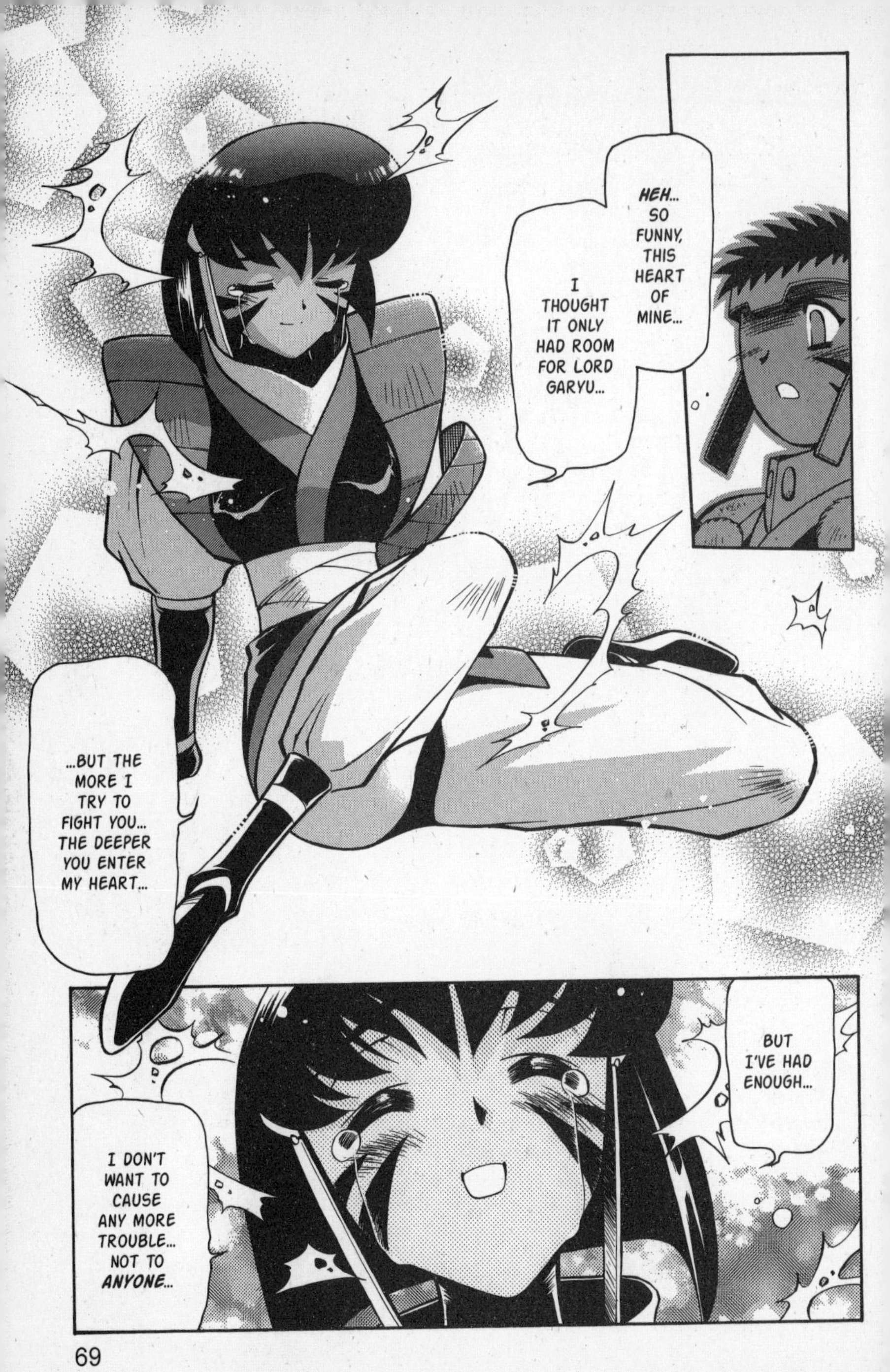
HEH... SO FUNNY, THIS HEART OF MINE...
I THOUGHT IT ONLY HAD ROOM FOR LORD GARYU...
...BUT THE MORE I TRY TO FIGHT YOU... THE DEEPER YOU ENTER MY HEART...
BUT I'VE HAD ENOUGH...
I DON'T WANT TO CAUSE ANY MORE TROUBLE... NOT TO ANYONE...

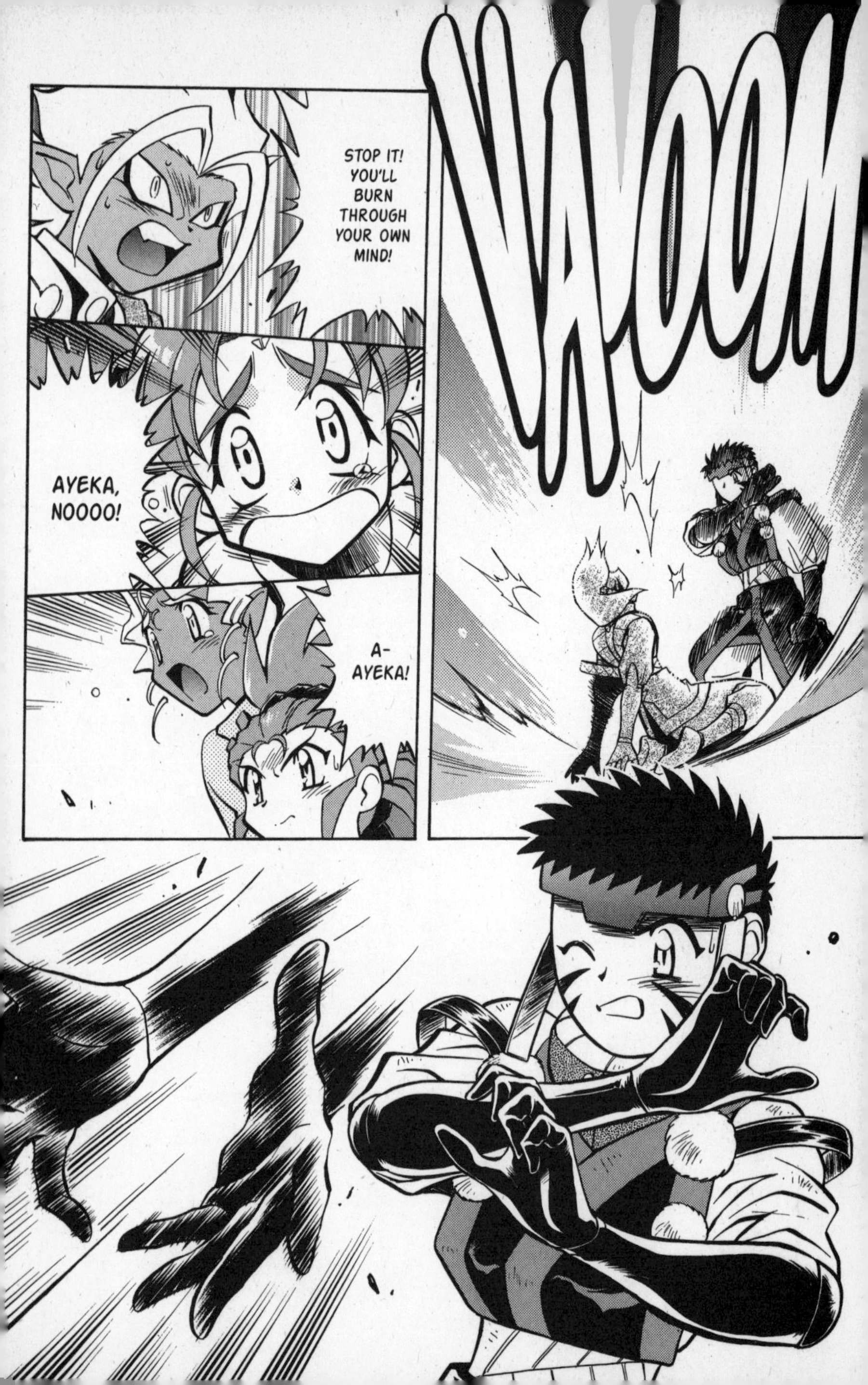
VAOOM
STOP IT! YOU'LL BURN THROUGH YOUR OWN MIND!
AYEKA, NOOOO!
A-AYEKA!

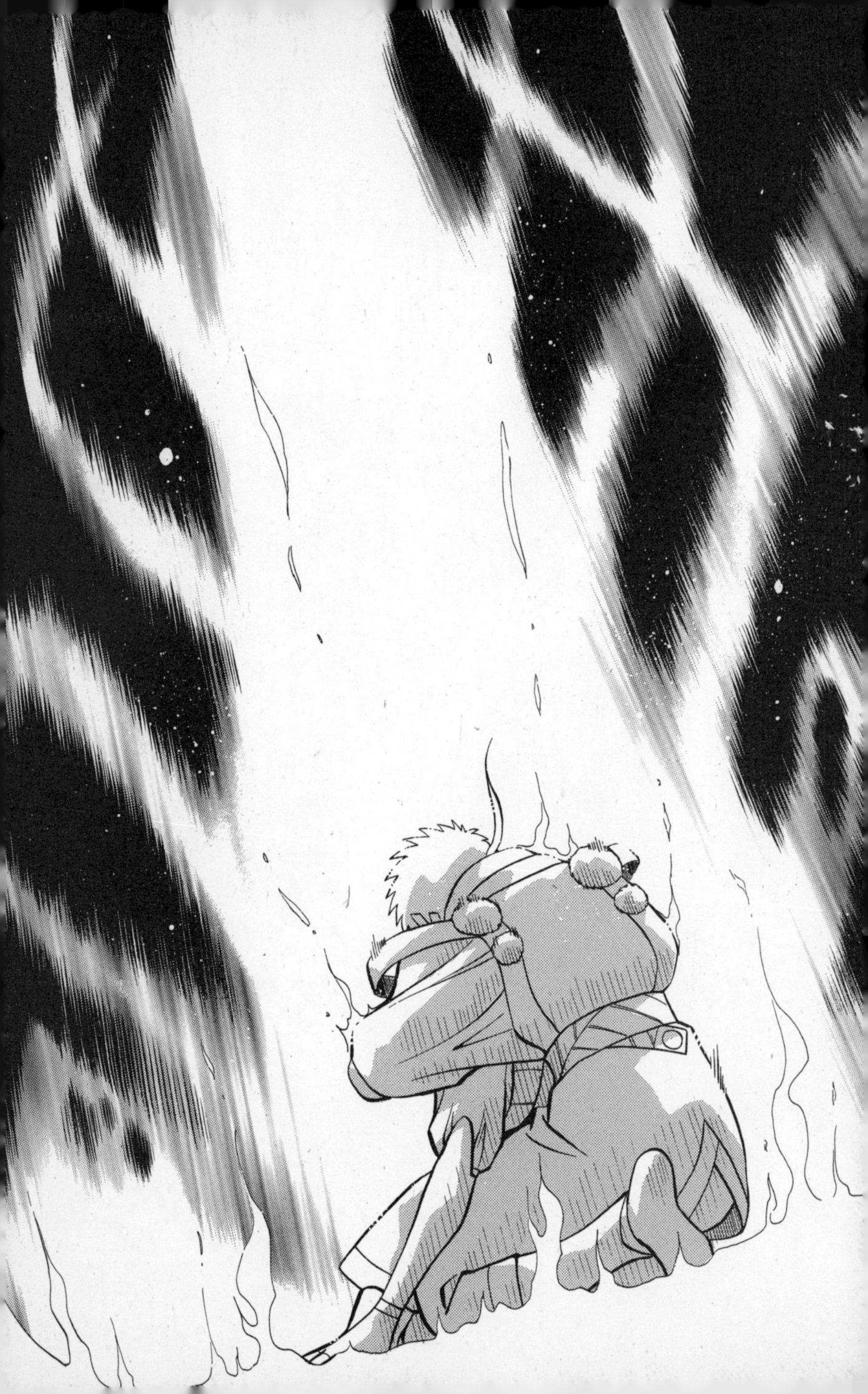

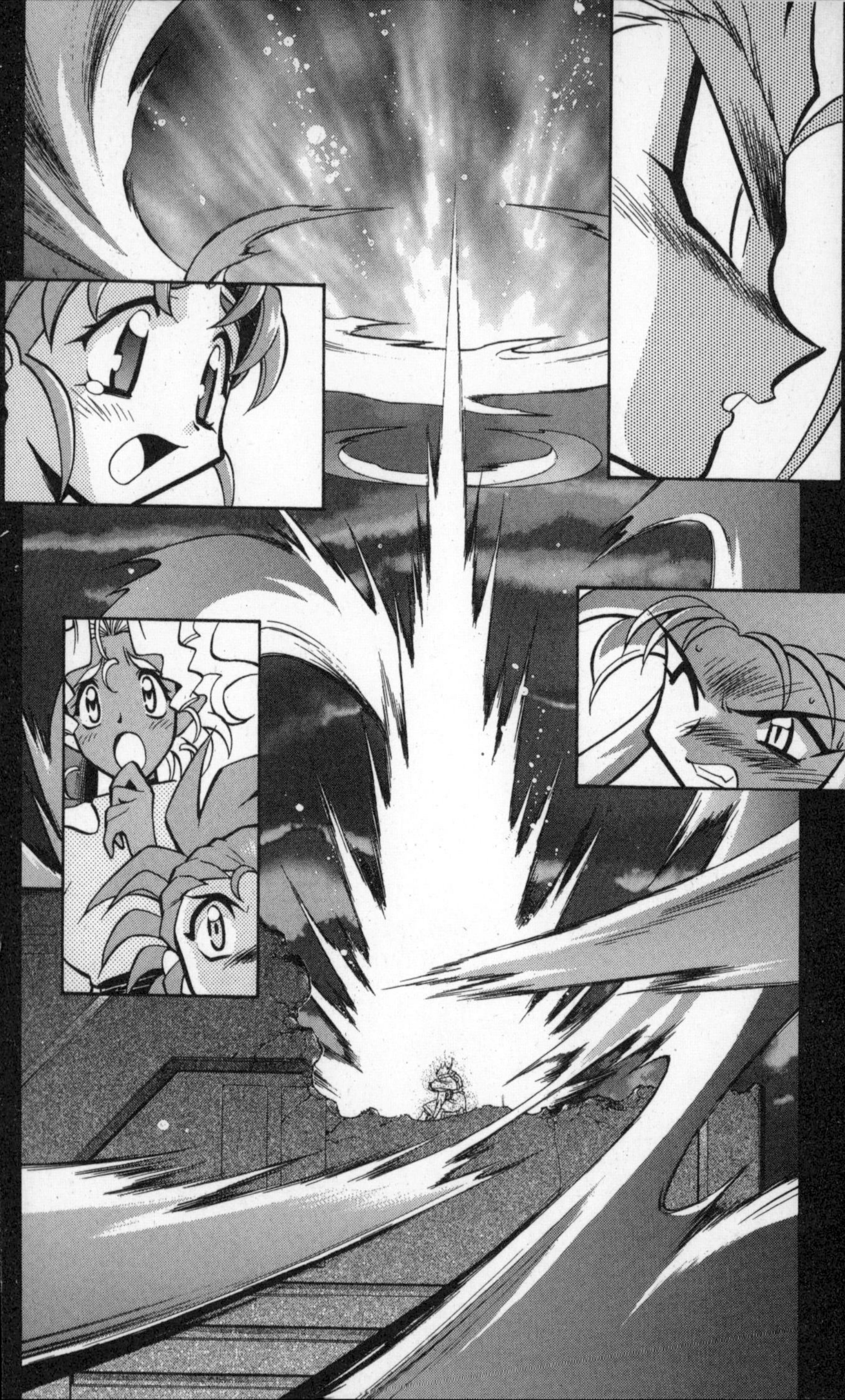

AYEKA
!!

SH HH   HH   HH   HH

Tales of Tenchi #5: EVERYONE

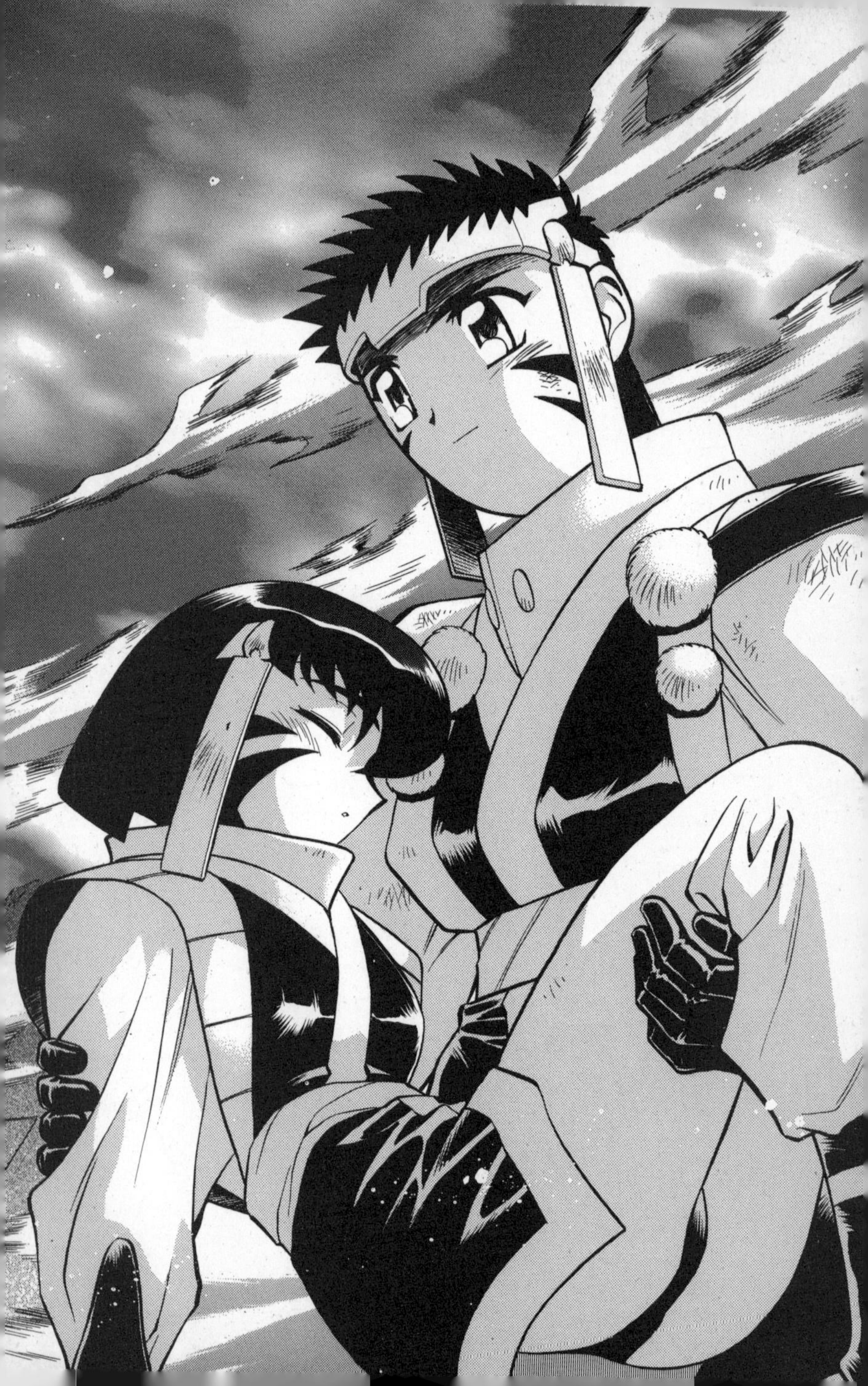

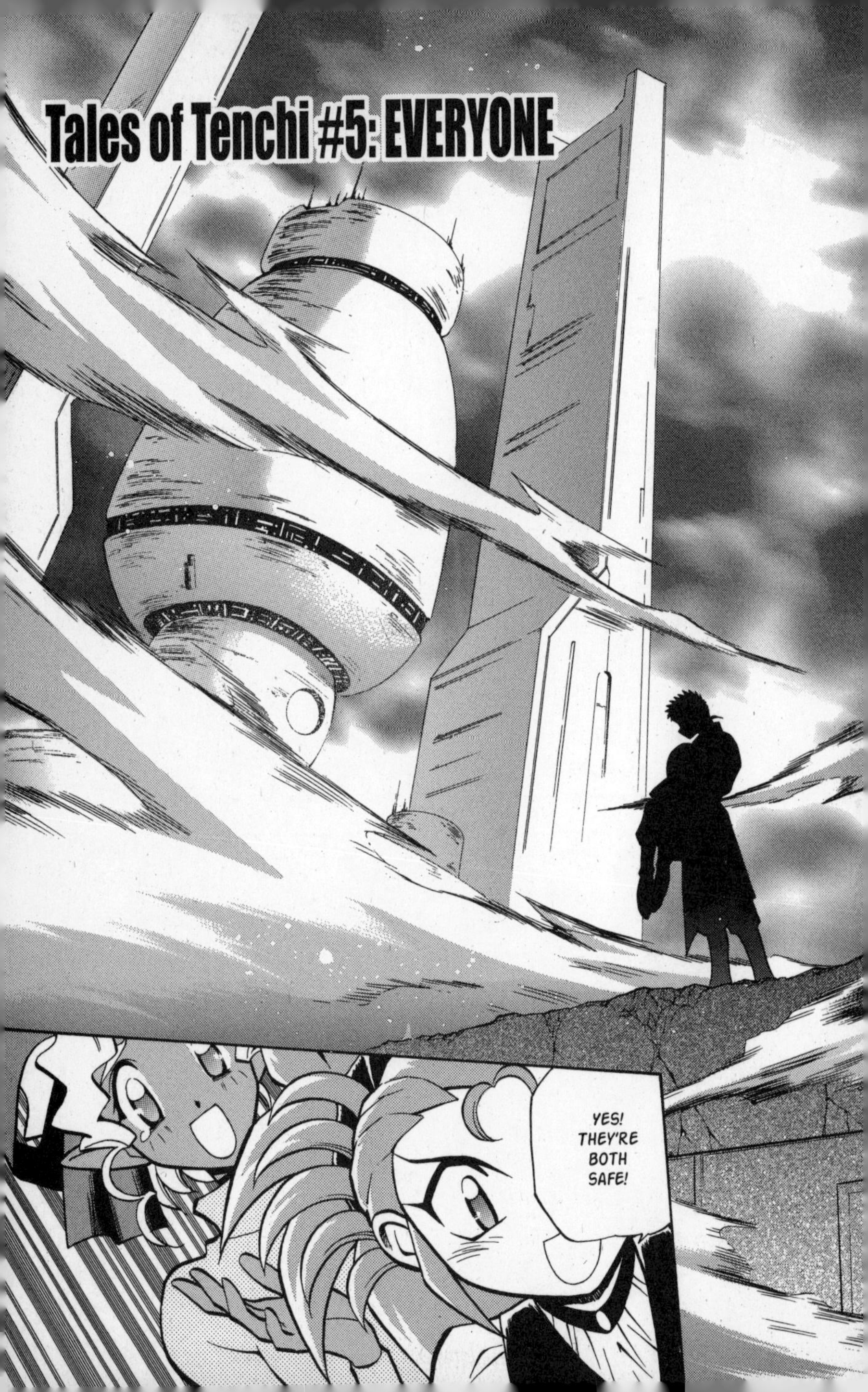
Tales of Tenchi #5: EVERYONE
YES! THEY'RE BOTH SAFE!

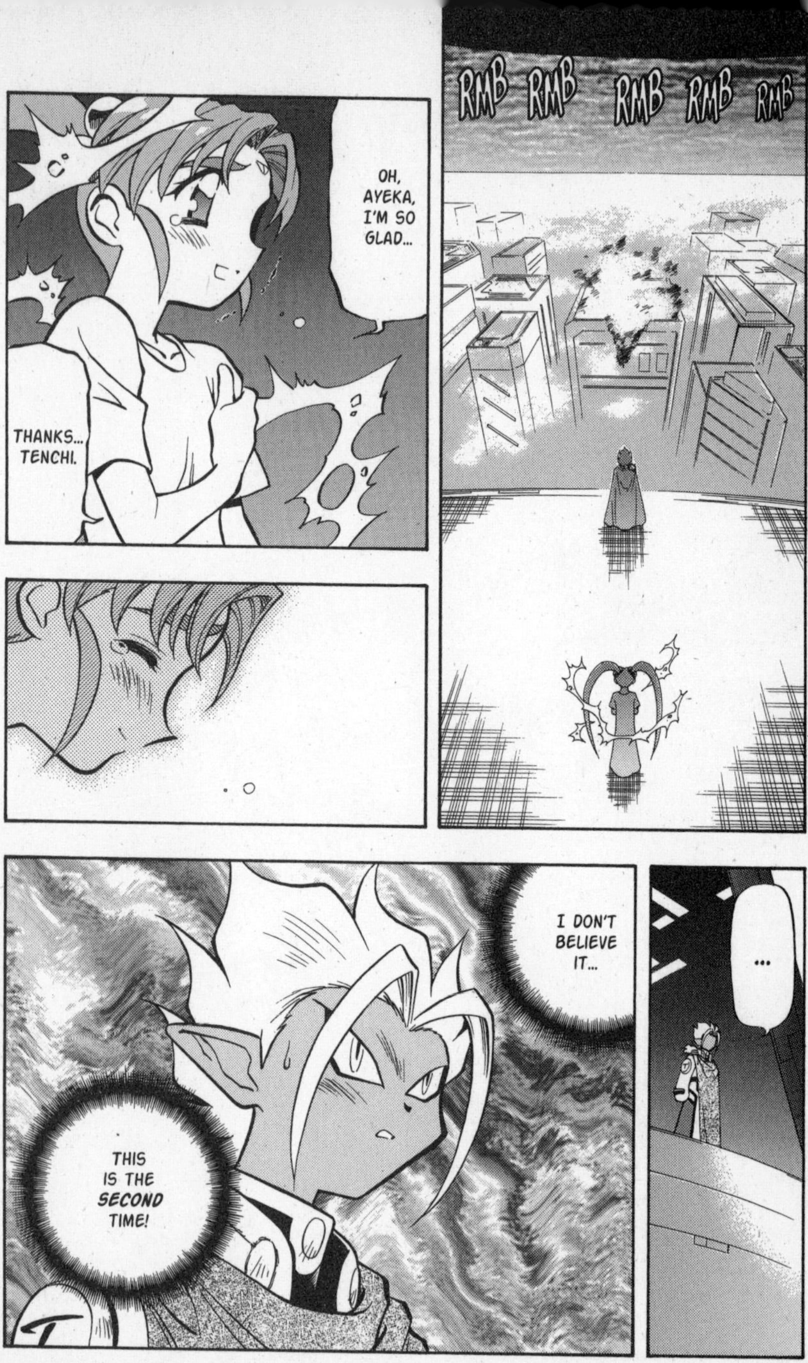
RMB RMB RMB RMB RMB
OH, AYEKA, I'M SO GLAD...
THANKS... TENCHI.
...
I DON'T BELIEVE IT...
THIS IS THE *SECOND* TIME!

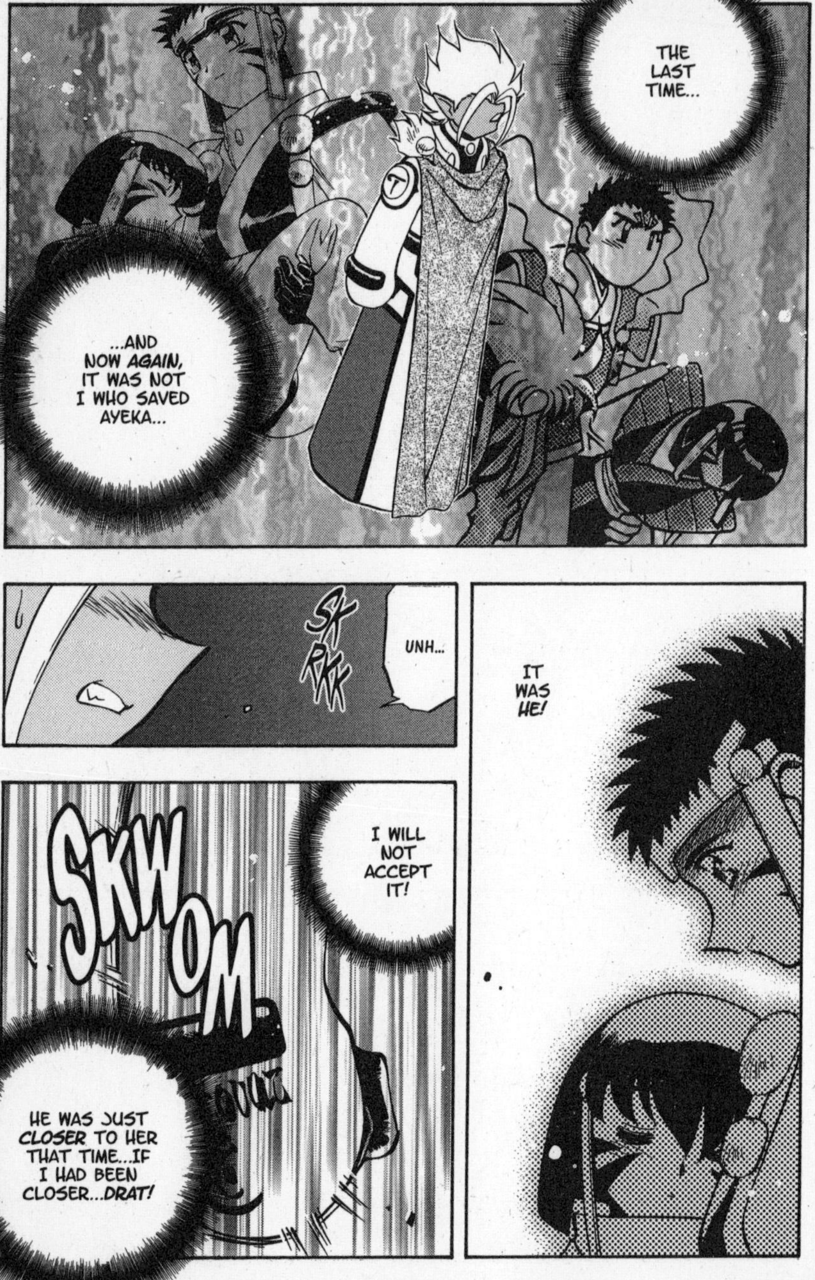
THE LAST TIME...
...AND NOW AGAIN, IT WAS NOT I WHO SAVED AYEKA...
IT WAS HE!
UNH...
SKRKK
I WILL NOT ACCEPT IT!
SKWOM
HE WAS JUST CLOSER TO HER THAT TIME...IF I HAD BEEN CLOSER...DRAT!

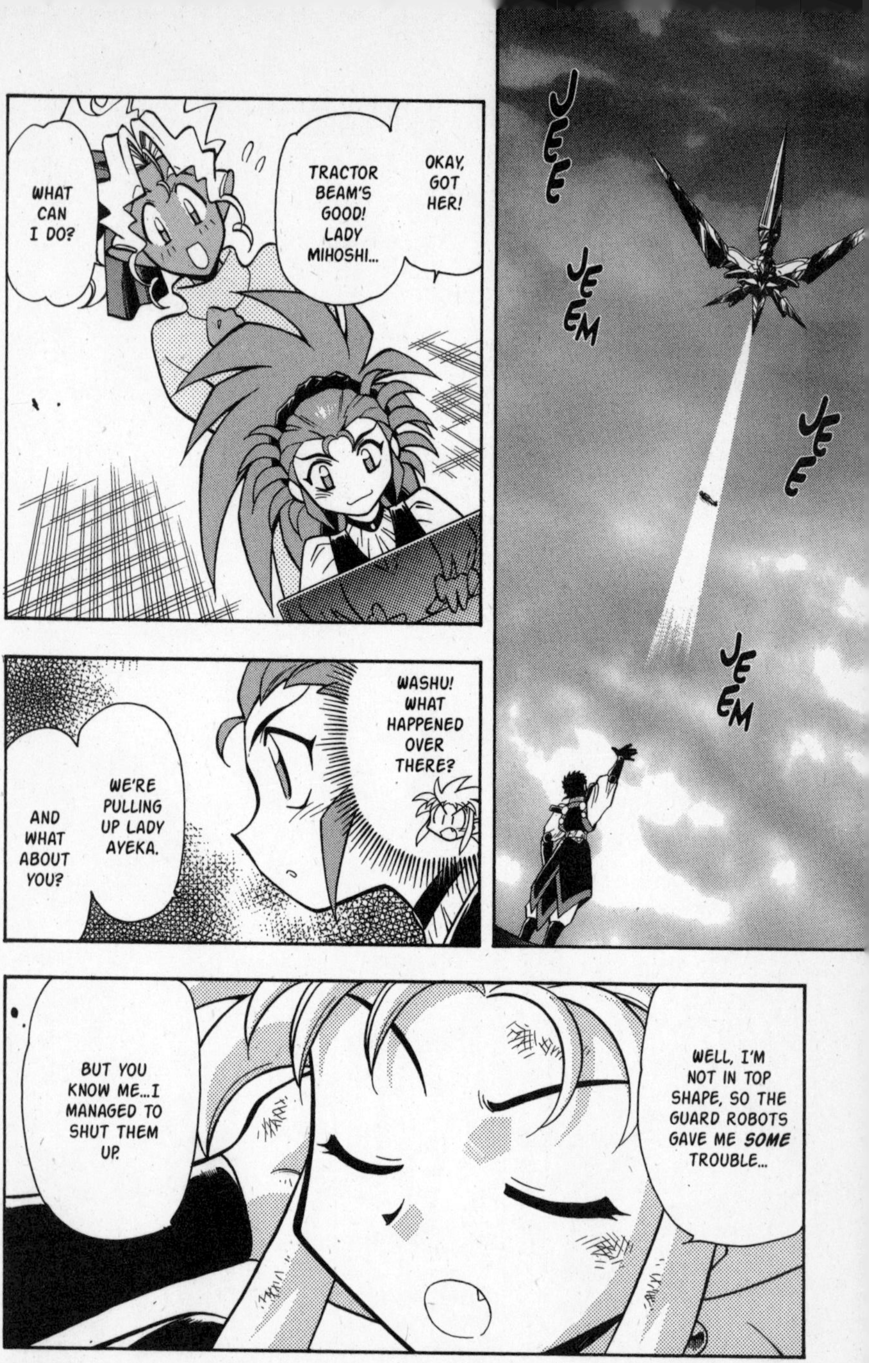
JEE
JEEM
JEE
JEEM
OKAY, GOT HER!
TRACTOR BEAM'S GOOD! LADY MIHOSHI...
WHAT CAN I DO?
WASHU! WHAT HAPPENED OVER THERE?
WE'RE PULLING UP LADY AYEKA.
AND WHAT ABOUT YOU?
WELL, I'M NOT IN TOP SHAPE, SO THE GUARD ROBOTS GAVE ME *SOME* TROUBLE...
BUT YOU KNOW ME...I MANAGED TO SHUT THEM UP.

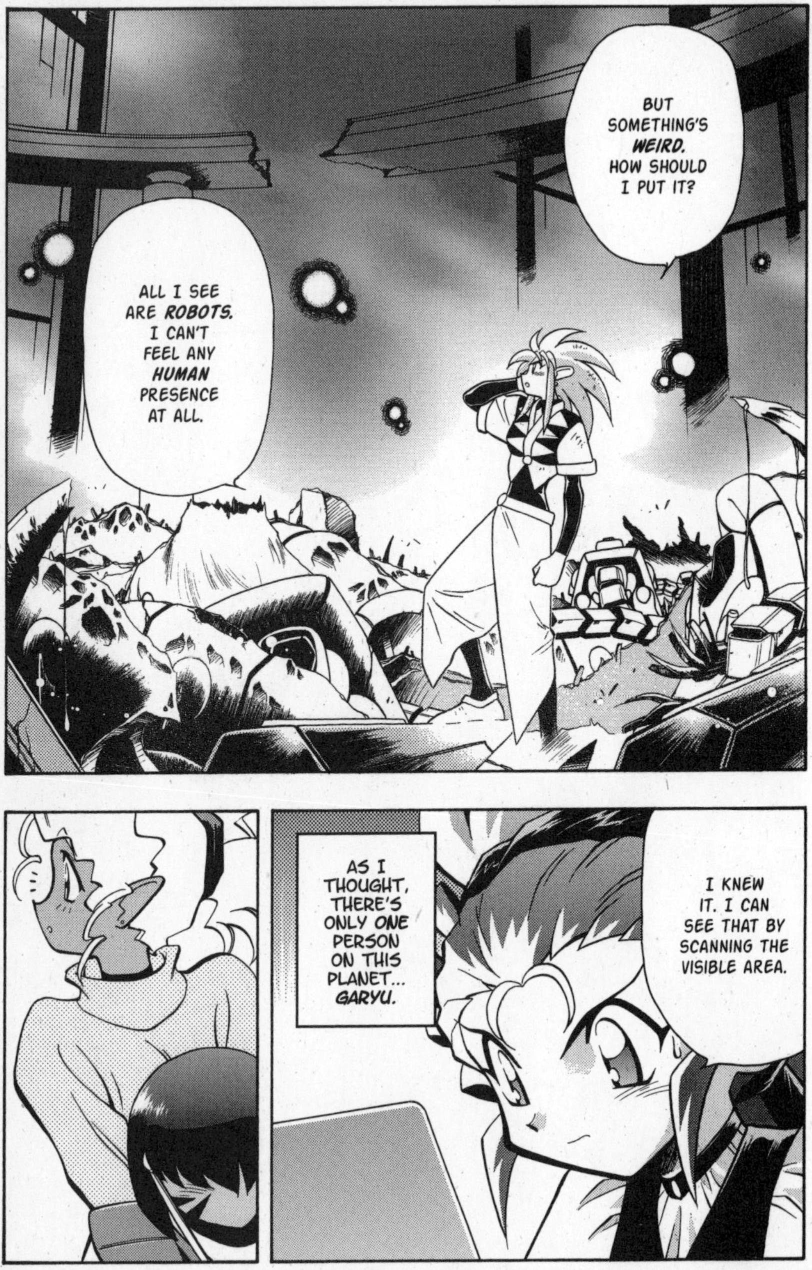
BUT SOMETHING'S WEIRD. HOW SHOULD I PUT IT?
ALL I SEE ARE ROBOTS. I CAN'T FEEL ANY HUMAN PRESENCE AT ALL.
I KNEW IT. I CAN SEE THAT BY SCANNING THE VISIBLE AREA.
AS I THOUGHT, THERE'S ONLY ONE PERSON ON THIS PLANET... GARYU.

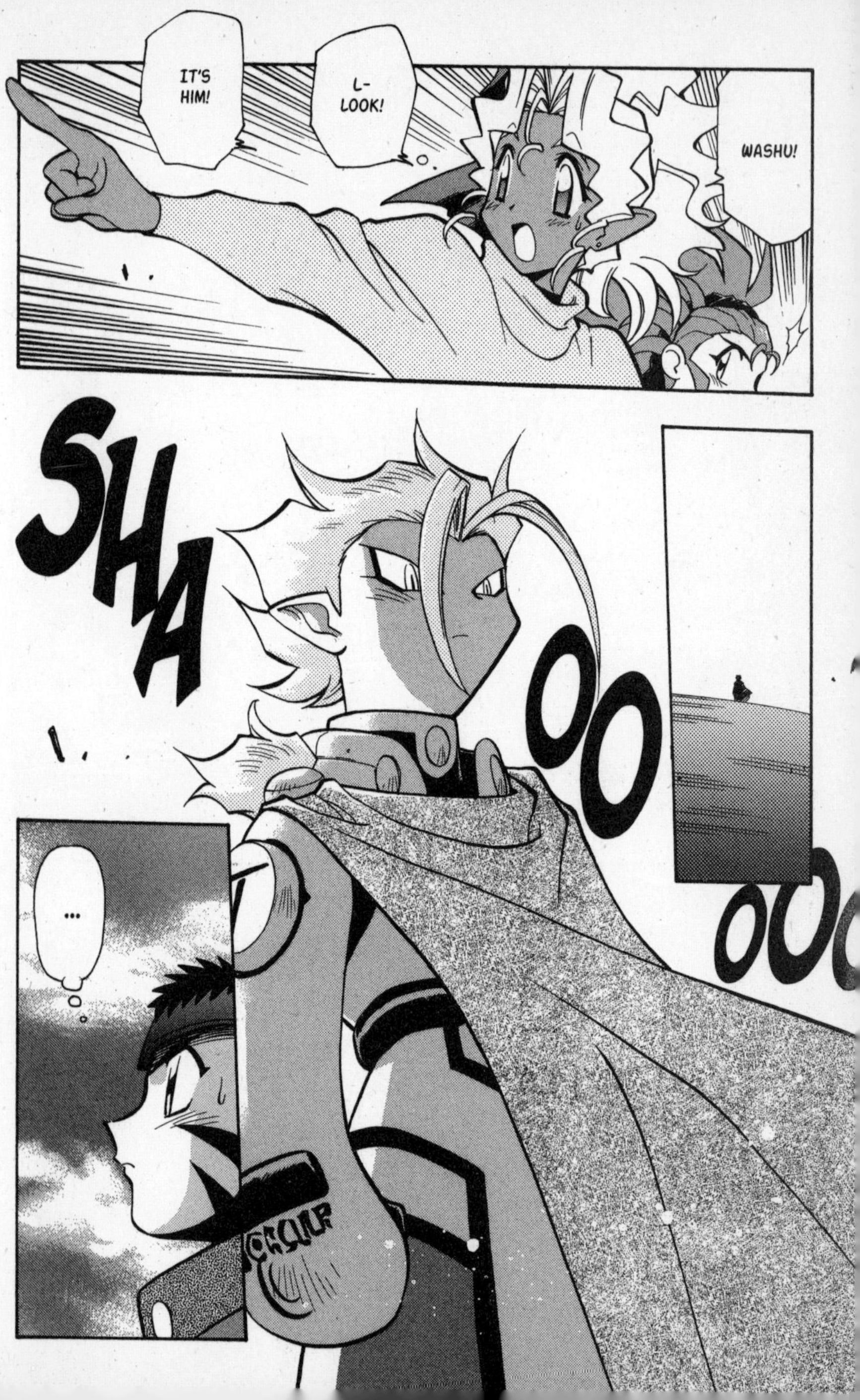
WASHU!
L- LOOK!
IT'S HIM!
SHA
OOOOO
...

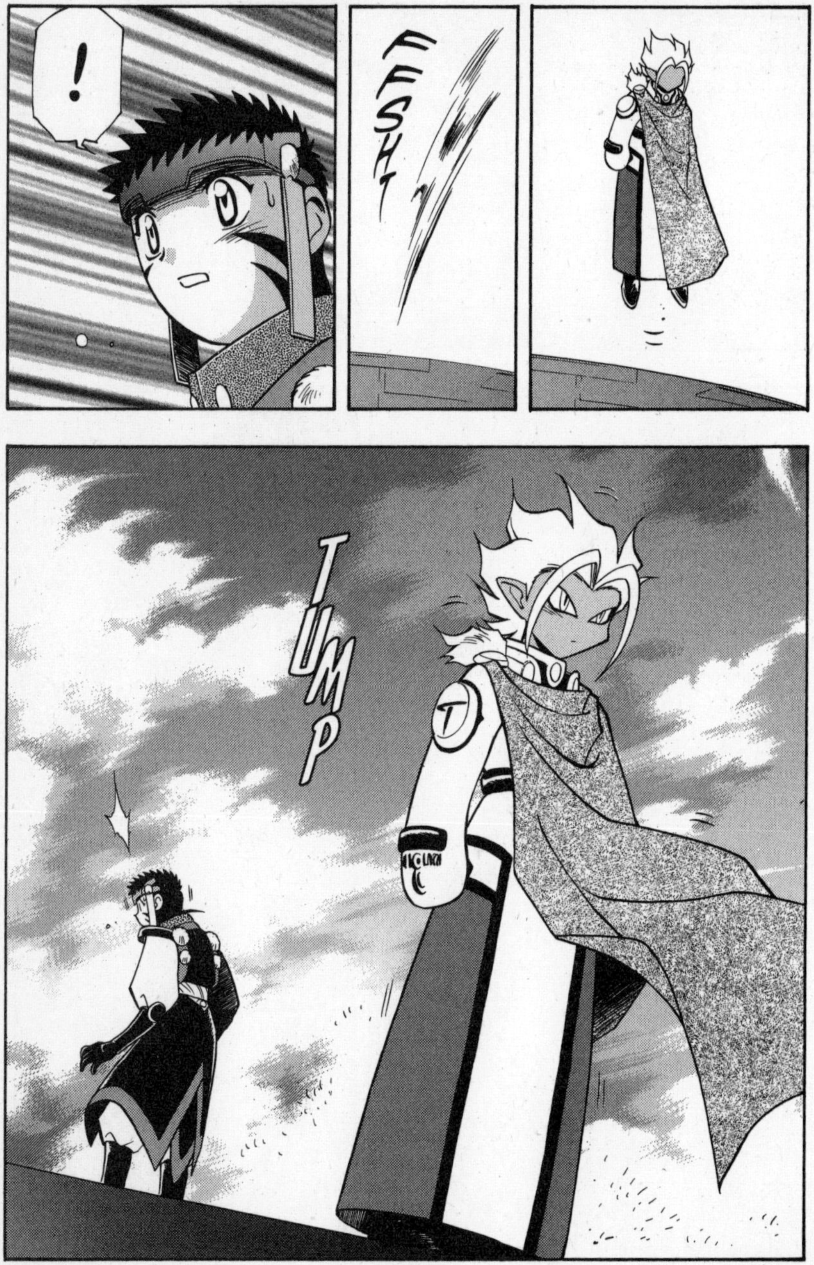
FFSHH
!
TUMP

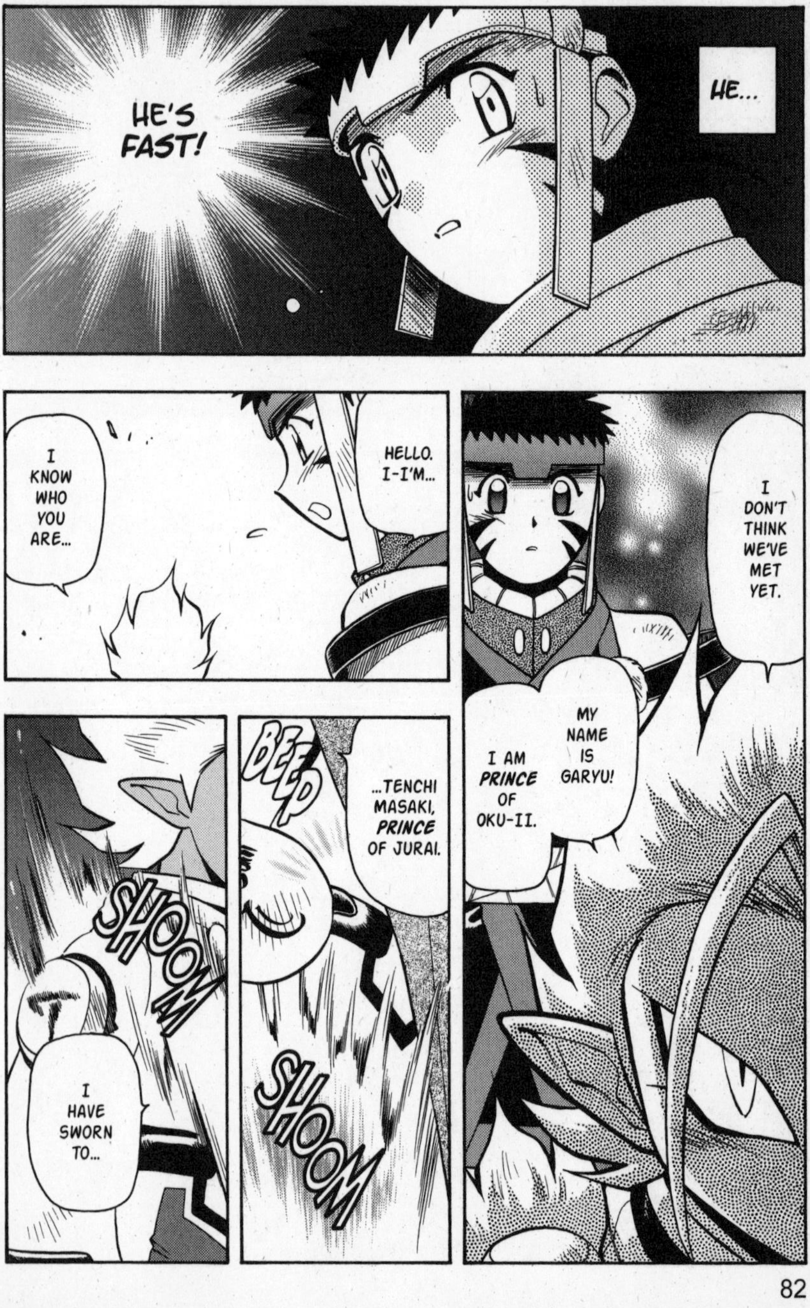
HE...
HE'S FAST!
I DON'T THINK WE'VE MET YET.
MY NAME IS GARYU!
I AM PRINCE OF OKU-II.
HELLO. I-I'M...
I KNOW WHO YOU ARE...
BEEP
...TENCHI MASAKI, PRINCE OF JURAI.
SHOOM
SHOOM
I HAVE SWORN TO...

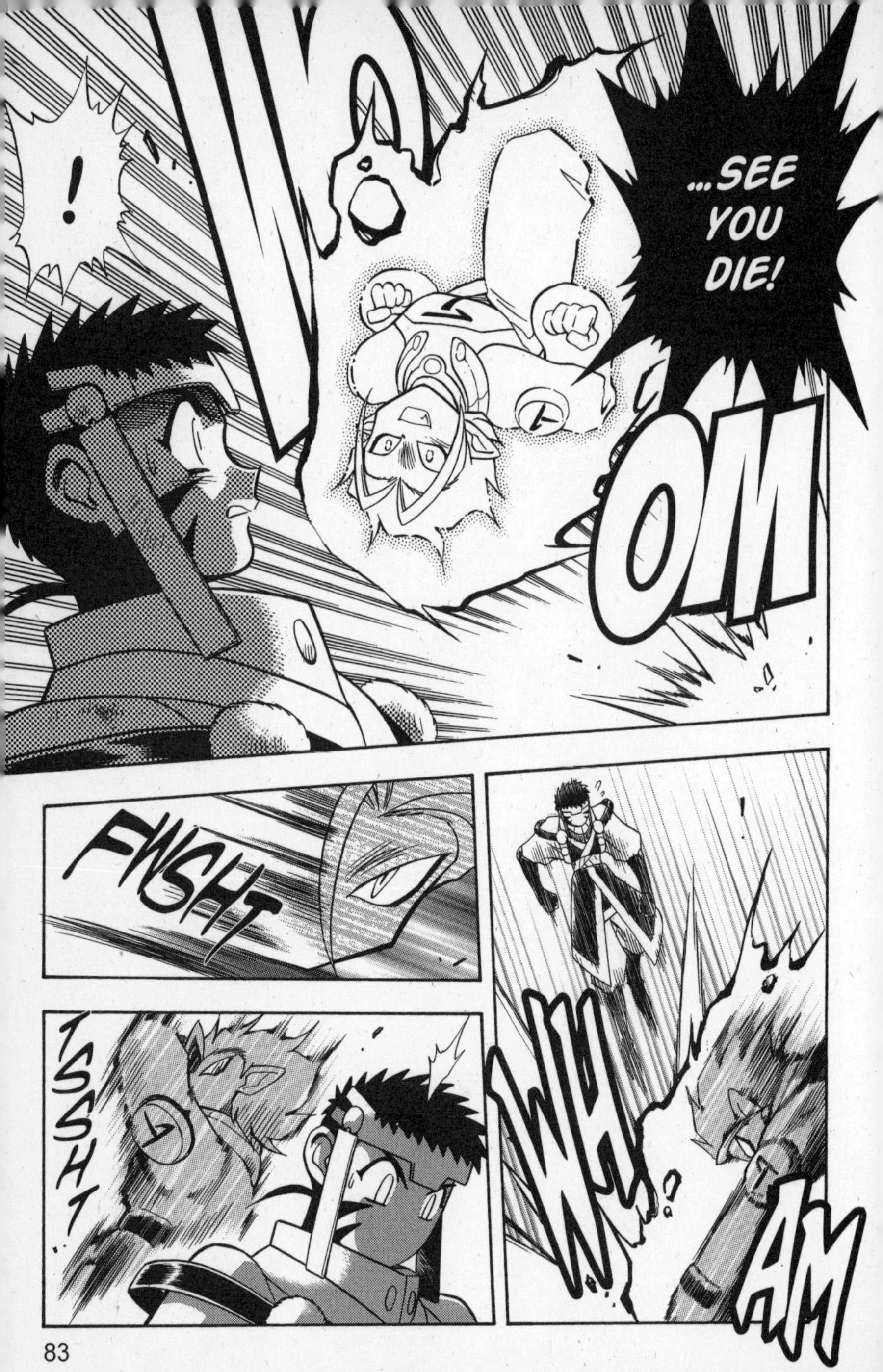

...SEE YOU DIE!
OM
!
?
WH
AM
FWSHT
TSSSH

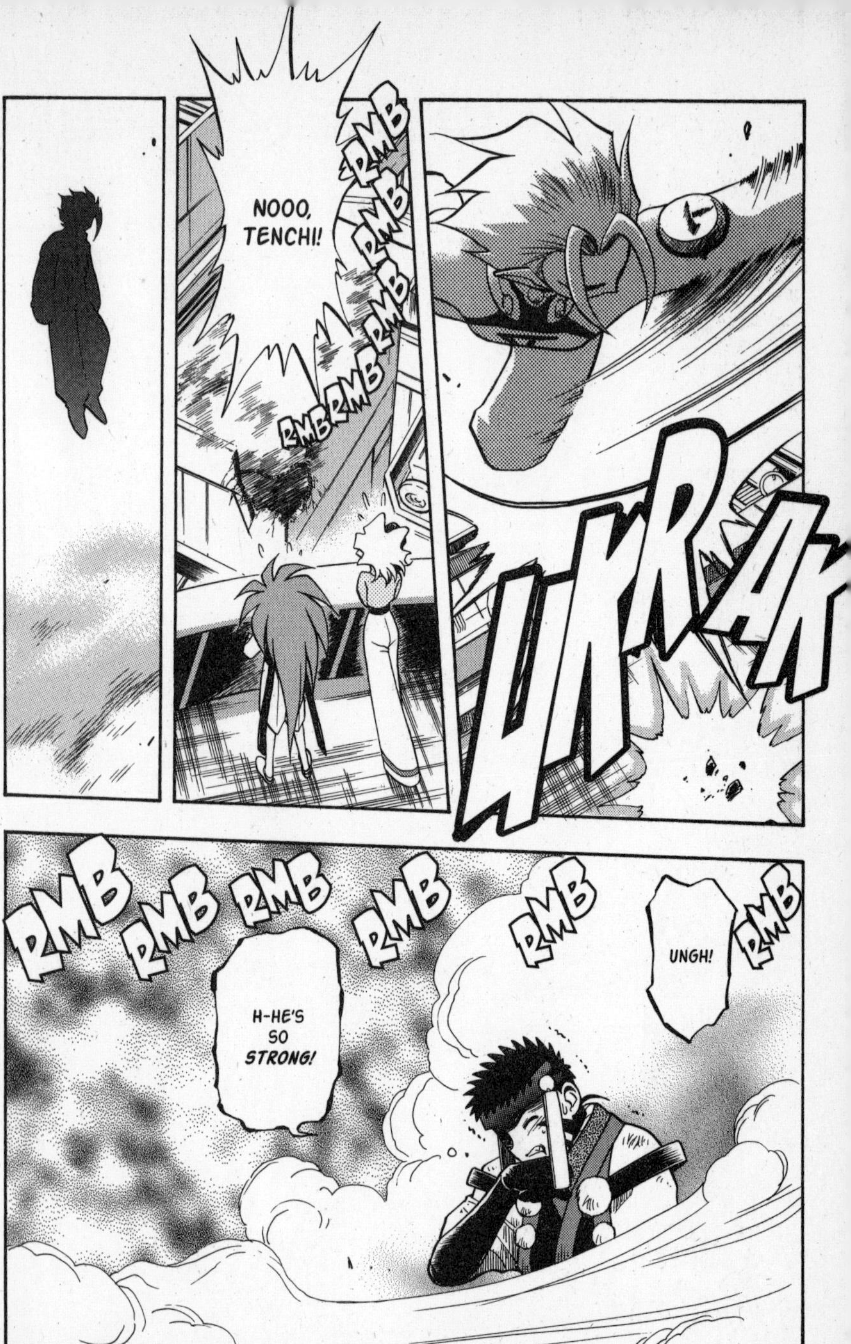
KRAK
NOOO, TENCHI!
RMB RMB RMB RMB RMB RMB RMB RMB
RMB
UNGH!
RMB
RMB
H-HE'S SO STRONG!
RMB RMB RMB

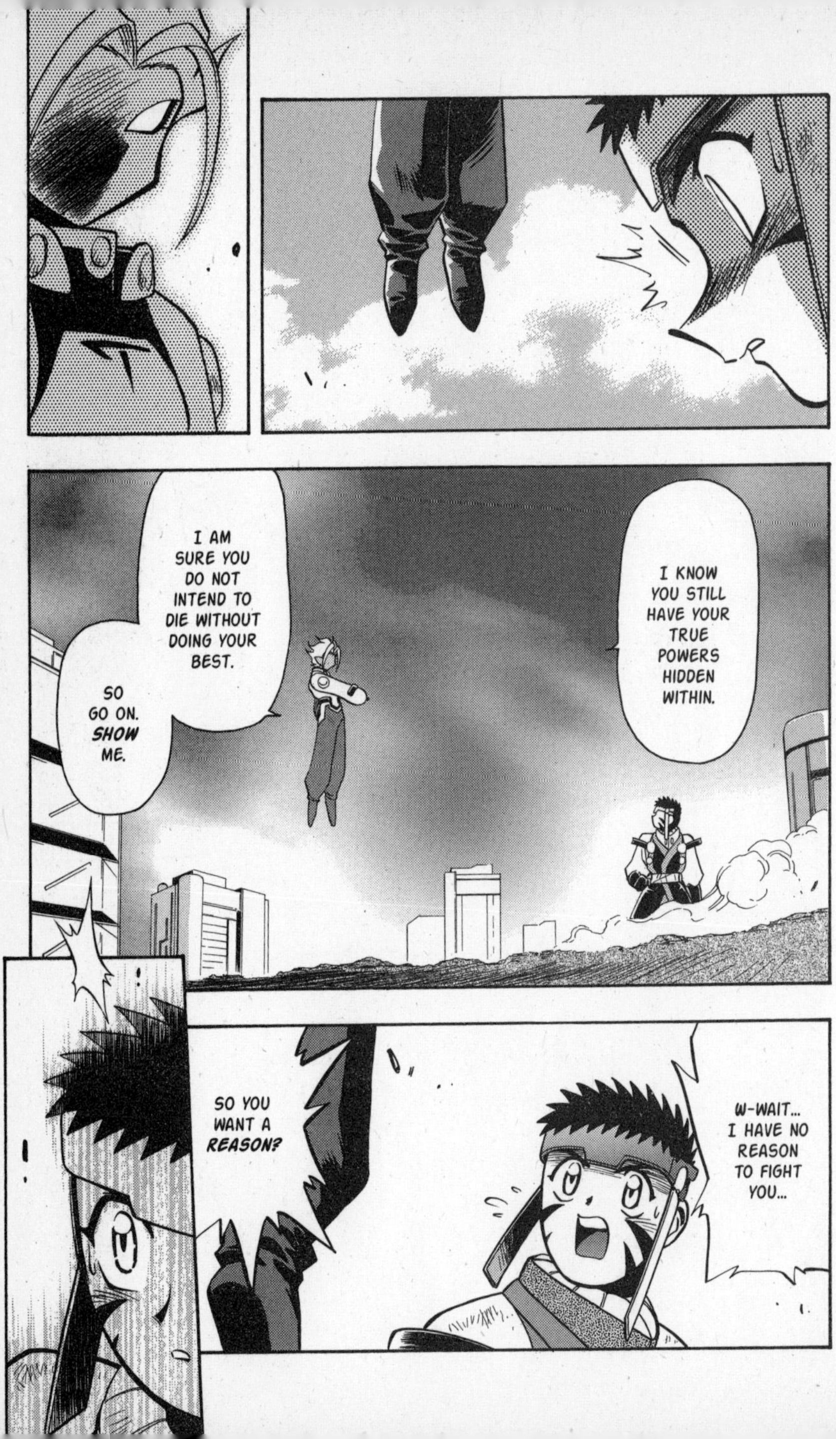
I KNOW YOU STILL HAVE YOUR TRUE POWERS HIDDEN WITHIN.
I AM SURE YOU DO NOT INTEND TO DIE WITHOUT DOING YOUR BEST.
SO GO ON. *SHOW* ME.
W-WAIT... I HAVE NO REASON TO FIGHT YOU...
SO YOU WANT A *REASON?*

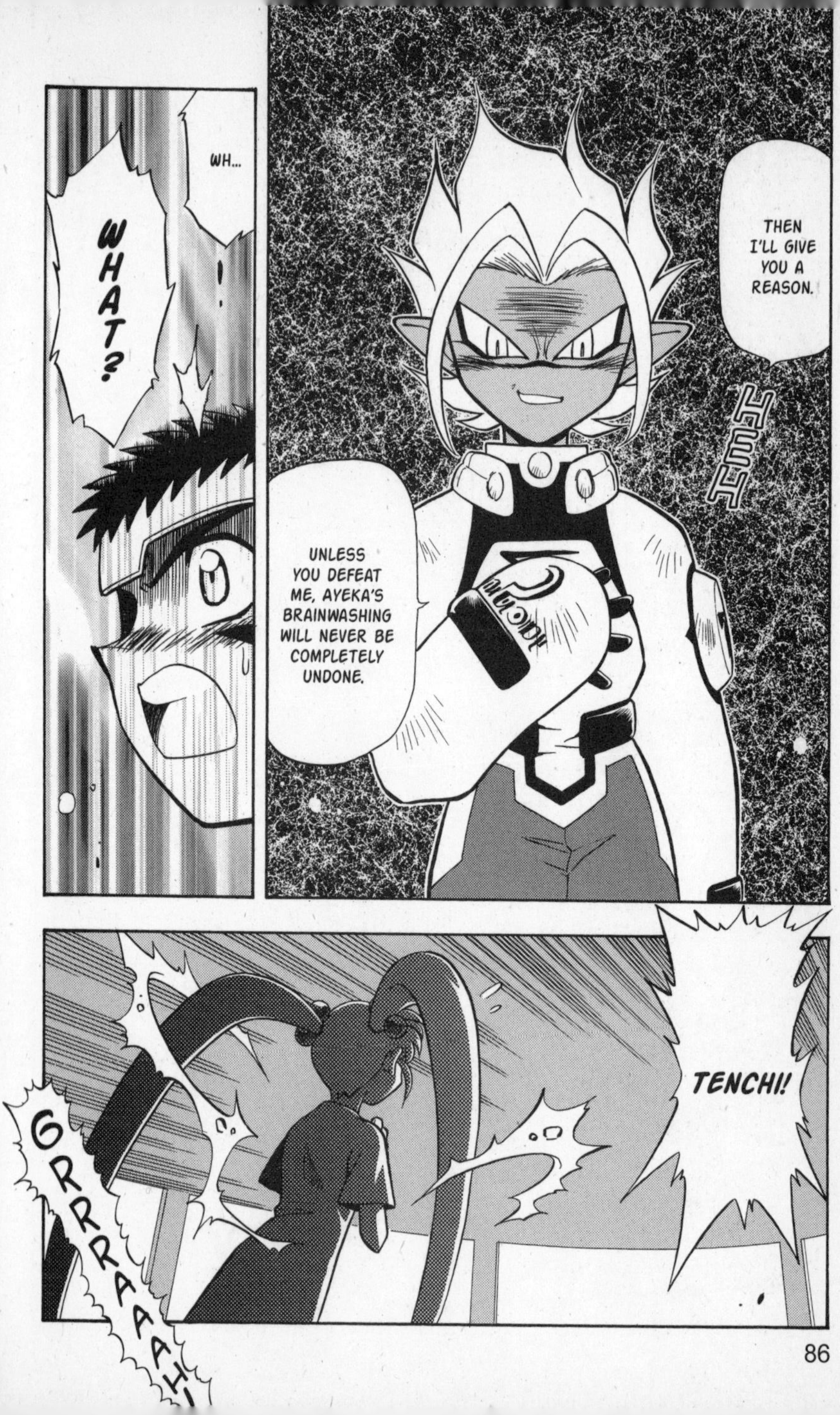
THEN I'LL GIVE YOU A REASON.
HEH
UNLESS YOU DEFEAT ME, AYEKA'S BRAINWASHING WILL NEVER BE COMPLETELY UNDONE.
WH...
WHAT?
TENCHI!
GRRRAAAH!

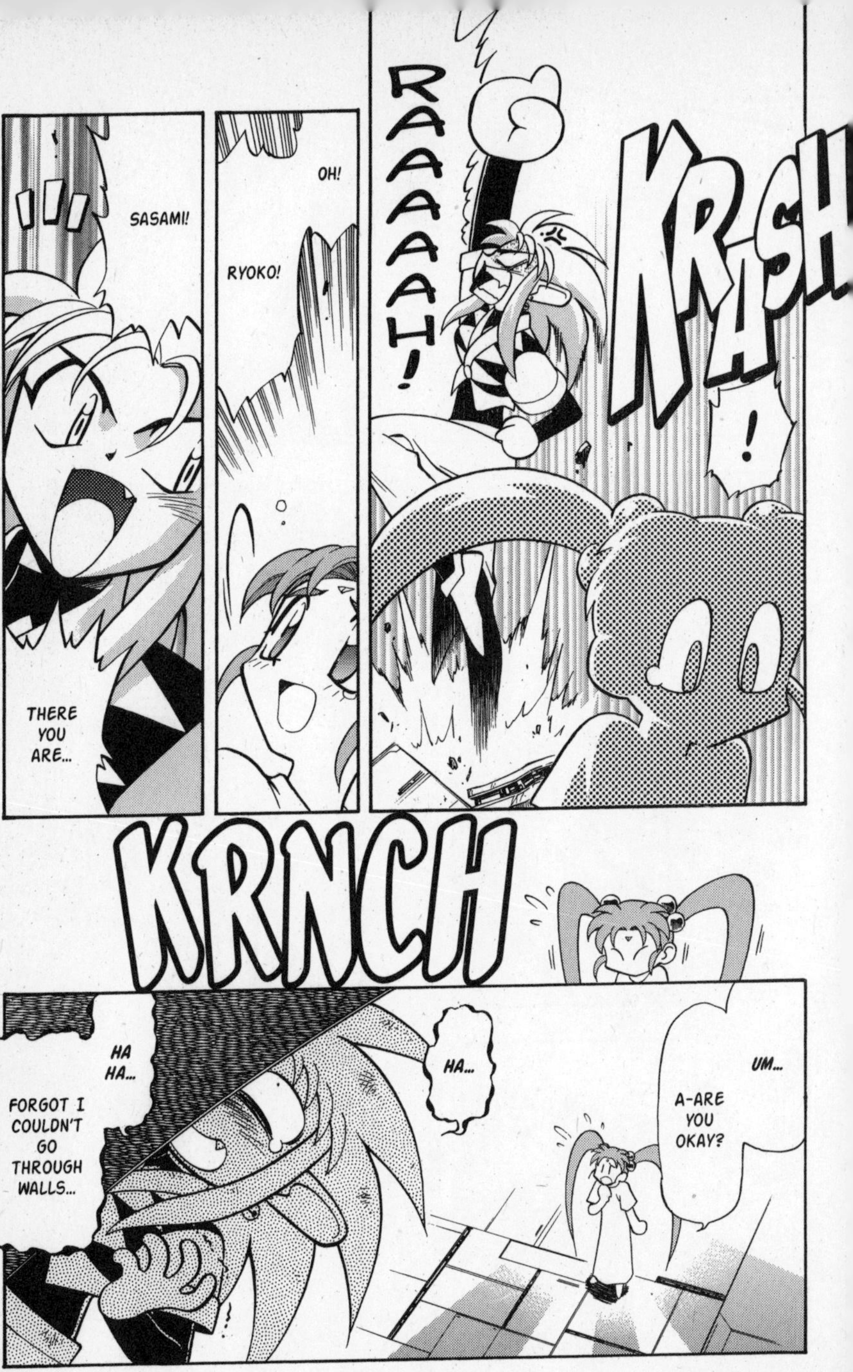
RAAAAAH!
KRASH
!
OH!
RYOKO!
SASAMI!
THERE YOU ARE...
KRNCH
UM...
A-ARE YOU OKAY?
HA...
HA HA...
FORGOT I COULDN'T GO THROUGH WALLS...

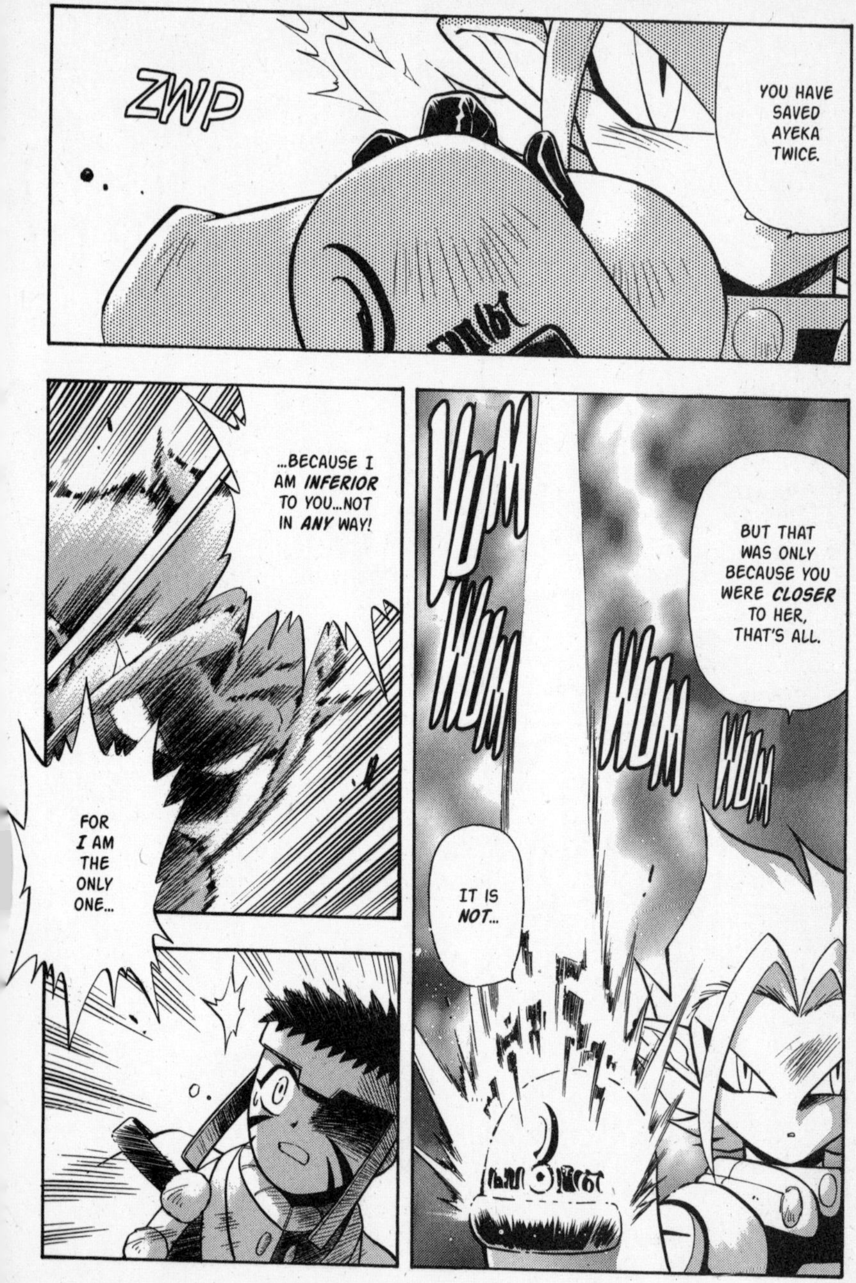
ZWP
YOU HAVE SAVED AYEKA TWICE.
BUT THAT WAS ONLY BECAUSE YOU WERE *CLOSER* TO HER, THAT'S ALL.
IT IS *NOT*...
...BECAUSE I AM *INFERIOR* TO YOU...NOT IN *ANY* WAY!
FOR *I* AM THE ONLY ONE...

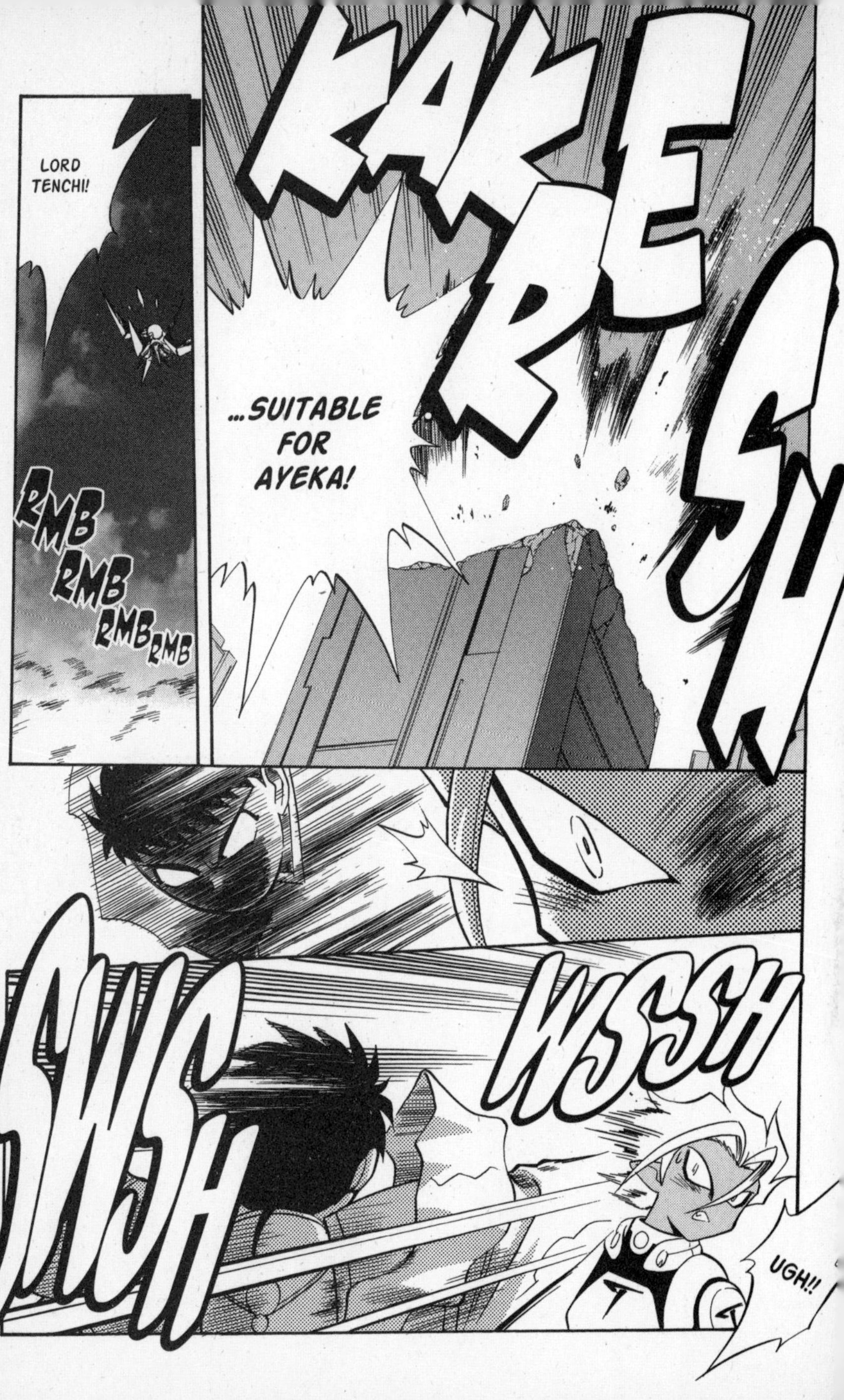
...SUITABLE FOR AYEKA!
LORD TENCHI!
RMB RMB RMB RMB
WSSH
UGH!!

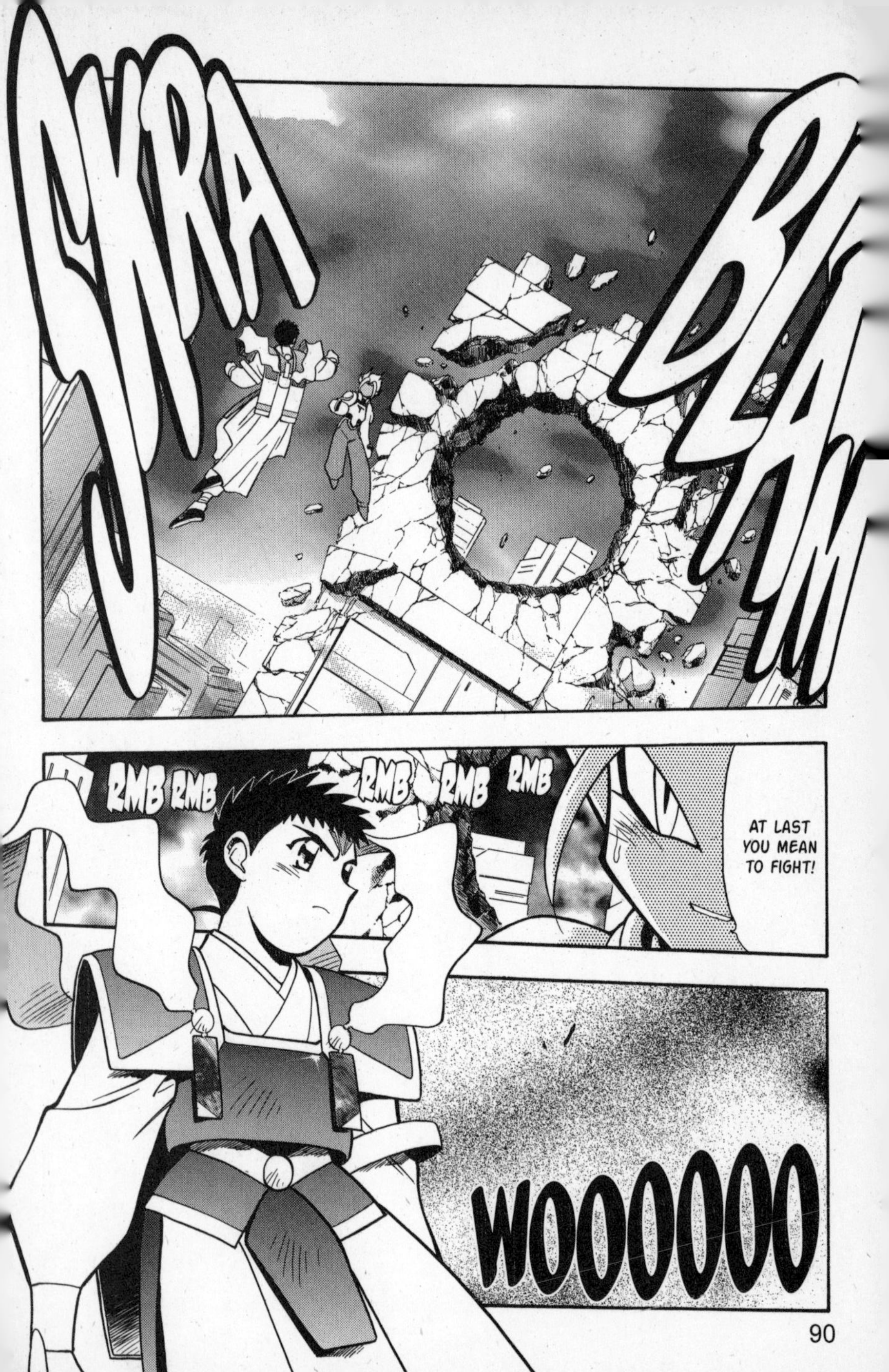
AT LAST YOU MEAN TO FIGHT!
WOOOOOO
RMB RMB RMB
RMB RMB

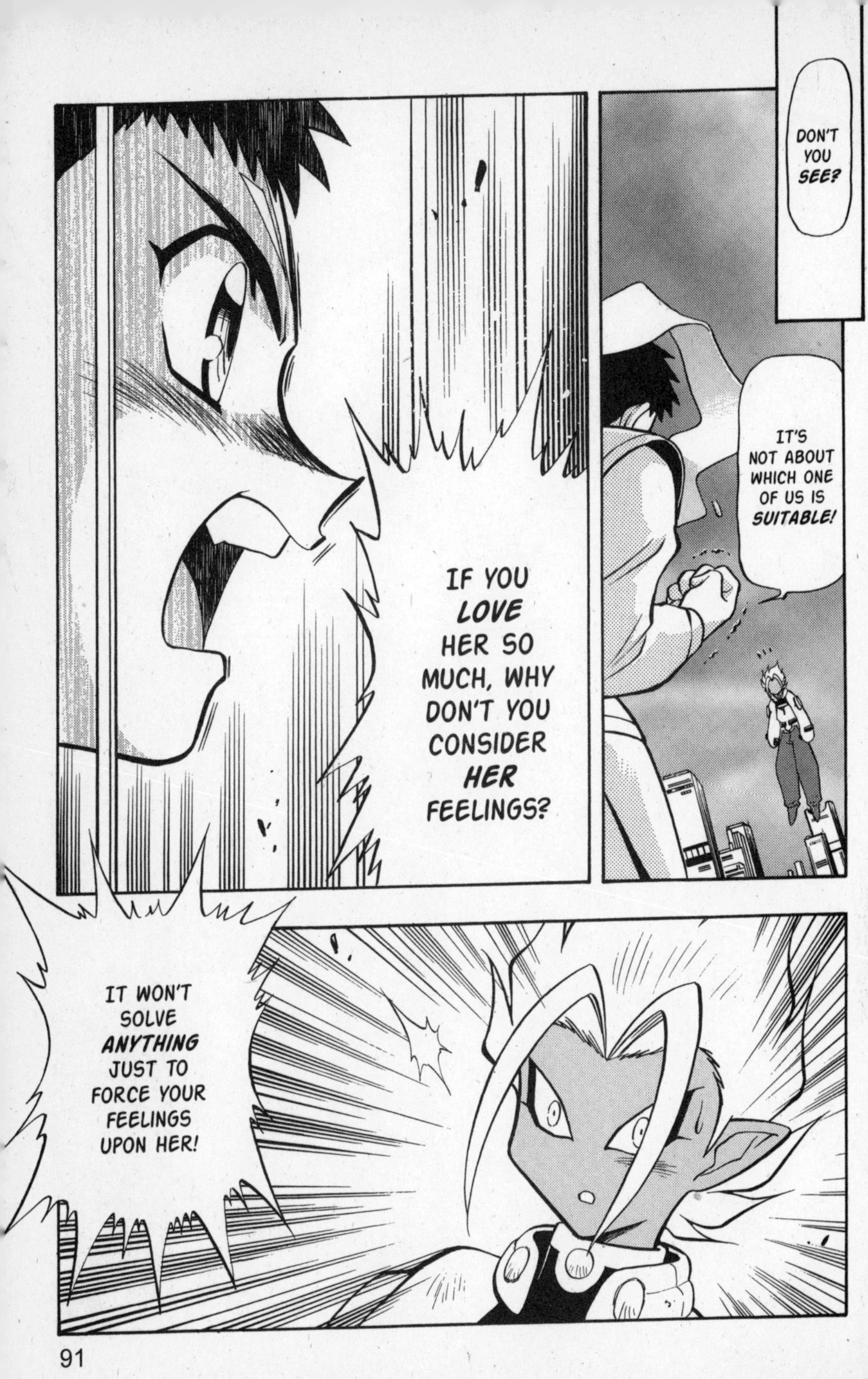

DON'T YOU SEE?
IT'S NOT ABOUT WHICH ONE OF US IS SUITABLE!
IF YOU LOVE HER SO MUCH, WHY DON'T YOU CONSIDER HER FEELINGS?
IT WON'T SOLVE ANYTHING JUST TO FORCE YOUR FEELINGS UPON HER!

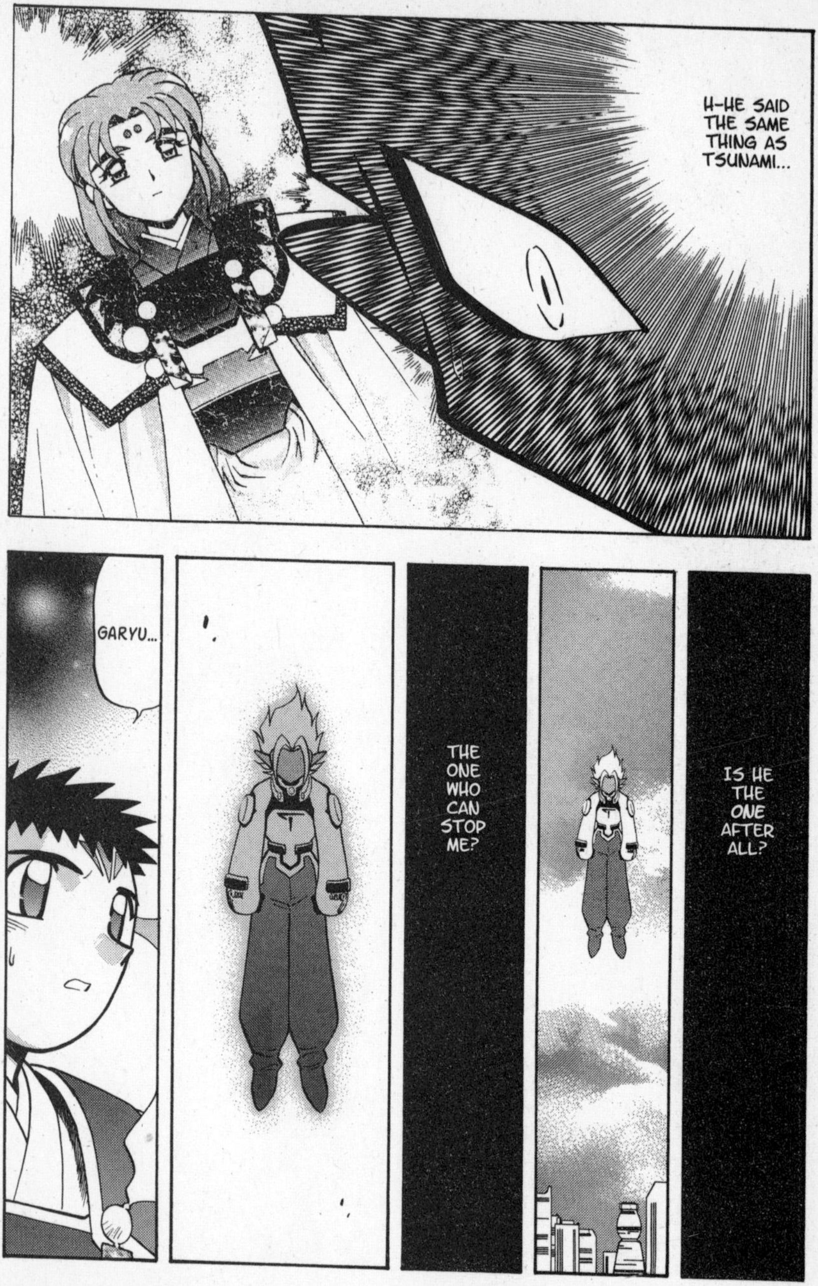
H-HE SAID THE SAME THING AS TSUNAMI...
IS HE THE ONE AFTER ALL?
THE ONE WHO CAN STOP ME?
GARYU...

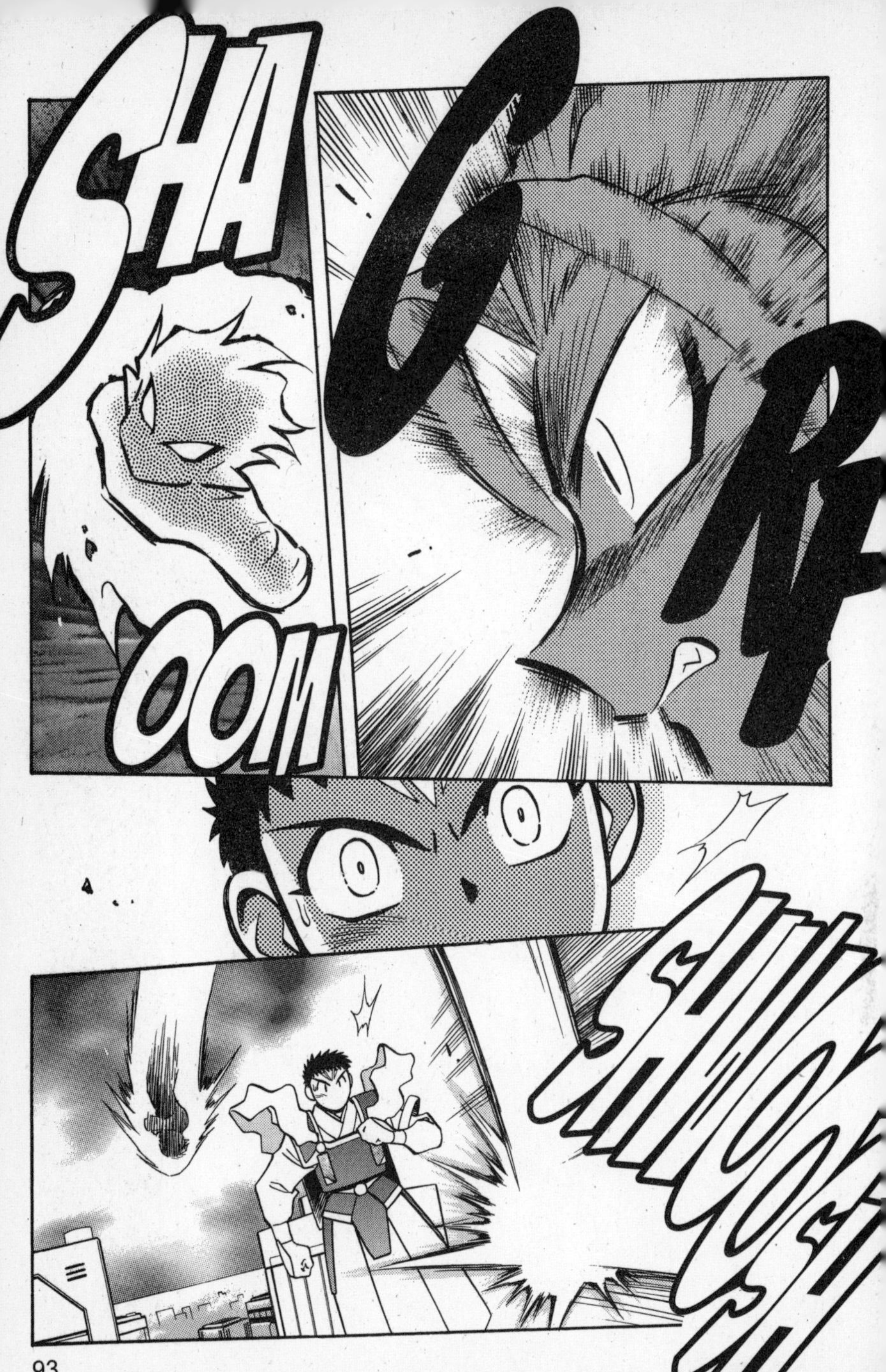
SHA
OOM

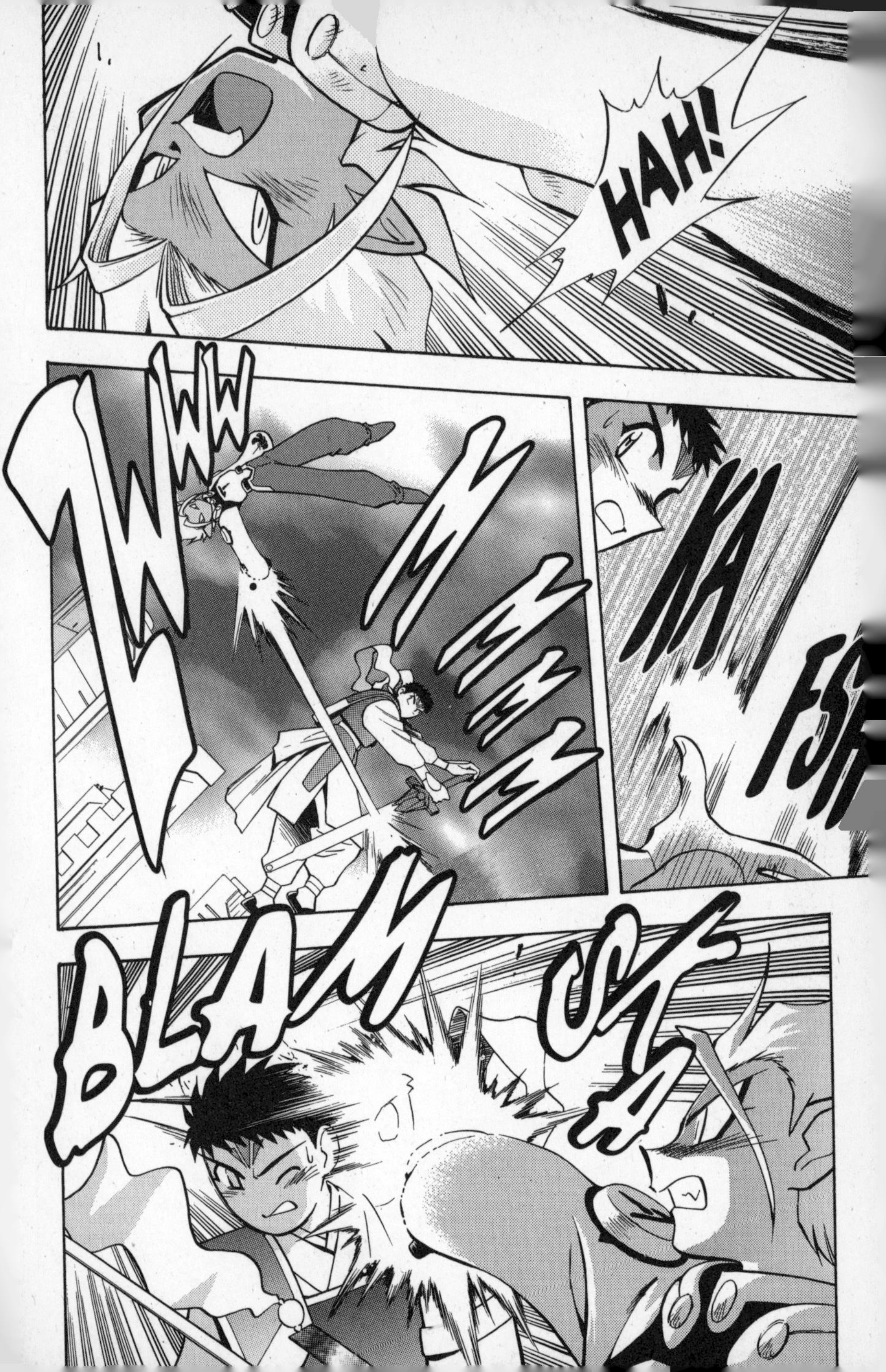
HAH!
BLAM

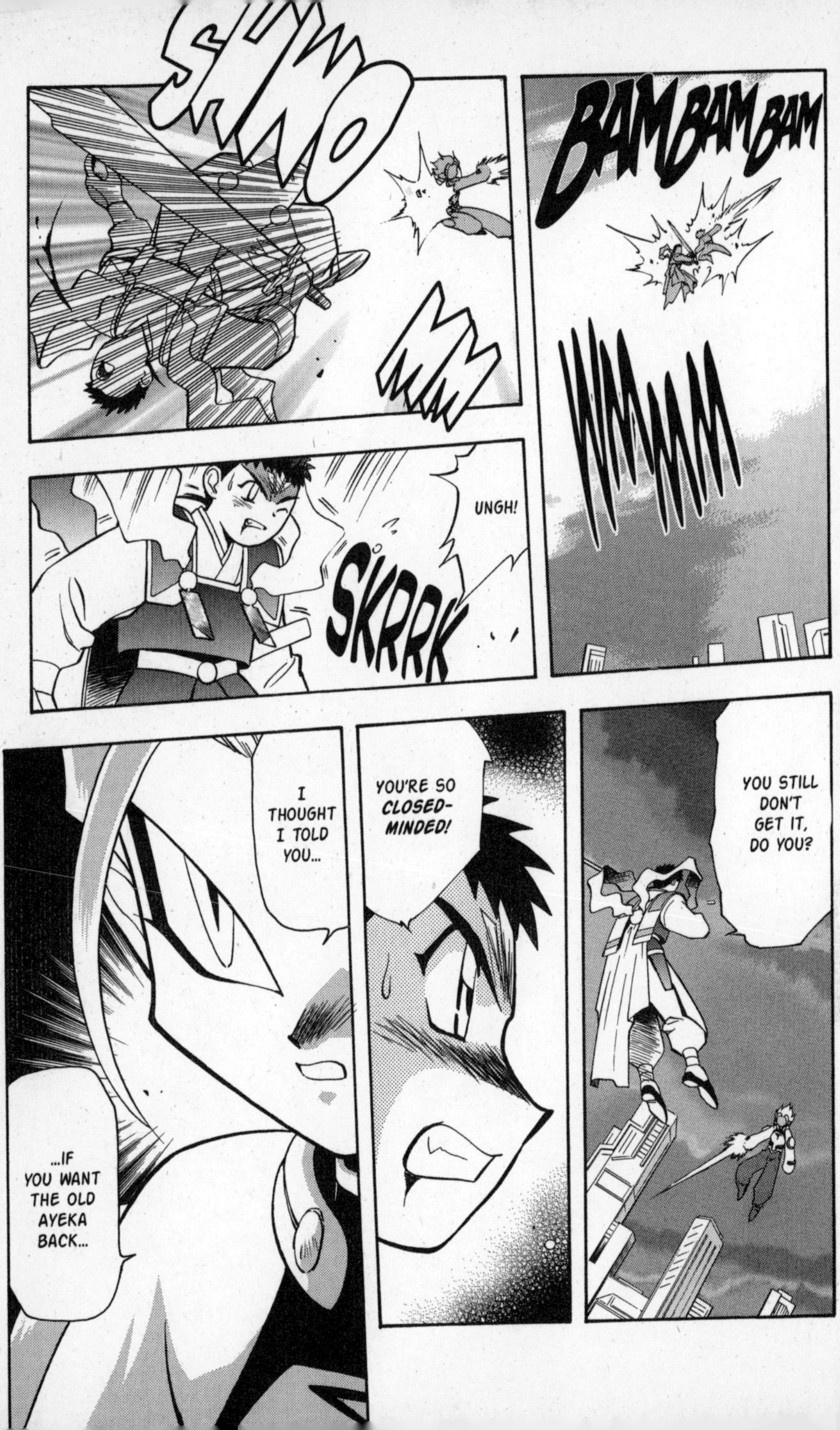
BAM BAM BAM
WMMMM
SHWO
MMM
UNGH!
SKRRK
YOU STILL DON'T GET IT, DO YOU?
YOU'RE SO CLOSED-MINDED!
I THOUGHT I TOLD YOU...
...IF YOU WANT THE OLD AYEKA BACK...

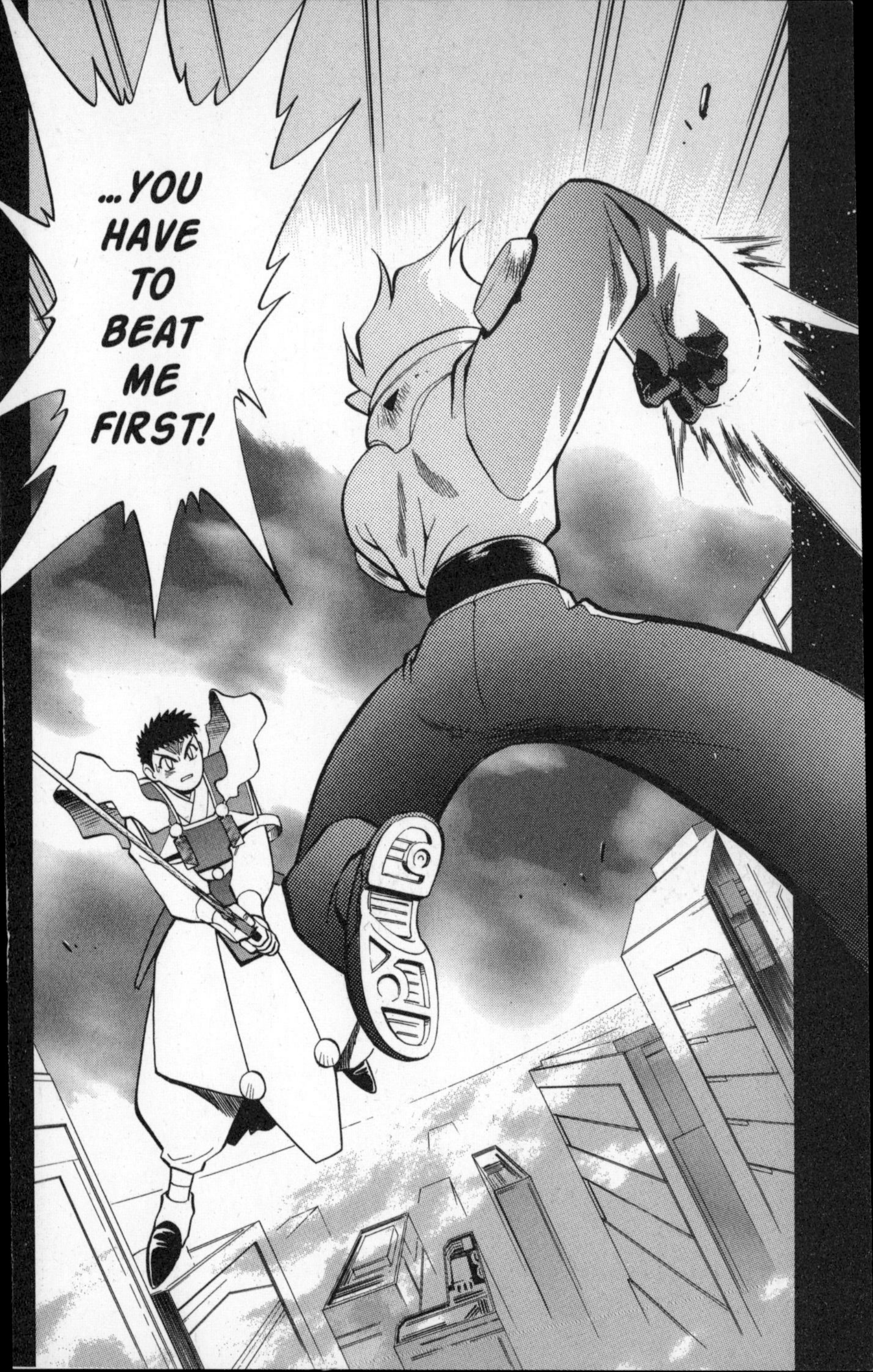
...YOU HAVE TO BEAT ME FIRST!

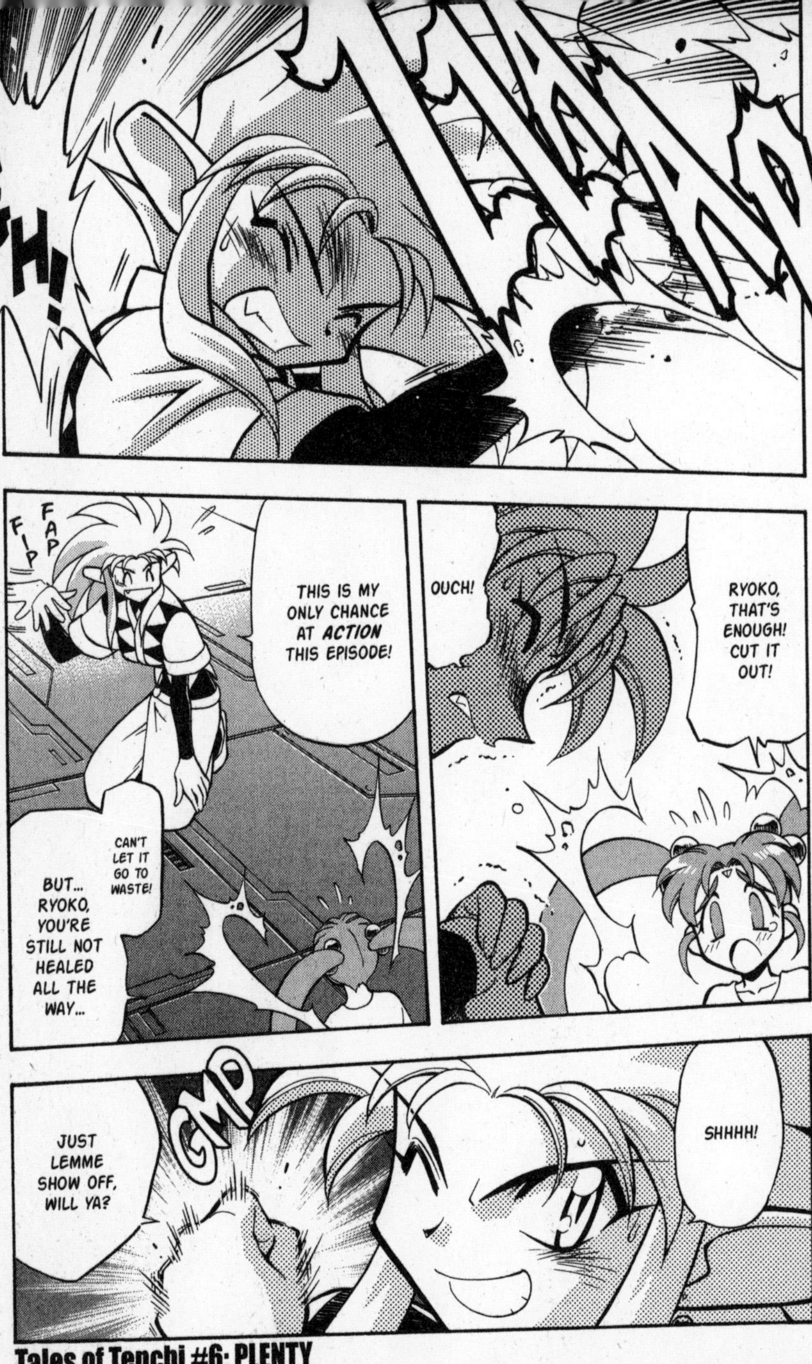
AGH!
RYOKO, THAT'S ENOUGH! CUT IT OUT!
OUCH!
THIS IS MY ONLY CHANCE AT *ACTION* THIS EPISODE!
FAP FIP
CAN'T LET IT GO TO WASTE!
BUT... RYOKO, YOU'RE STILL NOT HEALED ALL THE WAY...
SHHHH!
GMP
JUST LEMME SHOW OFF, WILL YA?

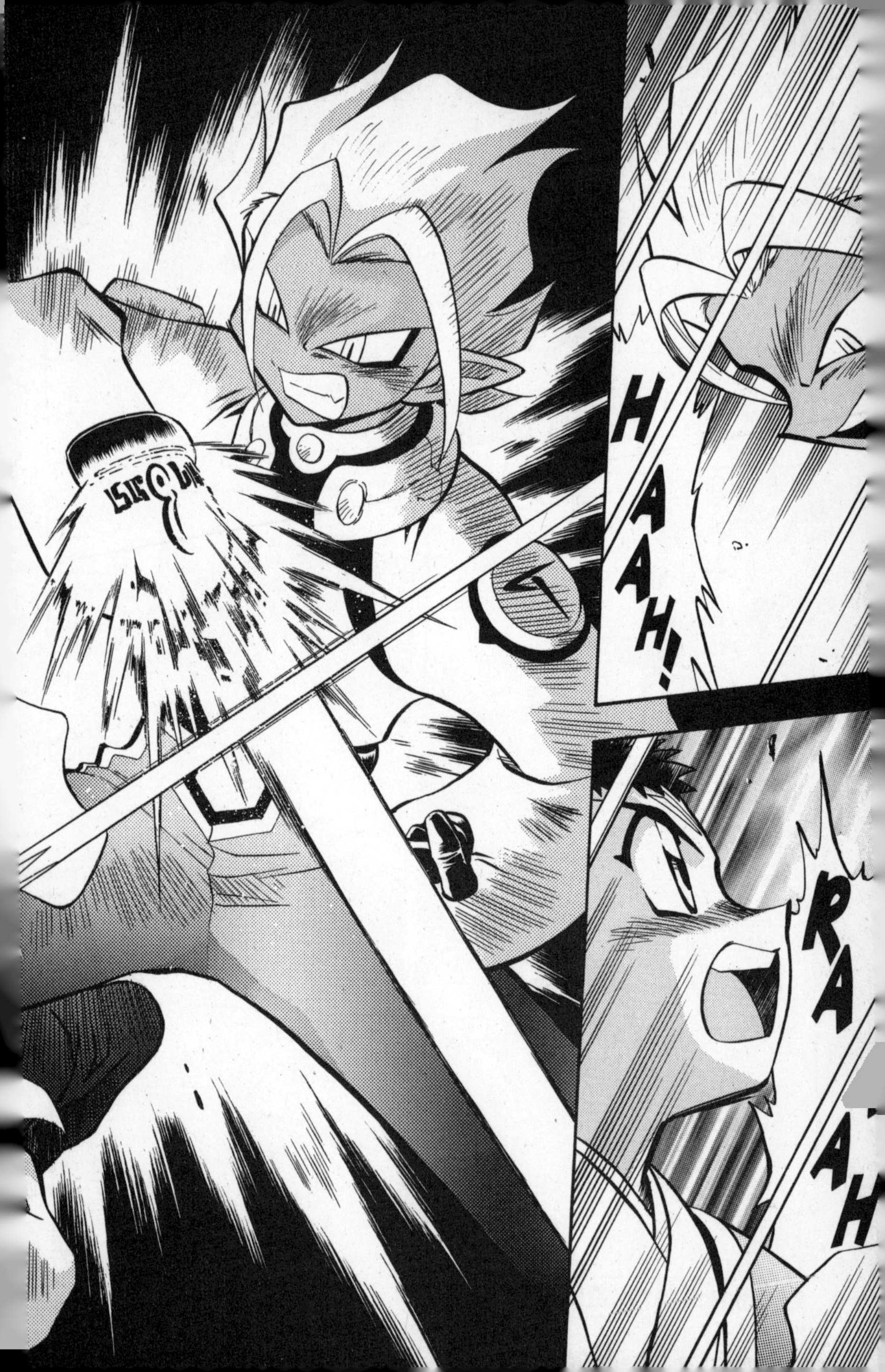
HAAAH!
RAAAH

Tales of Tenchi #6: PLENTY

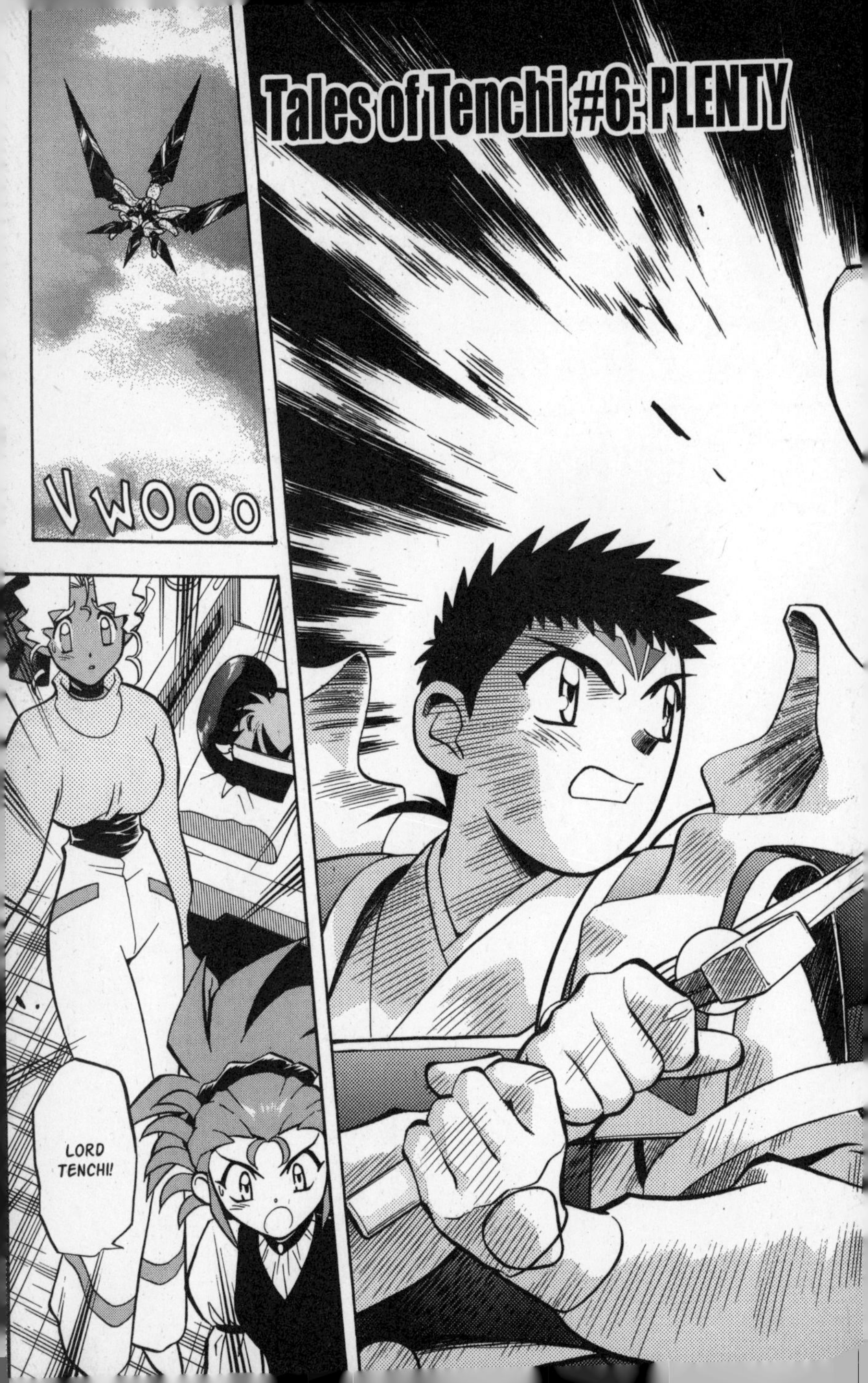
VWOOO
LORD TENCHI!

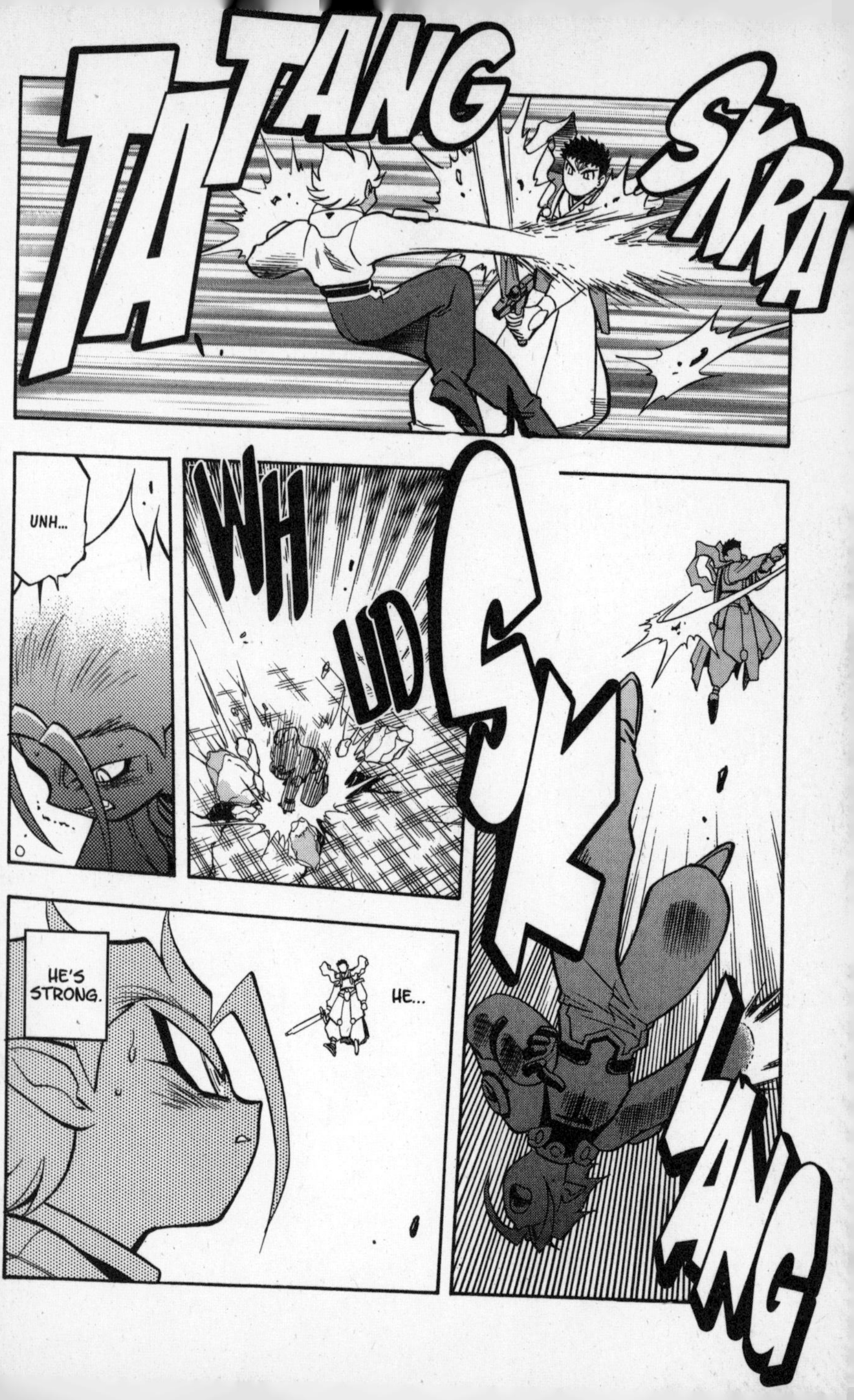

SKRA
TANG
TA
SK
LANG
WH
UD
UNH...
HE...
HE'S STRONG.

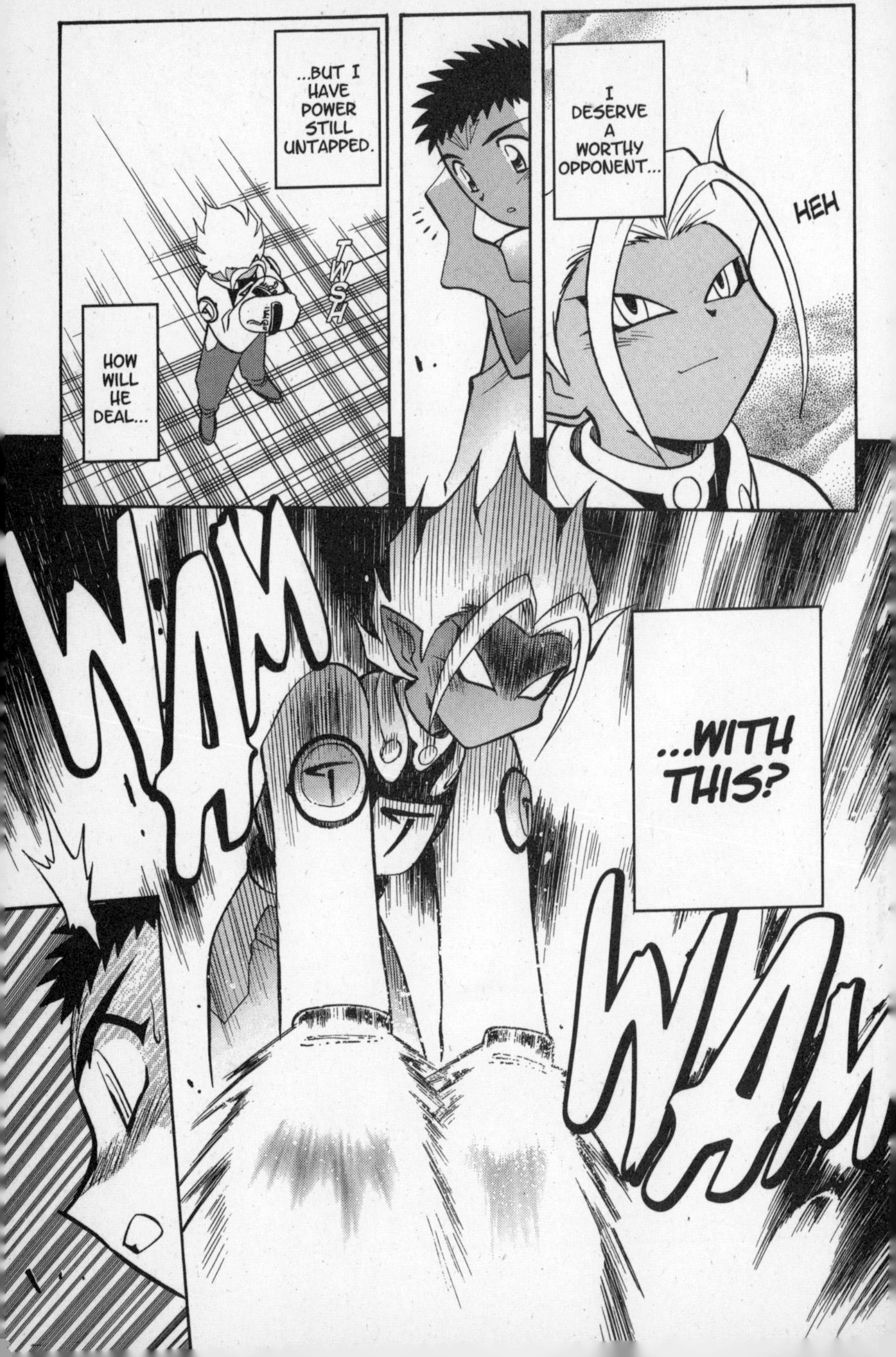
I DESERVE A WORTHY OPPONENT...
HEH
...BUT I HAVE POWER STILL UNTAPPED.
TWSH
HOW WILL HE DEAL...
...WITH THIS?
WAM
WAM

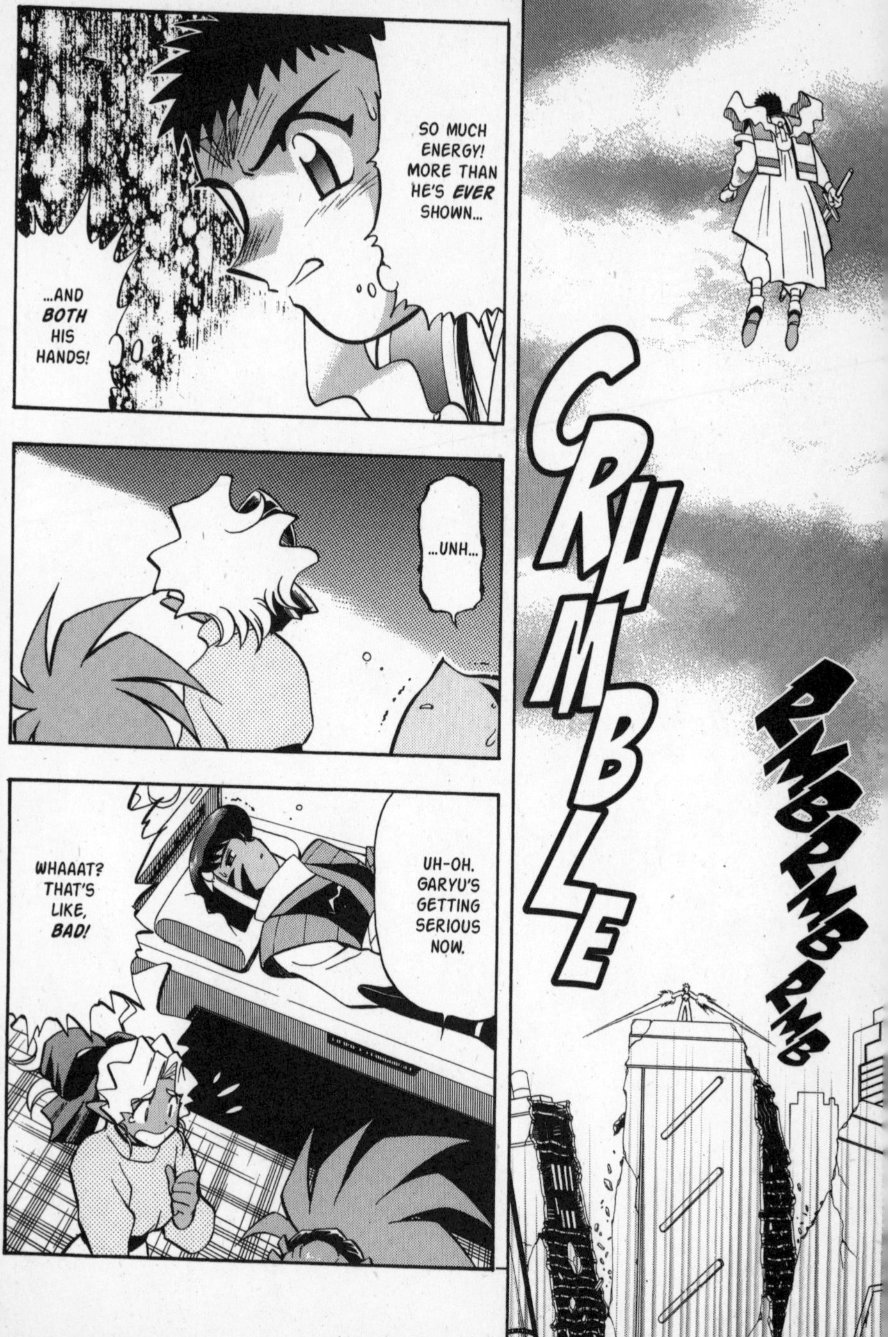
CRUMBLE
RMBRMBRMB
SO MUCH ENERGY! MORE THAN HE'S *EVER* SHOWN...
...AND *BOTH* HIS HANDS!
...UNH...
UH-OH. GARYU'S GETTING SERIOUS NOW.
WHAAAT? THAT'S LIKE, *BAD!*

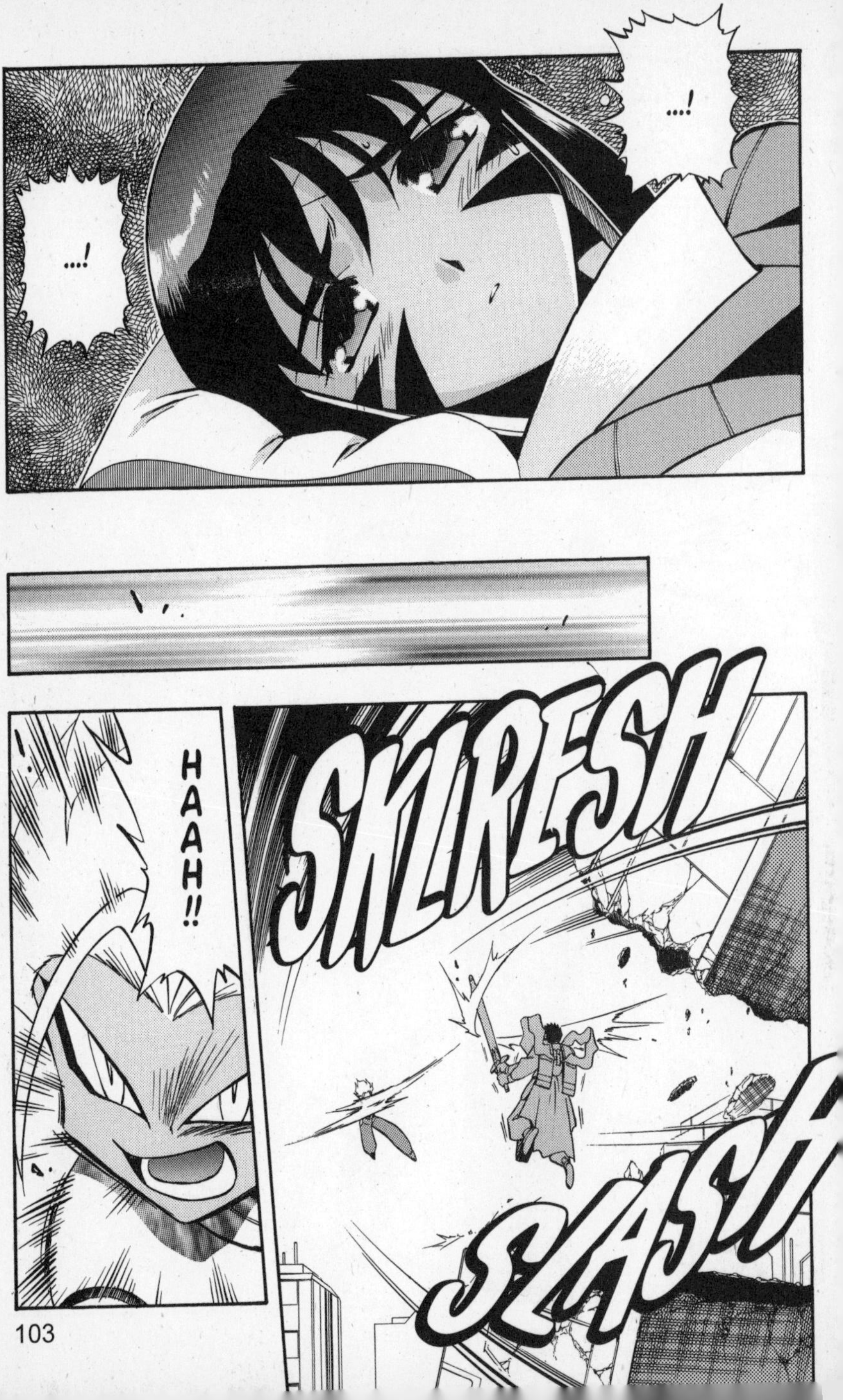
...!
...!
HAAAH!!

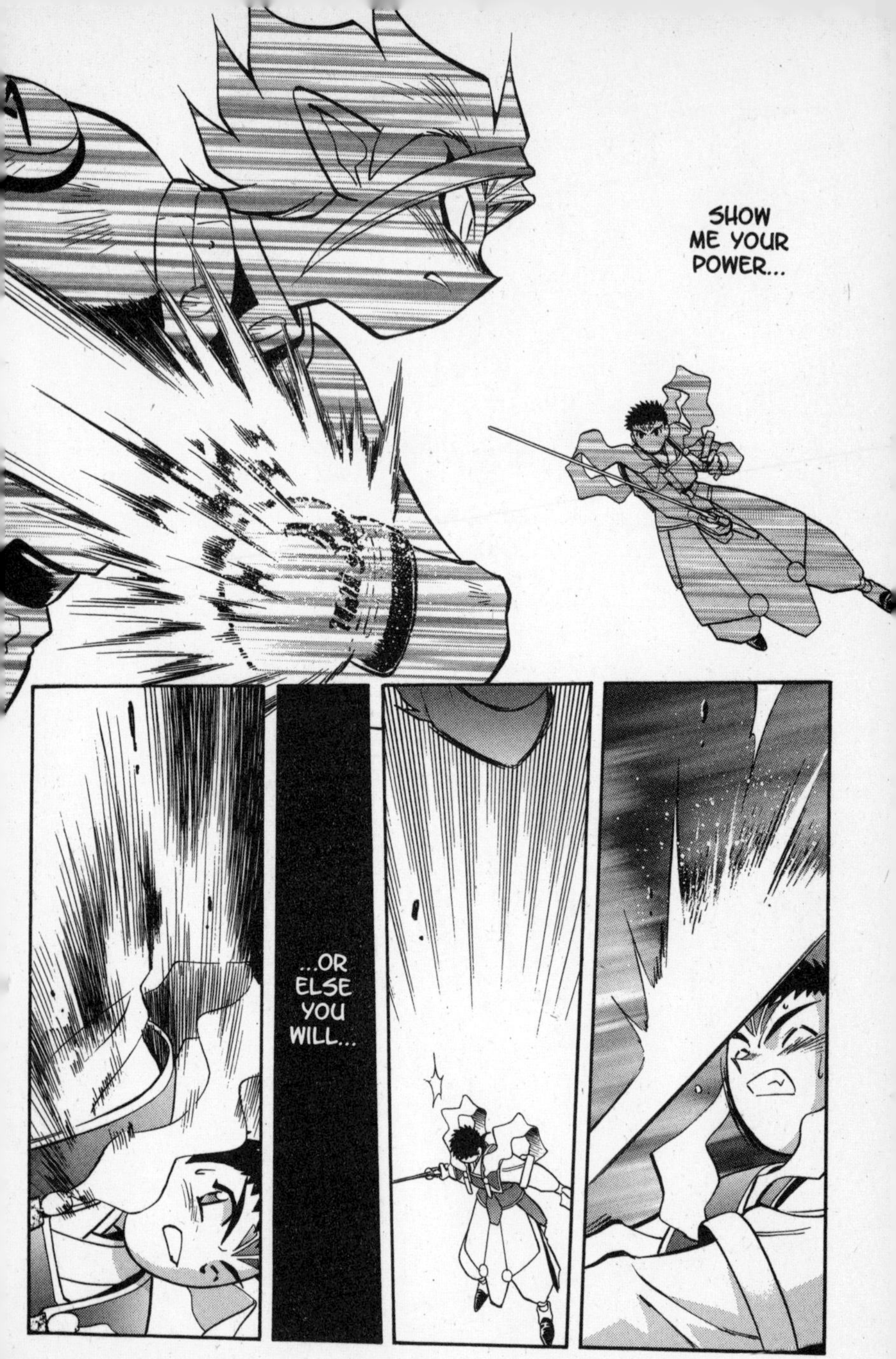
SHOW ME YOUR POWER...
...OR ELSE YOU WILL...

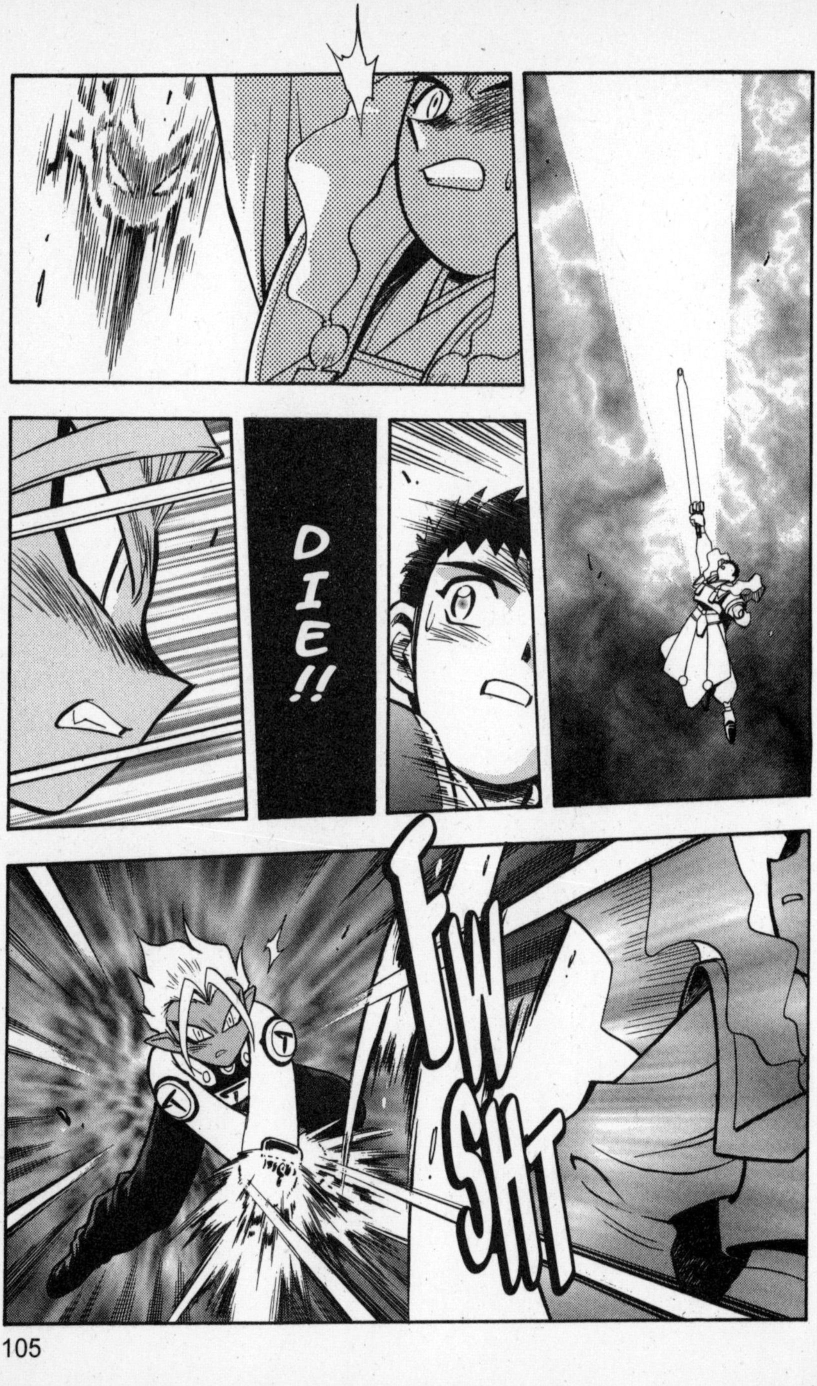
DIE!!
FWSHT

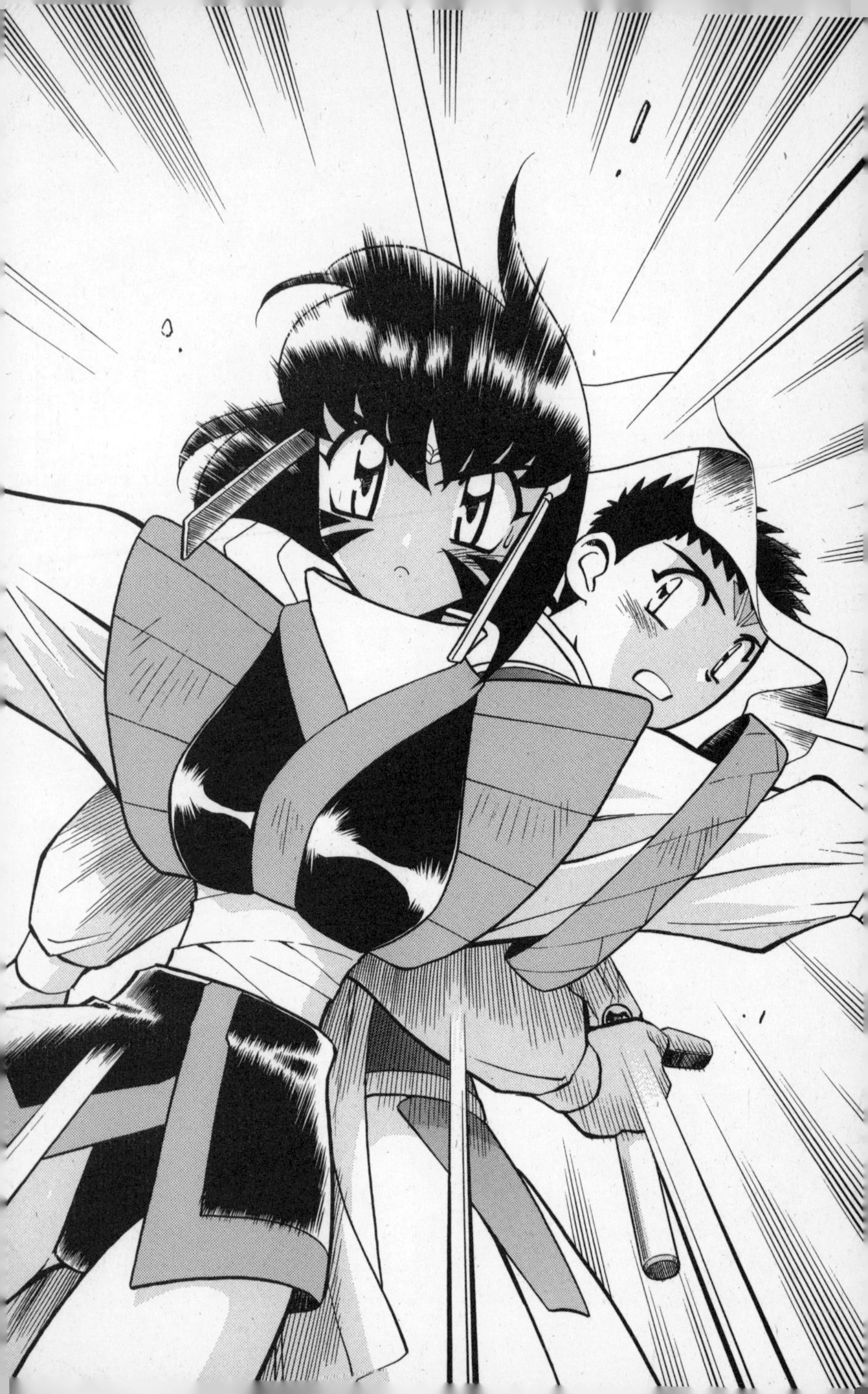

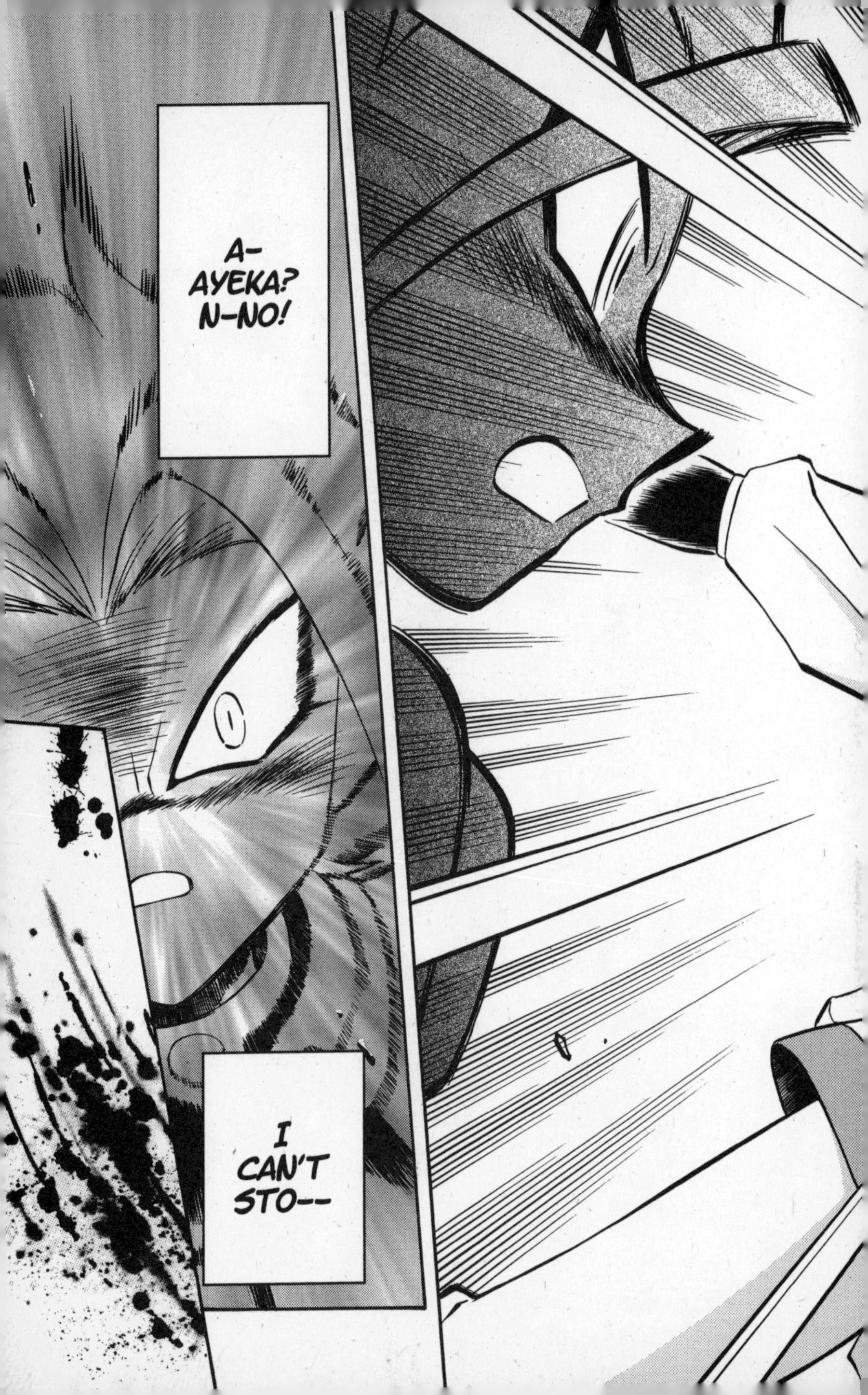
A- AYEKA? N-NO!
I CAN'T STO--

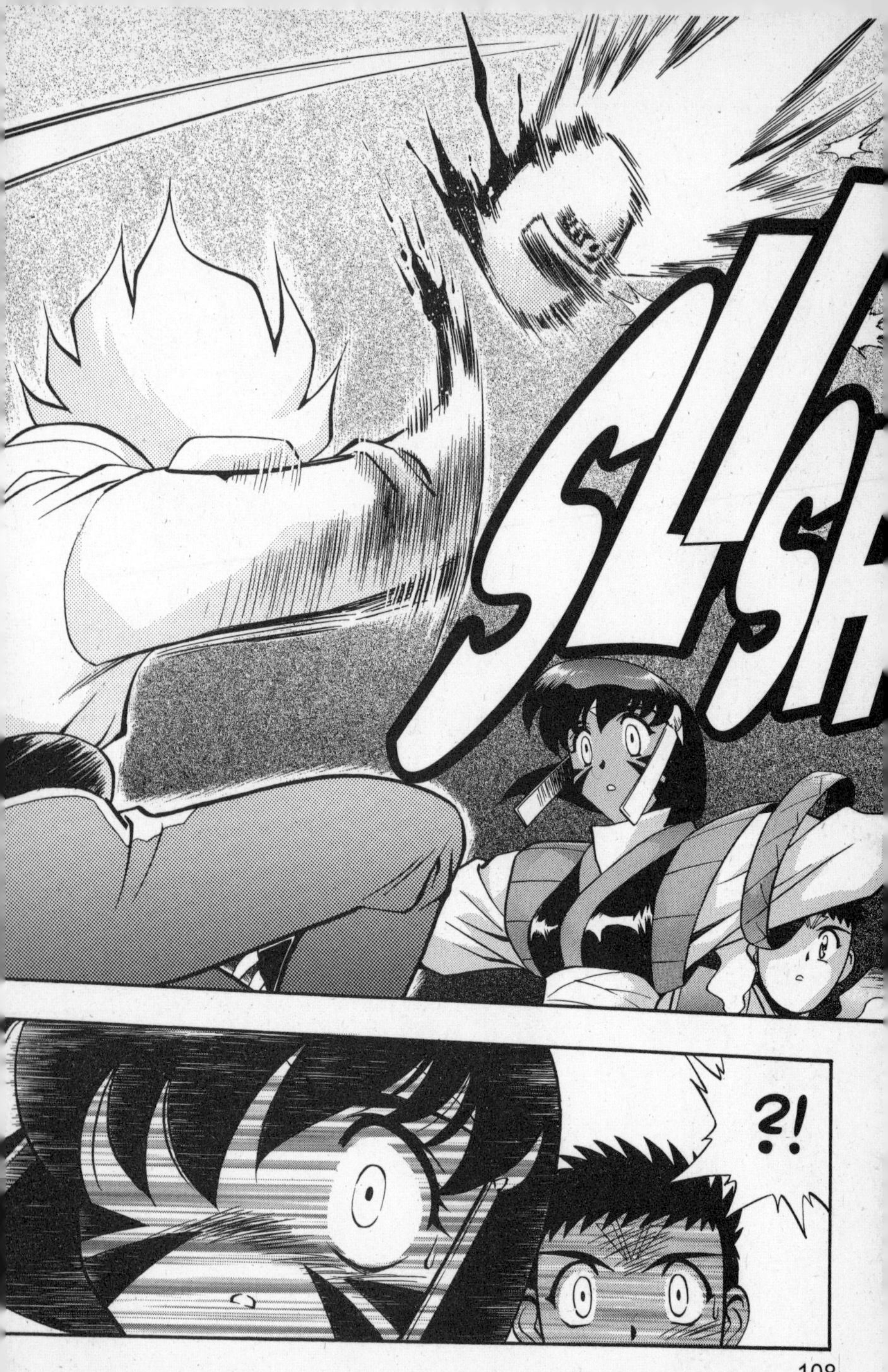
SLAS
?!

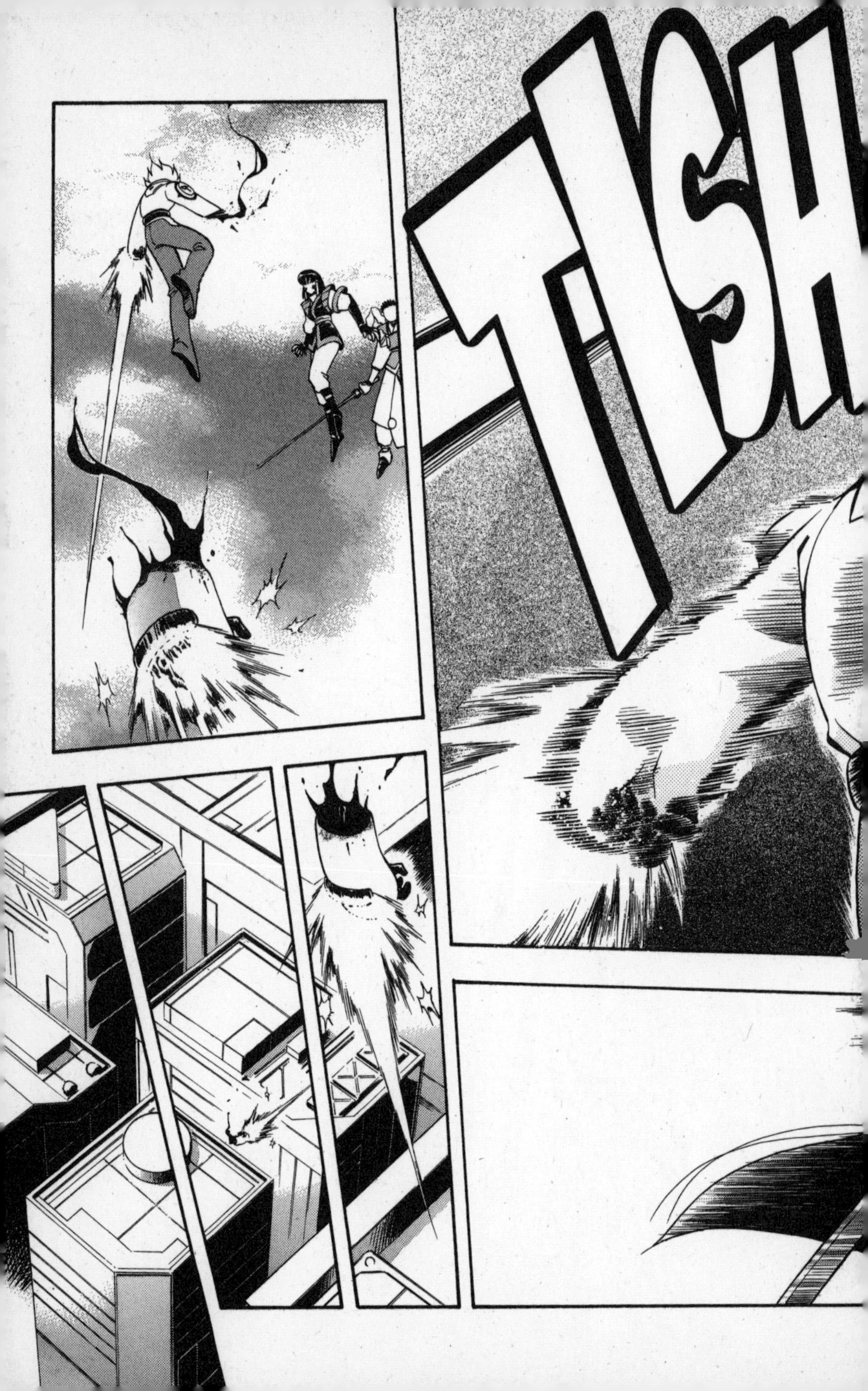
TISH

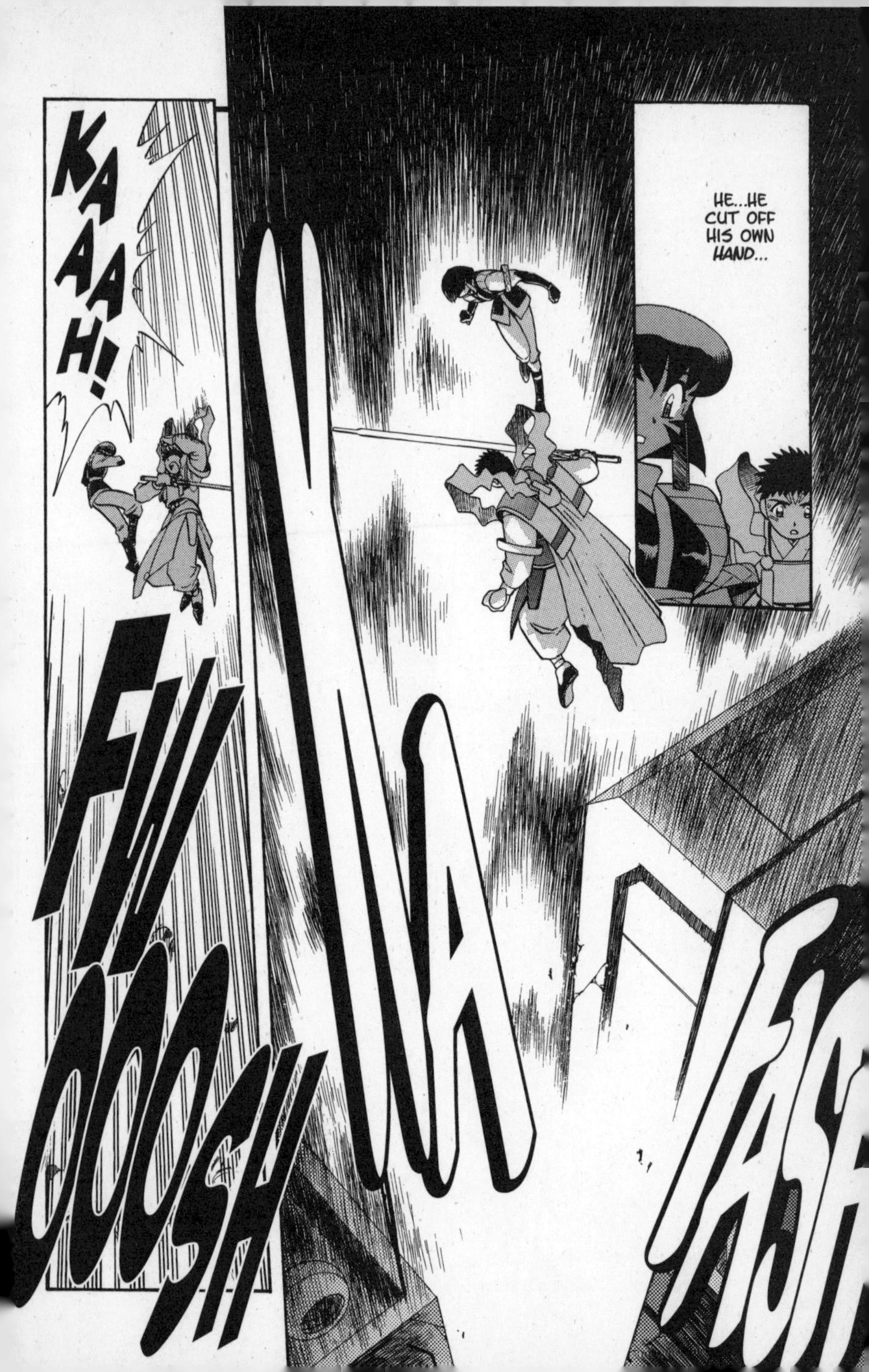
HE...HE CUT OFF HIS OWN HAND...
KAAAH!
FWOOOSH

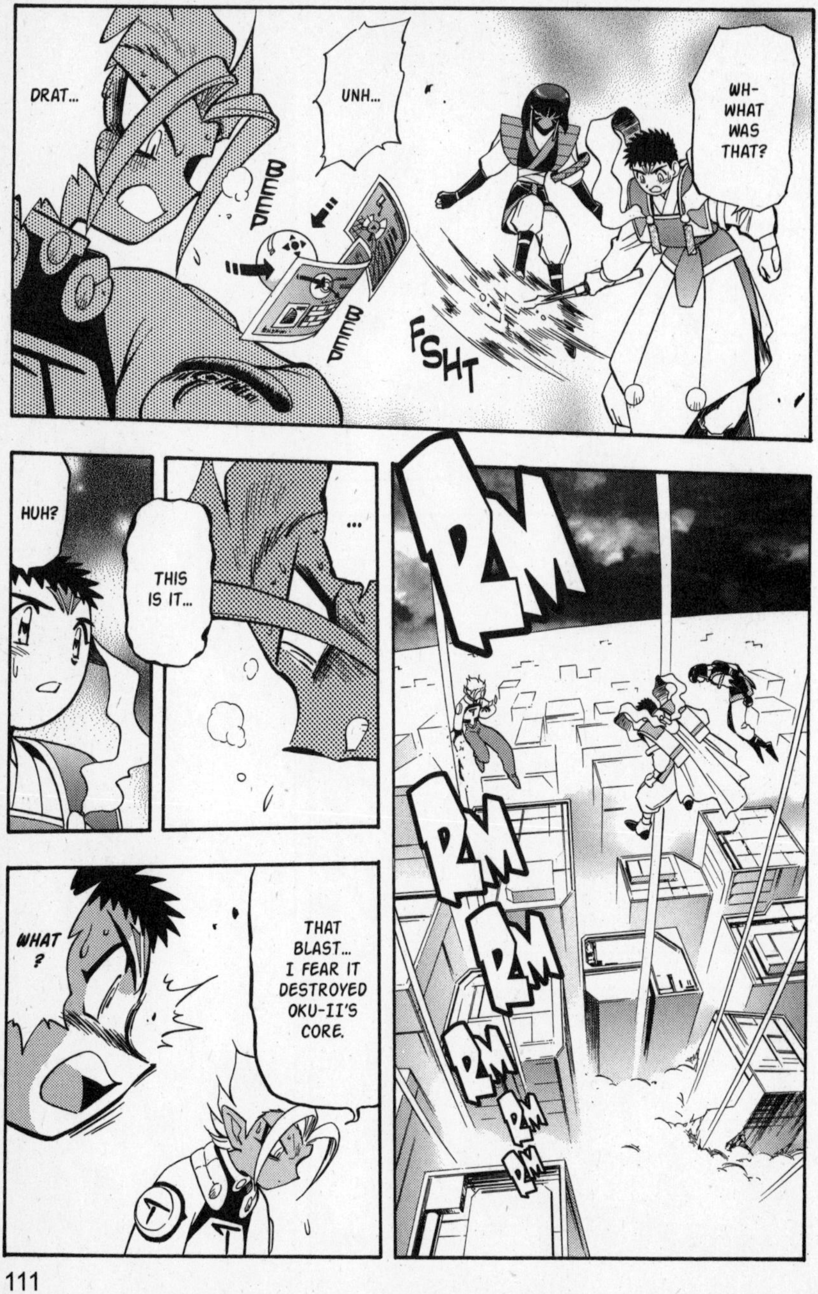
DRAT...
UNH...
BEEP
BEEP
FSHT
WH-WHAT WAS THAT?
HUH?
THIS IS IT...
...
DRM
DRM
DRM
DRM
DRM
DRM
WHAT?
THAT BLAST... I FEAR IT DESTROYED OKU-II'S CORE.

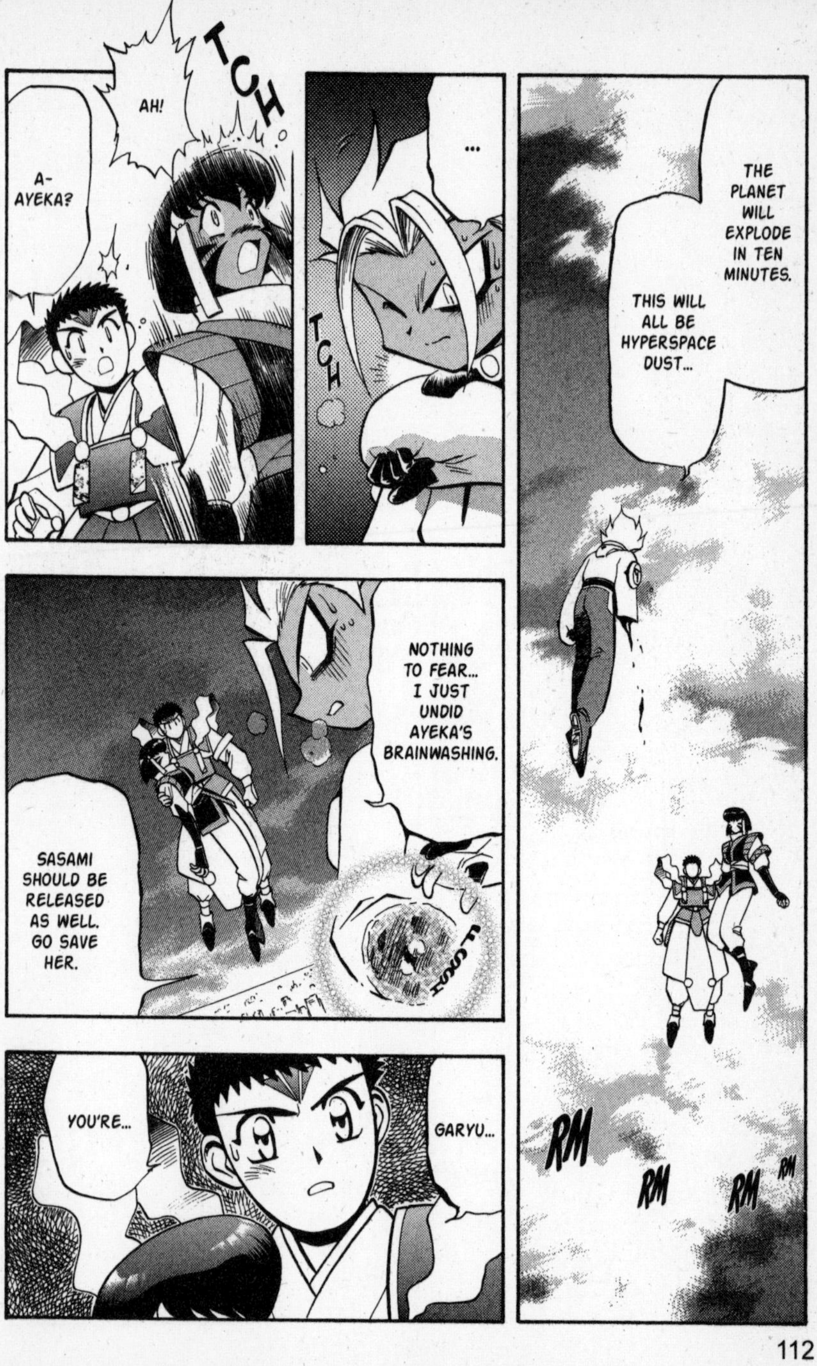
THE PLANET WILL EXPLODE IN TEN MINUTES.
THIS WILL ALL BE HYPERSPACE DUST...
RM
RM
RM
RM
...
TCH
TCH
AH!
A- AYEKA?
NOTHING TO FEAR... I JUST UNDID AYEKA'S BRAINWASHING.
SASAMI SHOULD BE RELEASED AS WELL. GO SAVE HER.
GARYU...
YOU'RE...

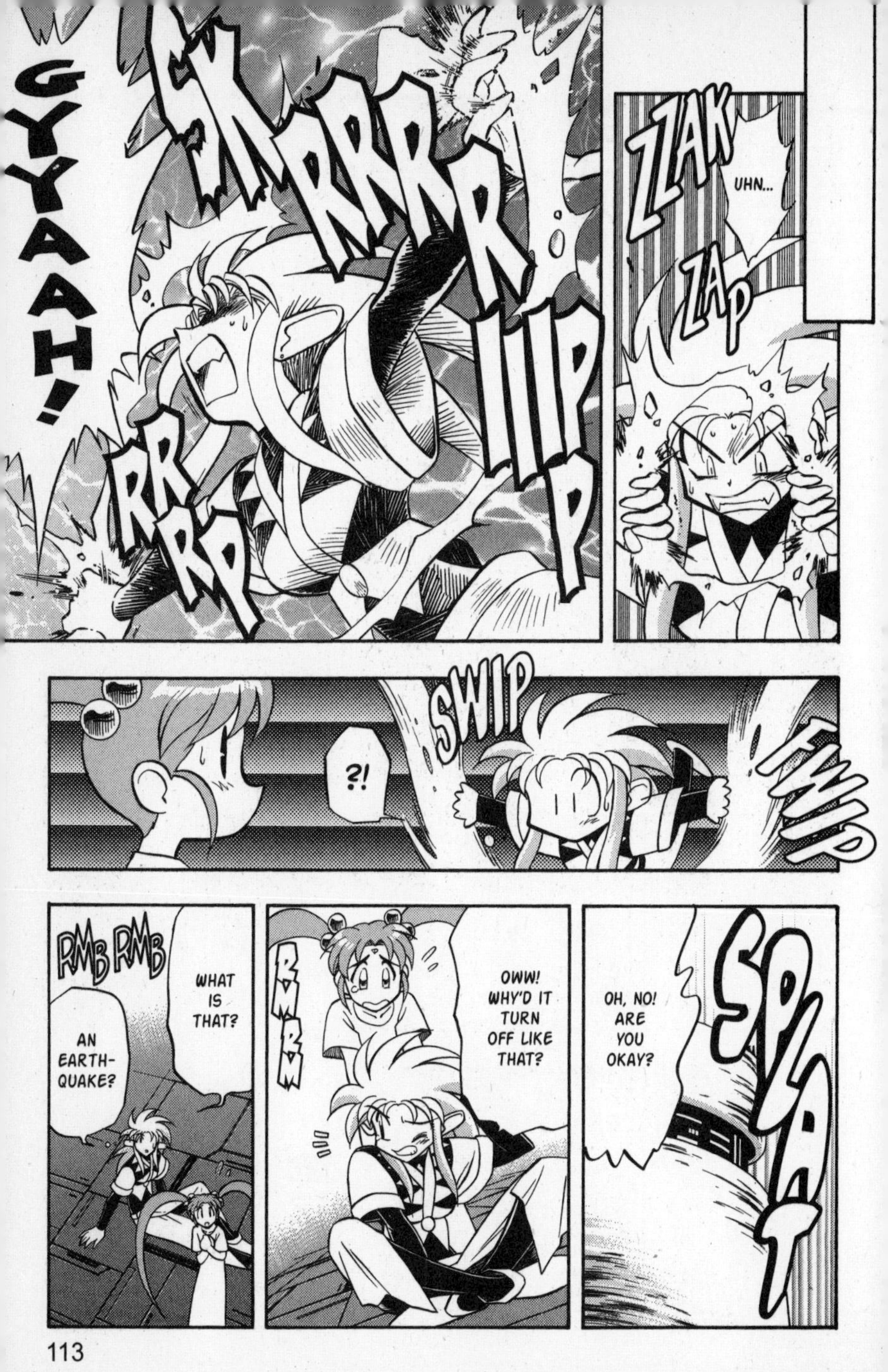
ZZAK
UHN...
ZAP
SKRRRRIIIP
GYYAAH!
RRRP
FWIP
SWIP
?!
SPLAT
OH, NO! ARE YOU OKAY?
OWW! WHY'D IT TURN OFF LIKE THAT?
RMB RMB
RMB RMB
WHAT IS THAT?
AN EARTH-QUAKE?

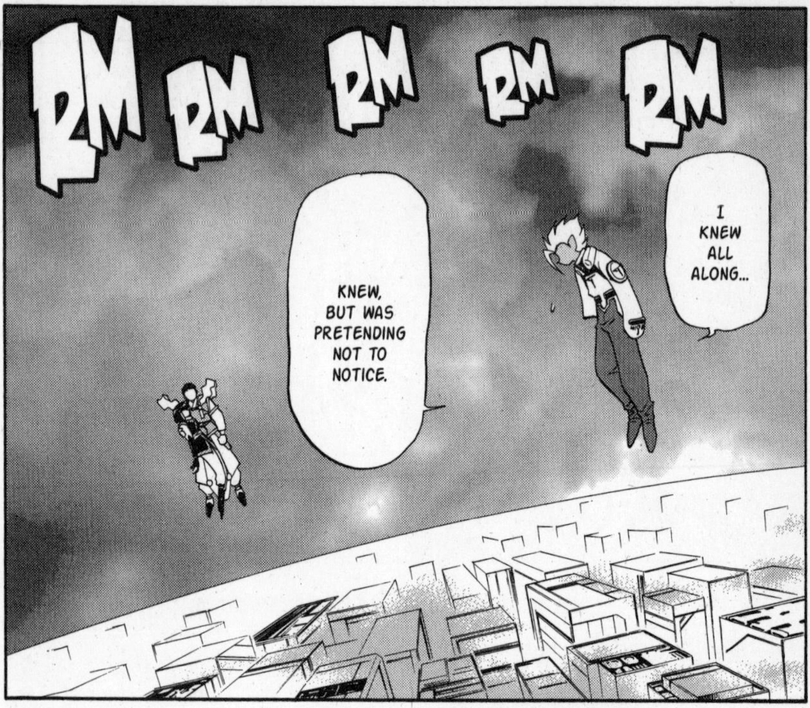
RM RM RM RM RM
I KNEW ALL ALONG...
KNEW, BUT WAS PRETENDING NOT TO NOTICE.

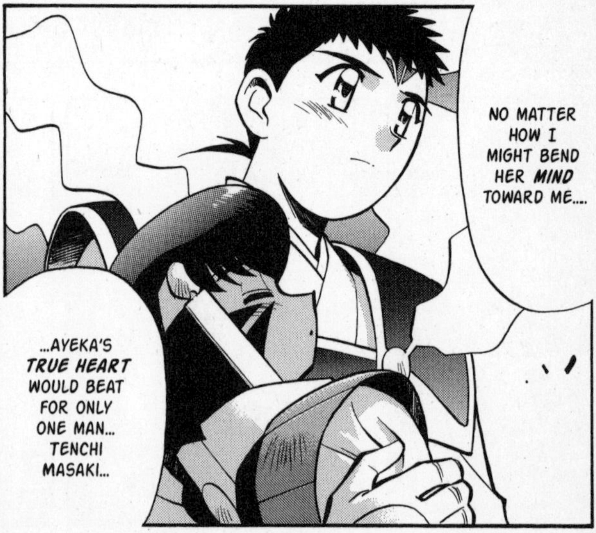
NO MATTER HOW I MIGHT BEND HER *MIND* TOWARD ME....
...AYEKA'S *TRUE HEART* WOULD BEAT FOR ONLY ONE MAN... TENCHI MASAKI...

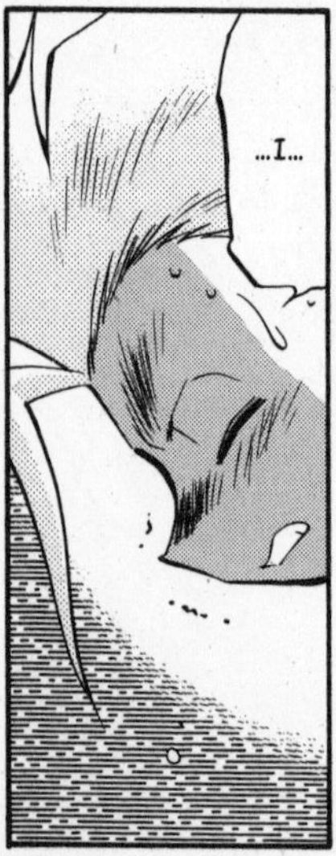
...I...

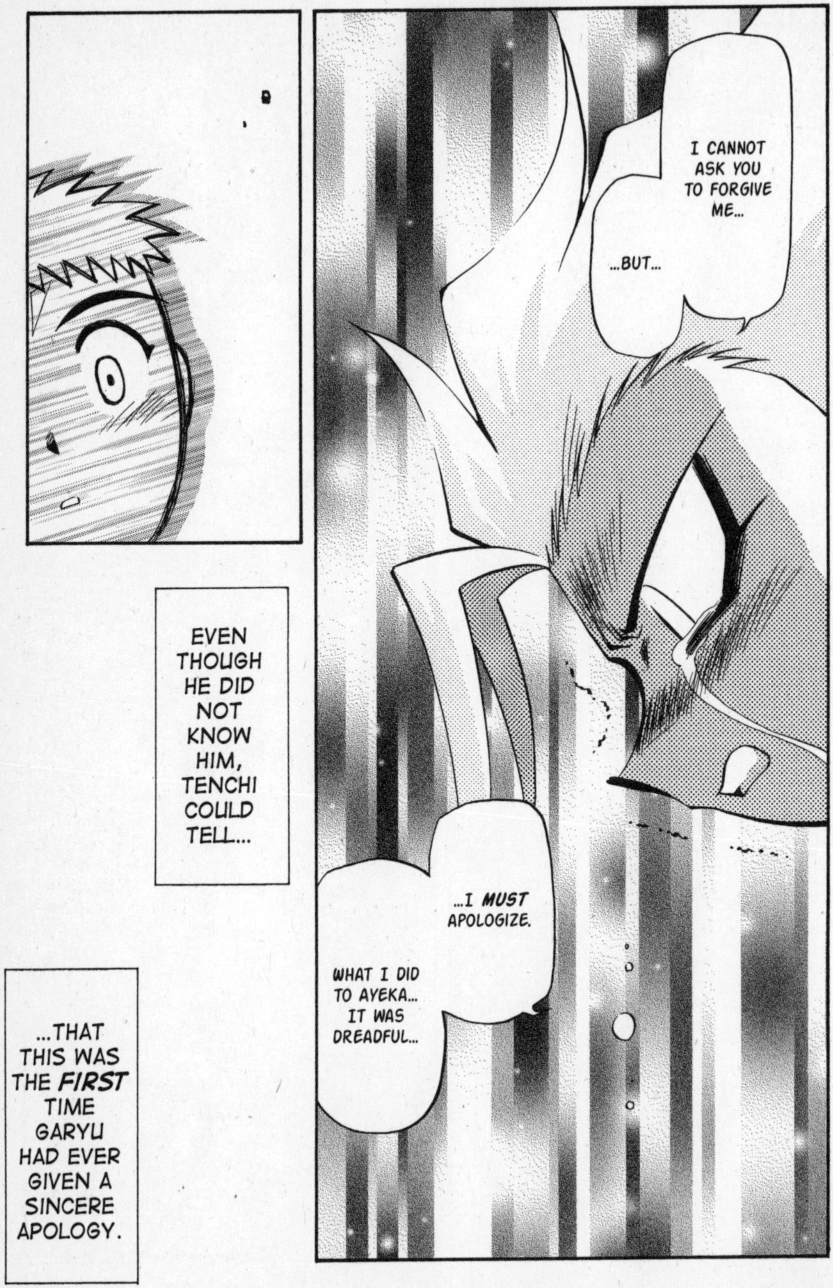
I CANNOT ASK YOU TO FORGIVE ME...
...BUT...
...I *MUST* APOLOGIZE.
WHAT I DID TO AYEKA... IT WAS DREADFUL...
EVEN THOUGH HE DID NOT KNOW HIM, TENCHI COULD TELL...
...THAT THIS WAS THE *FIRST* TIME GARYU HAD EVER GIVEN A SINCERE APOLOGY.

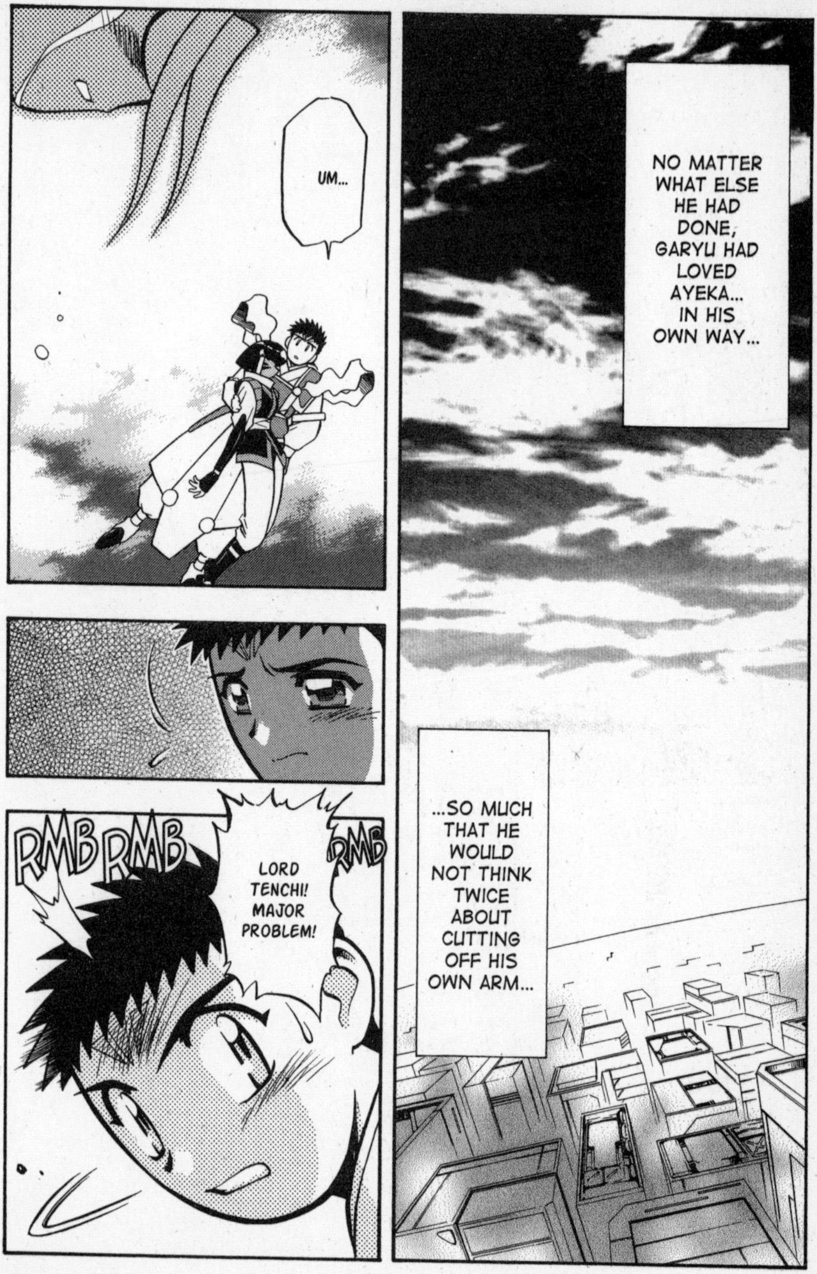
NO MATTER WHAT ELSE HE HAD DONE, GARYU HAD LOVED AYEKA... IN HIS OWN WAY...
...SO MUCH THAT HE WOULD NOT THINK TWICE ABOUT CUTTING OFF HIS OWN ARM...
UM...
RMB RMB
RMB
LORD TENCHI! MAJOR PROBLEM!

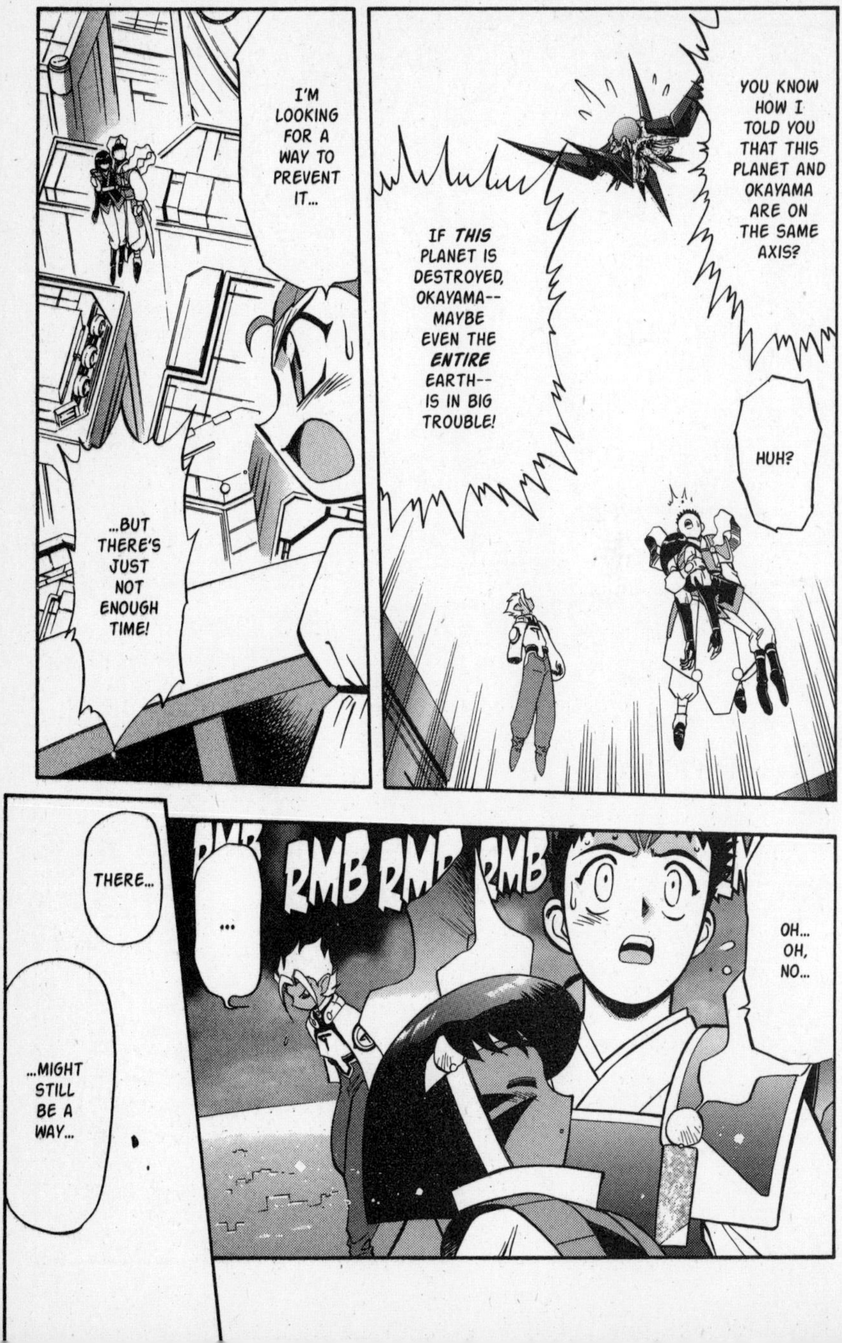
YOU KNOW HOW I TOLD YOU THAT THIS PLANET AND OKAYAMA ARE ON THE SAME AXIS?
IF *THIS* PLANET IS DESTROYED, OKAYAMA-- MAYBE EVEN THE *ENTIRE* EARTH-- IS IN BIG TROUBLE!
HUH?
I'M LOOKING FOR A WAY TO PREVENT IT...
...BUT THERE'S JUST NOT ENOUGH TIME!
OH... OH, NO...
RMB RMB RMB RMB
...
THERE...
...MIGHT STILL BE A WAY...

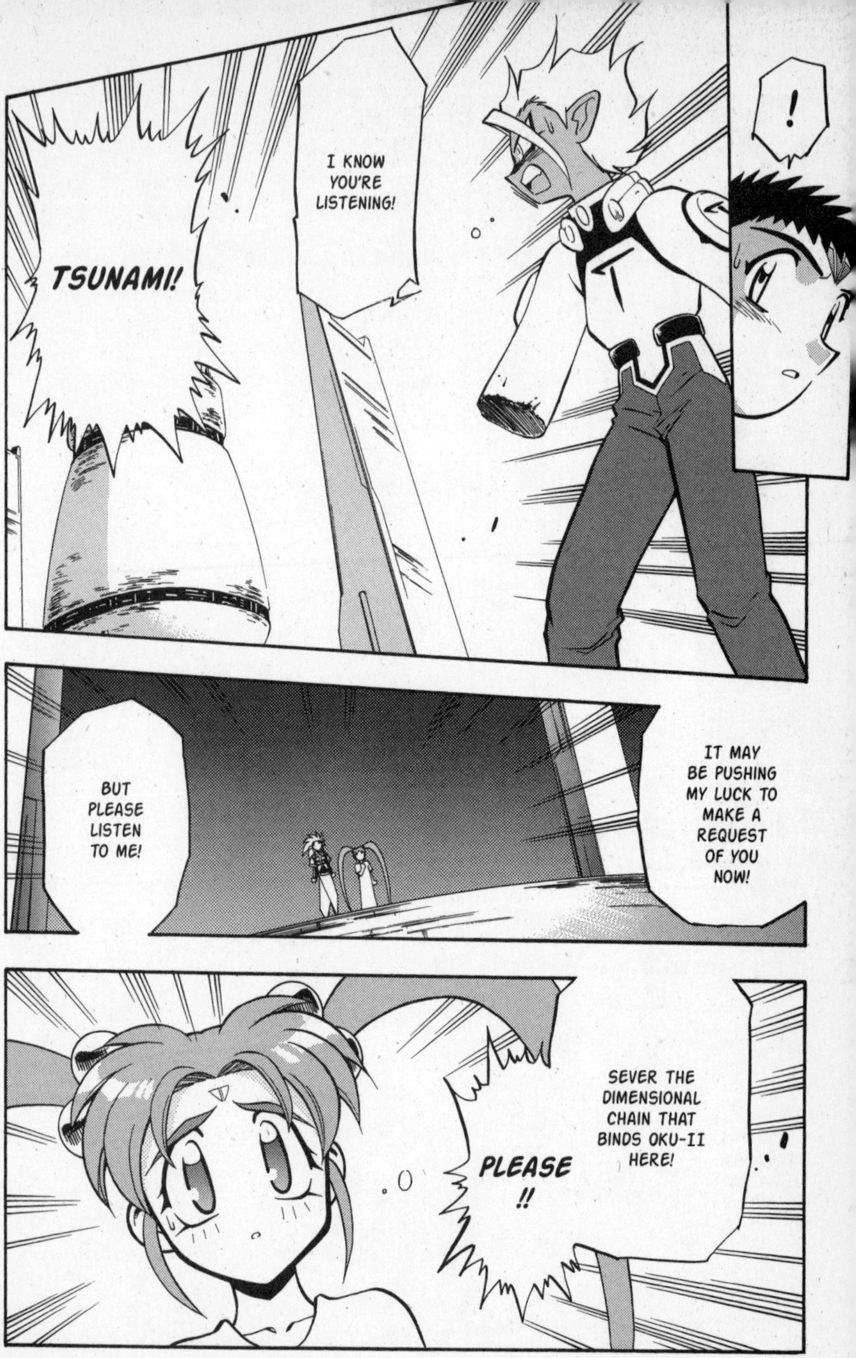
!
I KNOW YOU'RE LISTENING!
TSUNAMI!
IT MAY BE PUSHING MY LUCK TO MAKE A REQUEST OF YOU NOW!
BUT PLEASE LISTEN TO ME!
SEVER THE DIMENSIONAL CHAIN THAT BINDS OKU-II HERE!
PLEASE !!

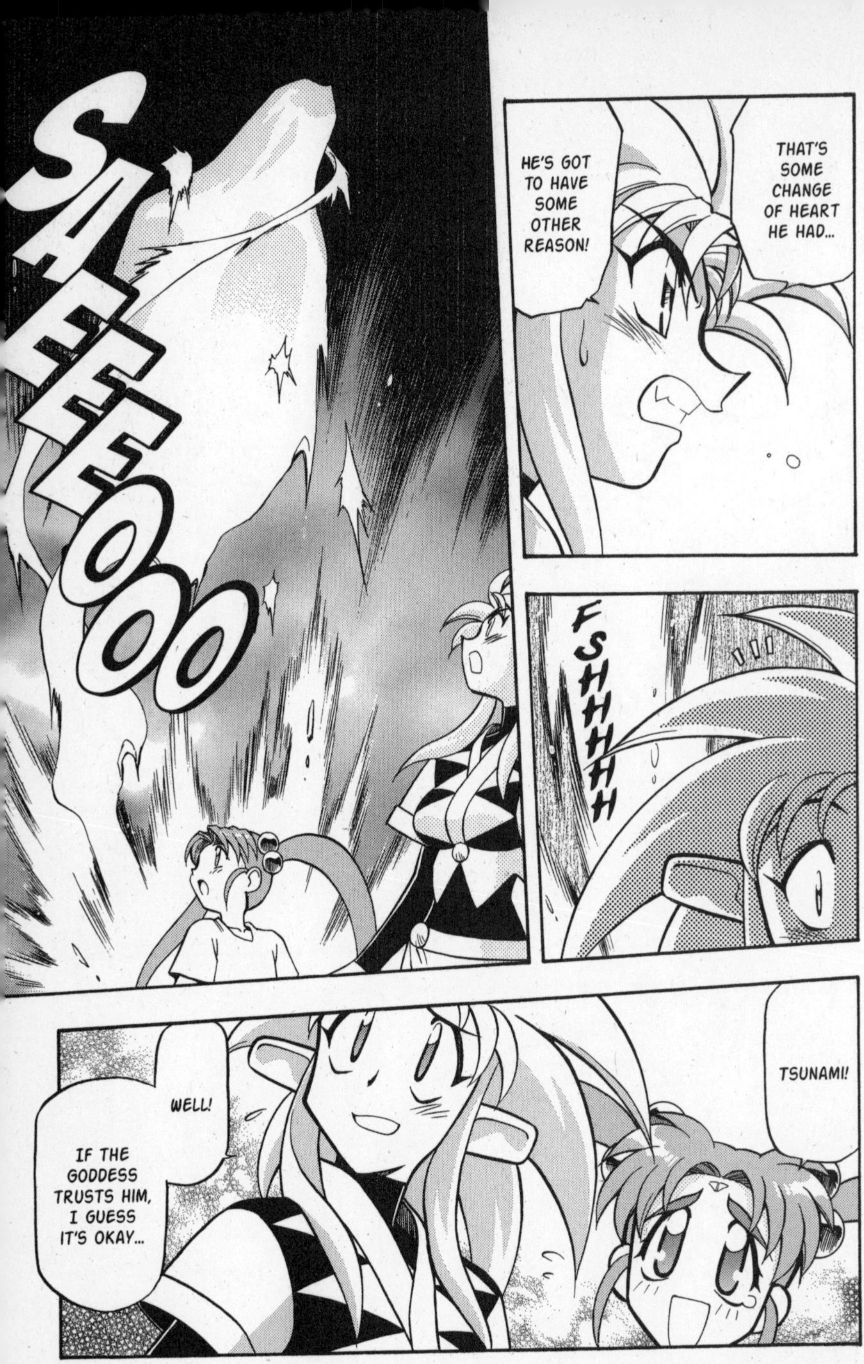
THAT'S SOME CHANGE OF HEART HE HAD...
HE'S GOT TO HAVE SOME OTHER REASON!
FSHHHHHH
SAEEEOOO
TSUNAMI!
WELL!
IF THE GODDESS TRUSTS HIM, I GUESS IT'S OKAY...

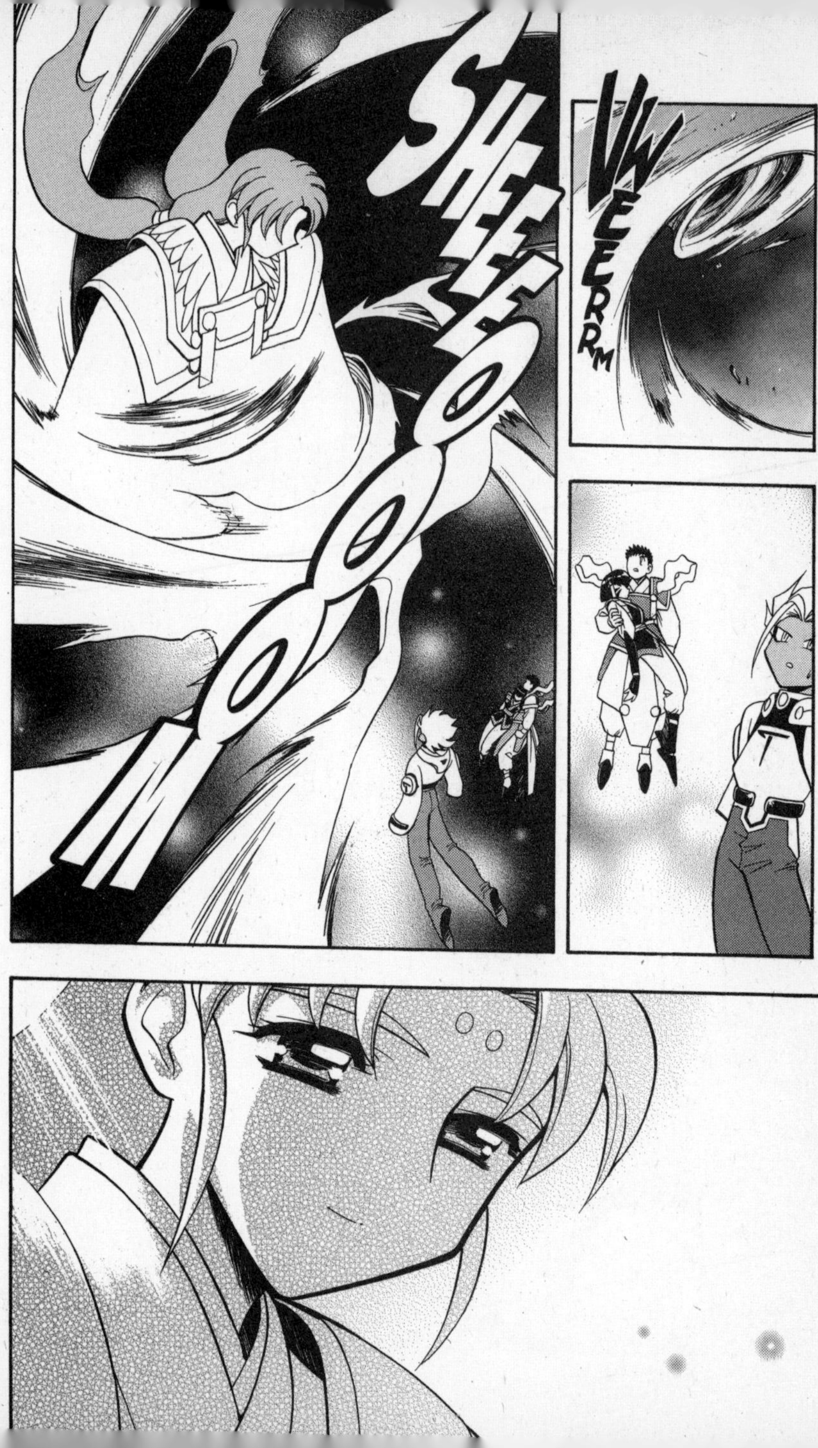
VWEEERRRM
SHEEEOOOOOM

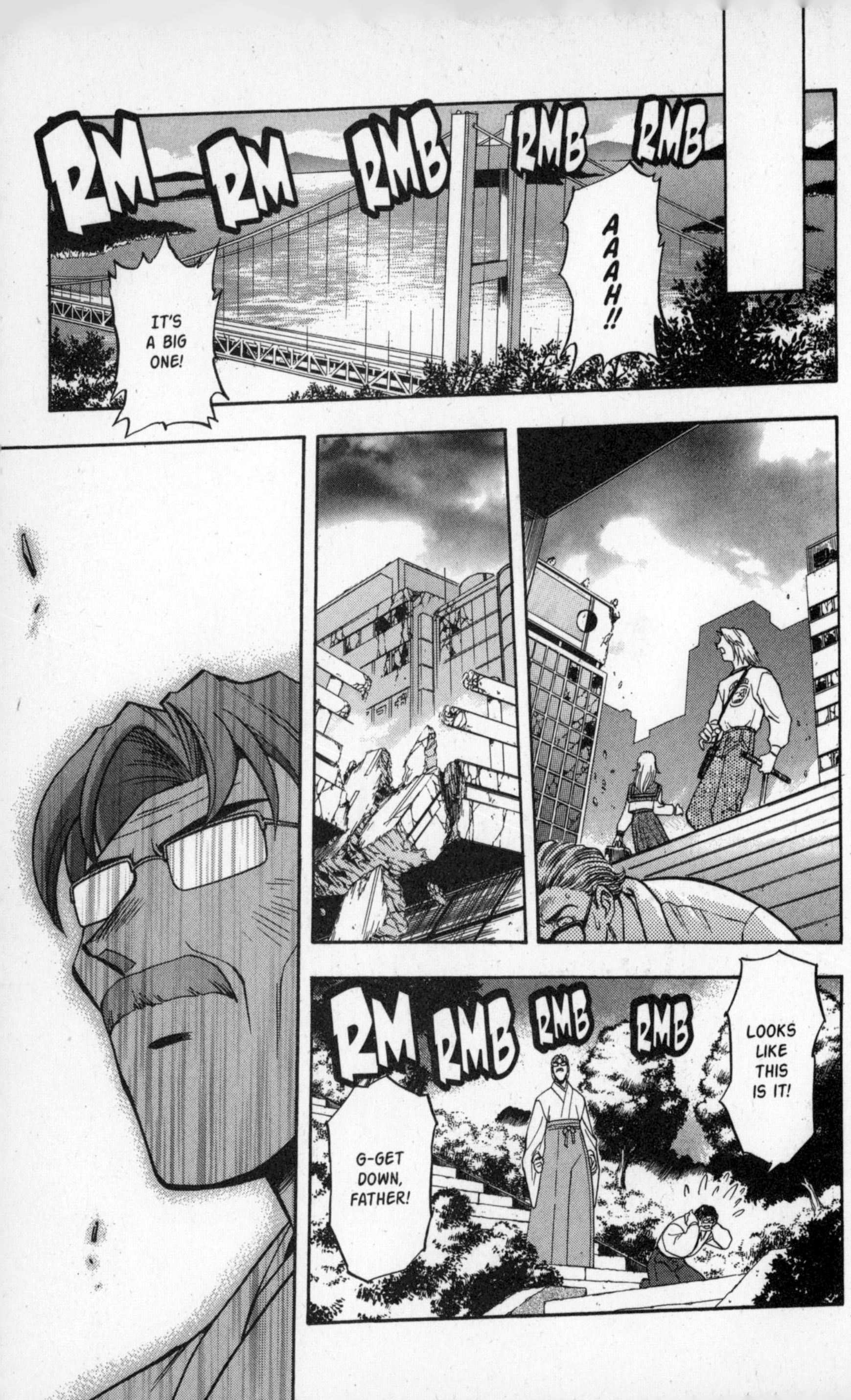
RM-RM RMB RMB RMB
AAAAH!!
IT'S A BIG ONE!
RM RMB RMB RMB
LOOKS LIKE THIS IS IT!
G-GET DOWN, FATHER!

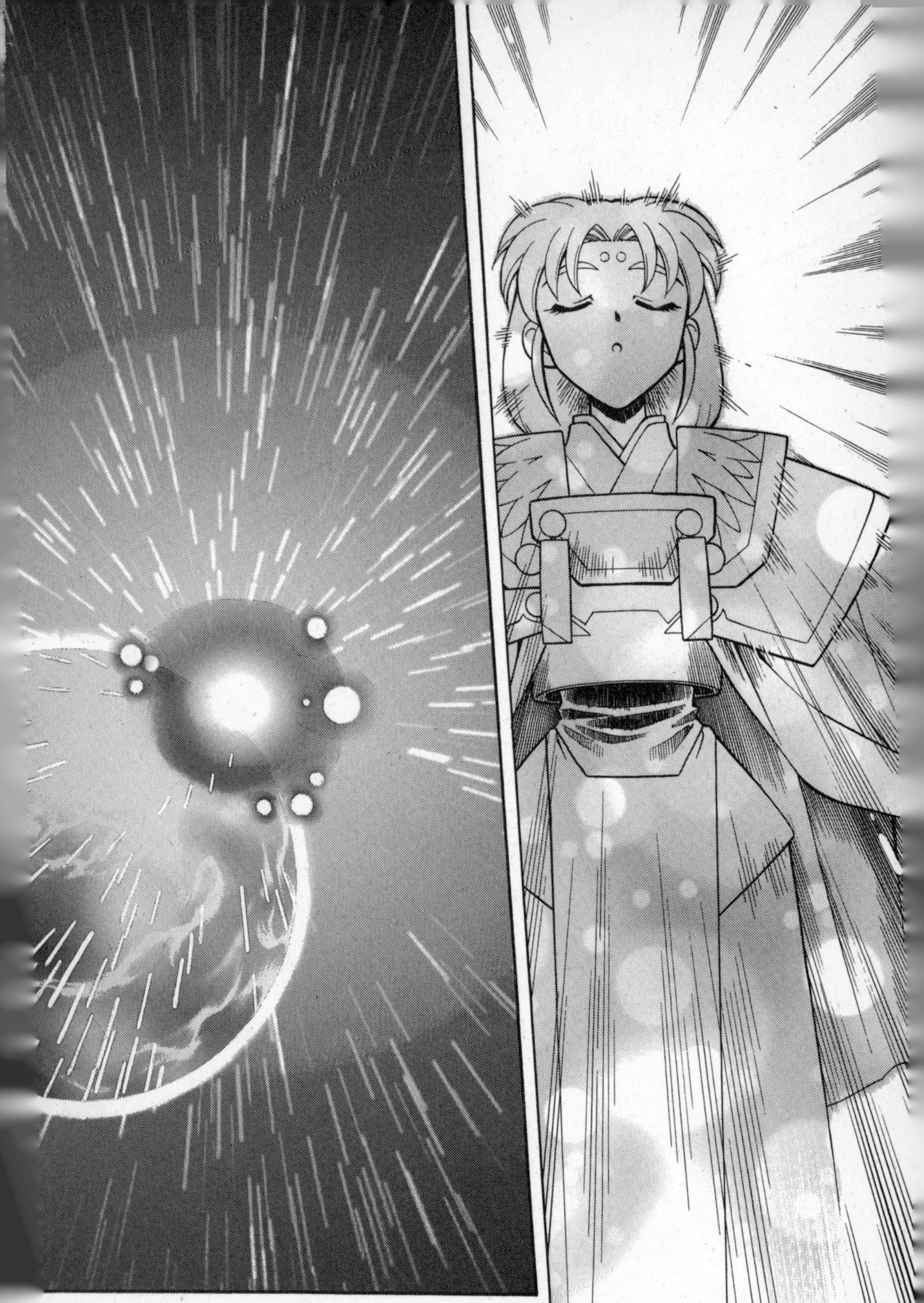

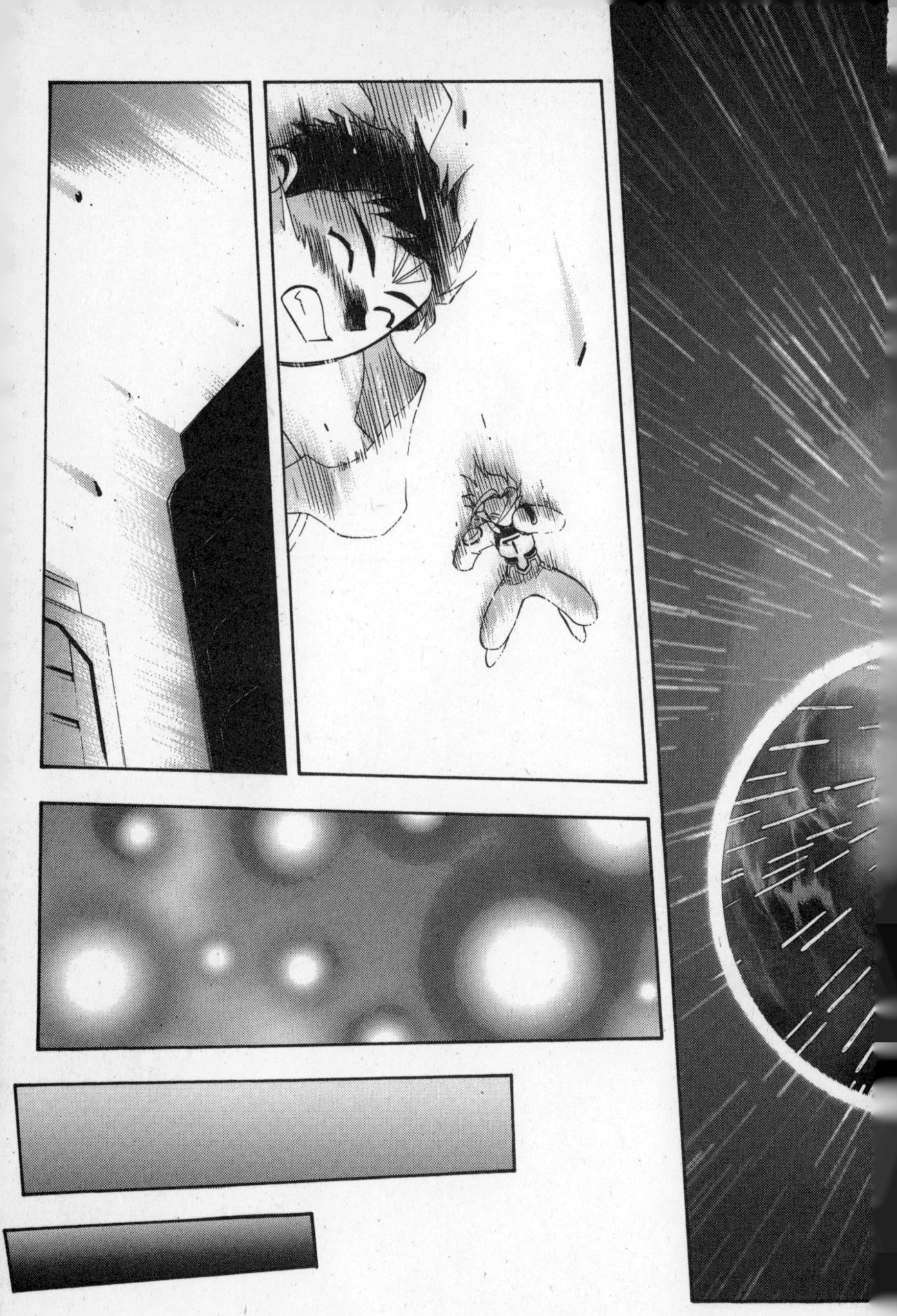

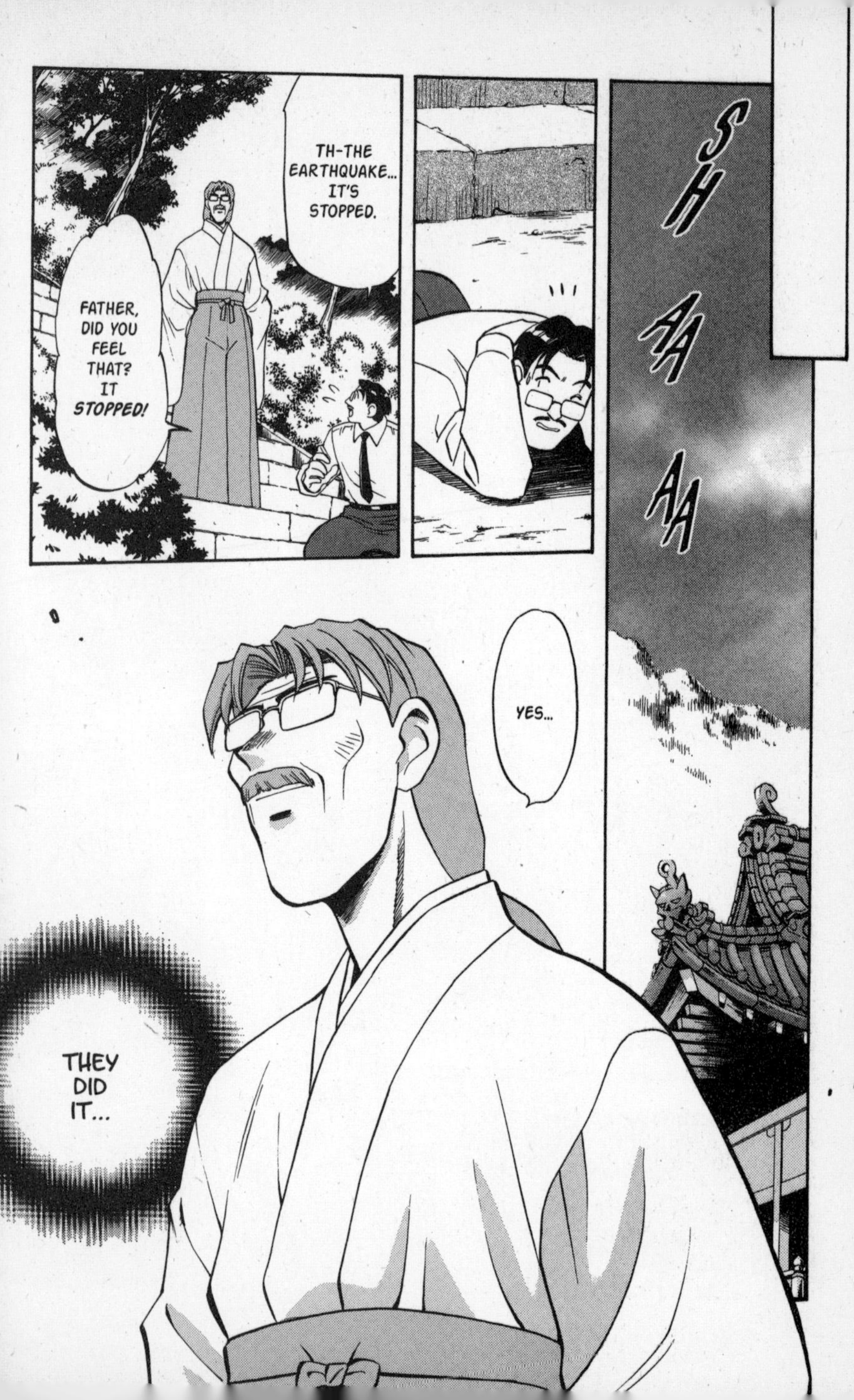
SHAAAA
TH-THE EARTHQUAKE... IT'S STOPPED.
FATHER, DID YOU FEEL THAT? IT STOPPED!
YES...
THEY DID IT...

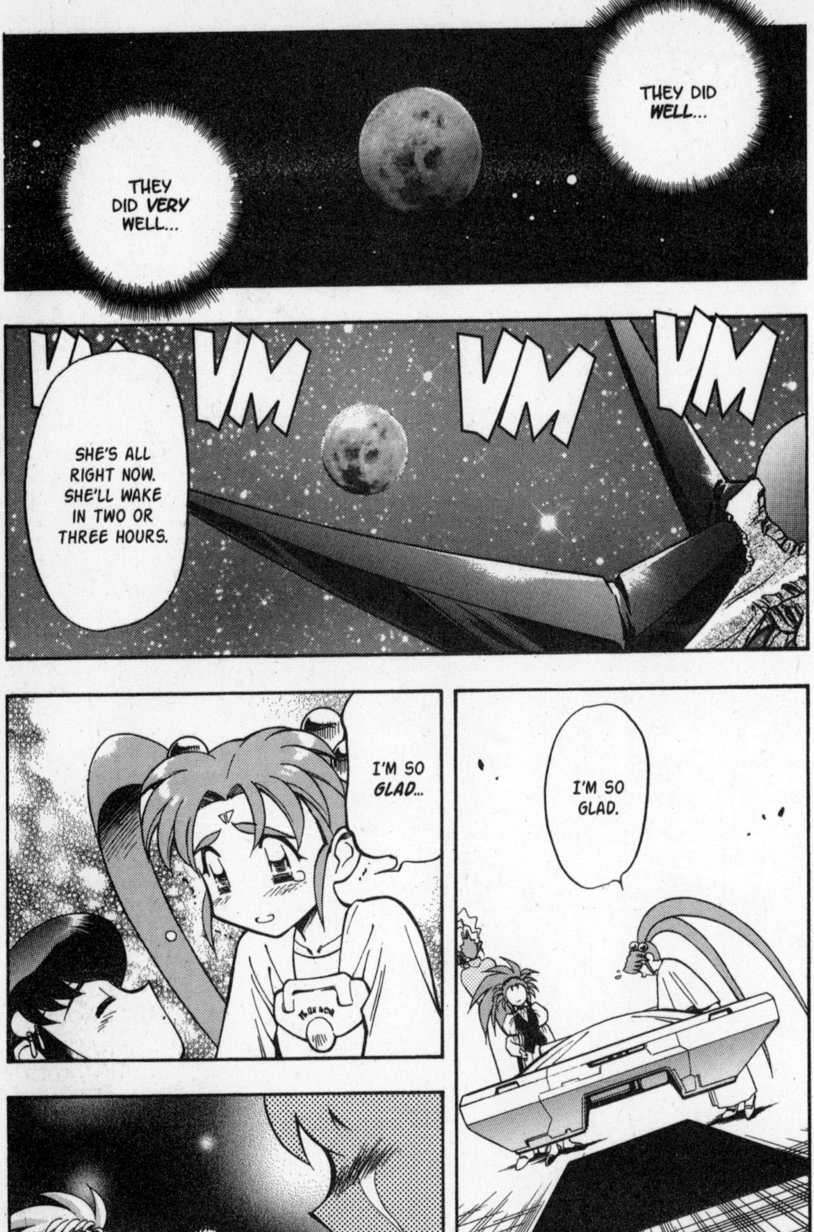
THEY DID WELL...
THEY DID VERY WELL...
VM VM
VM VM
SHE'S ALL RIGHT NOW. SHE'LL WAKE IN TWO OR THREE HOURS.
I'M SO GLAD.
I'M SO GLAD...

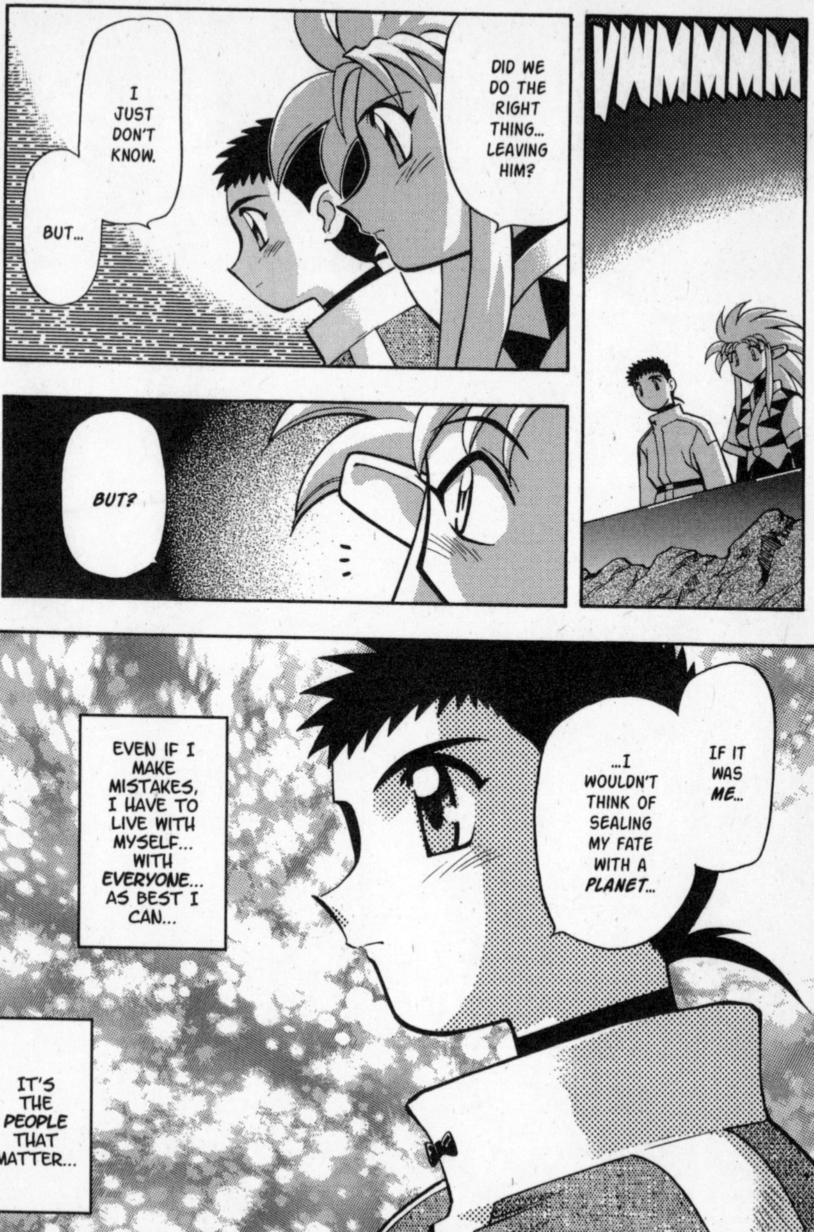
VWMMMM
DID WE DO THE RIGHT THING... LEAVING HIM?
I JUST DON'T KNOW.
BUT...
BUT?
IF IT WAS ME...
...I WOULDN'T THINK OF SEALING MY FATE WITH A PLANET...
EVEN IF I MAKE MISTAKES, I HAVE TO LIVE WITH MYSELF... WITH EVERYONE... AS BEST I CAN...
IT'S THE PEOPLE THAT MATTER...

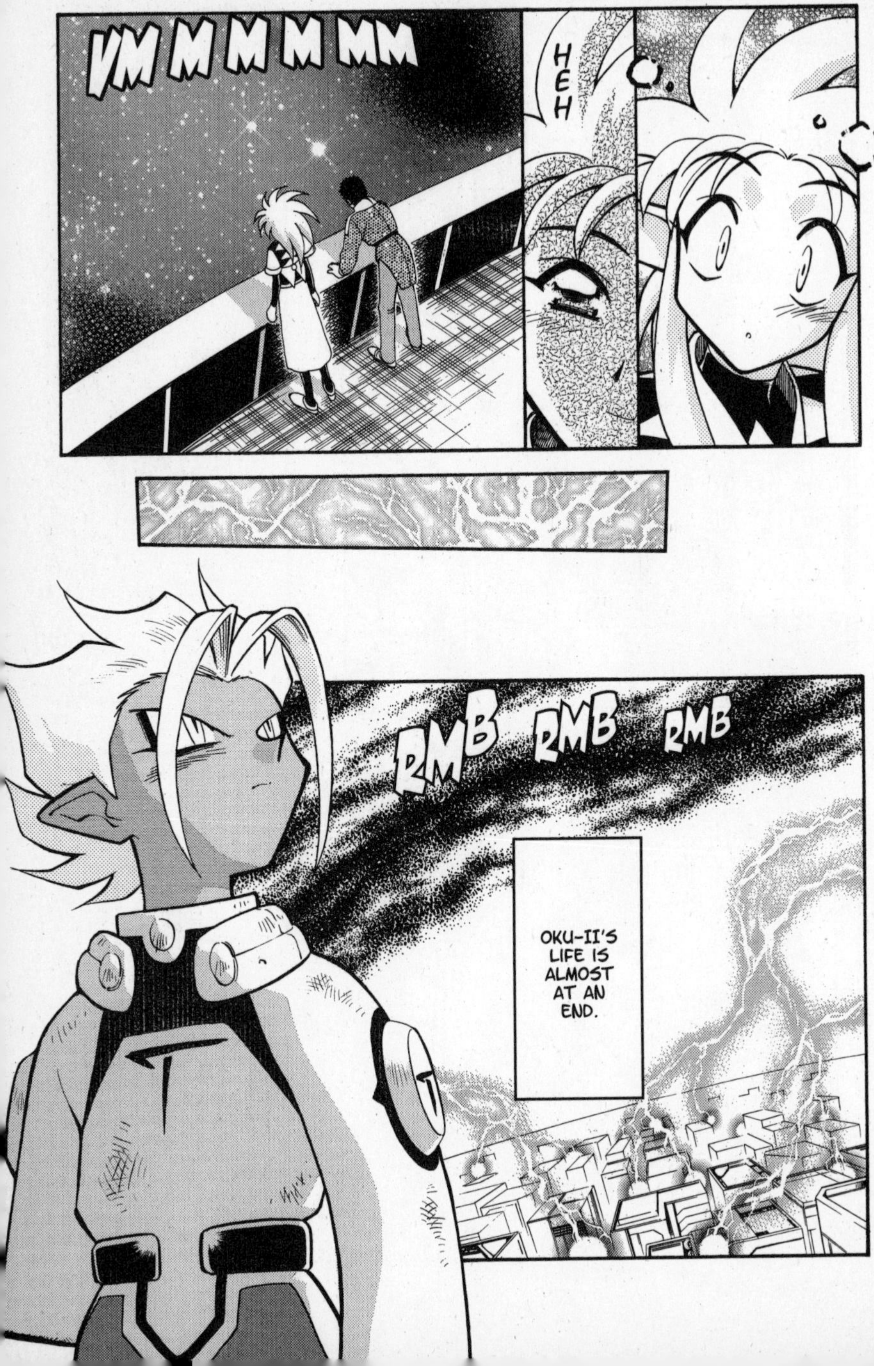
HEH
VM M M M MM
RMB RMB RMB
OKU-II'S LIFE IS ALMOST AT AN END.

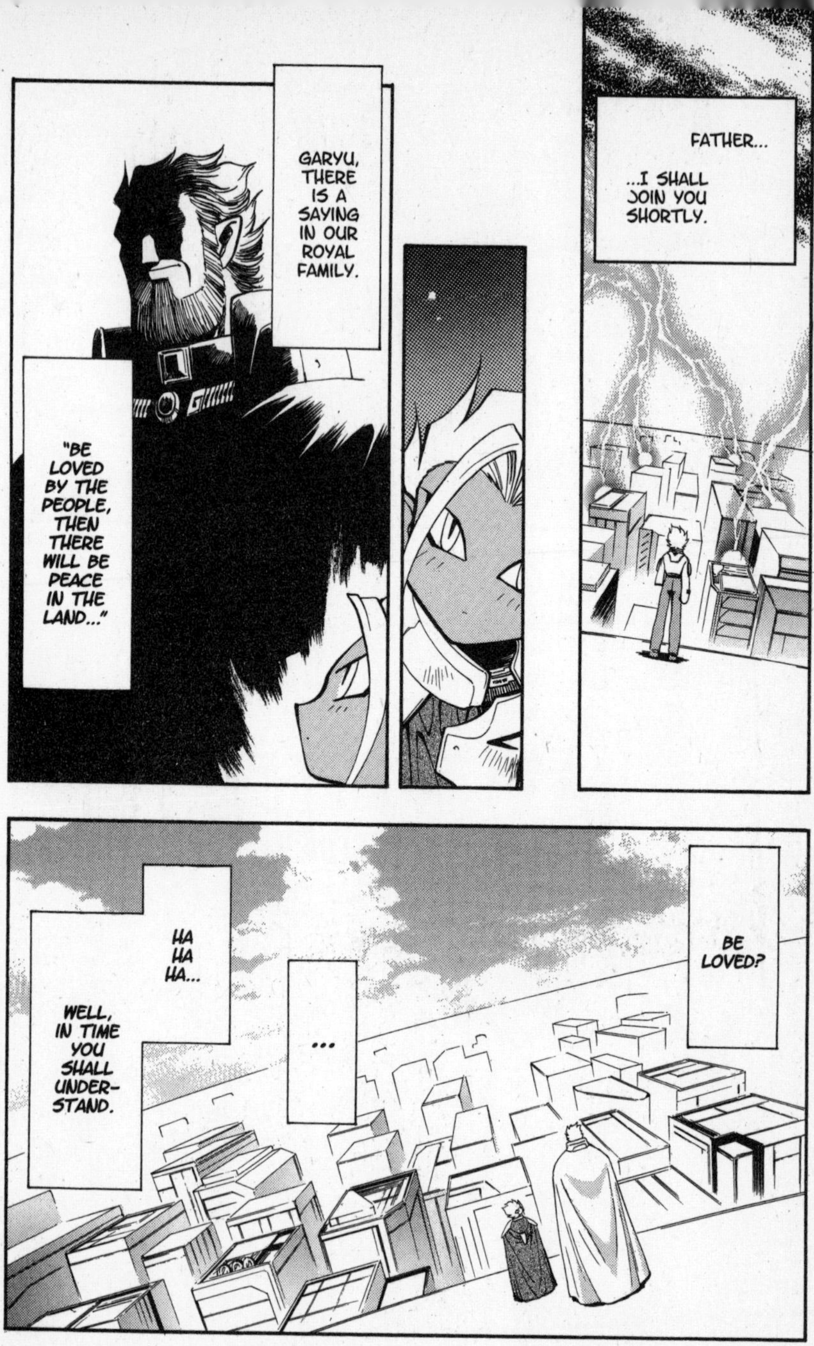
FATHER...
...I SHALL JOIN YOU SHORTLY.
GARYU, THERE IS A SAYING IN OUR ROYAL FAMILY.
"BE LOVED BY THE PEOPLE, THEN THERE WILL BE PEACE IN THE LAND..."
BE LOVED?
...
HA HA HA...
WELL, IN TIME YOU SHALL UNDER-STAND.

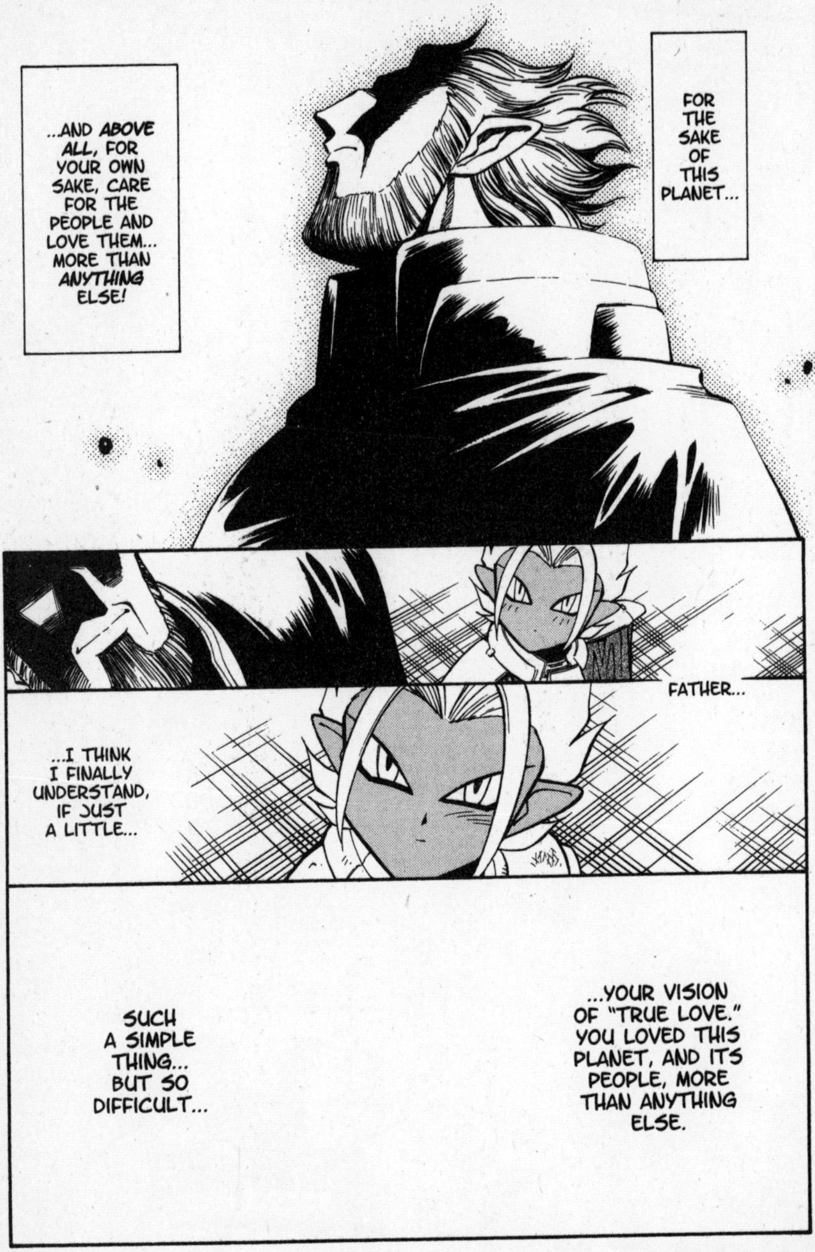
FOR THE SAKE OF THIS PLANET...
...AND ABOVE ALL, FOR YOUR OWN SAKE, CARE FOR THE PEOPLE AND LOVE THEM... MORE THAN ANYTHING ELSE!
FATHER...
...I THINK I FINALLY UNDERSTAND, IF JUST A LITTLE...
...YOUR VISION OF "TRUE LOVE." YOU LOVED THIS PLANET, AND ITS PEOPLE, MORE THAN ANYTHING ELSE.
SUCH A SIMPLE THING... BUT SO DIFFICULT...

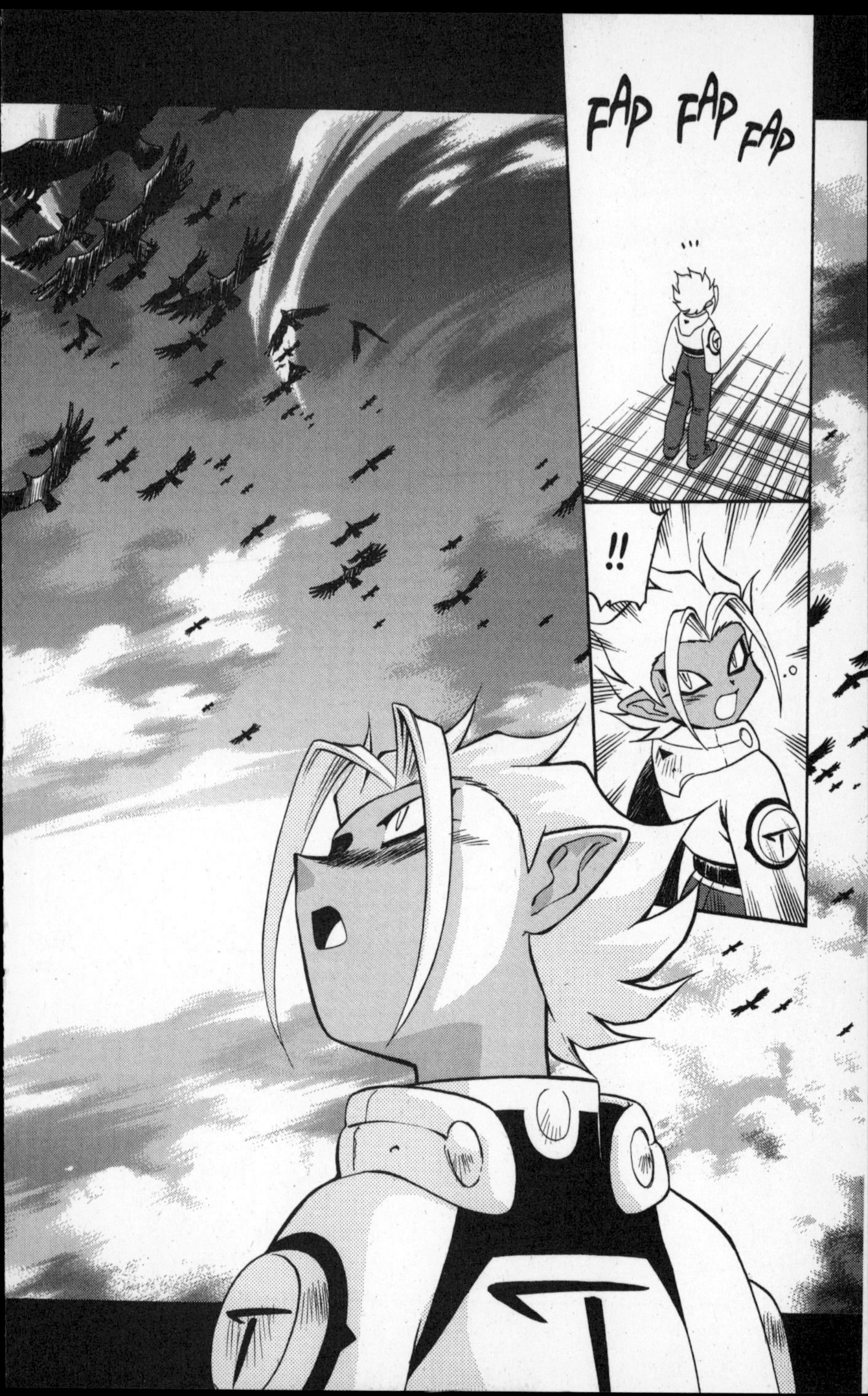
FAP FAP FAP
...
!!

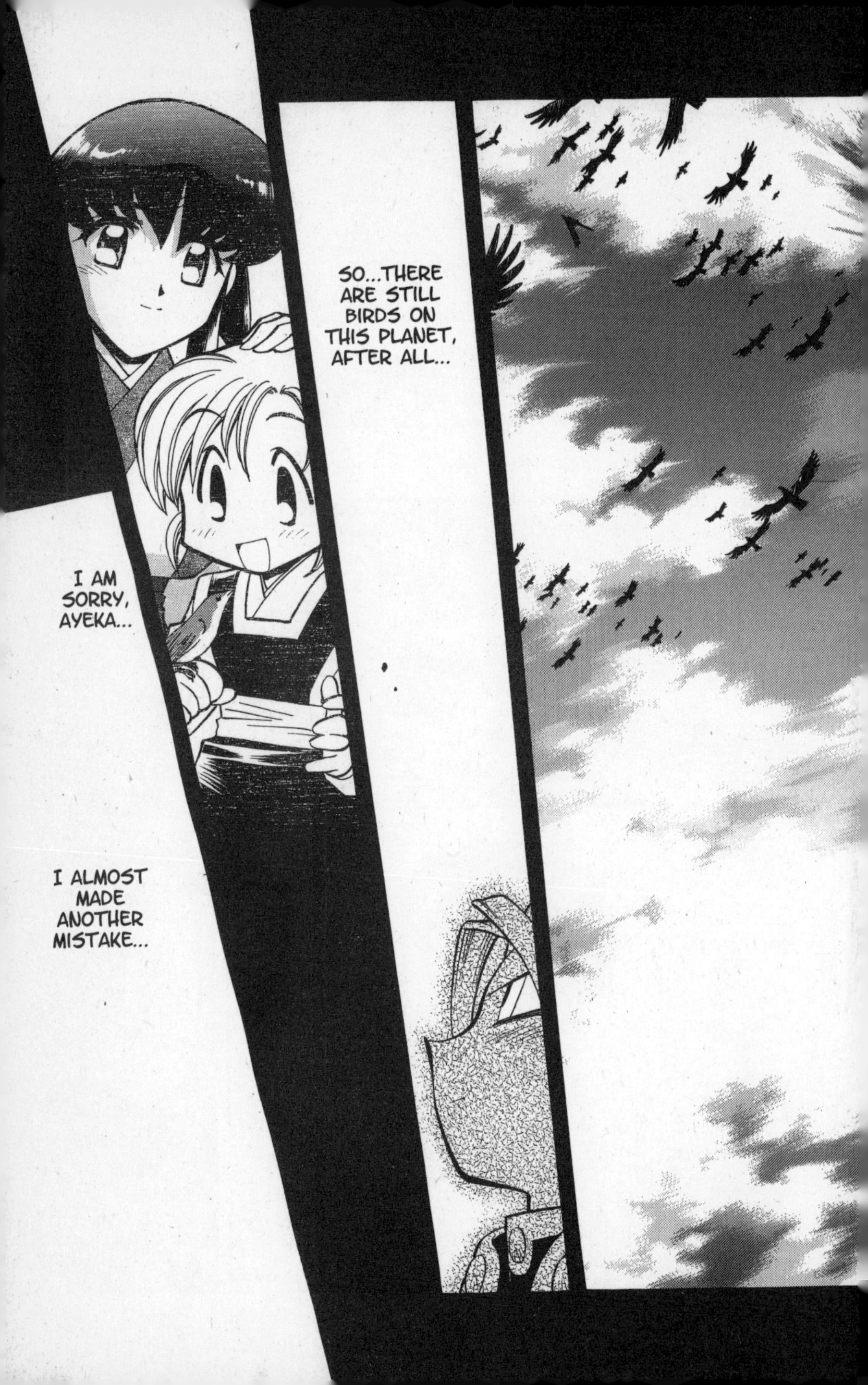
SO...THERE ARE STILL BIRDS ON THIS PLANET, AFTER ALL...
I AM SORRY, AYEKA...
I ALMOST MADE ANOTHER MISTAKE...

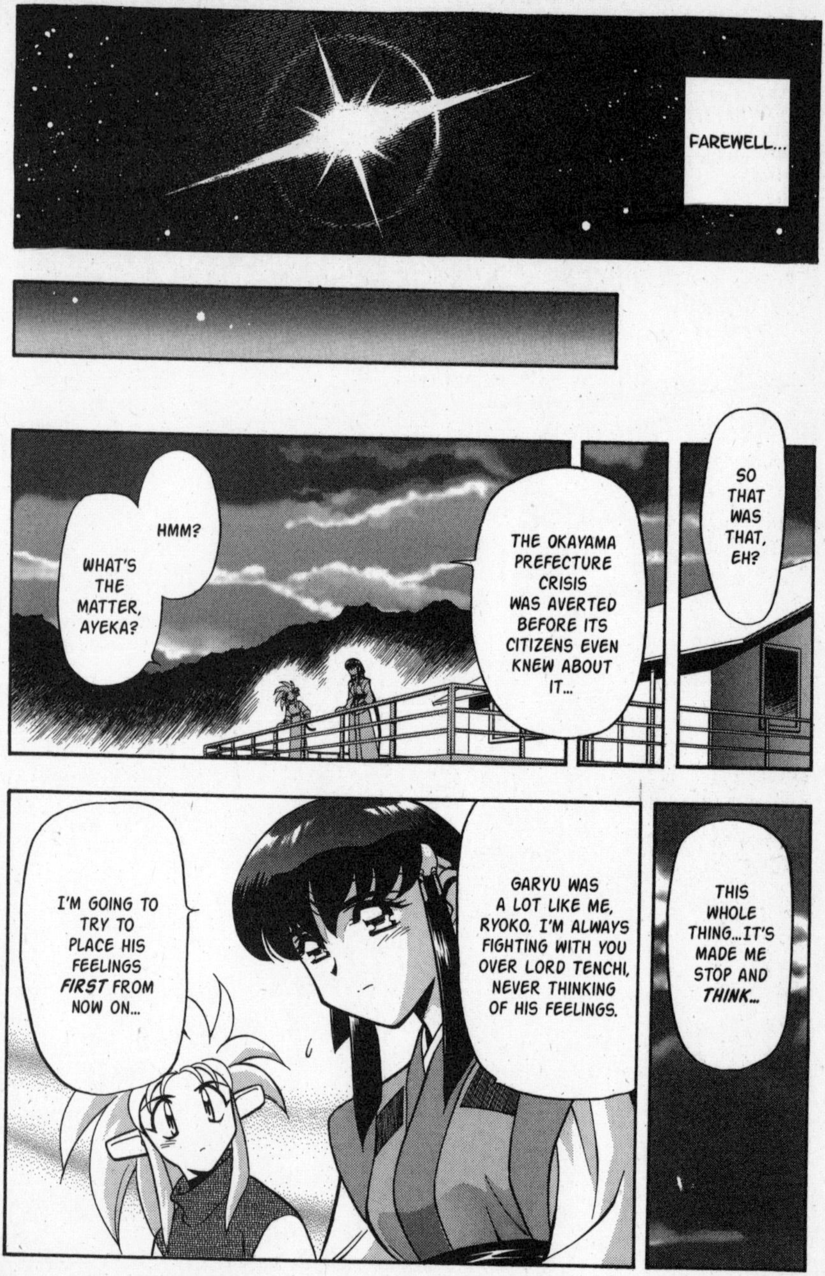
FAREWELL...
SO THAT WAS THAT, EH?
THE OKAYAMA PREFECTURE CRISIS WAS AVERTED BEFORE ITS CITIZENS EVEN KNEW ABOUT IT...
HMM? WHAT'S THE MATTER, AYEKA?
THIS WHOLE THING...IT'S MADE ME STOP AND *THINK*...
GARYU WAS A LOT LIKE ME, RYOKO. I'M ALWAYS FIGHTING WITH YOU OVER LORD TENCHI, NEVER THINKING OF HIS FEELINGS.
I'M GOING TO TRY TO PLACE HIS FEELINGS *FIRST* FROM NOW ON...

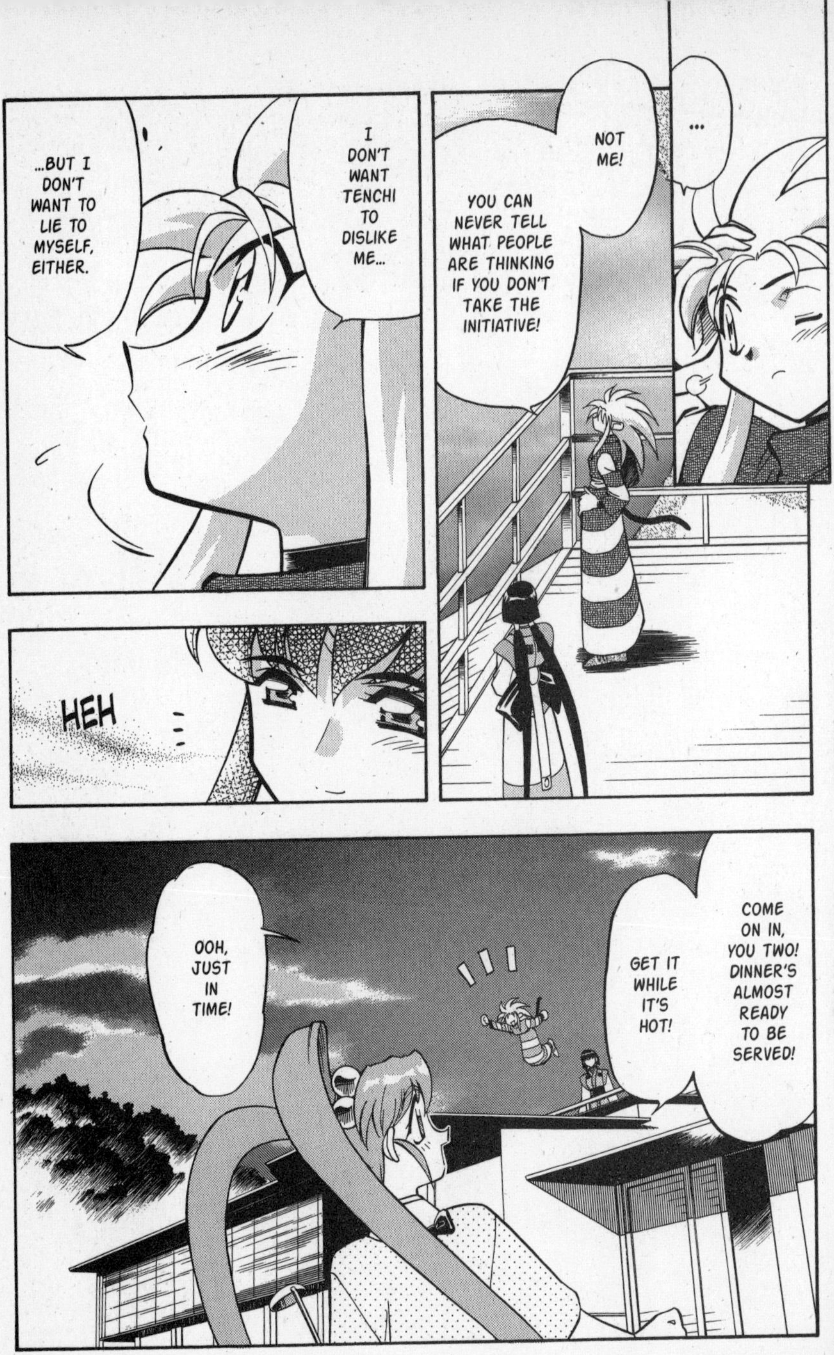
...
NOT ME!
YOU CAN NEVER TELL WHAT PEOPLE ARE THINKING IF YOU DON'T TAKE THE INITIATIVE!
I DON'T WANT TENCHI TO DISLIKE ME...
...BUT I DON'T WANT TO LIE TO MYSELF, EITHER.
HEH
COME ON IN, YOU TWO! DINNER'S ALMOST READY TO BE SERVED!
GET IT WHILE IT'S HOT!
OOH, JUST IN TIME!

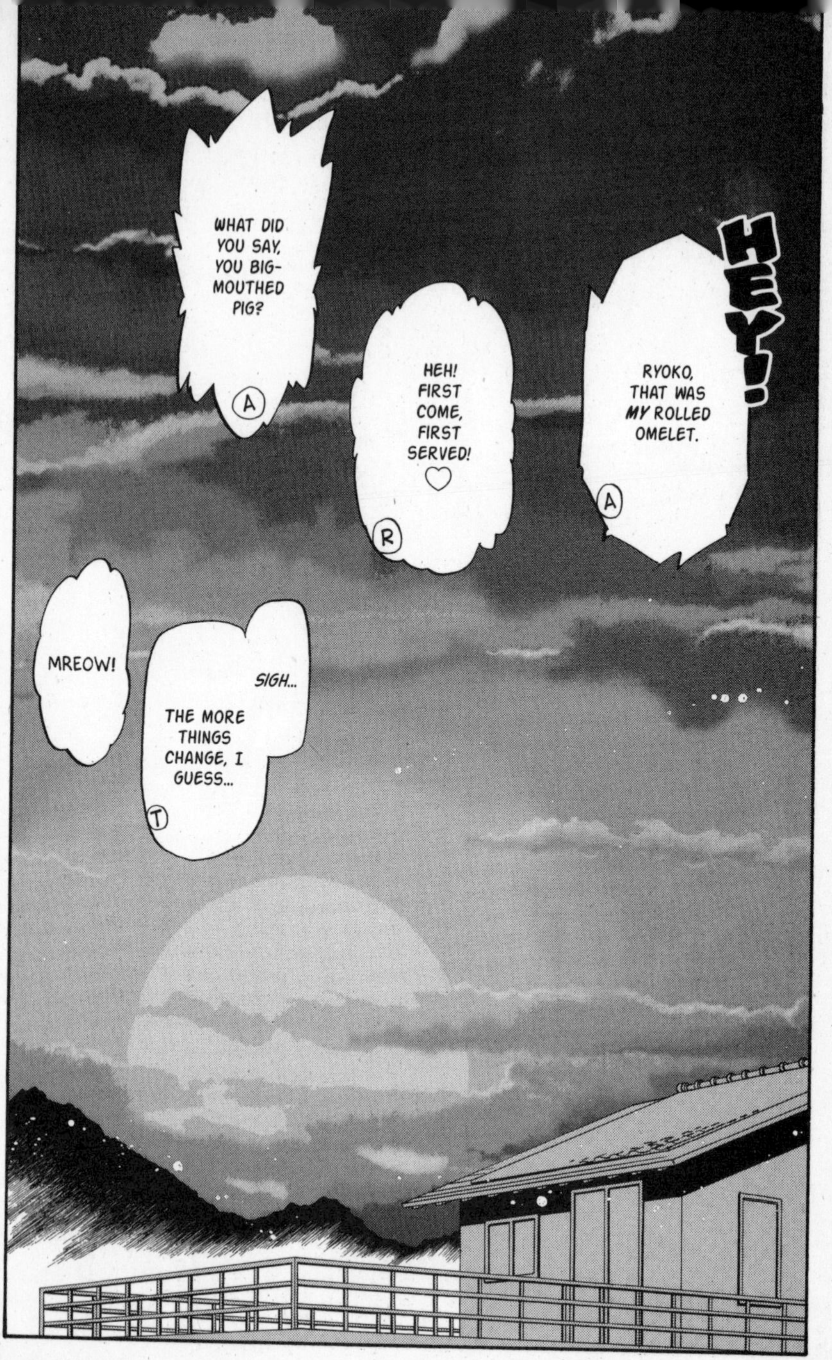
HEY!
RYOKO, THAT WAS MY ROLLED OMELET.
HEH! FIRST COME, FIRST SERVED! ♡
WHAT DID YOU SAY, YOU BIG-MOUTHED PIG?
SIGH... THE MORE THINGS CHANGE, I GUESS...
MREOW!

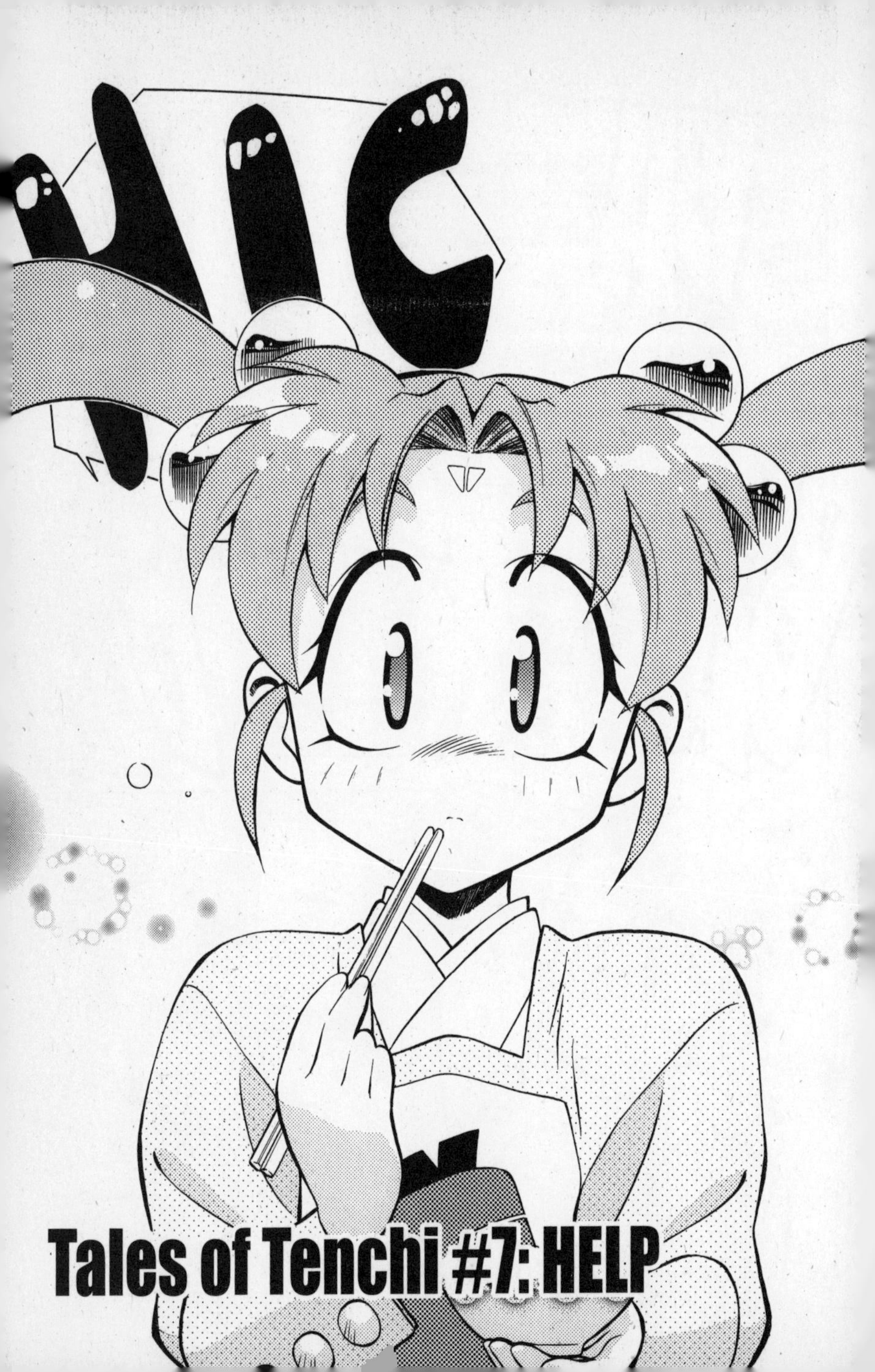
HIC

Tales of Tenchi #7: HELP

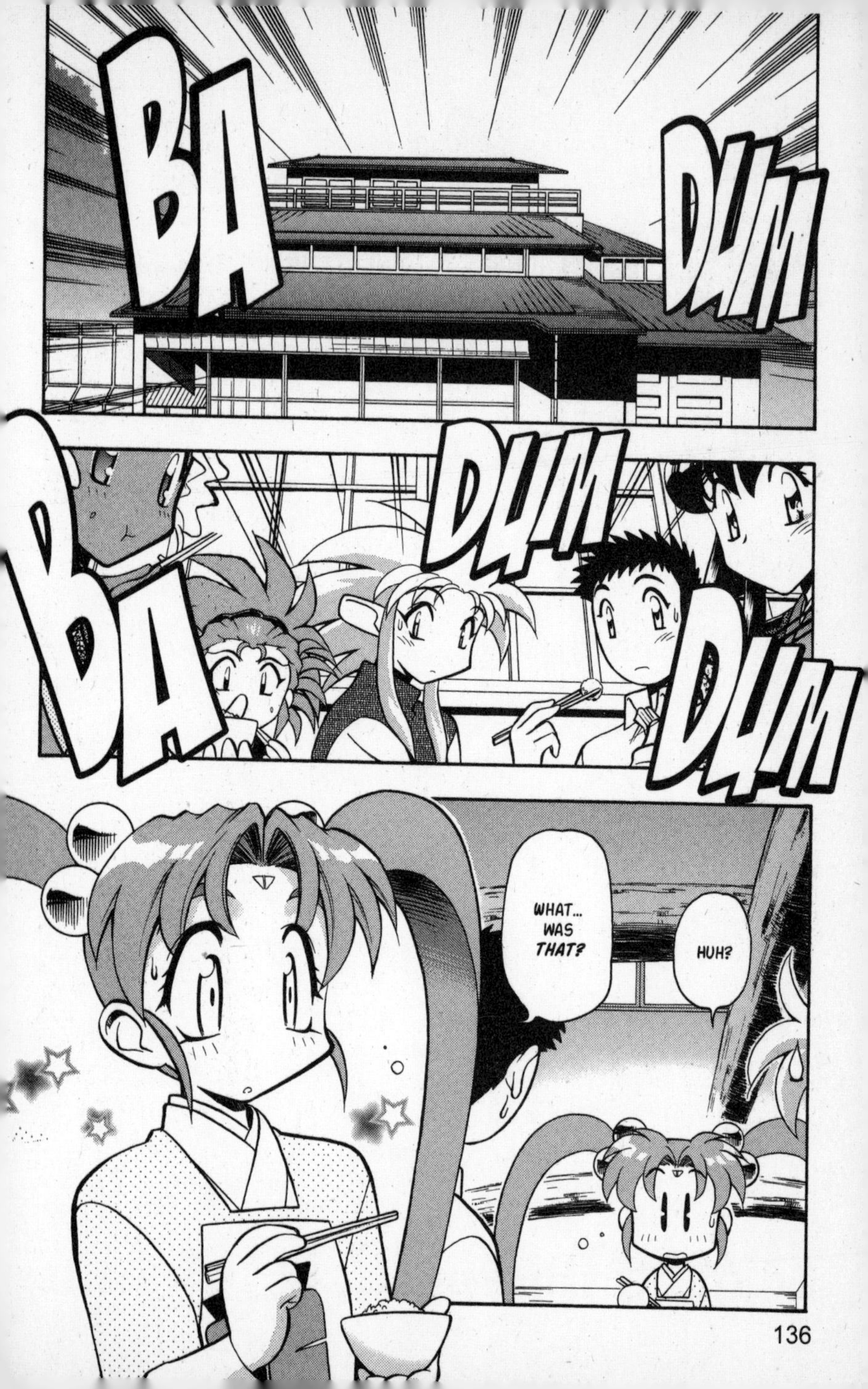
BA
DUM
DUM
BA
DUM
HUH?
WHAT... WAS *THAT?*

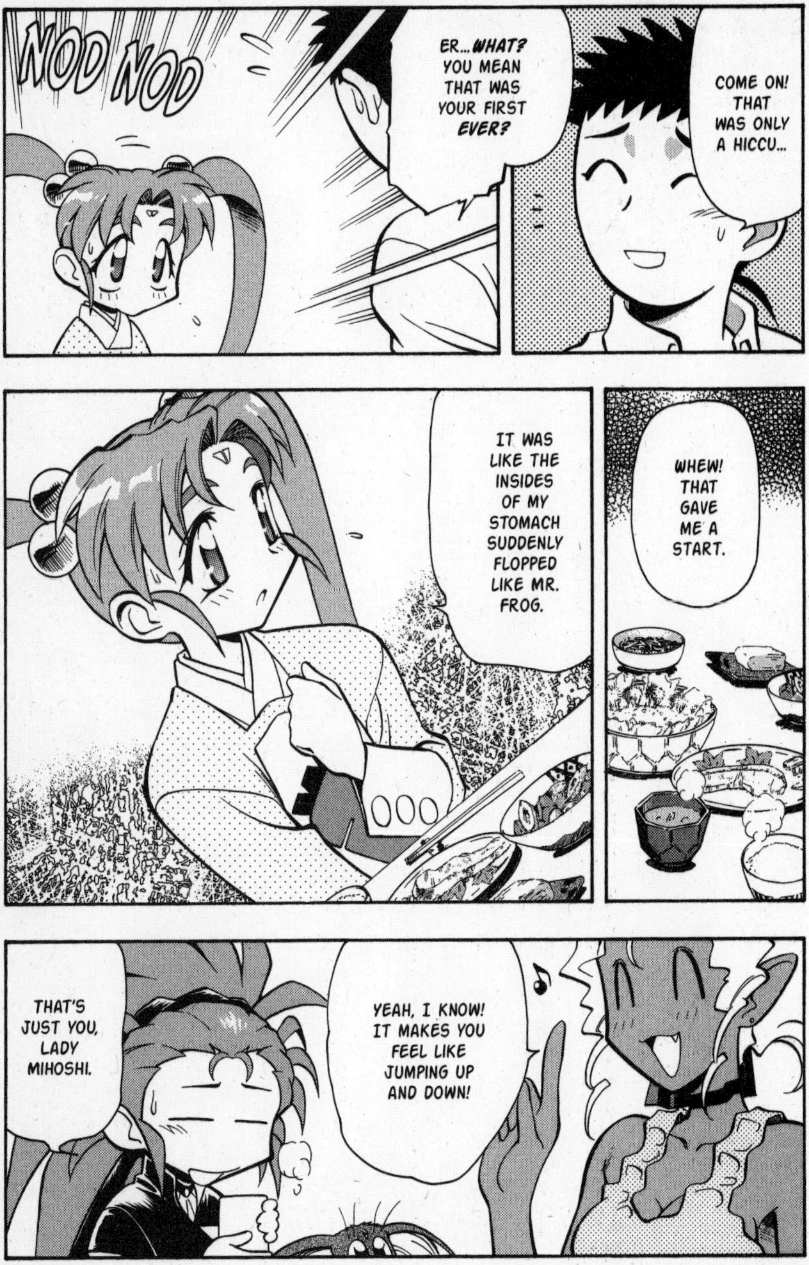

COME ON! THAT WAS ONLY A HICCU...
ER...WHAT? YOU MEAN THAT WAS YOUR FIRST EVER?
NOD NOD
WHEW! THAT GAVE ME A START.
IT WAS LIKE THE INSIDES OF MY STOMACH SUDDENLY FLOPPED LIKE MR. FROG.
YEAH, I KNOW! IT MAKES YOU FEEL LIKE JUMPING UP AND DOWN!
THAT'S JUST YOU, LADY MIHOSHI.

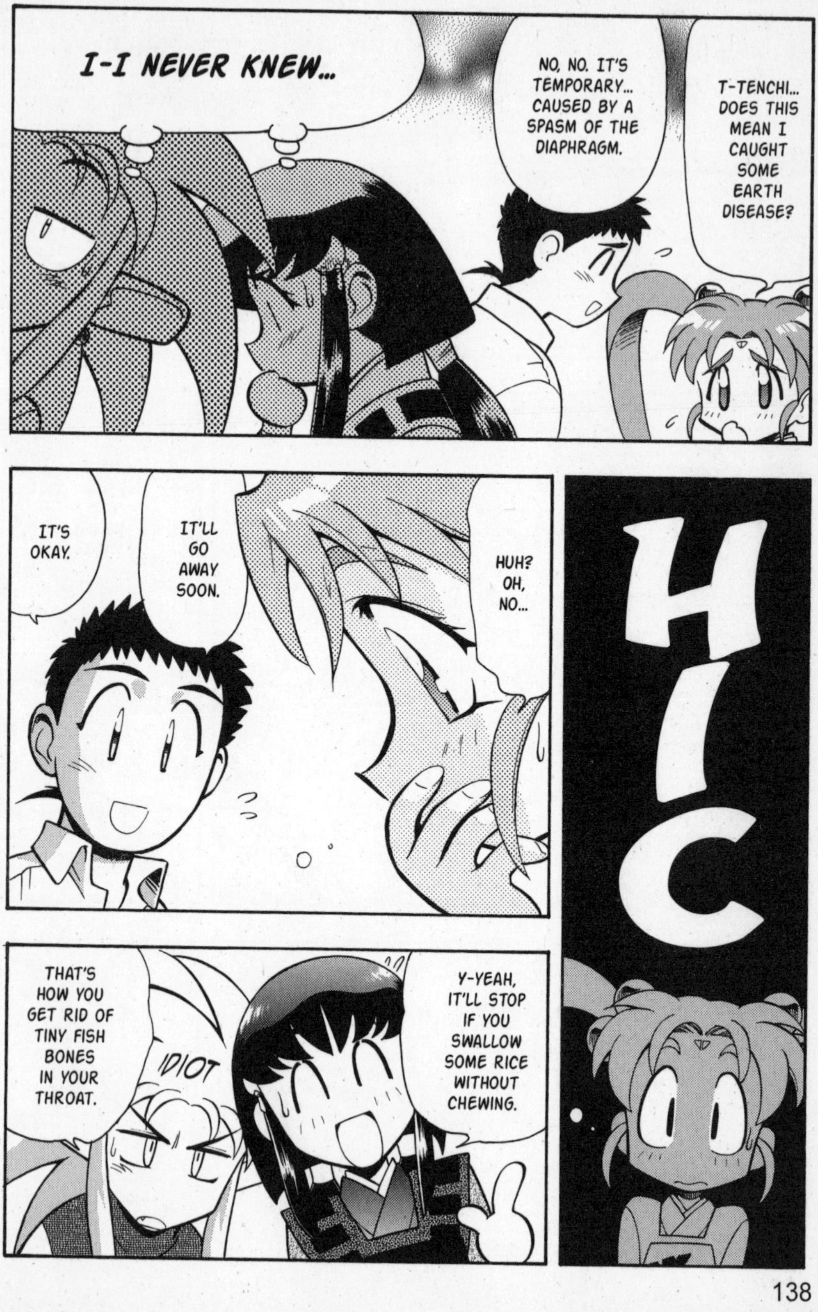
T-TENCHI... DOES THIS MEAN I CAUGHT SOME EARTH DISEASE?
NO, NO. IT'S TEMPORARY... CAUSED BY A SPASM OF THE DIAPHRAGM.
I-I NEVER KNEW...
HIC
HUH? OH, NO...
IT'LL GO AWAY SOON.
IT'S OKAY.
Y-YEAH, IT'LL STOP IF YOU SWALLOW SOME RICE WITHOUT CHEWING.
IDIOT
THAT'S HOW YOU GET RID OF TINY FISH BONES IN YOUR THROAT.

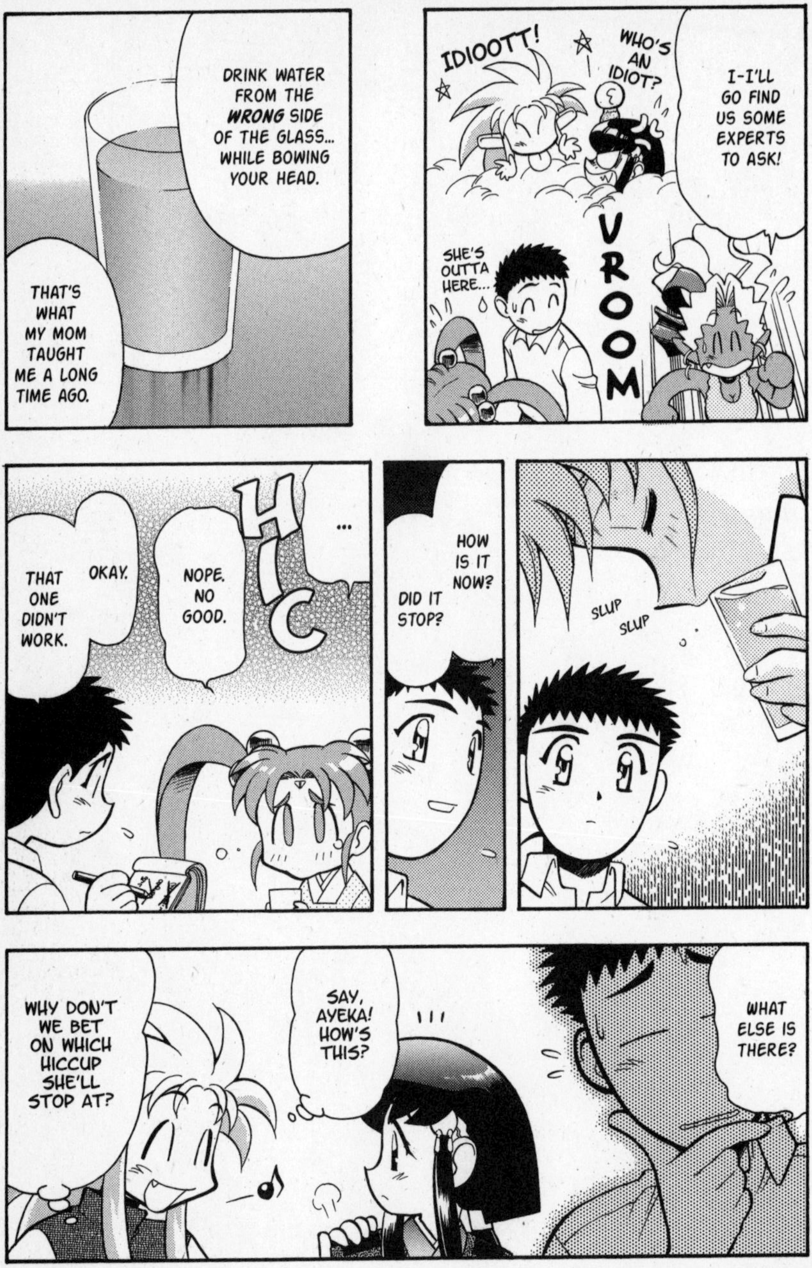
I-I'LL GO FIND US SOME EXPERTS TO ASK!
WHO'S AN IDIOT?
IDIOOTT!
VROOM
SHE'S OUTTA HERE...
DRINK WATER FROM THE ***WRONG*** SIDE OF THE GLASS... WHILE BOWING YOUR HEAD.
THAT'S WHAT MY MOM TAUGHT ME A LONG TIME AGO.
SLUP
SLUP
HOW IS IT NOW?
DID IT STOP?
...
HIC
NOPE. NO GOOD.
OKAY.
THAT ONE DIDN'T WORK.
WHAT ELSE IS THERE?
SAY, AYEKA! HOW'S THIS?
WHY DON'T WE BET ON WHICH HICCUP SHE'LL STOP AT?

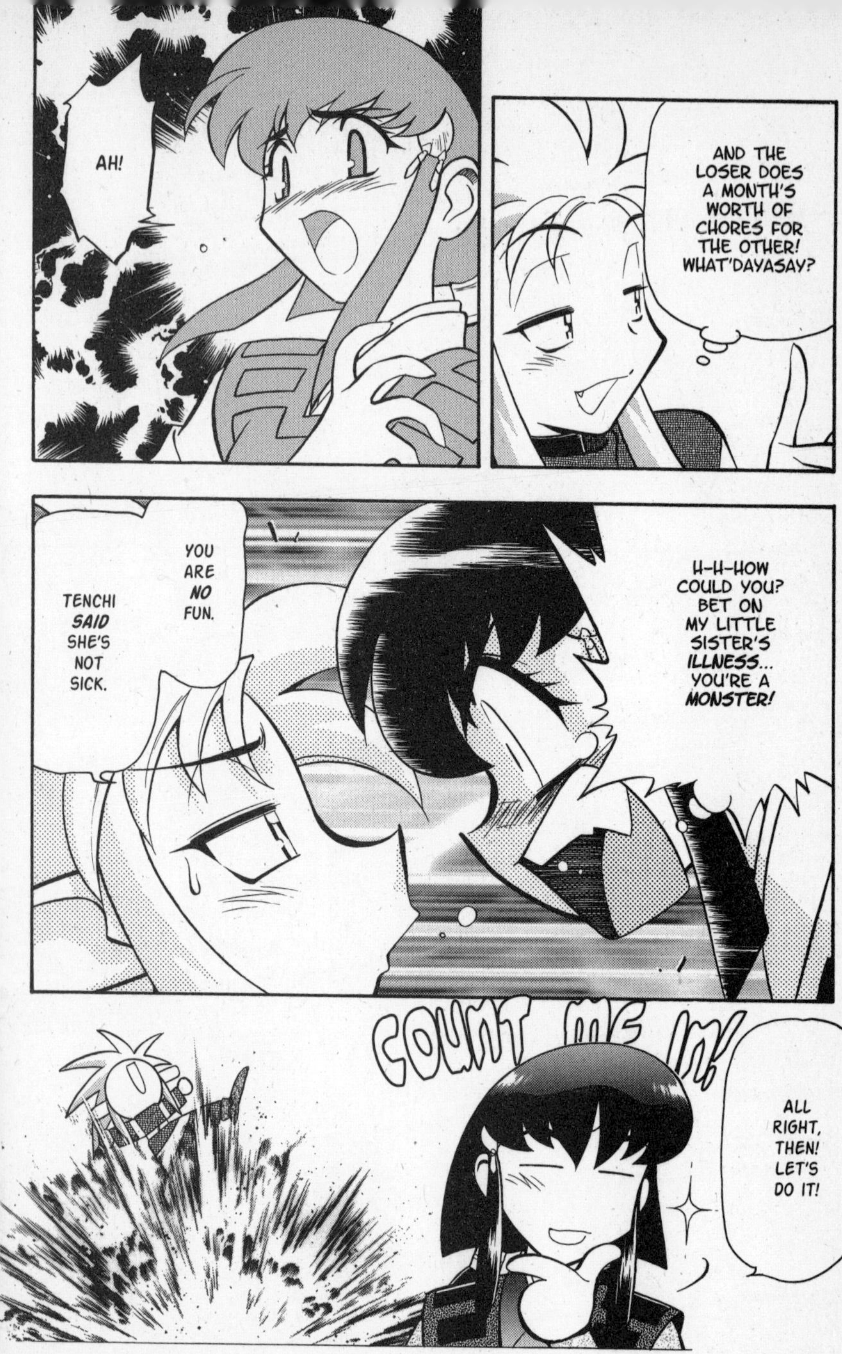
AND THE LOSER DOES A MONTH'S WORTH OF CHORES FOR THE OTHER! WHAT'DAYASAY?
AH!
H-H-HOW COULD YOU? BET ON MY LITTLE SISTER'S *ILLNESS*... YOU'RE A *MONSTER!*
YOU ARE *NO* FUN.
TENCHI *SAID* SHE'S NOT SICK.
ALL RIGHT, THEN! LET'S DO IT!
COUNT ME IN!

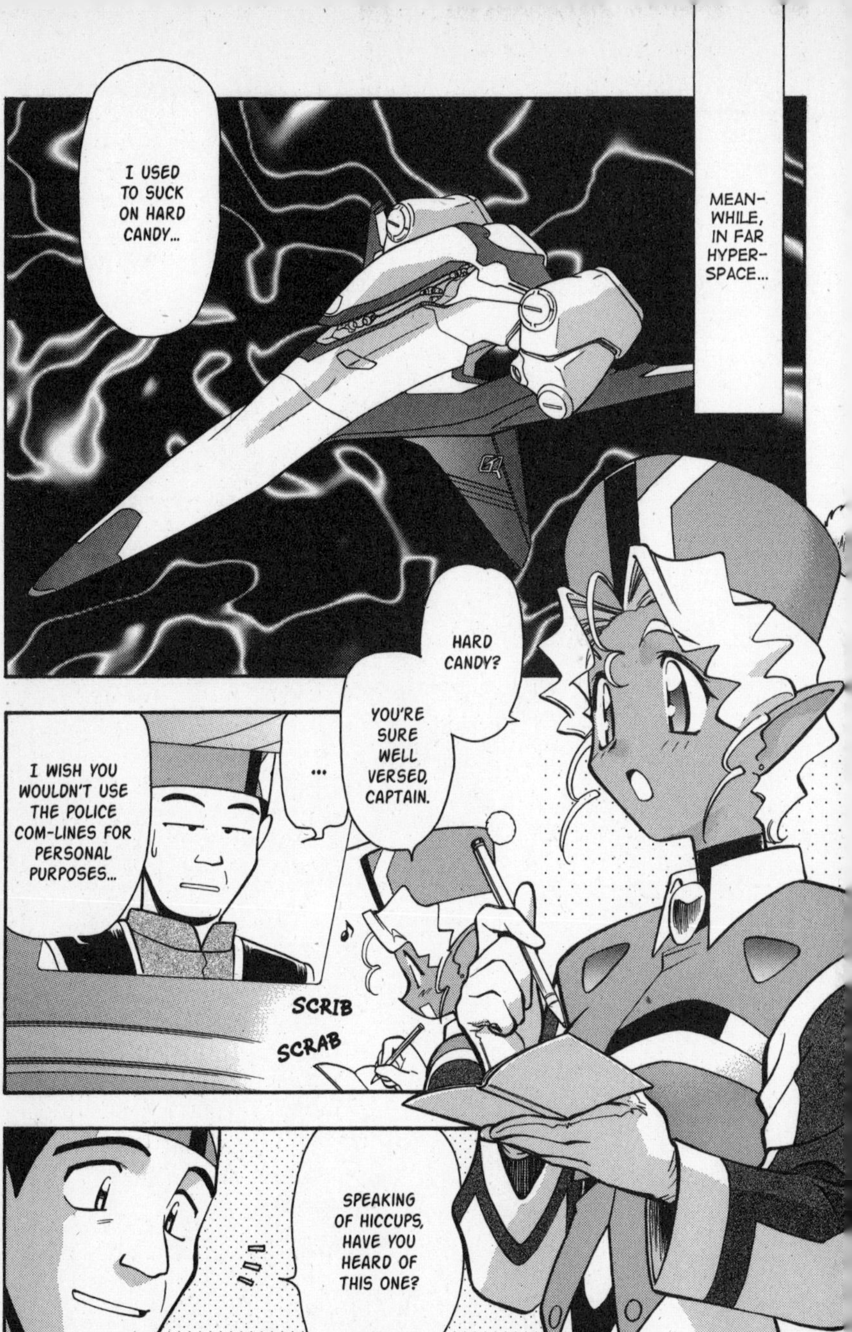
MEAN-WHILE, IN FAR HYPER-SPACE...
I USED TO SUCK ON HARD CANDY...
HARD CANDY?
YOU'RE SURE WELL VERSED, CAPTAIN.
...
I WISH YOU WOULDN'T USE THE POLICE COM-LINES FOR PERSONAL PURPOSES...
SCRIB
SCRAB
SPEAKING OF HICCUPS, HAVE YOU HEARD OF THIS ONE?

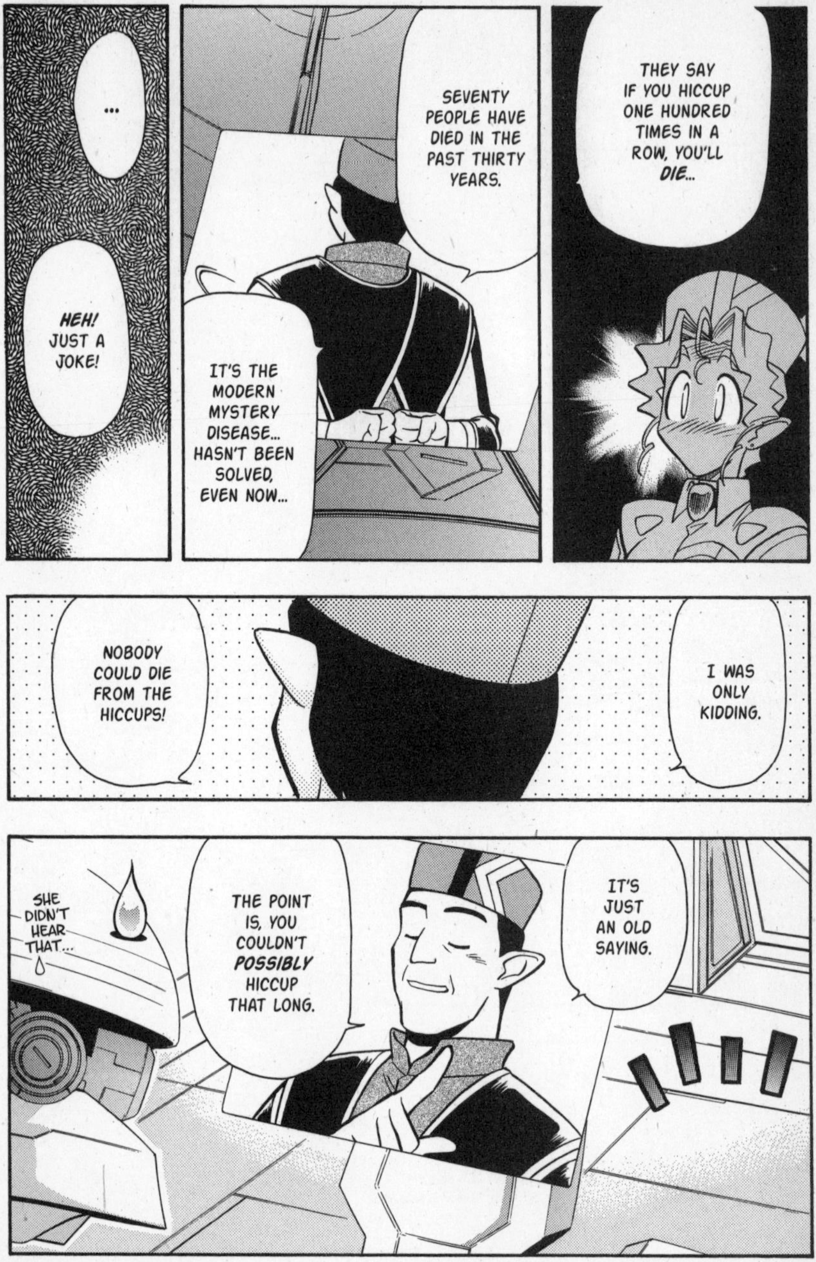
THEY SAY IF YOU HICCUP ONE HUNDRED TIMES IN A ROW, YOU'LL *DIE*...
SEVENTY PEOPLE HAVE DIED IN THE PAST THIRTY YEARS.
IT'S THE MODERN MYSTERY DISEASE... HASN'T BEEN SOLVED, EVEN NOW...
...
HEH! JUST A JOKE!
I WAS ONLY KIDDING.
NOBODY COULD DIE FROM THE HICCUPS!
IT'S JUST AN OLD SAYING.
THE POINT IS, YOU COULDN'T *POSSIBLY* HICCUP THAT LONG.
SHE DIDN'T HEAR THAT...

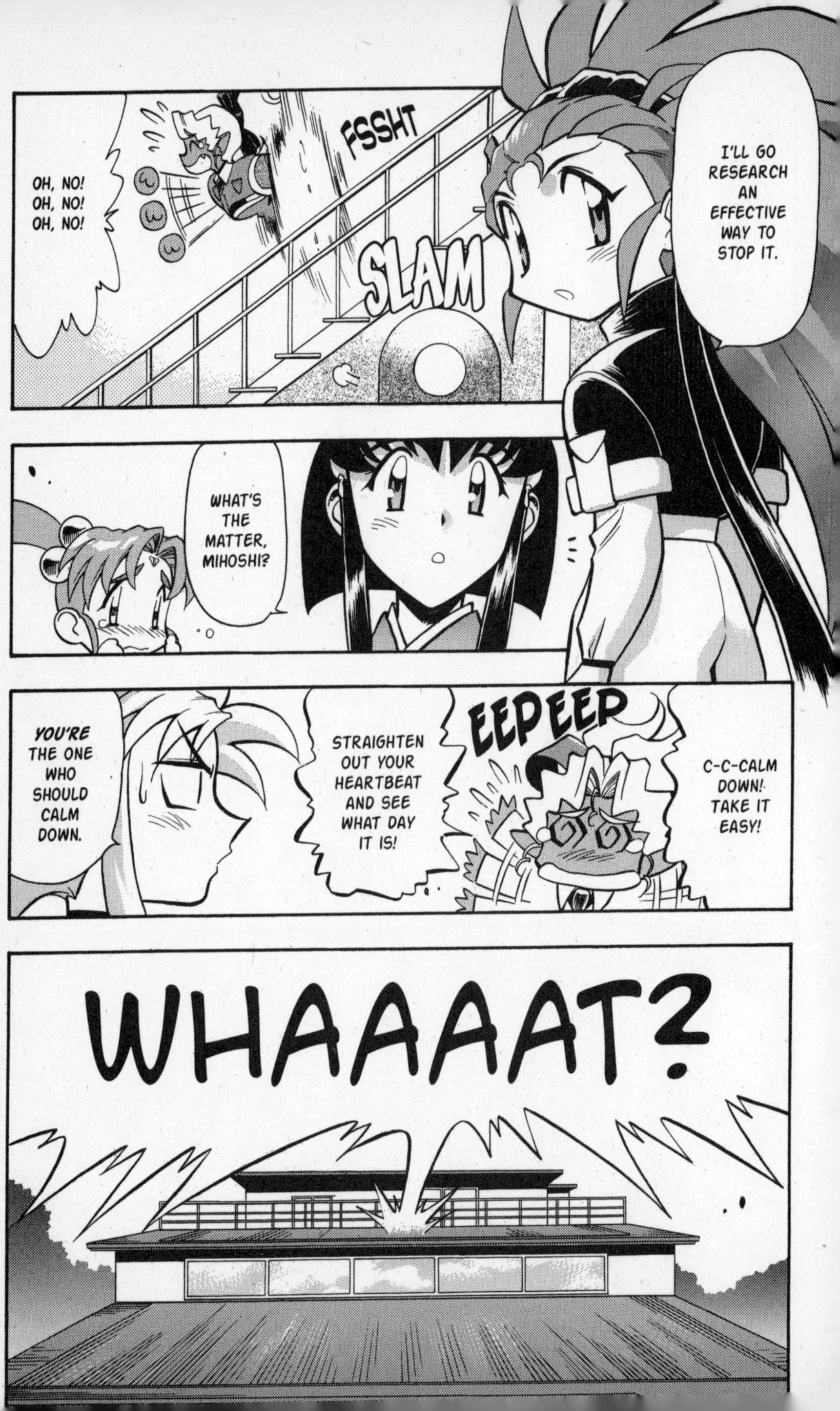

I'LL GO RESEARCH AN EFFECTIVE WAY TO STOP IT.
FSSHT
SLAM
OH, NO! OH, NO! OH, NO!
WHAT'S THE MATTER, MIHOSHI?
C-C-CALM DOWN! TAKE IT EASY!
EEPEEP
STRAIGHTEN OUT YOUR HEARTBEAT AND SEE WHAT DAY IT IS!
YOU'RE THE ONE WHO SHOULD CALM DOWN.
WHAAAAT?

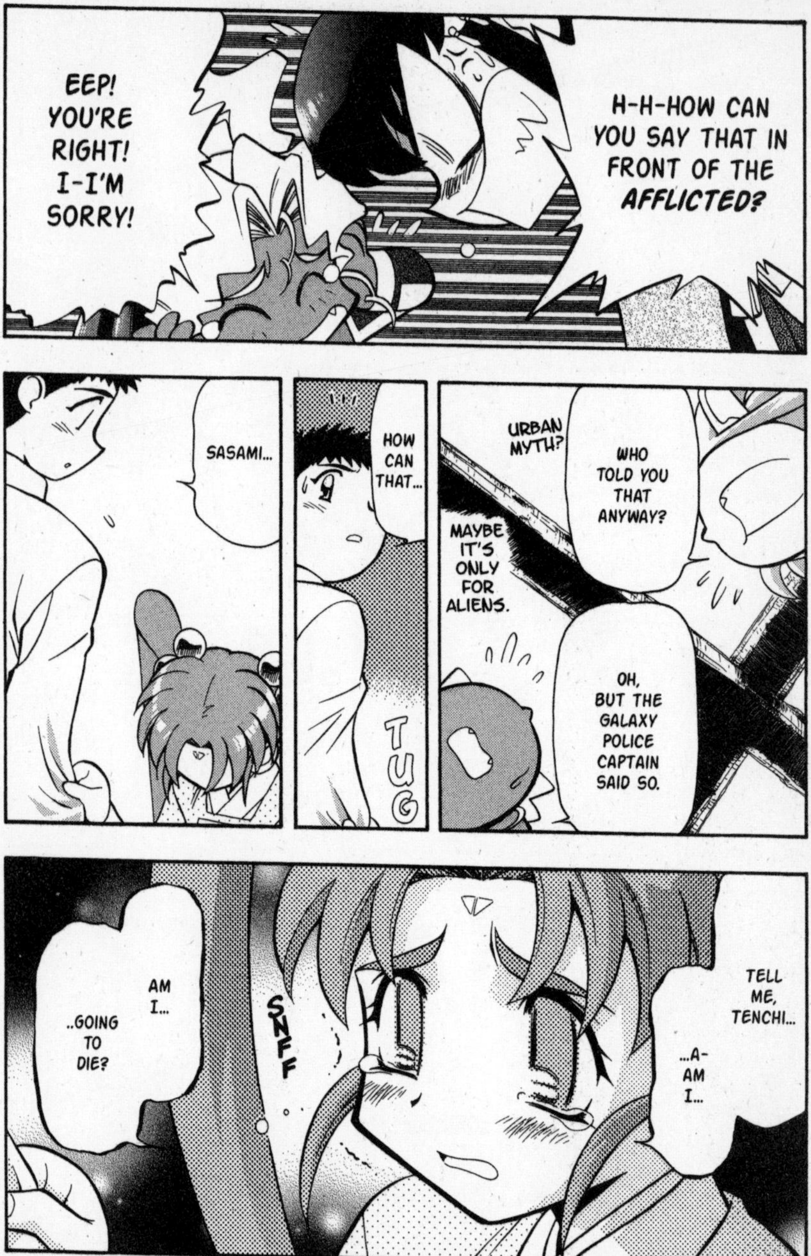
H-H-HOW CAN YOU SAY THAT IN FRONT OF THE *AFFLICTED?*
EEP! YOU'RE RIGHT! I-I'M SORRY!
WHO TOLD YOU THAT ANYWAY?
URBAN MYTH?
MAYBE IT'S ONLY FOR ALIENS.
OH, BUT THE GALAXY POLICE CAPTAIN SAID SO.
HOW CAN THAT...
TUG
SASAMI...
TELL ME, TENCHI...
...A- AM I...
SNFF
AM I...
..GOING TO DIE?

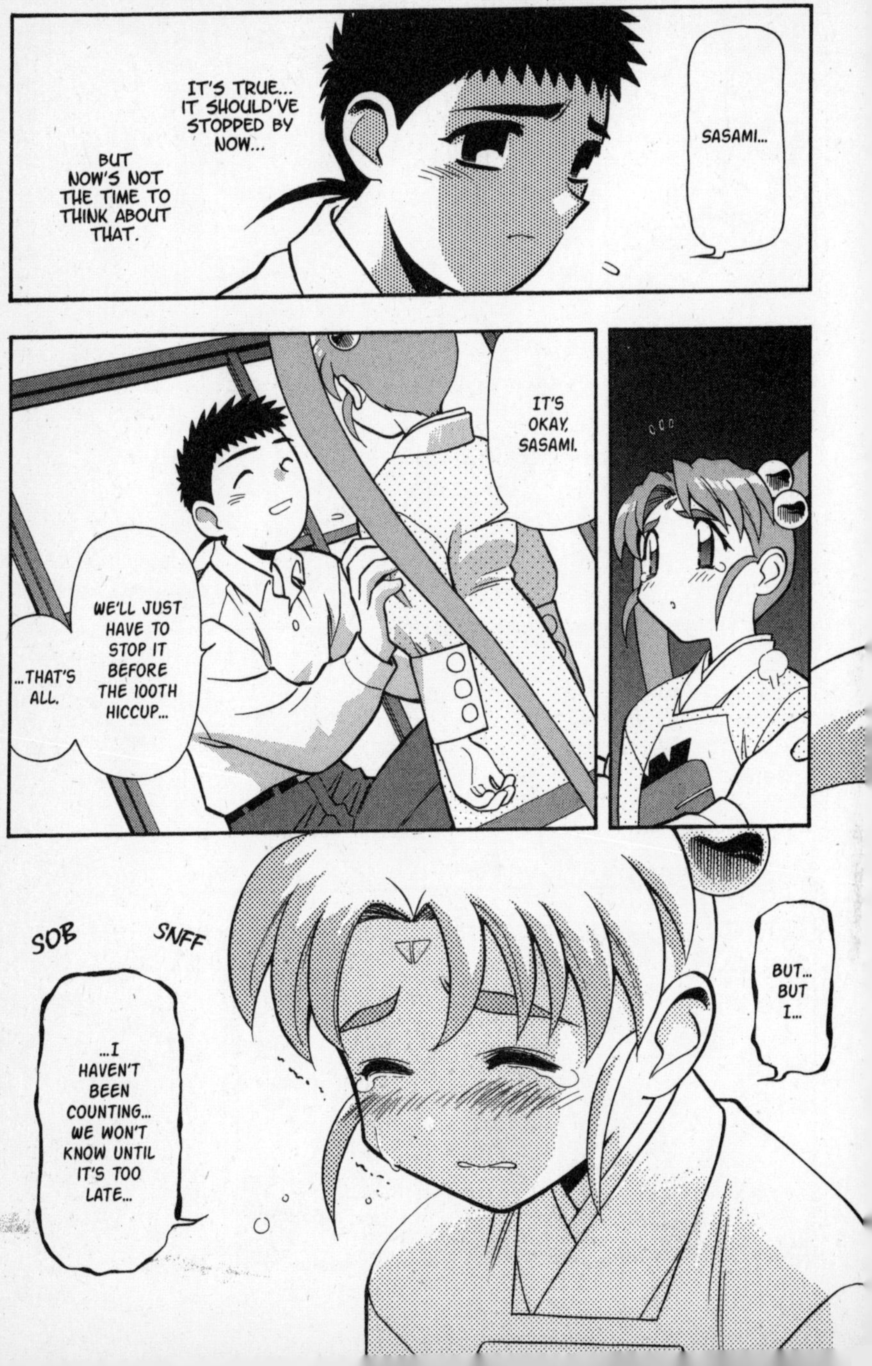
SASAMI...
IT'S TRUE... IT SHOULD'VE STOPPED BY NOW...
BUT NOW'S NOT THE TIME TO THINK ABOUT THAT.
IT'S OKAY, SASAMI.
WE'LL JUST HAVE TO STOP IT BEFORE THE 100TH HICCUP...
...THAT'S ALL.
BUT... BUT I...
SNFF
SOB
...I HAVEN'T BEEN COUNTING... WE WON'T KNOW UNTIL IT'S TOO LATE...

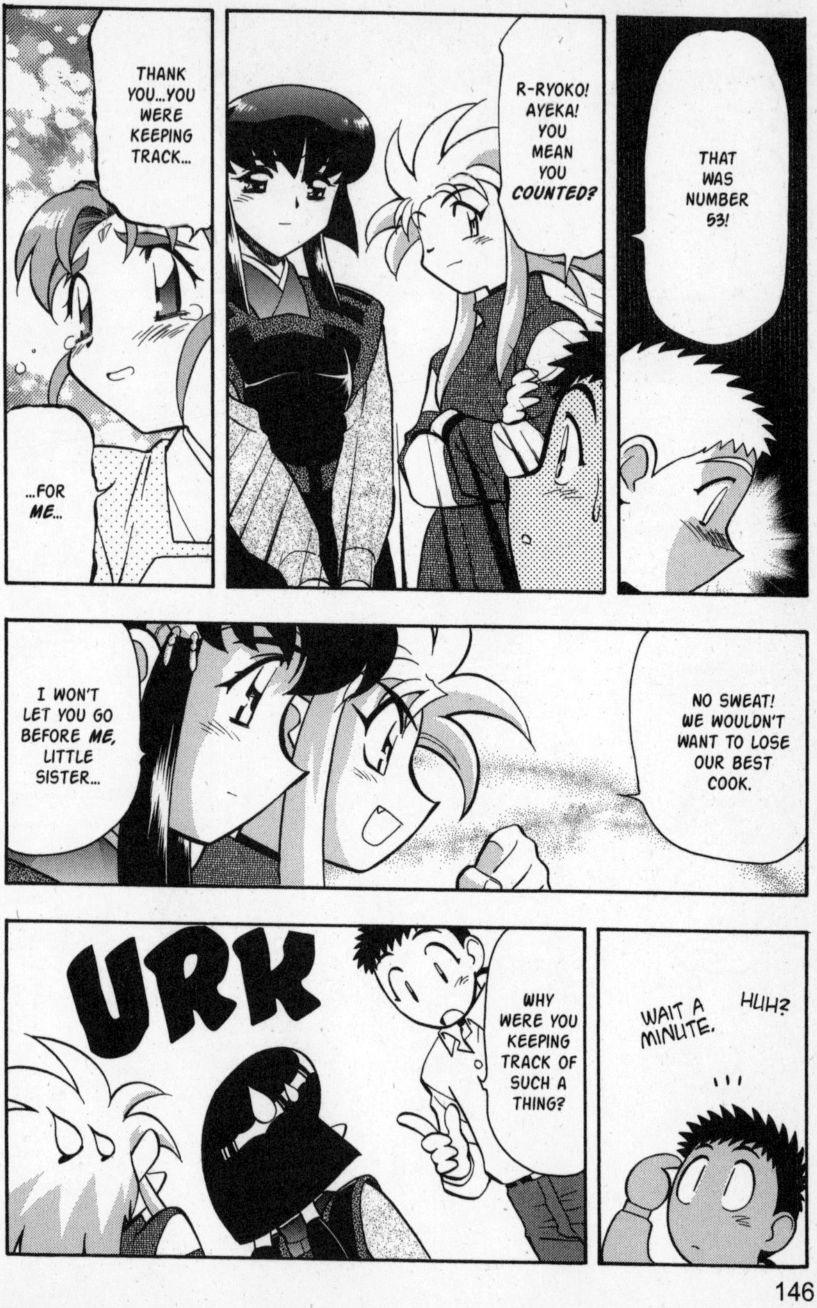
THAT WAS NUMBER 53!
R-RYOKO! AYEKA! YOU MEAN YOU *COUNTED?*
THANK YOU...YOU WERE KEEPING TRACK...
...FOR *ME*...
NO SWEAT! WE WOULDN'T WANT TO LOSE OUR BEST COOK.
I WON'T LET YOU GO BEFORE *ME*, LITTLE SISTER...
HUH?
WAIT A MINUTE.
WHY WERE YOU KEEPING TRACK OF SUCH A THING?
URK

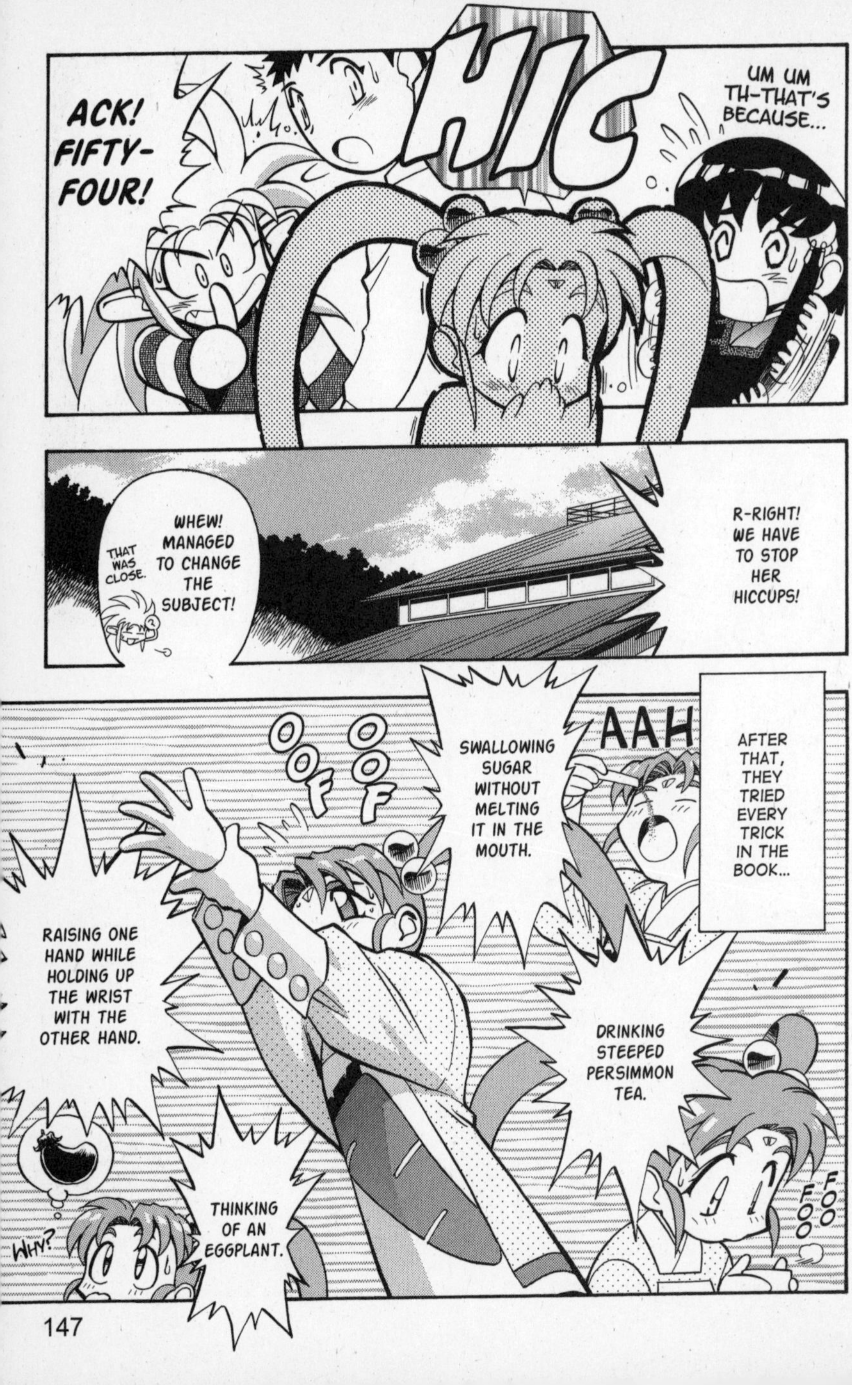
UM UM TH-THAT'S BECAUSE...
HIC
ACK! FIFTY-FOUR!
R-RIGHT! WE HAVE TO STOP HER HICCUPS!
WHEW! MANAGED TO CHANGE THE SUBJECT!
THAT WAS CLOSE.
AFTER THAT, THEY TRIED EVERY TRICK IN THE BOOK...
AAH
SWALLOWING SUGAR WITHOUT MELTING IT IN THE MOUTH.
OOF OOF
RAISING ONE HAND WHILE HOLDING UP THE WRIST WITH THE OTHER HAND.
DRINKING STEEPED PERSIMMON TEA.
FOO FOO FOO
THINKING OF AN EGGPLANT.
WHY?

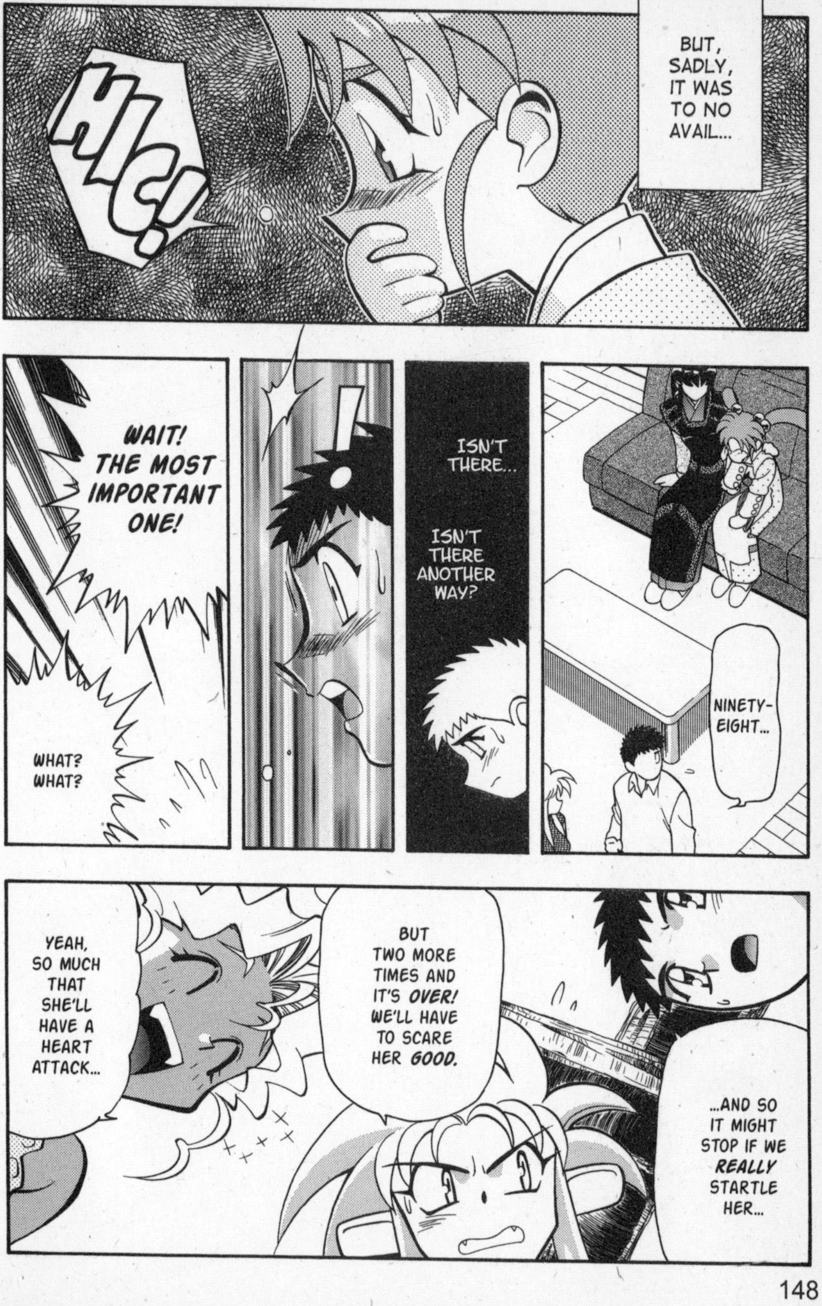
BUT, SADLY, IT WAS TO NO AVAIL...
HIC!
NINETY-EIGHT...
ISN'T THERE...
ISN'T THERE ANOTHER WAY?
!
WAIT! THE MOST IMPORTANT ONE!
WHAT? WHAT?
BUT TWO MORE TIMES AND IT'S *OVER!* WE'LL HAVE TO SCARE HER *GOOD.*
...AND SO IT MIGHT STOP IF WE *REALLY* STARTLE HER...
YEAH, SO MUCH THAT SHE'LL HAVE A HEART ATTACK...

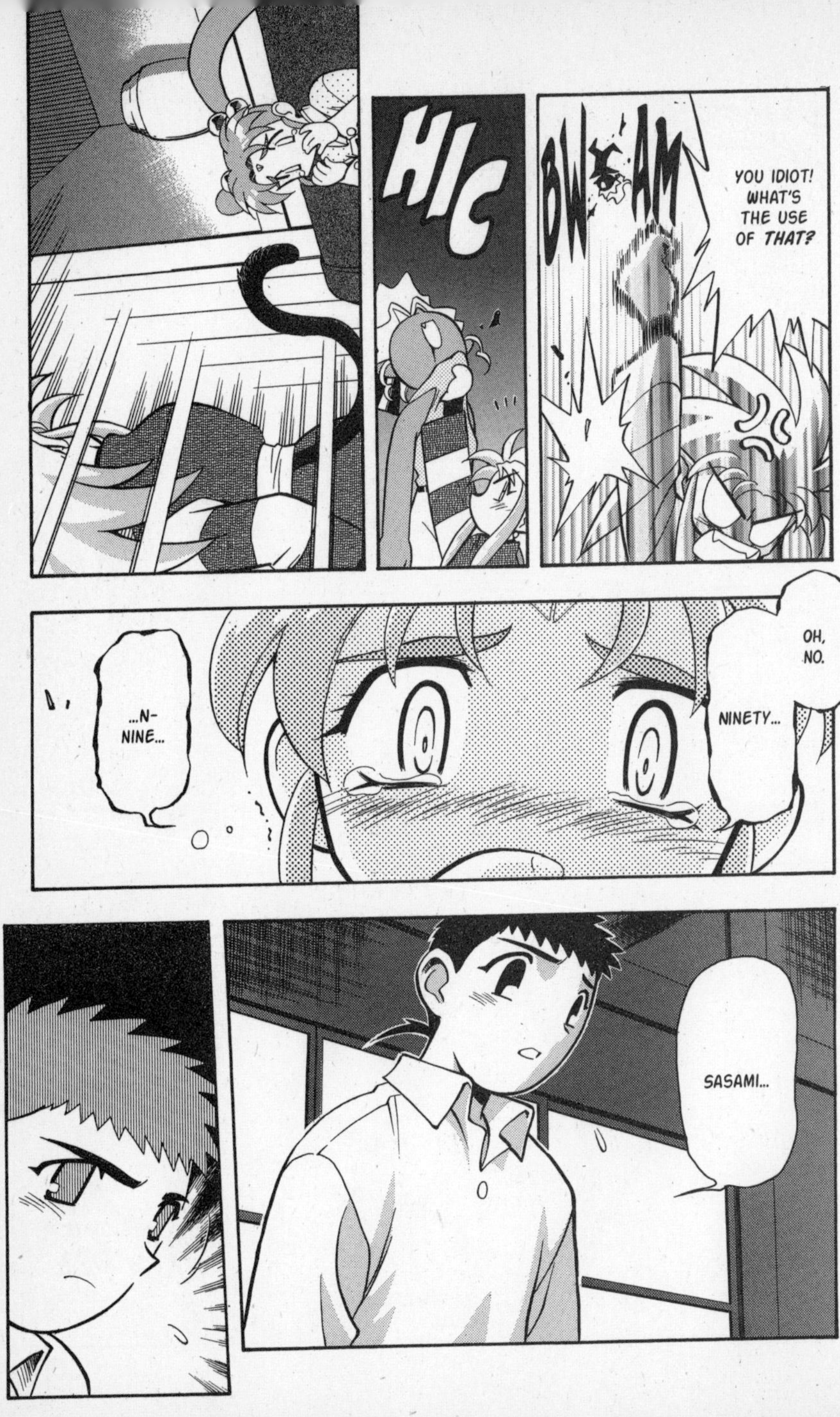
BWAM
YOU IDIOT! WHAT'S THE USE OF *THAT?*
HIC
OH, NO. NINETY...
...N- NINE...
SASAMI...

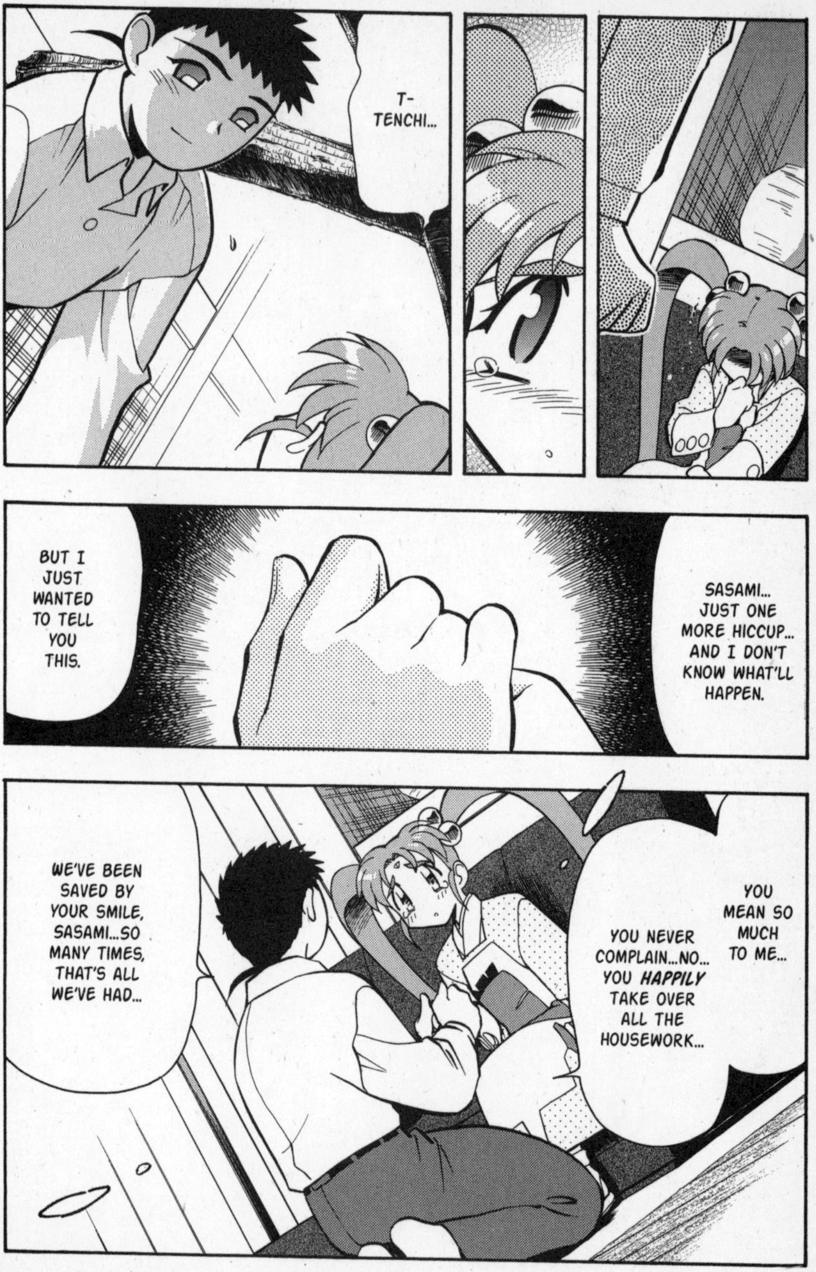
T- TENCHI...
SASAMI... JUST ONE MORE HICCUP... AND I DON'T KNOW WHAT'LL HAPPEN.
BUT I JUST WANTED TO TELL YOU THIS.
YOU MEAN SO MUCH TO ME...
YOU NEVER COMPLAIN...NO... YOU *HAPPILY* TAKE OVER ALL THE HOUSEWORK...
WE'VE BEEN SAVED BY YOUR SMILE, SASAMI...SO MANY TIMES, THAT'S ALL WE'VE HAD...

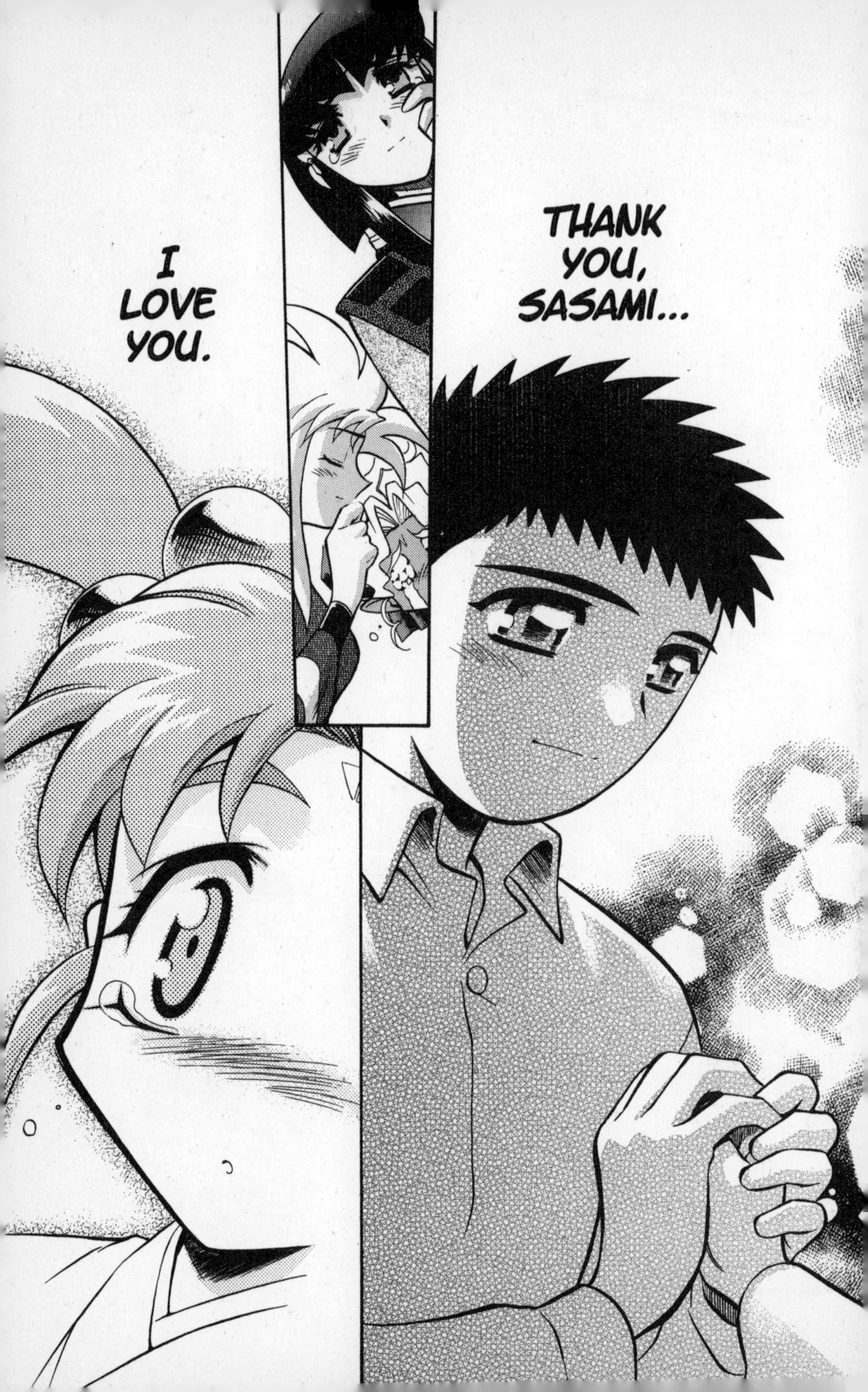
THANK YOU, SASAMI...
I LOVE YOU.

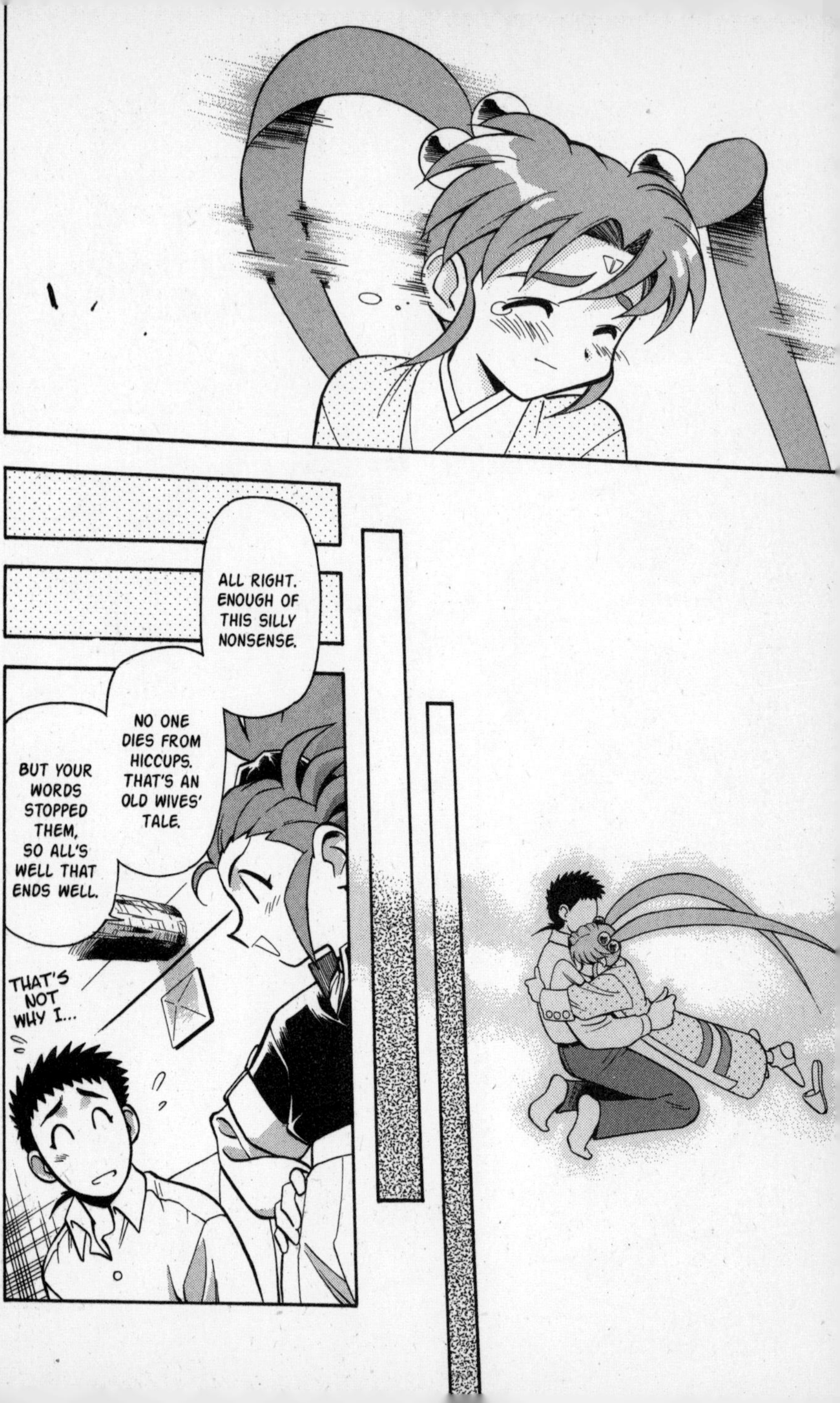
ALL RIGHT. ENOUGH OF THIS SILLY NONSENSE.
NO ONE DIES FROM HICCUPS. THAT'S AN OLD WIVES' TALE.
BUT YOUR WORDS STOPPED THEM, SO ALL'S WELL THAT ENDS WELL.
THAT'S NOT WHY I...

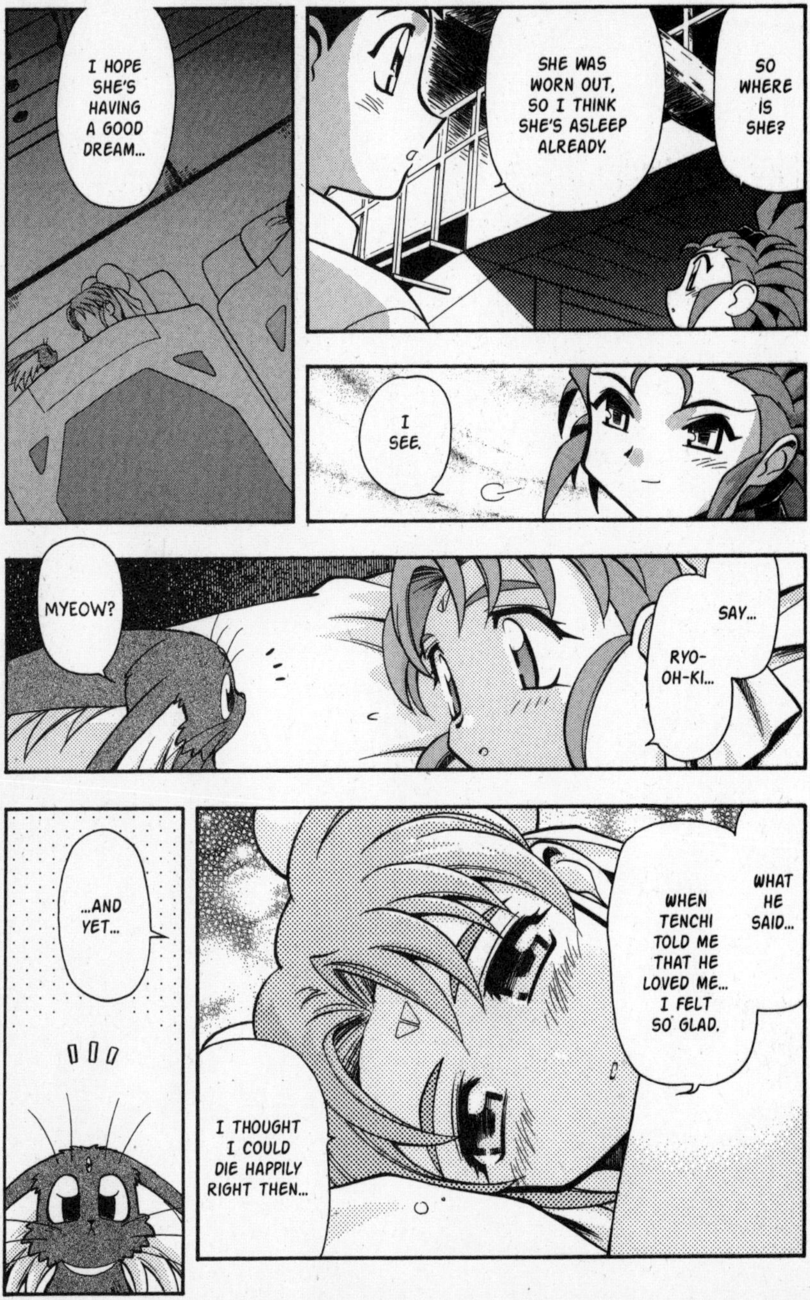
SO WHERE IS SHE?
SHE WAS WORN OUT, SO I THINK SHE'S ASLEEP ALREADY.
I SEE.
I HOPE SHE'S HAVING A GOOD DREAM...
SAY... RYO-OH-KI...
MYEOW?
WHAT HE SAID...
WHEN TENCHI TOLD ME THAT HE LOVED ME... I FELT SO GLAD.
I THOUGHT I COULD DIE HAPPILY RIGHT THEN...
...AND YET...

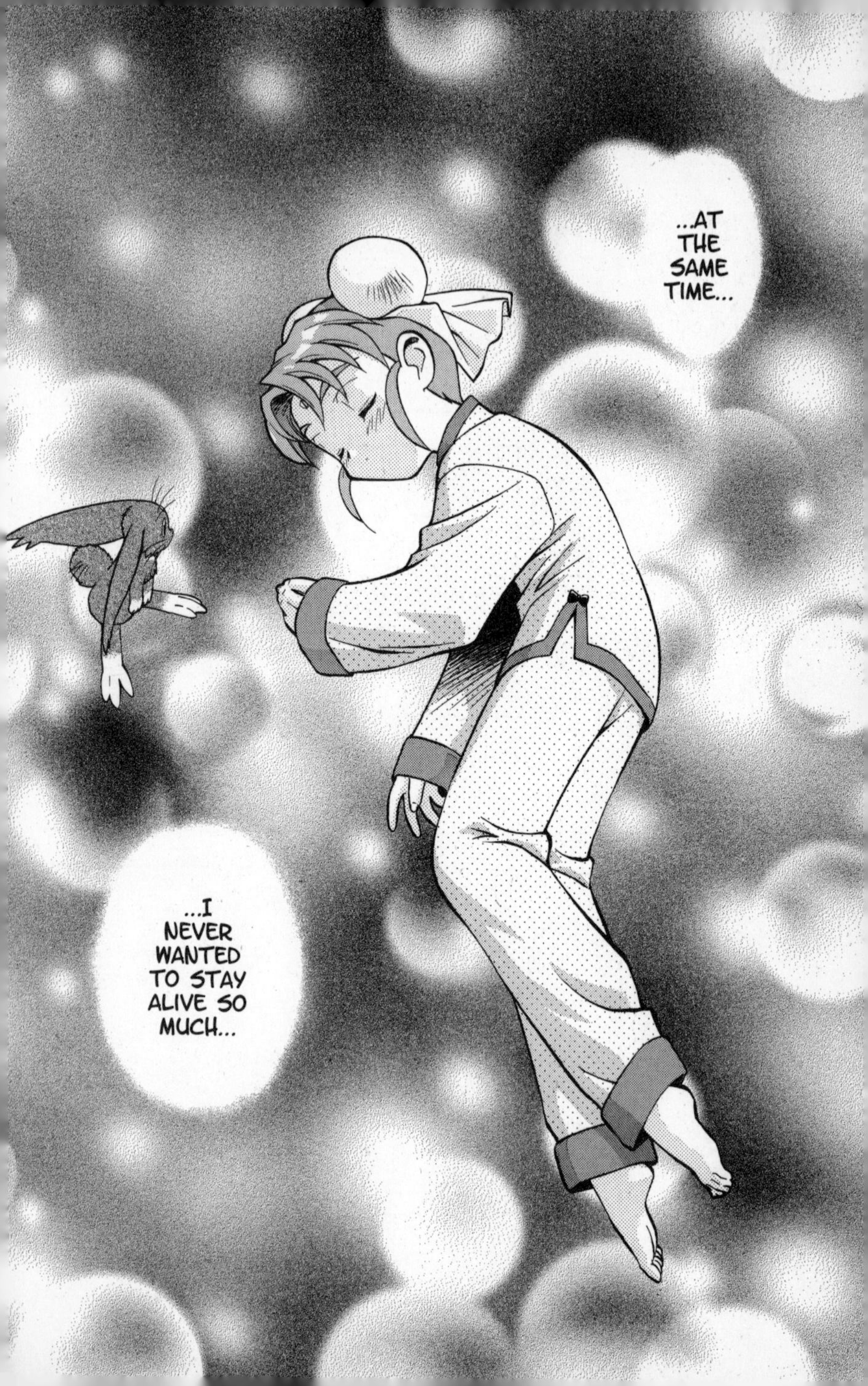
...AT THE SAME TIME...
...I NEVER WANTED TO STAY ALIVE SO MUCH...

Tales of Tenchi #8: OUT OF THE PAST

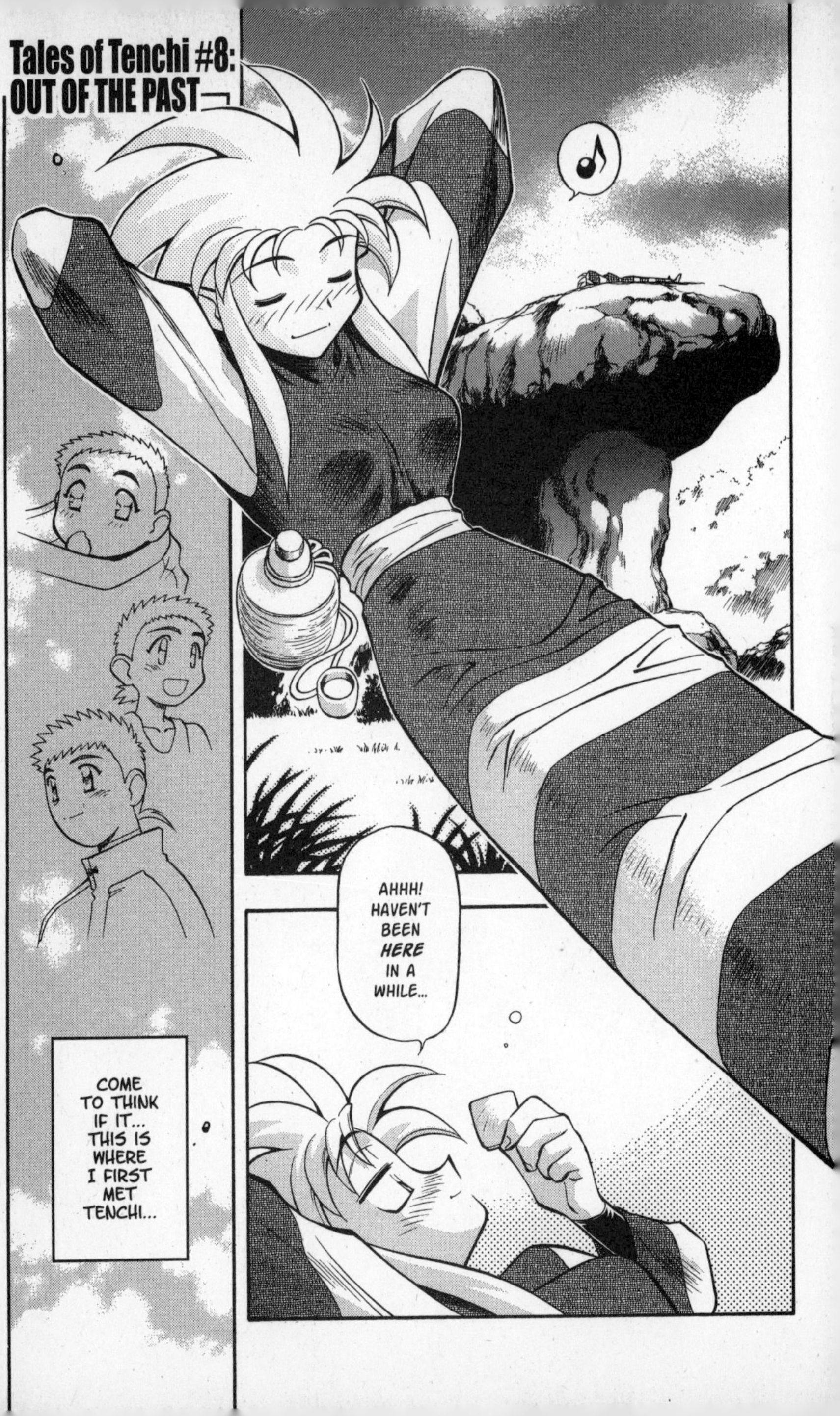
♪
AHHH! HAVEN'T BEEN *HERE* IN A WHILE...
COME TO THINK IF IT... THIS IS WHERE I FIRST MET TENCHI...

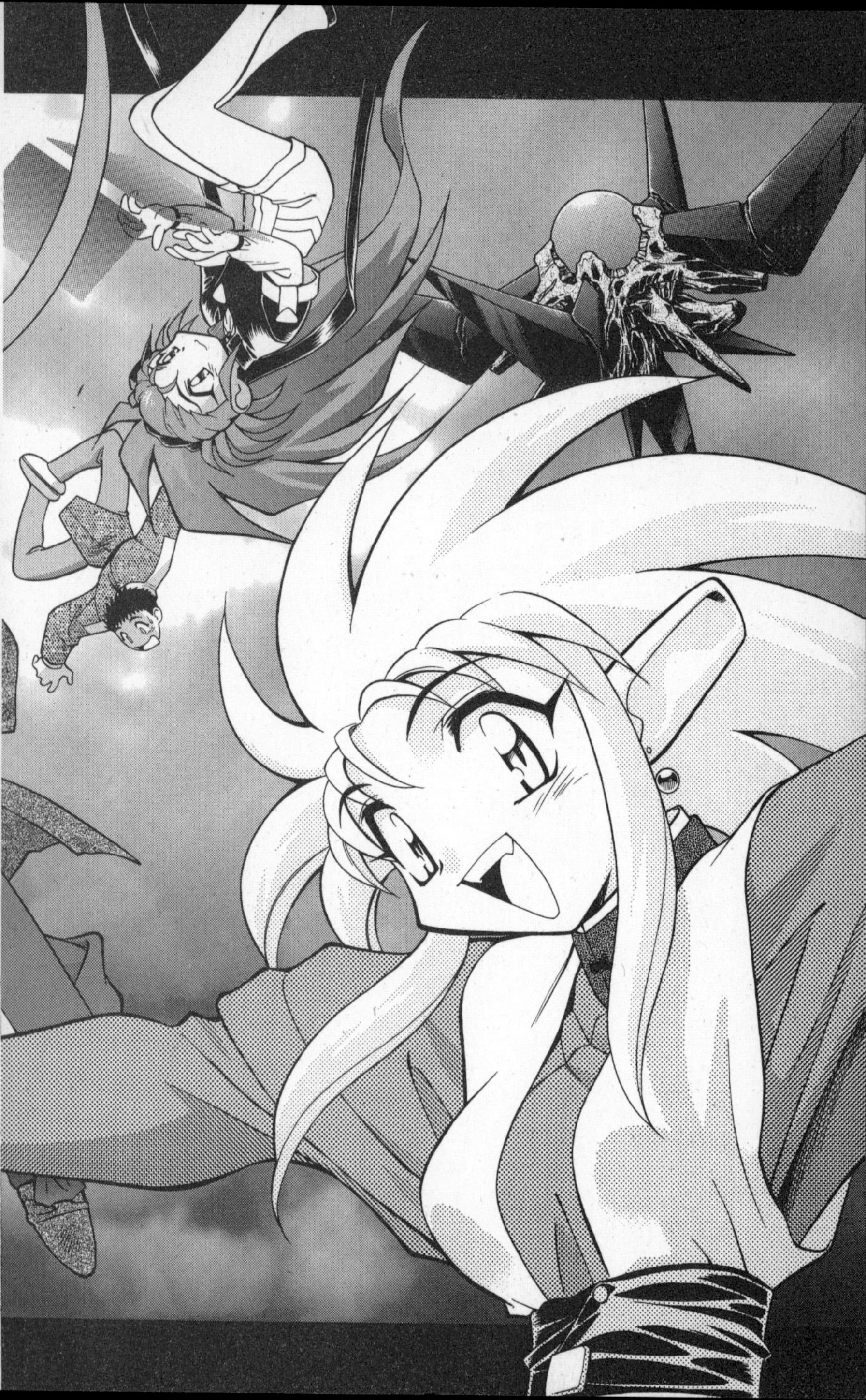

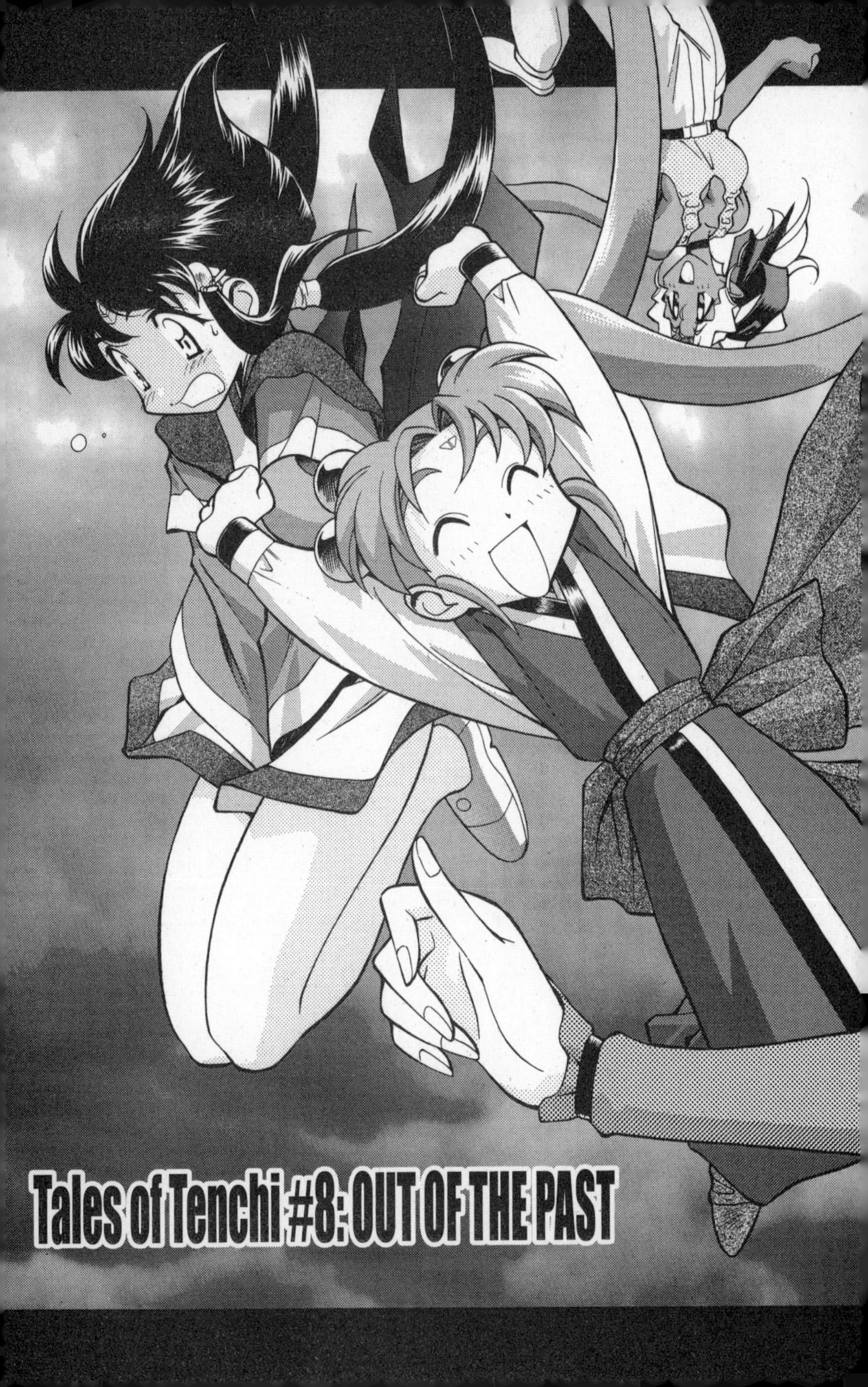
Tales of Tenchi #8: OUT OF THE PAST

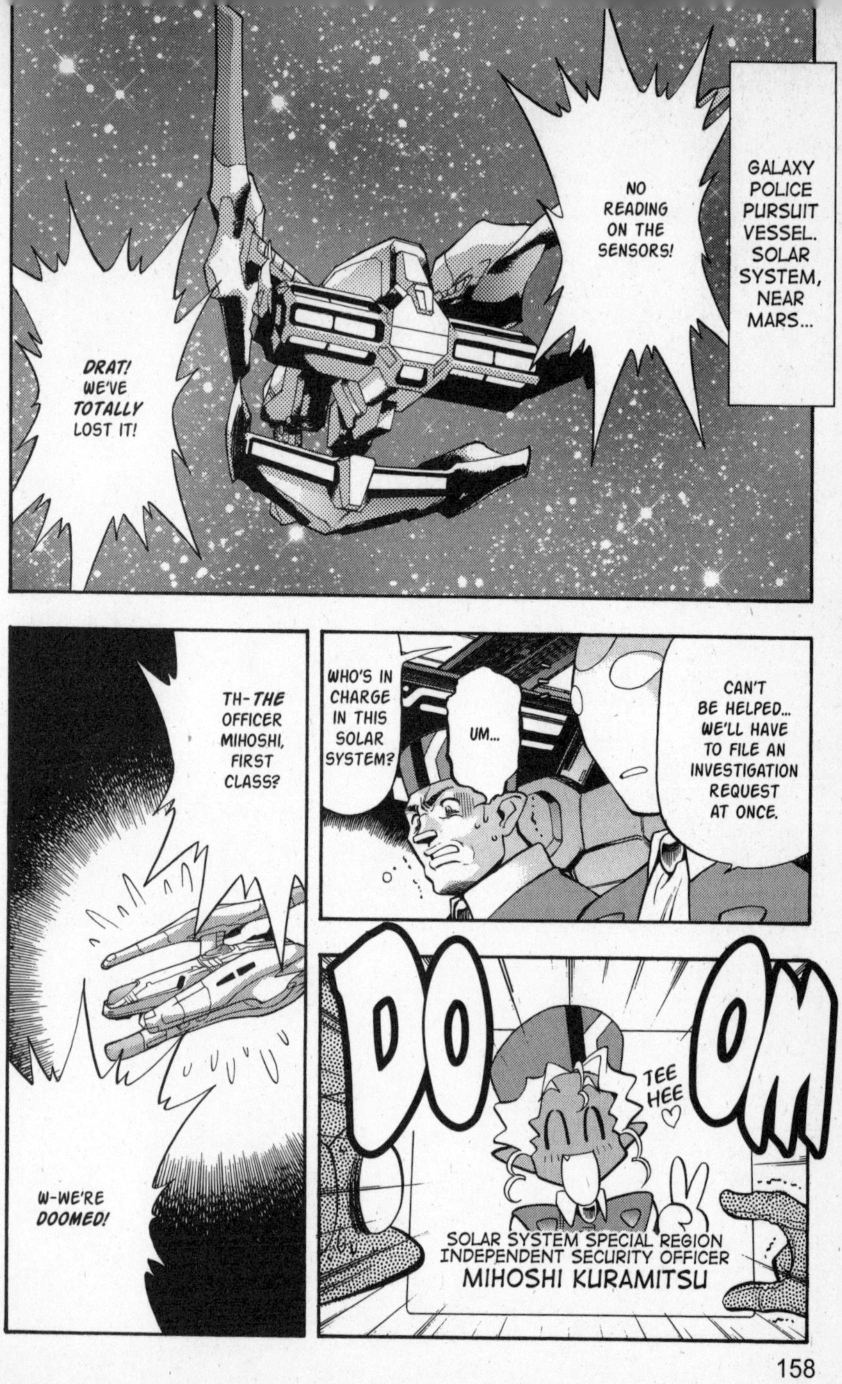
GALAXY POLICE PURSUIT VESSEL. SOLAR SYSTEM, NEAR MARS...
NO READING ON THE SENSORS!
DRAT! WE'VE *TOTALLY* LOST IT!
CAN'T BE HELPED... WE'LL HAVE TO FILE AN INVESTIGATION REQUEST AT ONCE.
UM...
WHO'S IN CHARGE IN THIS SOLAR SYSTEM?
DOOOM
TEE HEE ♡
SOLAR SYSTEM SPECIAL REGION INDEPENDENT SECURITY OFFICER
MIHOSHI KURAMITSU
TH-*THE* OFFICER MIHOSHI, FIRST CLASS?
W-WE'RE *DOOMED!*

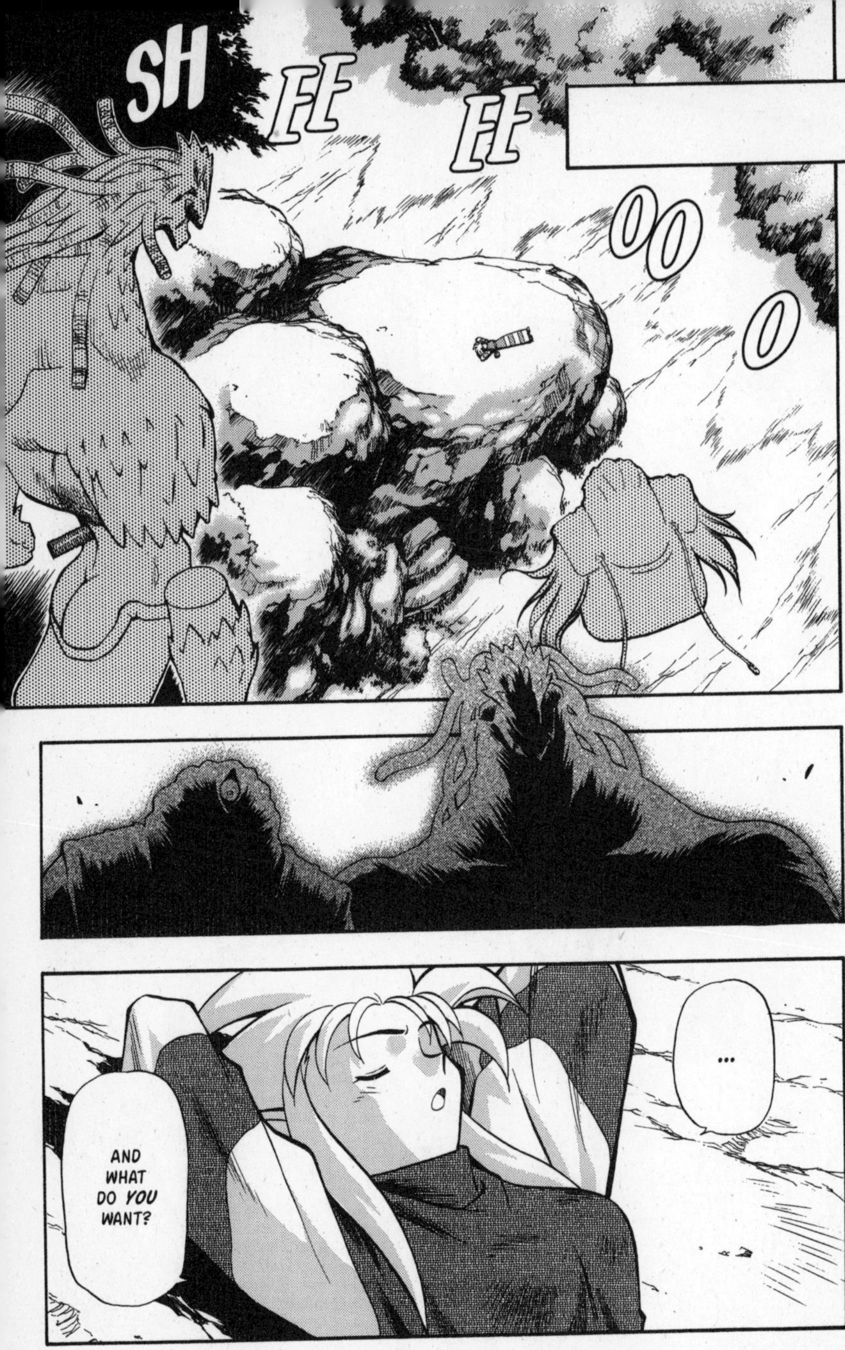
SH
EE
EE
OO
O
...
AND WHAT DO YOU WANT?

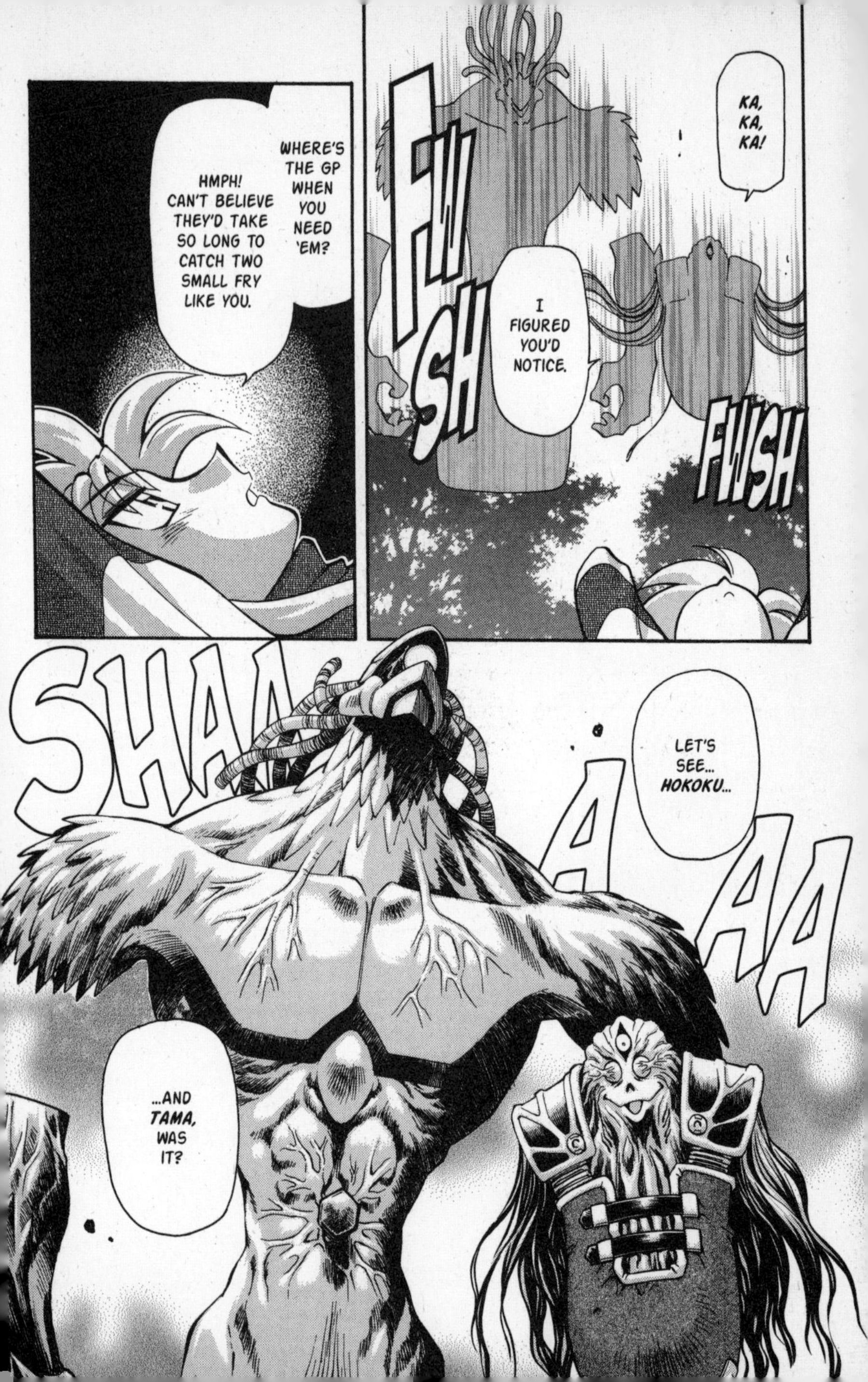
KA, KA, KA!
FWISH
I FIGURED YOU'D NOTICE.
FWISH
WHERE'S THE GP WHEN YOU NEED 'EM?
HMPH! CAN'T BELIEVE THEY'D TAKE SO LONG TO CATCH TWO SMALL FRY LIKE YOU.
LET'S SEE... HOKOKU...
SHAAAAAA
...AND TAMA, WAS IT?

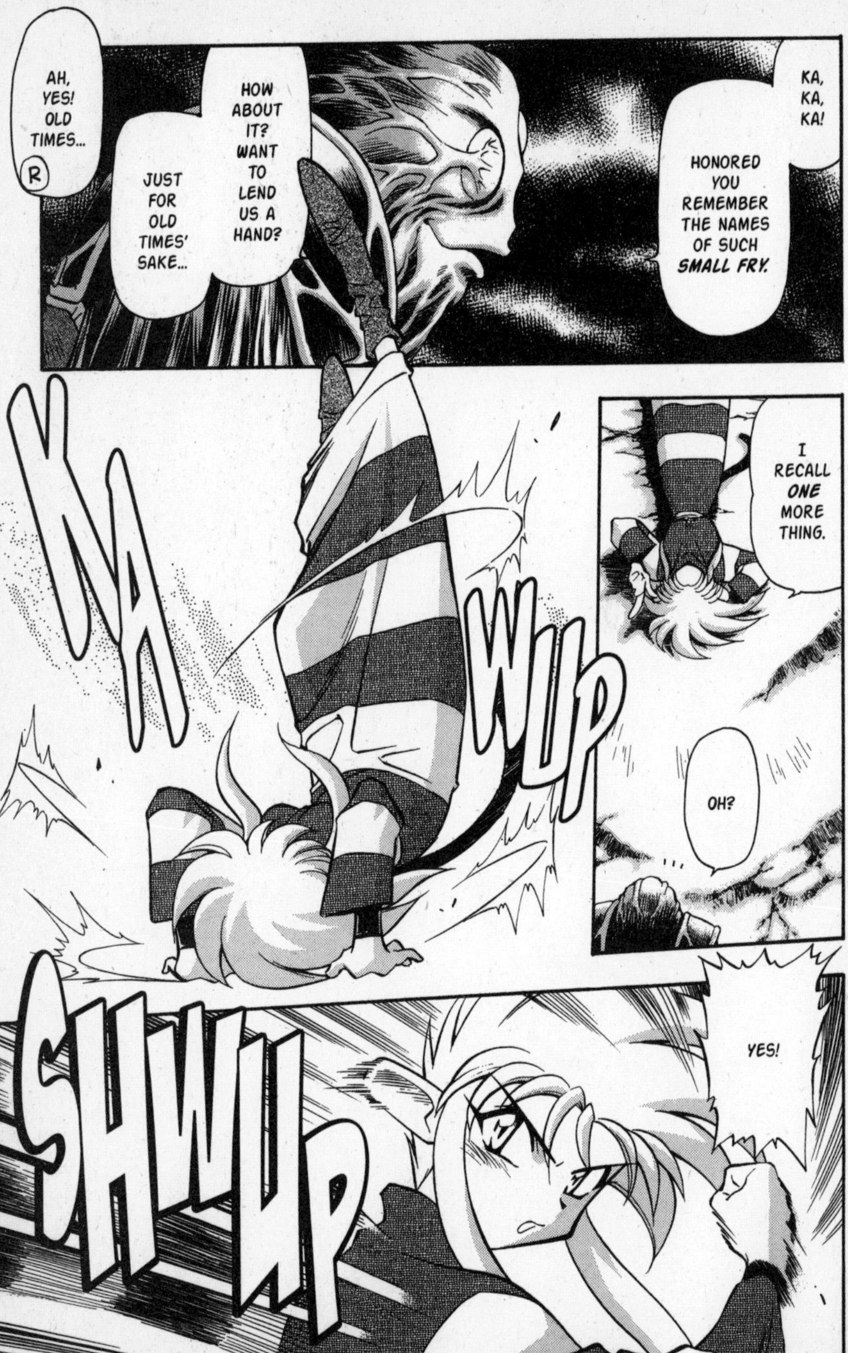

KA, KA, KA!
HONORED YOU REMEMBER THE NAMES OF SUCH *SMALL FRY.*
HOW ABOUT IT? WANT TO LEND US A HAND?
JUST FOR OLD TIMES' SAKE...
AH, YES! OLD TIMES...
I RECALL *ONE* MORE THING.
OH?
...
KA
WUP
YES!
SHWUP

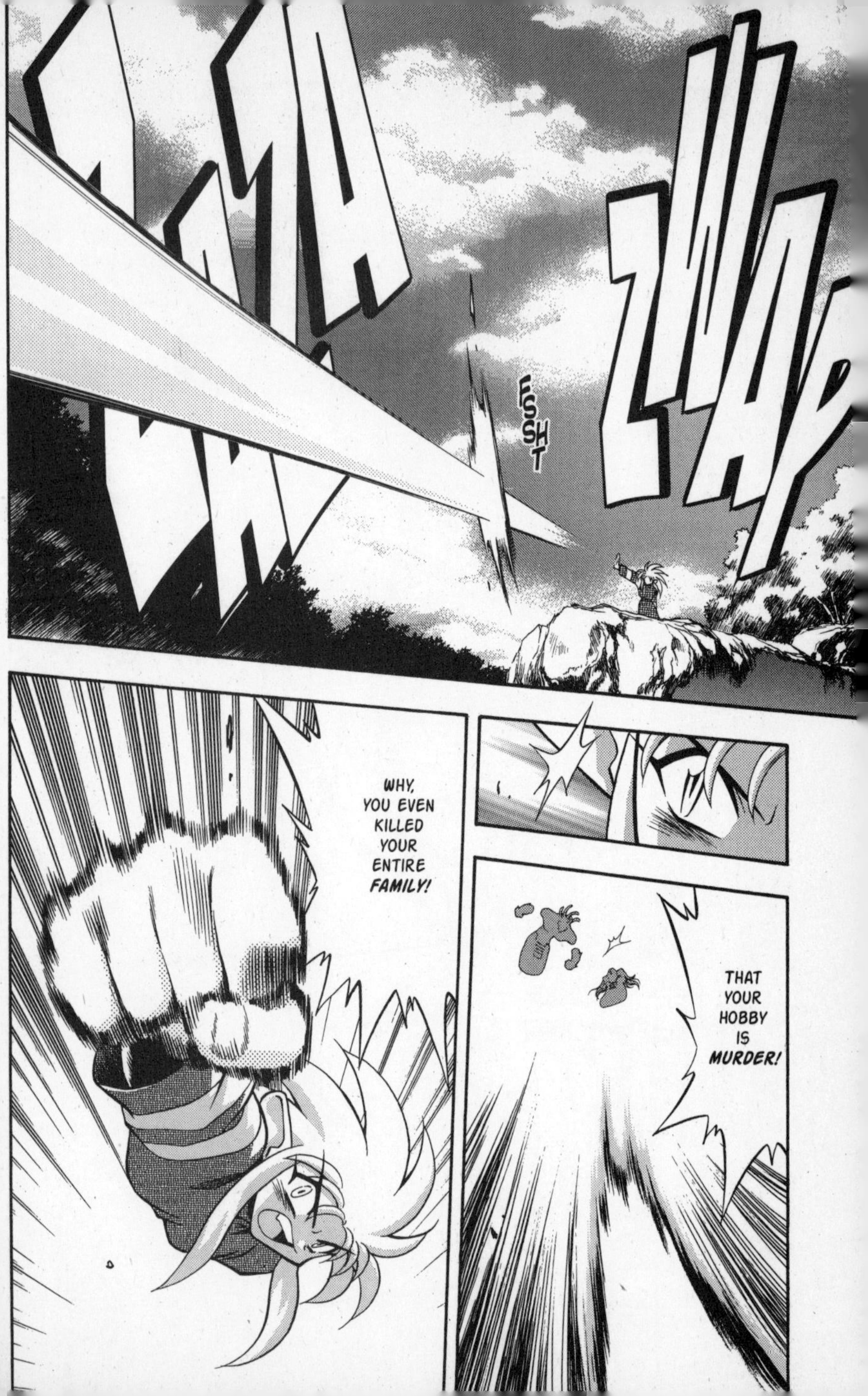
FSSHT
THAT YOUR HOBBY IS *MURDER!*
WHY, YOU EVEN KILLED YOUR ENTIRE *FAMILY!*

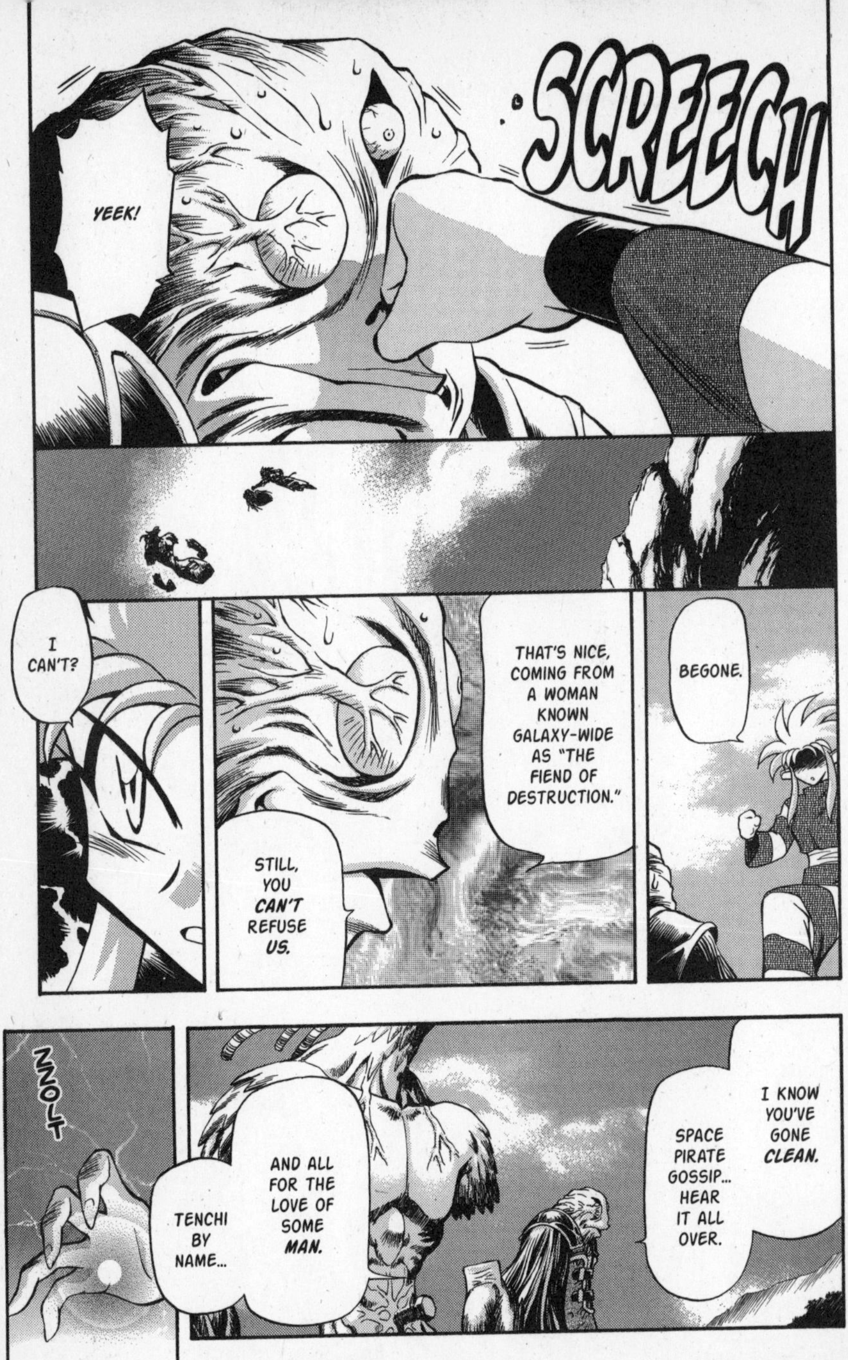
SCREECH
YEEK!
BEGONE.
THAT'S NICE, COMING FROM A WOMAN KNOWN GALAXY-WIDE AS "THE FIEND OF DESTRUCTION."
STILL, YOU *CAN'T* REFUSE *US.*
I CAN'T?
I KNOW YOU'VE GONE *CLEAN.*
SPACE PIRATE GOSSIP... HEAR IT ALL OVER.
AND ALL FOR THE LOVE OF SOME *MAN.*
TENCHI BY NAME...
ZZOLT

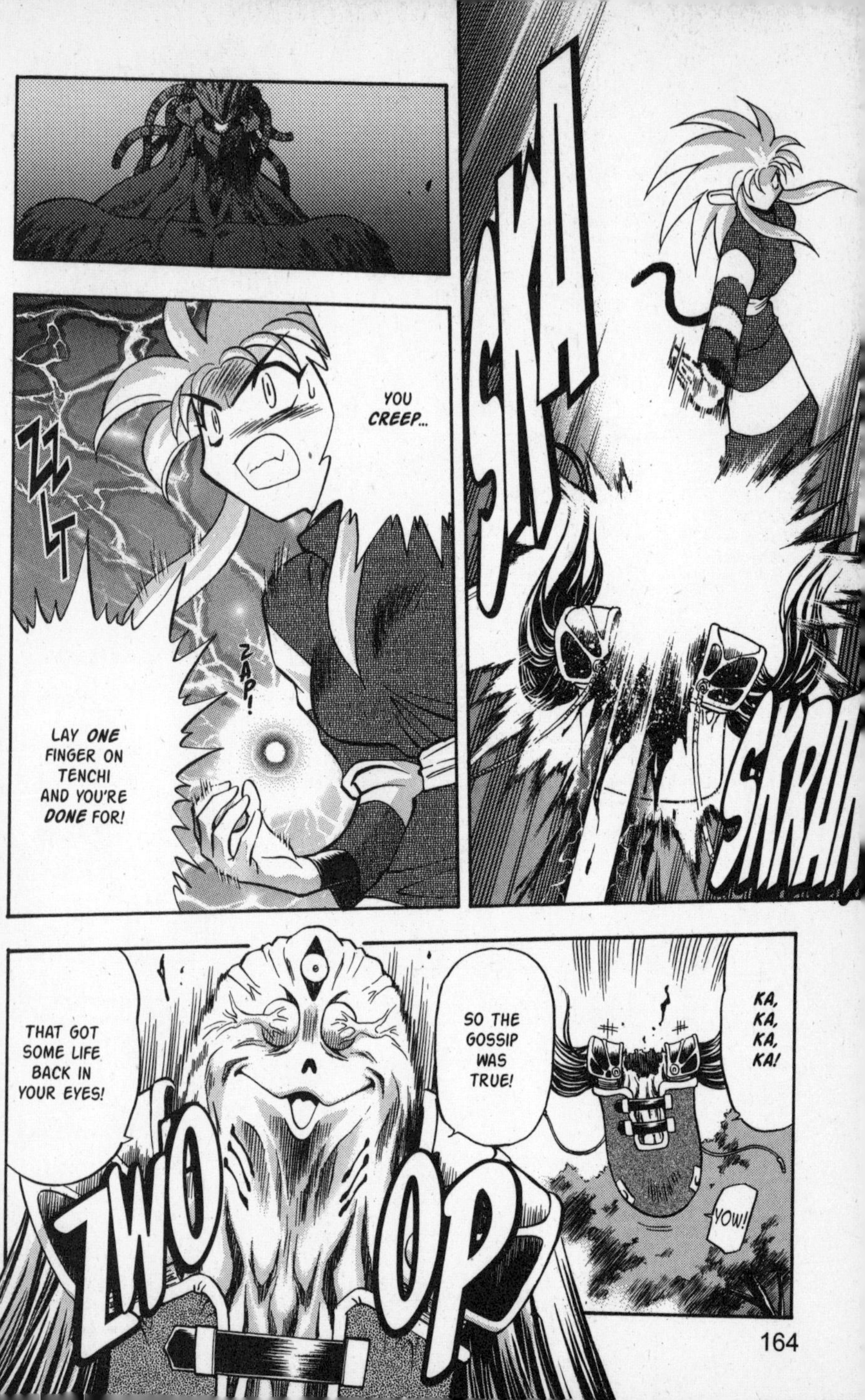
SKA
SKRA
YOU CREEP...
ZZLT
ZAP!
LAY ONE FINGER ON TENCHI AND YOU'RE DONE FOR!
KA, KA, KA, KA!
YOW!
SO THE GOSSIP WAS TRUE!
THAT GOT SOME LIFE BACK IN YOUR EYES!
ZWOOP

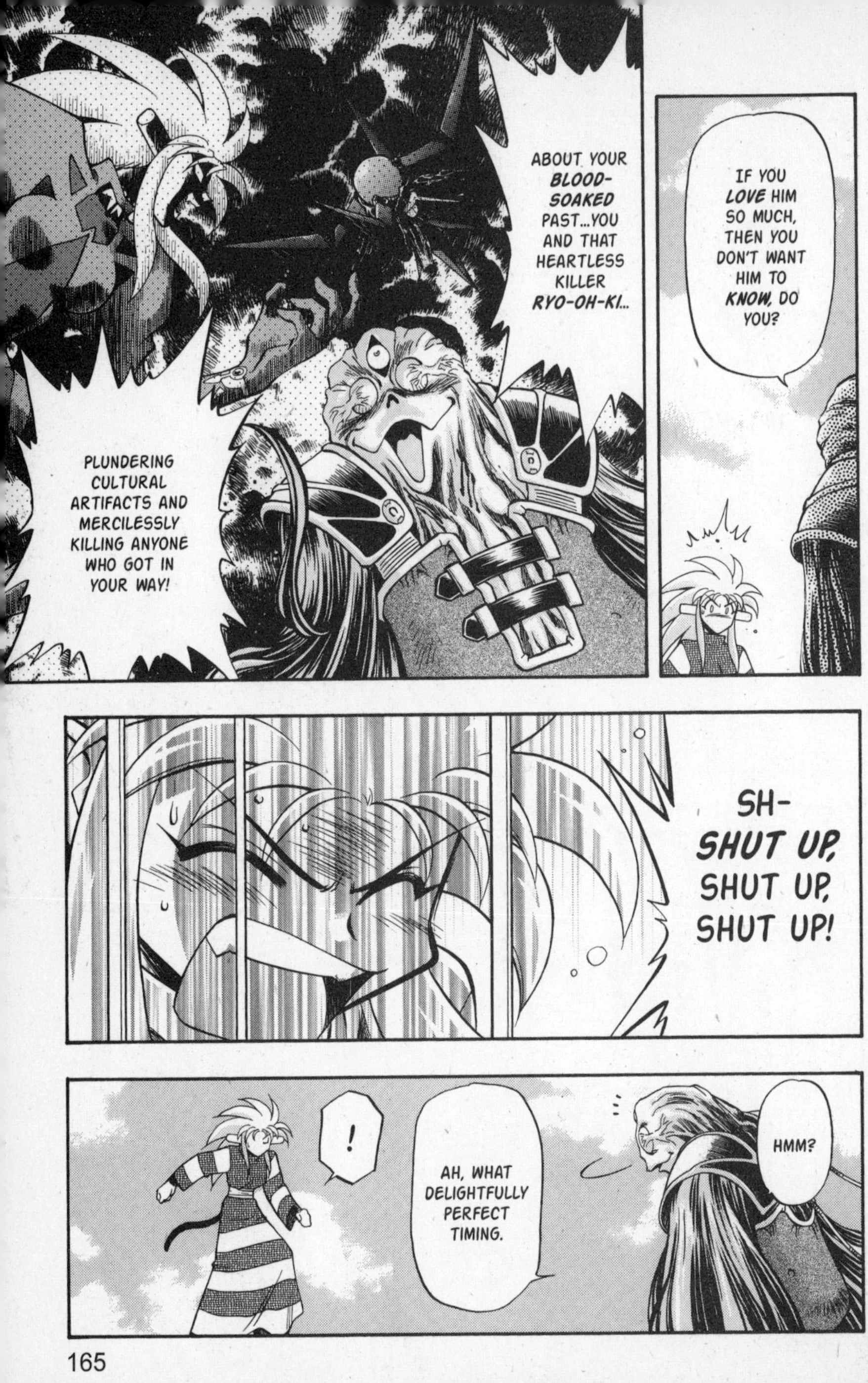
IF YOU LOVE HIM SO MUCH, THEN YOU DON'T WANT HIM TO KNOW, DO YOU?
ABOUT YOUR BLOOD-SOAKED PAST...YOU AND THAT HEARTLESS KILLER RYO-OH-KI...
PLUNDERING CULTURAL ARTIFACTS AND MERCILESSLY KILLING ANYONE WHO GOT IN YOUR WAY!
SH- SHUT UP, SHUT UP, SHUT UP!
HMM?
AH, WHAT DELIGHTFULLY PERFECT TIMING.
!

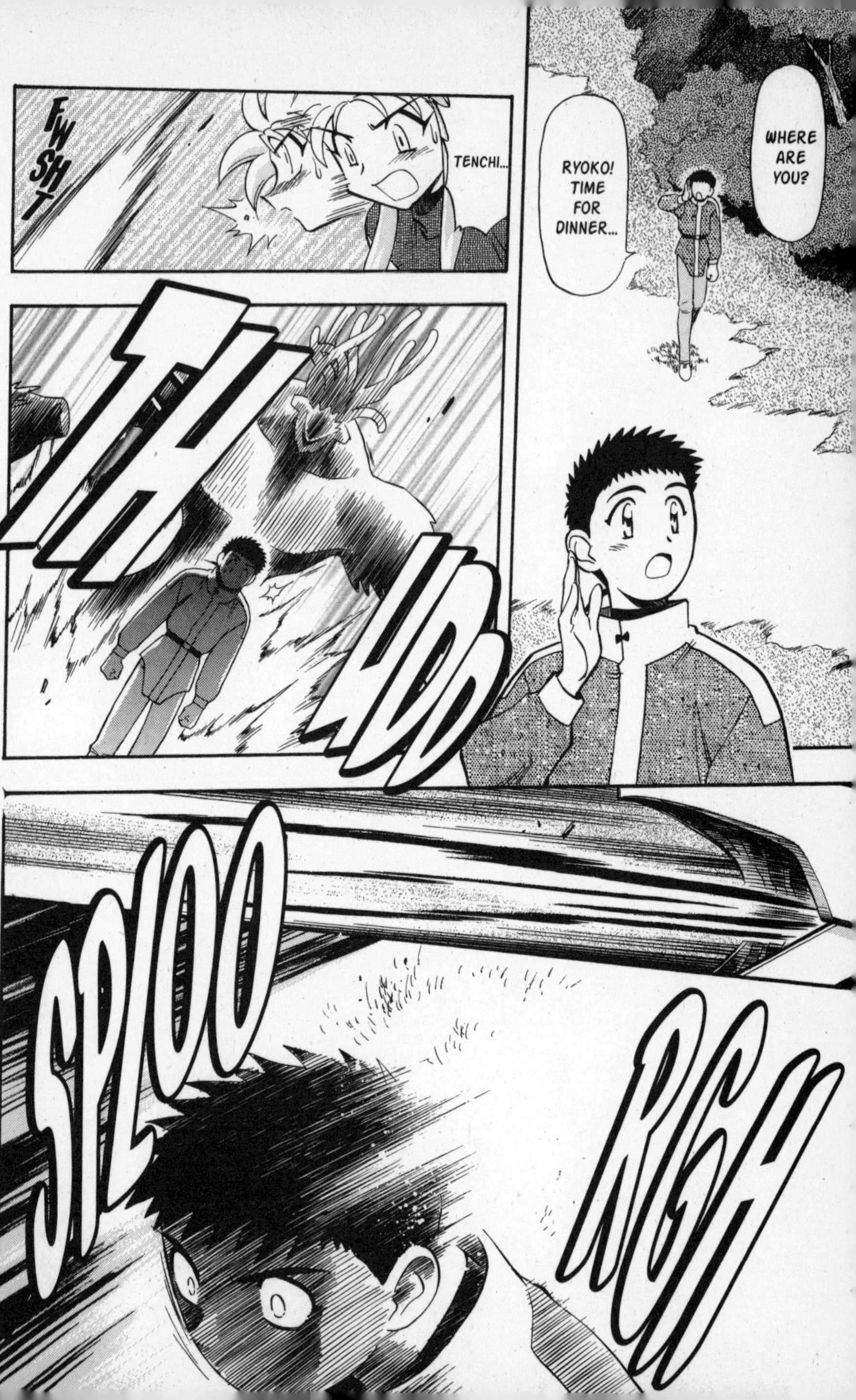
WHERE ARE YOU?
RYOKO! TIME FOR DINNER...
FWSHT
TENCHI...
THUDD
SPLOOO

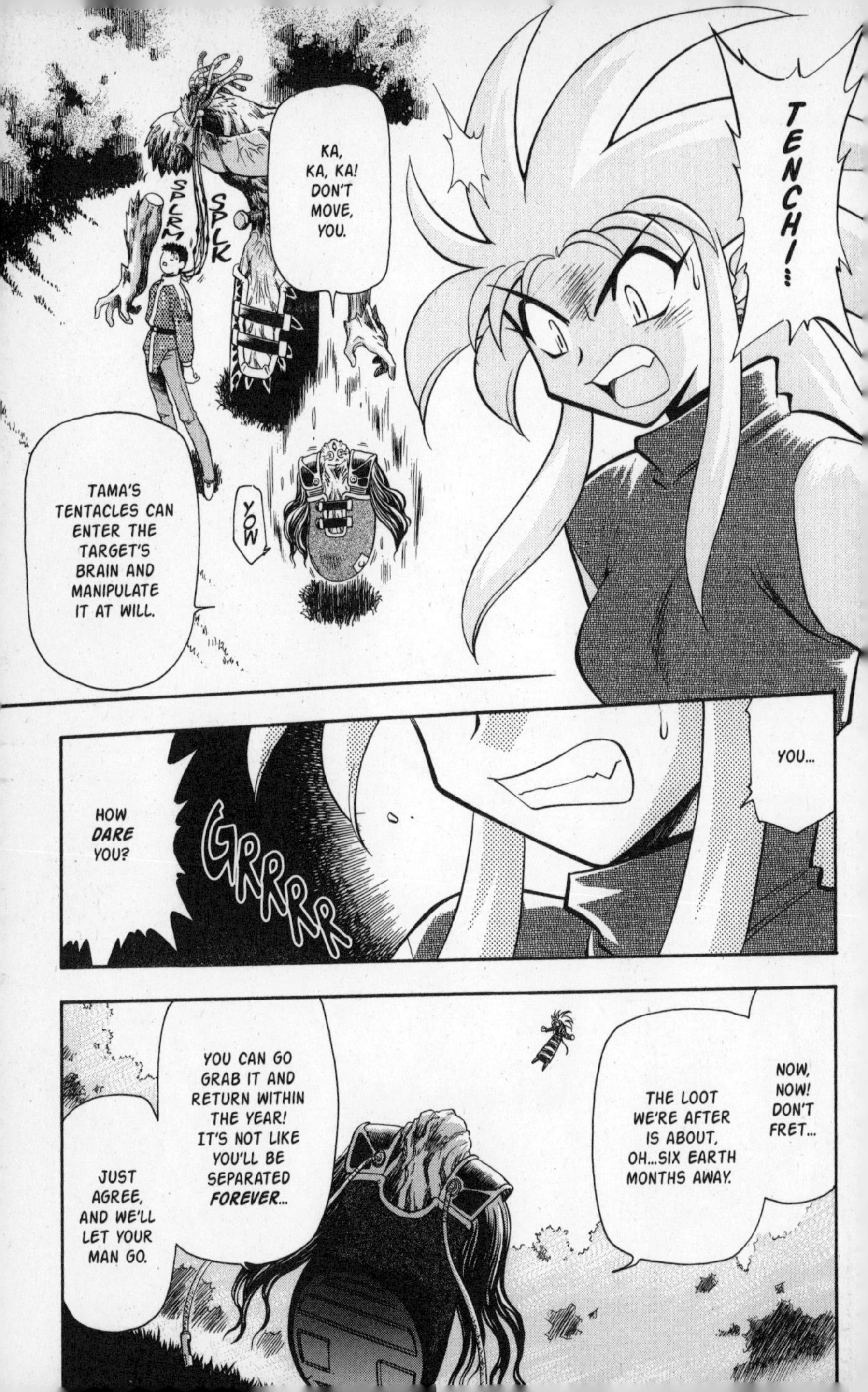
TENCHI!!
KA, KA, KA! DON'T MOVE, YOU.
SPLK
SPLRM
YOW
TAMA'S TENTACLES CAN ENTER THE TARGET'S BRAIN AND MANIPULATE IT AT WILL.
YOU...
GRRRR
HOW *DARE* YOU?
NOW, NOW! DON'T FRET...
THE LOOT WE'RE AFTER IS ABOUT, OH...SIX EARTH MONTHS AWAY.
YOU CAN GO GRAB IT AND RETURN WITHIN THE YEAR! IT'S NOT LIKE YOU'LL BE SEPARATED ***FOREVER***...
JUST AGREE, AND WE'LL LET YOUR MAN GO.

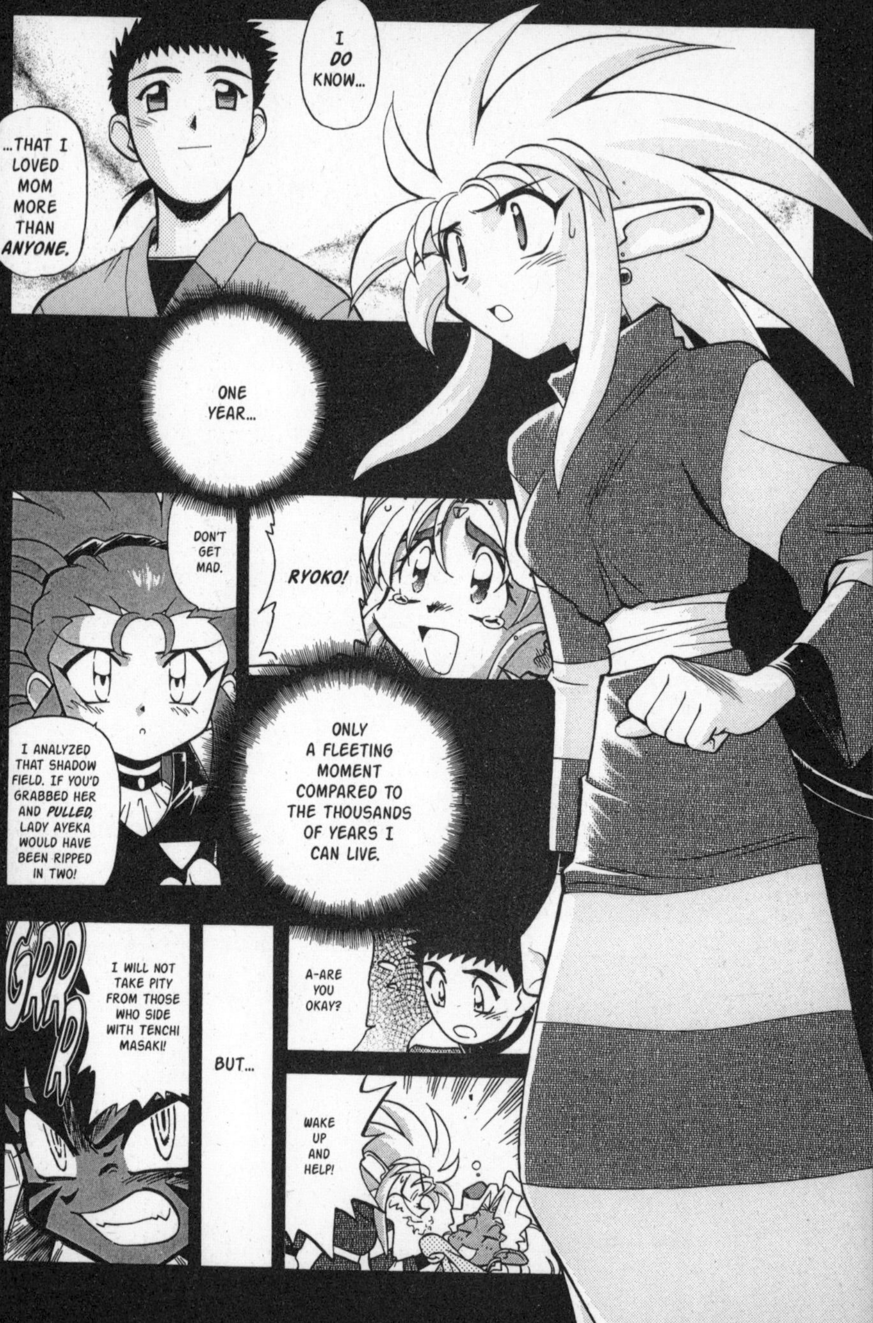

I DO KNOW...
...THAT I LOVED MOM MORE THAN ANYONE.
ONE YEAR...
RYOKO!
DON'T GET MAD.
I ANALYZED THAT SHADOW FIELD. IF YOU'D GRABBED HER AND PULLED, LADY AYEKA WOULD HAVE BEEN RIPPED IN TWO!
ONLY A FLEETING MOMENT COMPARED TO THE THOUSANDS OF YEARS I CAN LIVE.
A-ARE YOU OKAY?
WAKE UP AND HELP!
BUT...
GRRR
I WILL NOT TAKE PITY FROM THOSE WHO SIDE WITH TENCHI MASAKI!

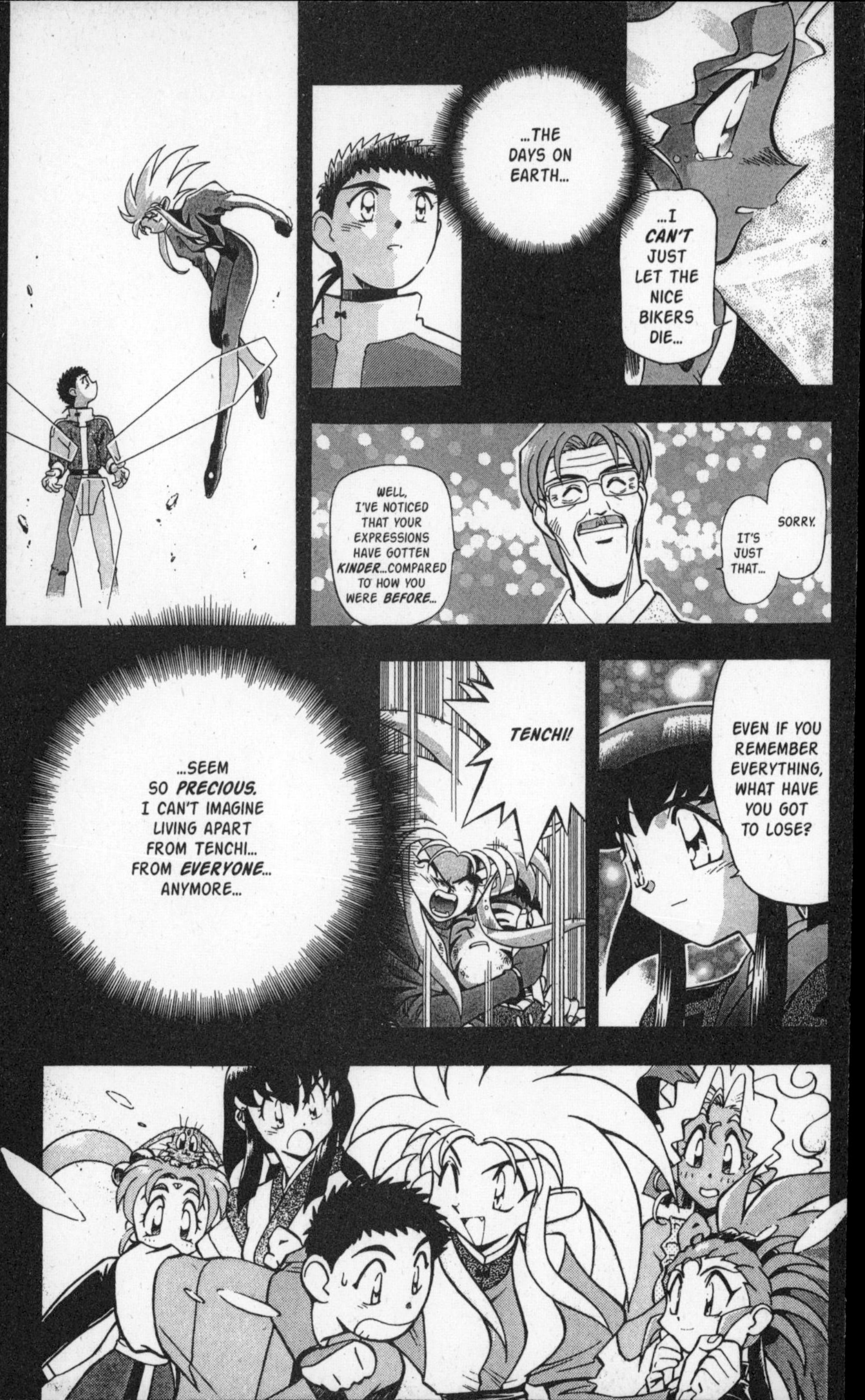
...I CAN'T JUST LET THE NICE BIKERS DIE...
...THE DAYS ON EARTH...
SORRY. IT'S JUST THAT...
WELL, I'VE NOTICED THAT YOUR EXPRESSIONS HAVE GOTTEN KINDER...COMPARED TO HOW YOU WERE BEFORE...
EVEN IF YOU REMEMBER EVERYTHING, WHAT HAVE YOU GOT TO LOSE?
TENCHI!
...SEEM SO PRECIOUS. I CAN'T IMAGINE LIVING APART FROM TENCHI... FROM EVERYONE... ANYMORE...

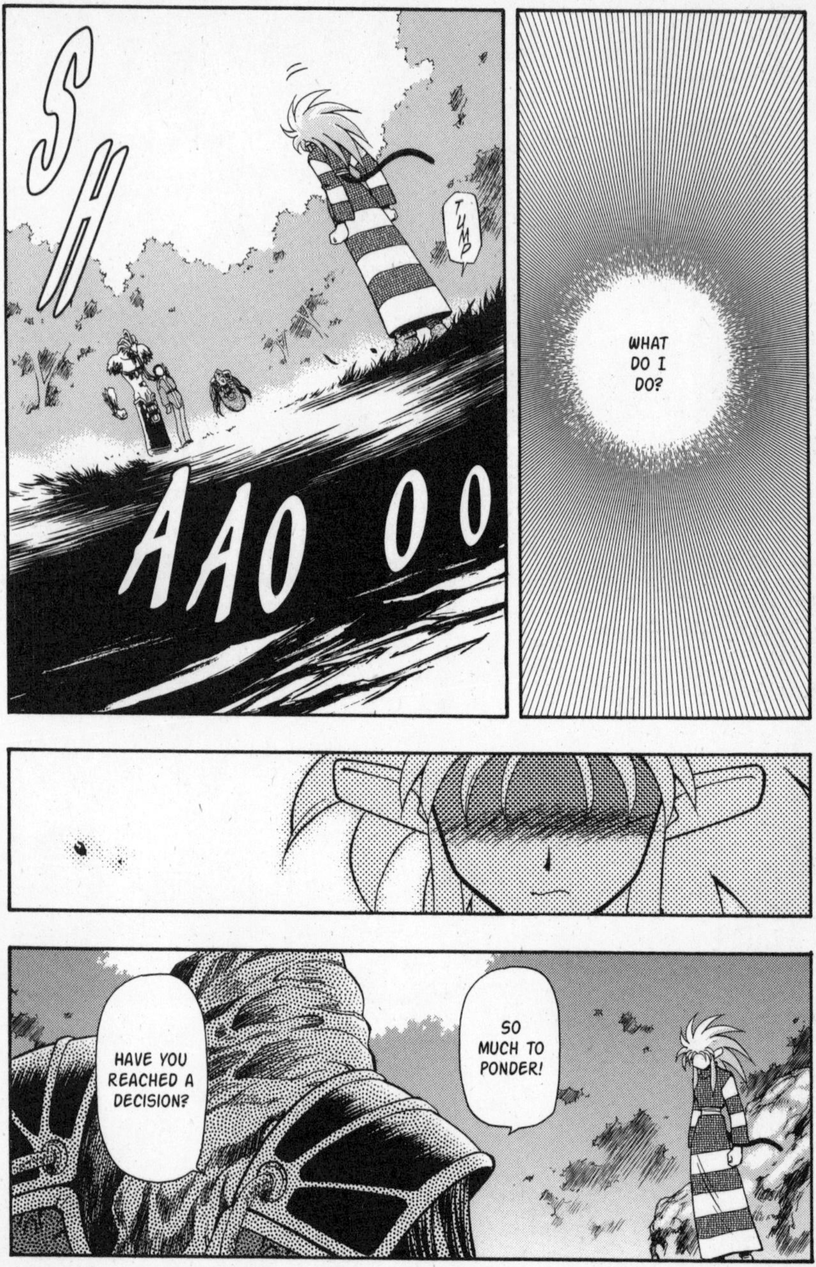
WHAT DO I DO?
TUMP
SH
AAO OO
SO MUCH TO PONDER!
HAVE YOU REACHED A DECISION?

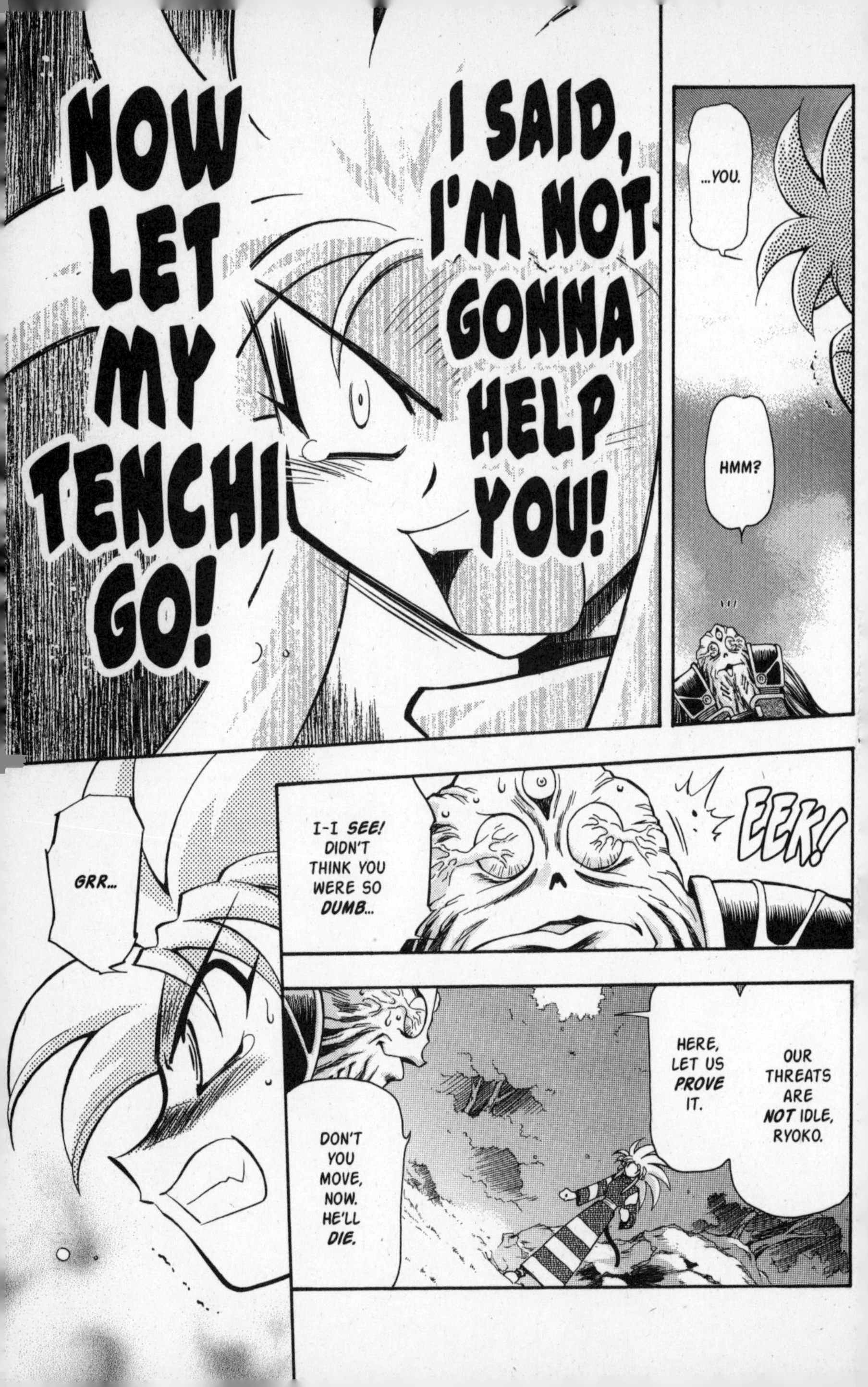

...YOU.
HMM?
I SAID, I'M NOT GONNA HELP YOU!
NOW LET MY TENCHI GO!
EEK!
I-I *SEE!* DIDN'T THINK YOU WERE SO *DUMB*...
OUR THREATS ARE *NOT* IDLE, RYOKO.
HERE, LET US *PROVE* IT.
DON'T YOU MOVE, NOW. HE'LL *DIE.*
GRR...

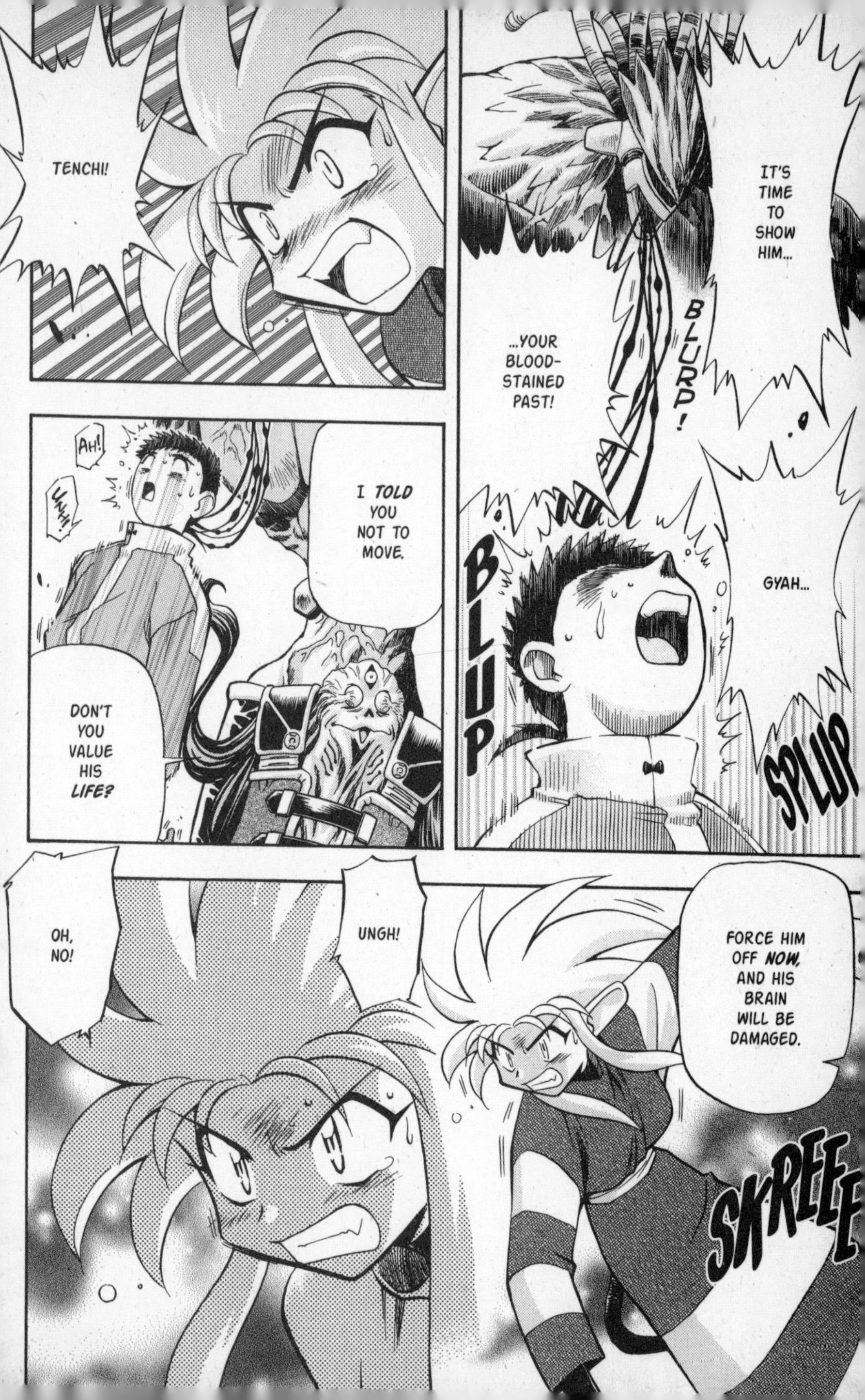
IT'S TIME TO SHOW HIM...
BLURP!
...YOUR BLOOD-STAINED PAST!
GYAH...
BLUP
SPLUP
TENCHI!
I *TOLD* YOU NOT TO MOVE.
AH!
UNH!
DON'T YOU VALUE HIS *LIFE?*
FORCE HIM OFF *NOW,* AND HIS BRAIN WILL BE DAMAGED.
UNGH!
OH, NO!
SKREEE

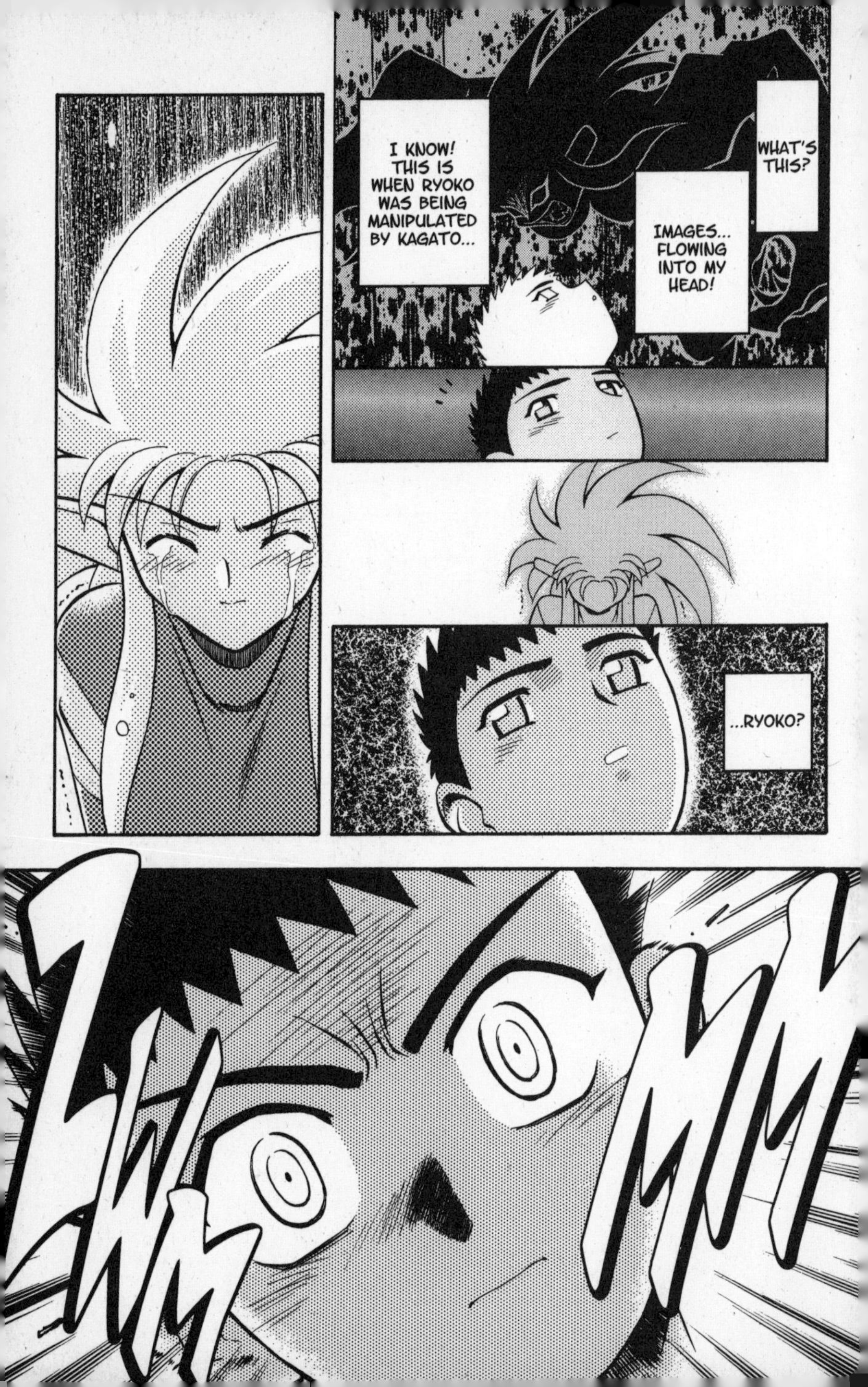
WHAT'S THIS?
IMAGES... FLOWING INTO MY HEAD!
I KNOW! THIS IS WHEN RYOKO WAS BEING MANIPULATED BY KAGATO...
...RYOKO?

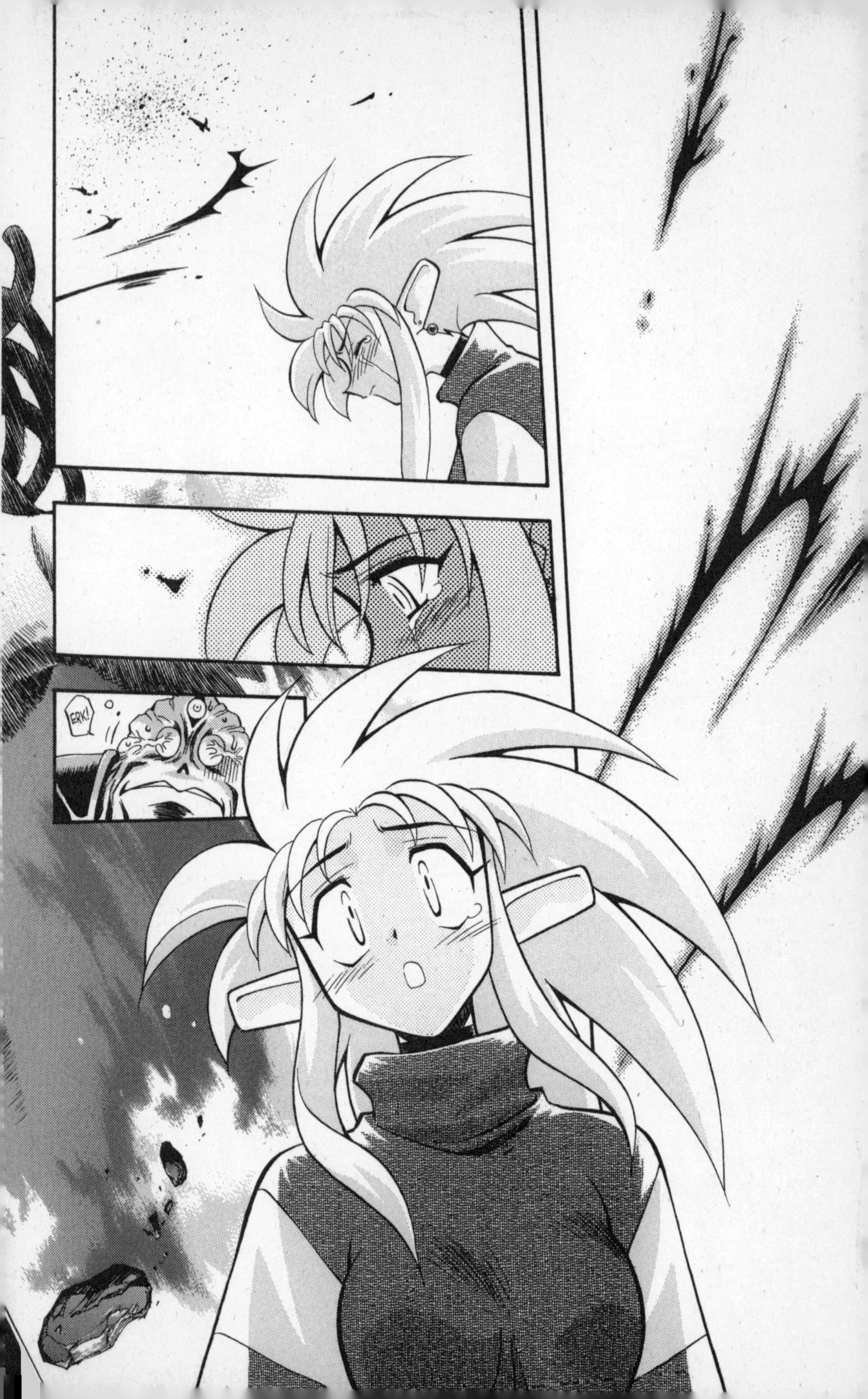
ERK!

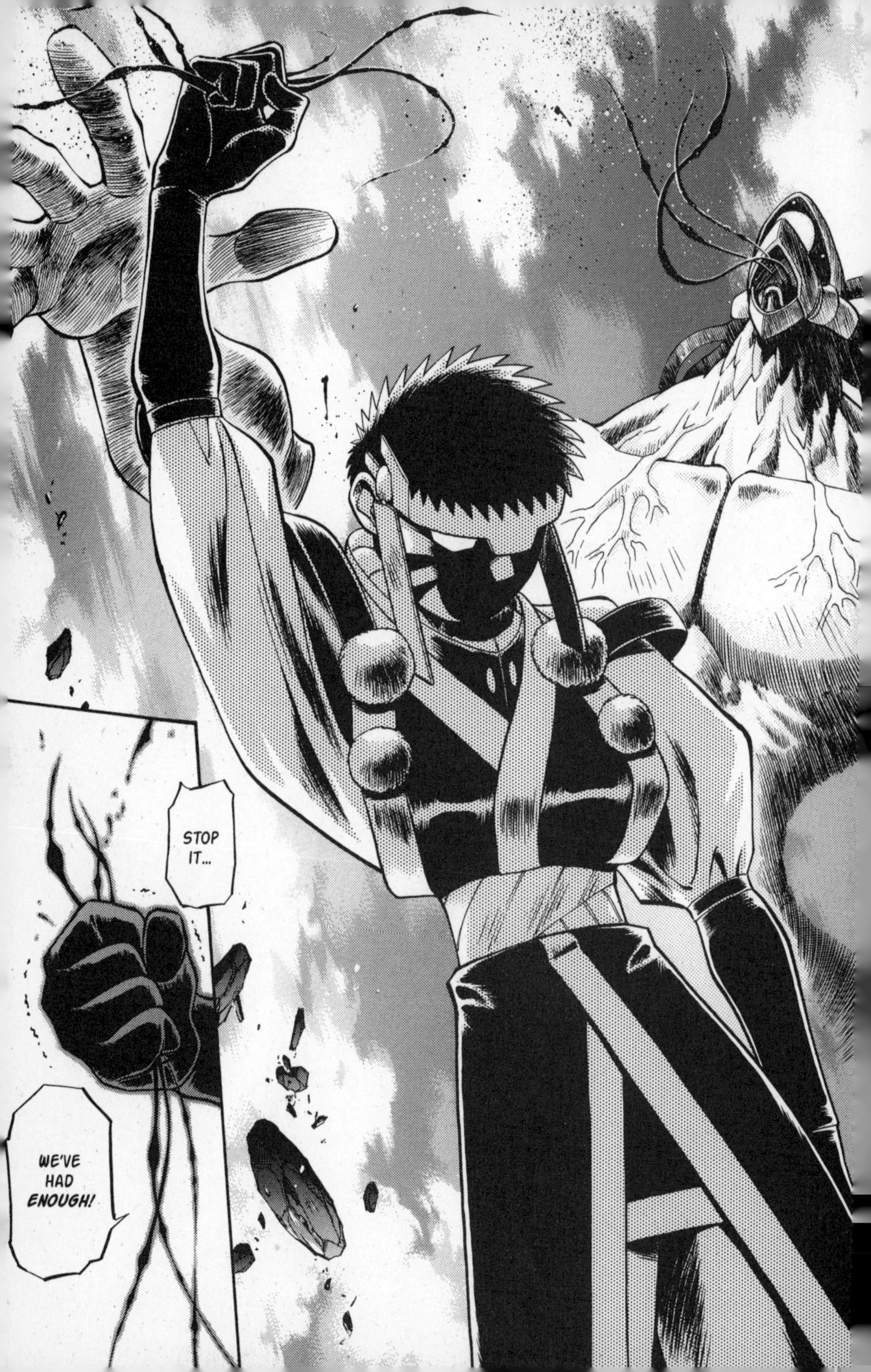
STOP IT...
WE'VE HAD ENOUGH!

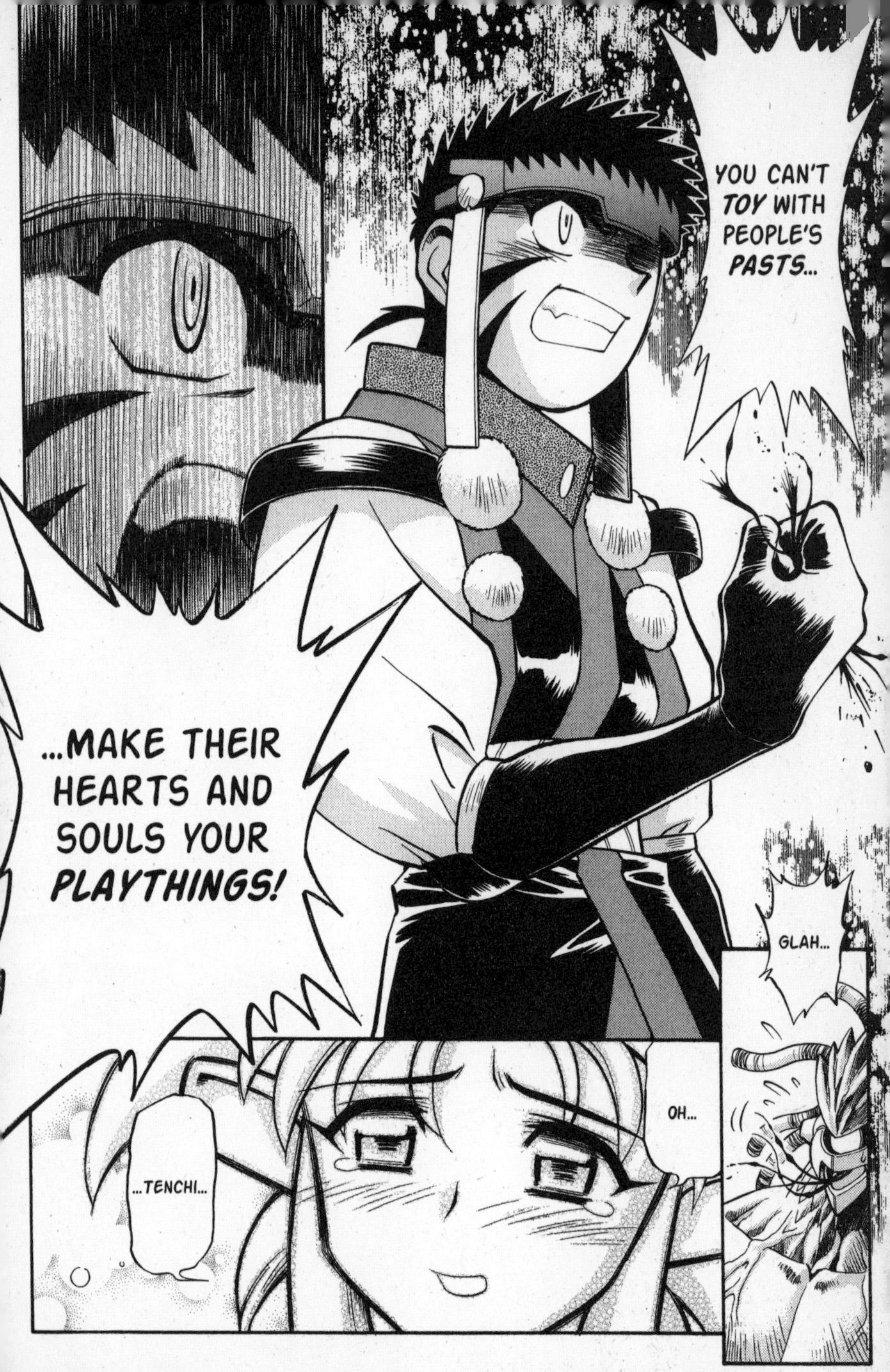
YOU CAN'T TOY WITH PEOPLE'S PASTS...
...MAKE THEIR HEARTS AND SOULS YOUR PLAYTHINGS!
GLAH...
OH...
...TENCHI...

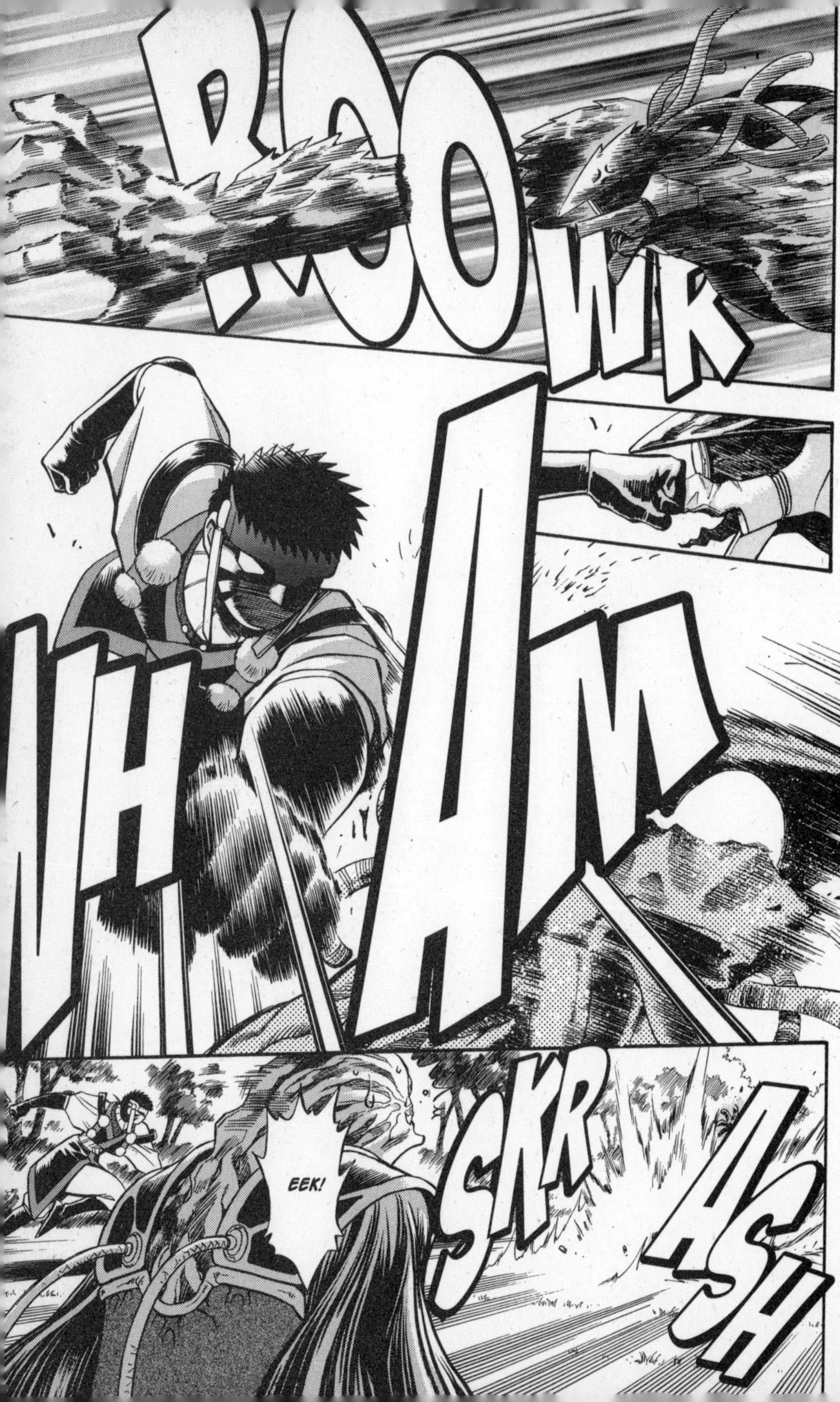
ROOWR
WHAM
EEK!
SKRASH

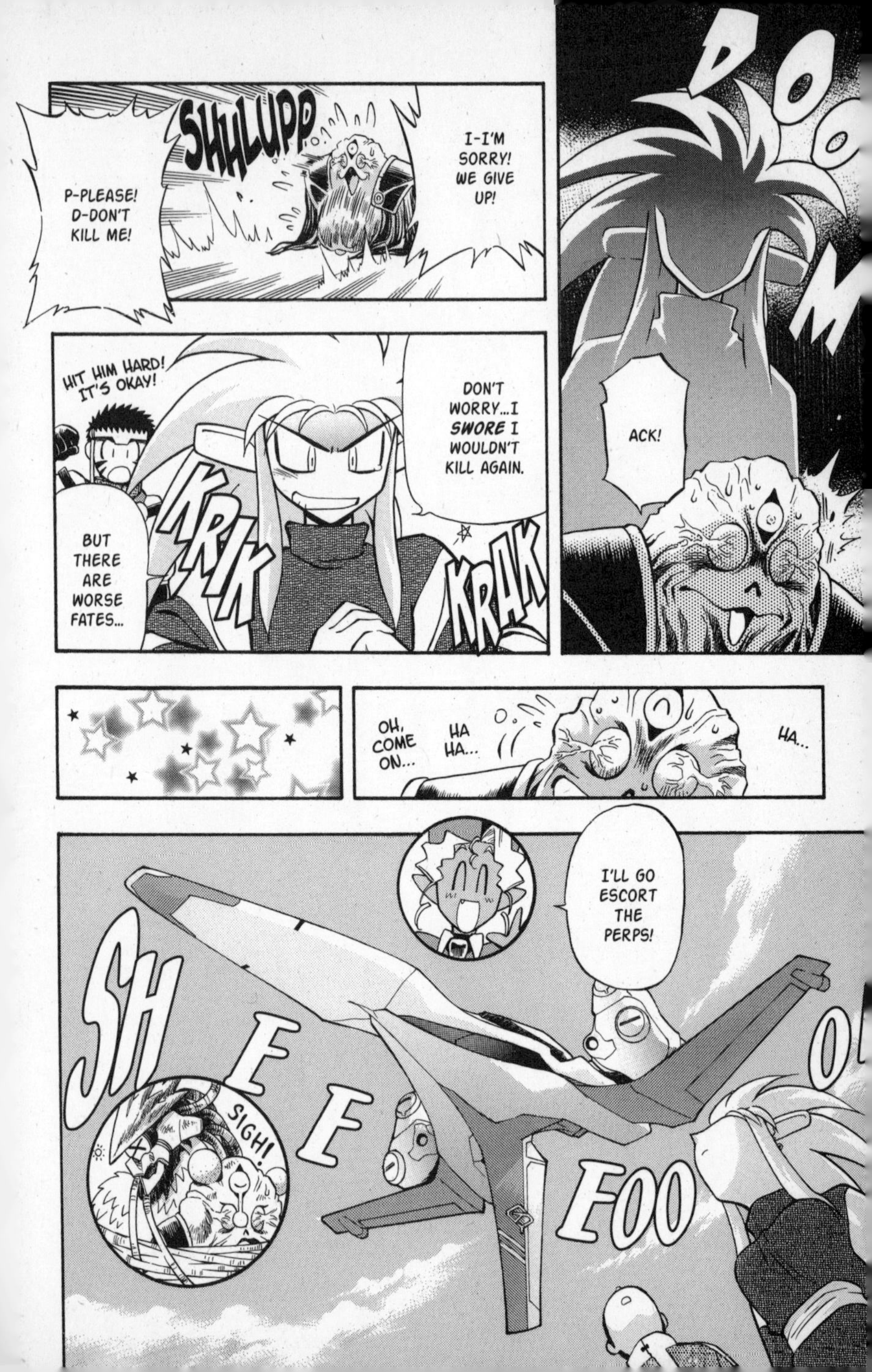
DOOOM
ACK!
SHHLUPP
I-I'M SORRY! WE GIVE UP!
P-PLEASE! D-DON'T KILL ME!
DON'T WORRY...I SWORE I WOULDN'T KILL AGAIN.
KRAK
KRIK
HIT HIM HARD! IT'S OKAY!
BUT THERE ARE WORSE FATES...
HA...
HA HA...
OH, COME ON...
I'LL GO ESCORT THE PERPS!
SHEEEEOO
SIGH!

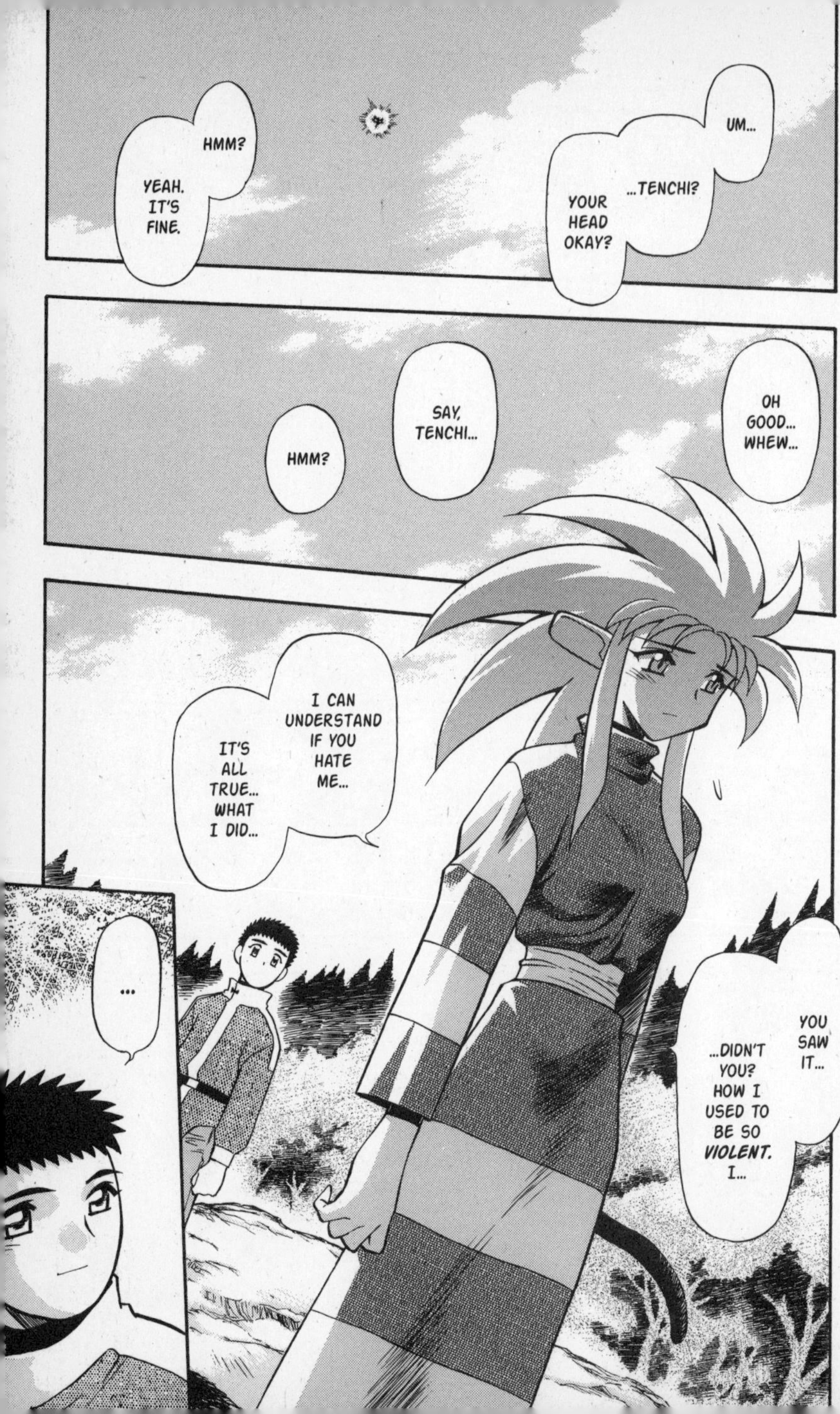

UM...
...TENCHI?
YOUR HEAD OKAY?
HMM?
YEAH. IT'S FINE.
OH GOOD... WHEW...
SAY, TENCHI...
HMM?
YOU SAW IT...
...DIDN'T YOU? HOW I USED TO BE SO *VIOLENT*. I...
I CAN UNDERSTAND IF YOU HATE ME...
IT'S ALL TRUE... WHAT I DID...
...

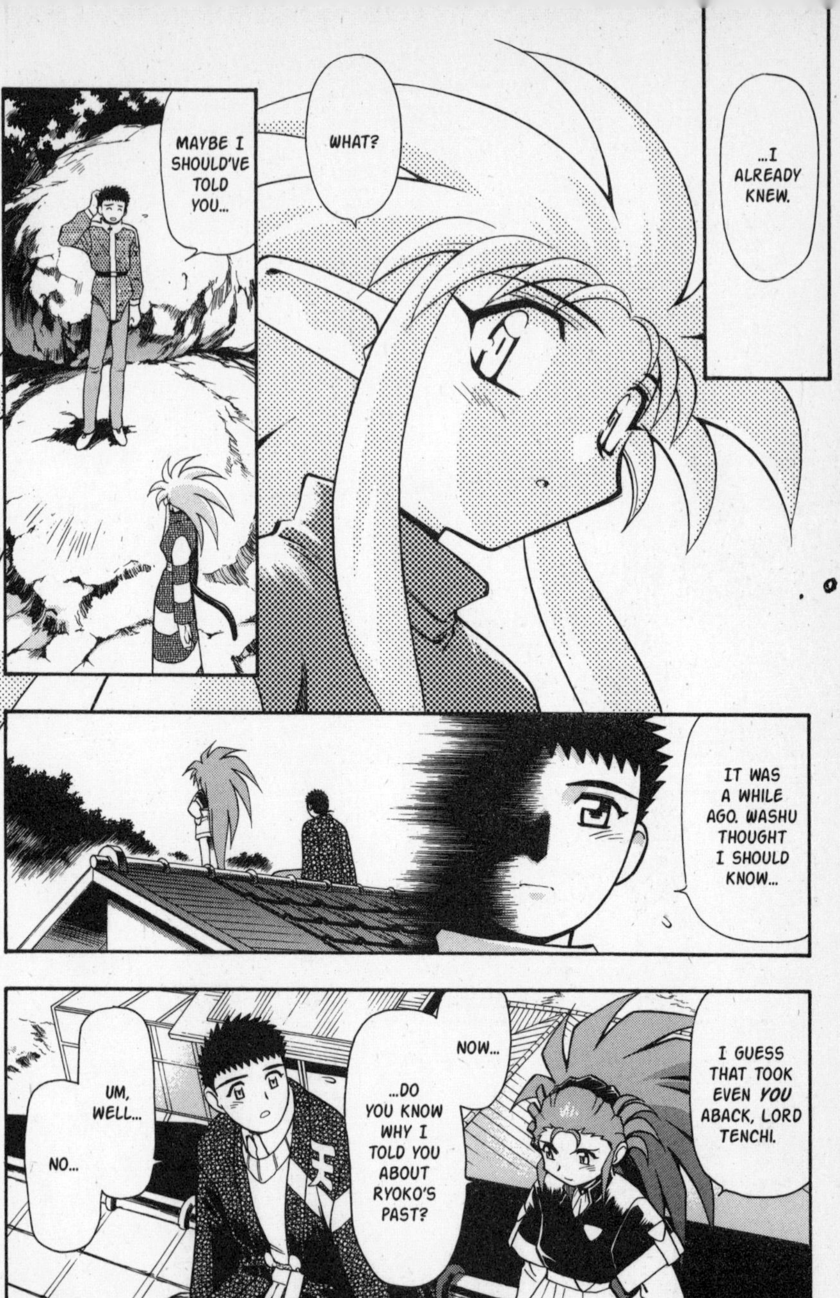
...I ALREADY KNEW.
WHAT?
MAYBE I SHOULD'VE TOLD YOU...
IT WAS A WHILE AGO. WASHU THOUGHT I SHOULD KNOW...
I GUESS THAT TOOK EVEN *YOU* ABACK, LORD TENCHI.
NOW...
...DO YOU KNOW WHY I TOLD YOU ABOUT RYOKO'S PAST?
UM, WELL...
NO...

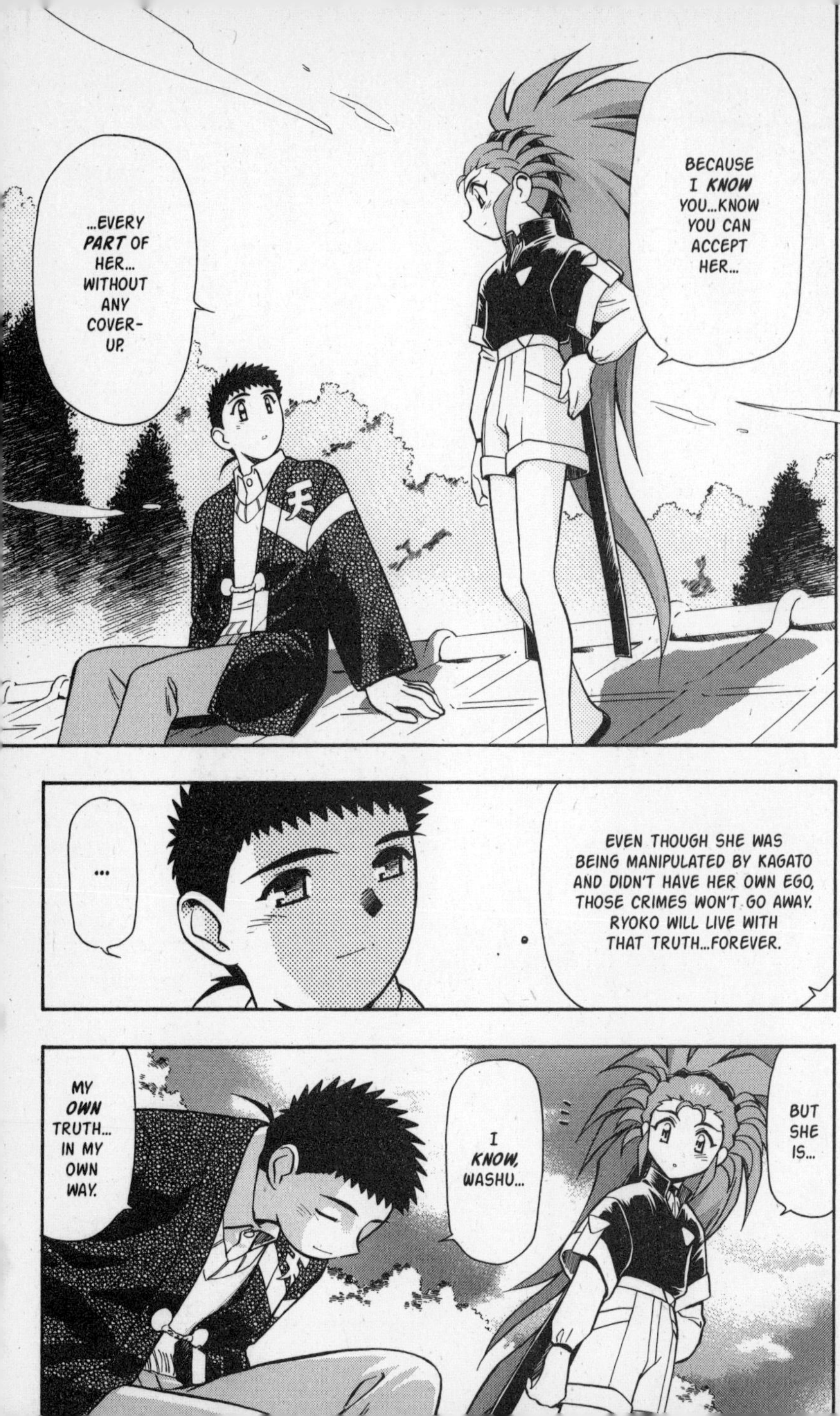
BECAUSE I *KNOW* YOU...KNOW YOU CAN ACCEPT HER...
...EVERY *PART* OF HER... WITHOUT ANY COVER-UP.
EVEN THOUGH SHE WAS BEING MANIPULATED BY KAGATO AND DIDN'T HAVE HER OWN EGO, THOSE CRIMES WON'T GO AWAY. RYOKO WILL LIVE WITH THAT TRUTH...FOREVER.
...
BUT SHE IS...
I *KNOW,* WASHU...
MY *OWN* TRUTH... IN MY OWN WAY.

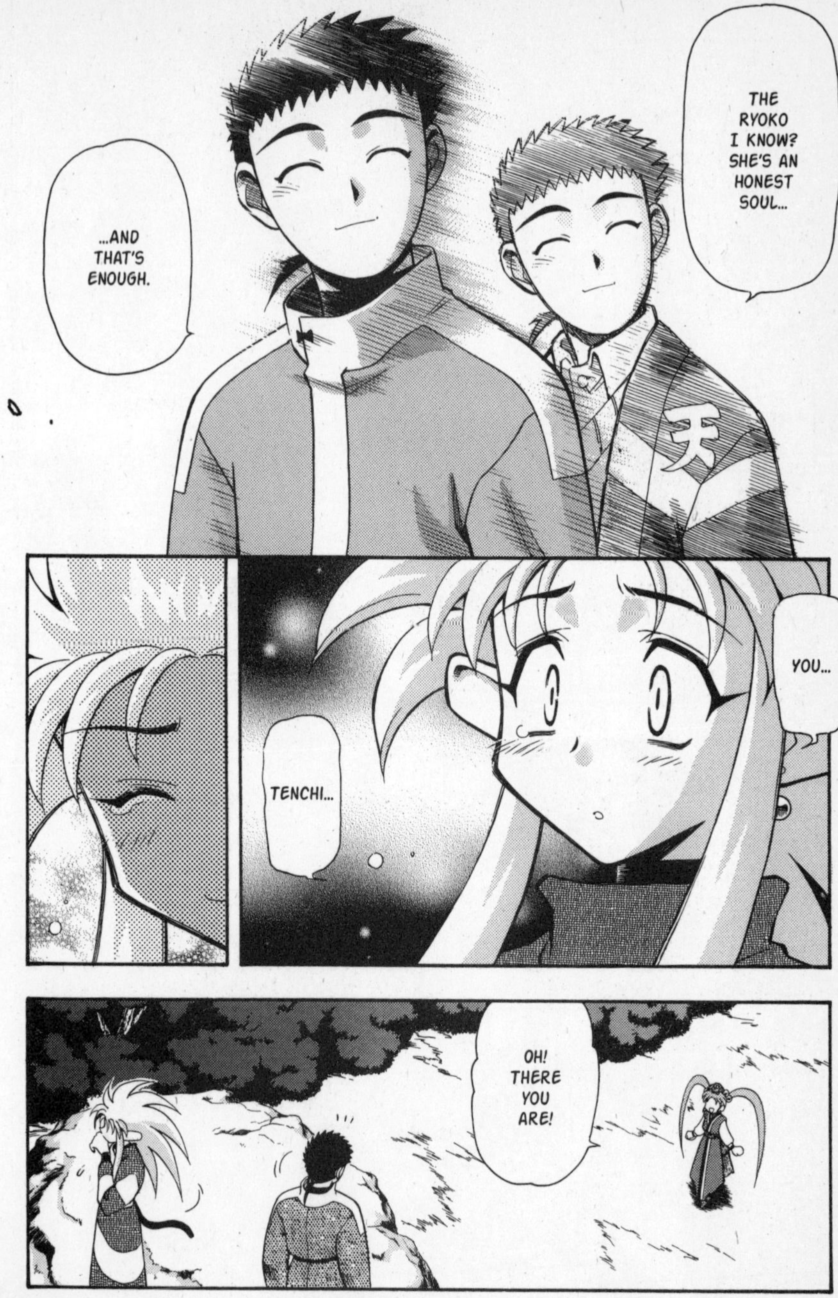
THE RYOKO I KNOW? SHE'S AN HONEST SOUL...
...AND THAT'S ENOUGH.
YOU...
TENCHI...
OH! THERE YOU ARE!

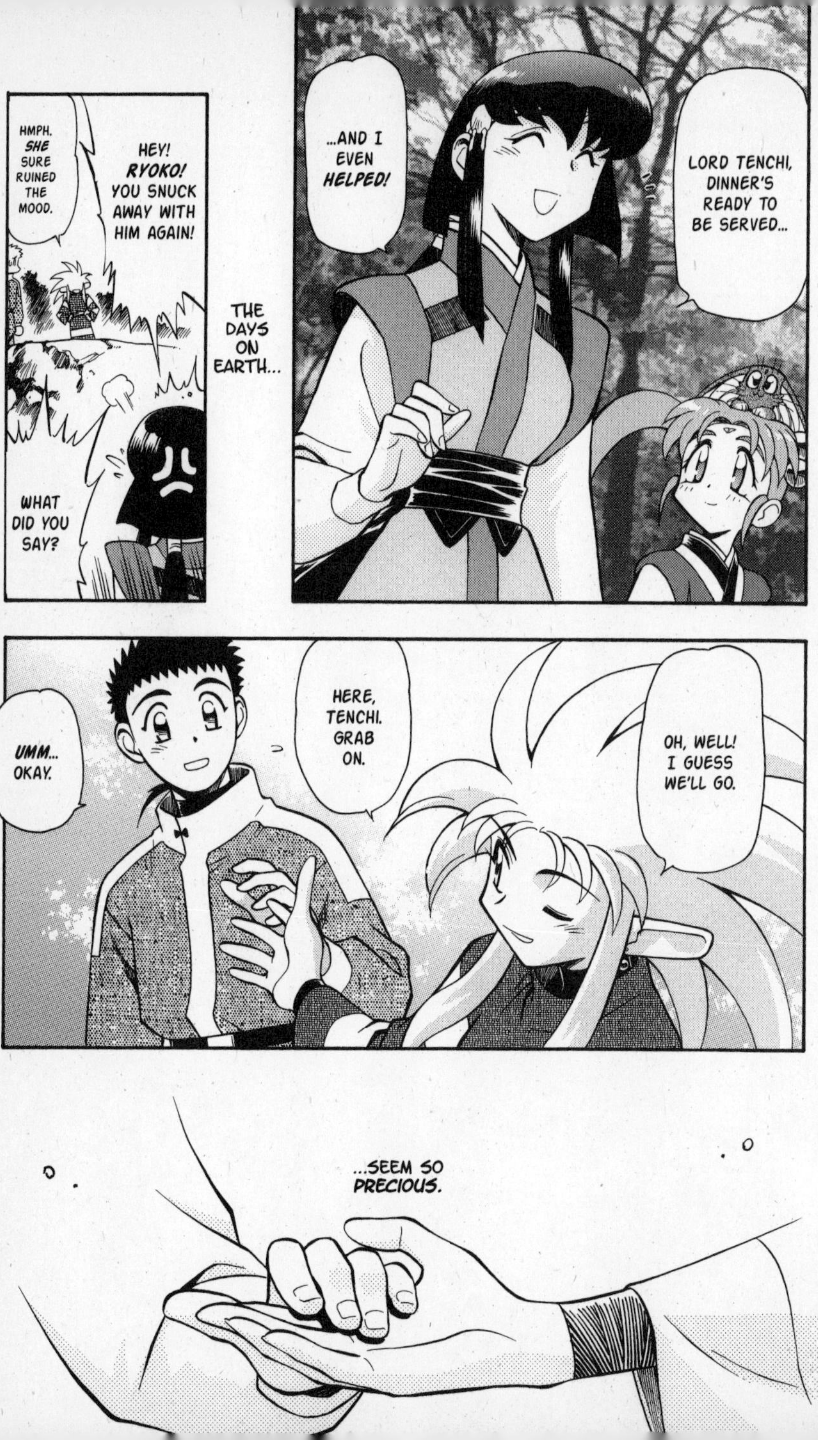
LORD TENCHI, DINNER'S READY TO BE SERVED...
...AND I EVEN HELPED!
THE DAYS ON EARTH...
HEY! RYOKO! YOU SNUCK AWAY WITH HIM AGAIN!
HMPH. SHE SURE RUINED THE MOOD.
WHAT DID YOU SAY?
OH, WELL! I GUESS WE'LL GO.
HERE, TENCHI. GRAB ON.
UMM... OKAY.
...SEEM SO PRECIOUS.

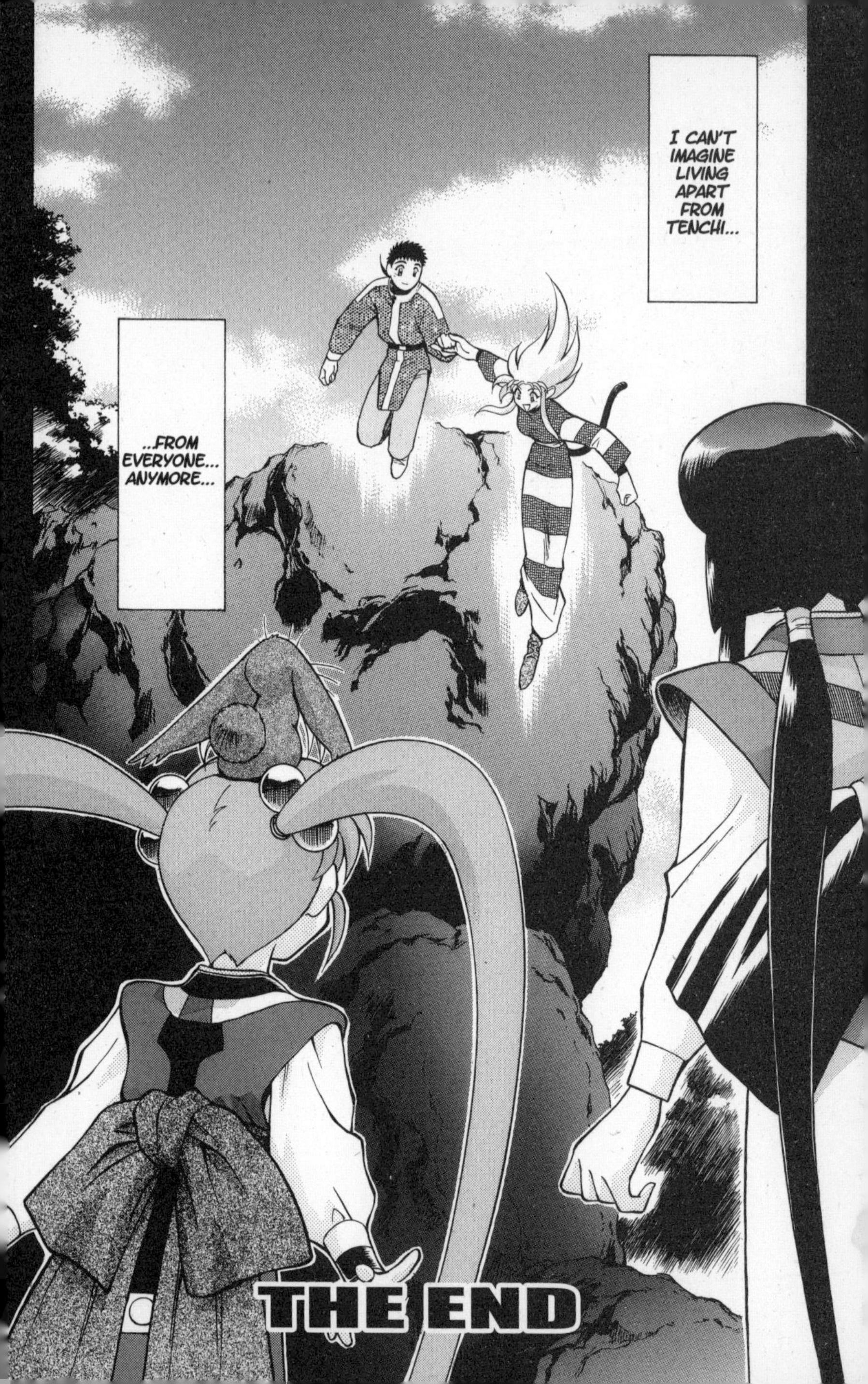
I CAN'T IMAGINE LIVING APART FROM TENCHI...
...FROM EVERYONE... ANYMORE...
THE END

No Need for Tenchi!: The (Sort Of) Ending

THANK YOU SO MUCH, EVERYONE! FORTUNATELY, I WAS ABLE TO HAVE A LOT OF FUN DRAWING TENCHI FOR SIX AND A HALF YEARS.

RIGHT AFTER IT STARTED, THERE WERE HARSH CRITICISMS (WELL, MAYBE JUSTIFIED) LIKE, "IS HITOSHI OKUDA REALLY FIT FOR IT?" "NO, THERE MUST BE A MORE SUITABLE ARTIST." BUT NOW THAT I LOOK BACK, SUCH WORDS MAY HAVE MADE ME TRY HARDER...THERE WERE MANY CRISES, BUT I WAS ABLE TO HOLD OUT AND STRUGGLE MY WAY THROUGH THEM.

WHAT ENCOURAGED ME MOST OF ALL WERE EVERYONE'S LETTERS! YOU CAN'T IMAGINE HOW THEY'VE UPLIFTED ME...AND I'D LIKE TO TAKE THIS OPPORTUNITY TO SHOW MY GRATITUDE. THANK YOU SO MUCH!

WE'RE TAKING A BREAK FOR THE TIME BEING AND CALLING THIS THE FINAL VOLUME, BUT ***NO NEED FOR TENCHI!*** ISN'T OVER YET! WE'VE TURNED OVER A NEW LEAF, SWITCHED TO THE MONTHLY MAGAZINE ***DRAGON JR.***, AND ARE CURRENTLY STILL RUNNING! (YOU CAN READ THE NEW ADVENTURES OF TENCHI AND COMPANY IN ***THE ALL-NEW TENCHI MUYO!***, NOW AVAILABLE FROM VIZ. -ED.)

SO I WON'T SAY GOODBYE. SEE YOU AGAIN!

FALL 2000 奥田ひとし HITOSHI OKUDA

ERASE!
ERASE!
HEY, WHAT ARE YOU DOING?

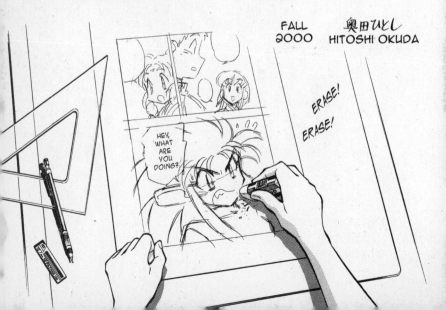

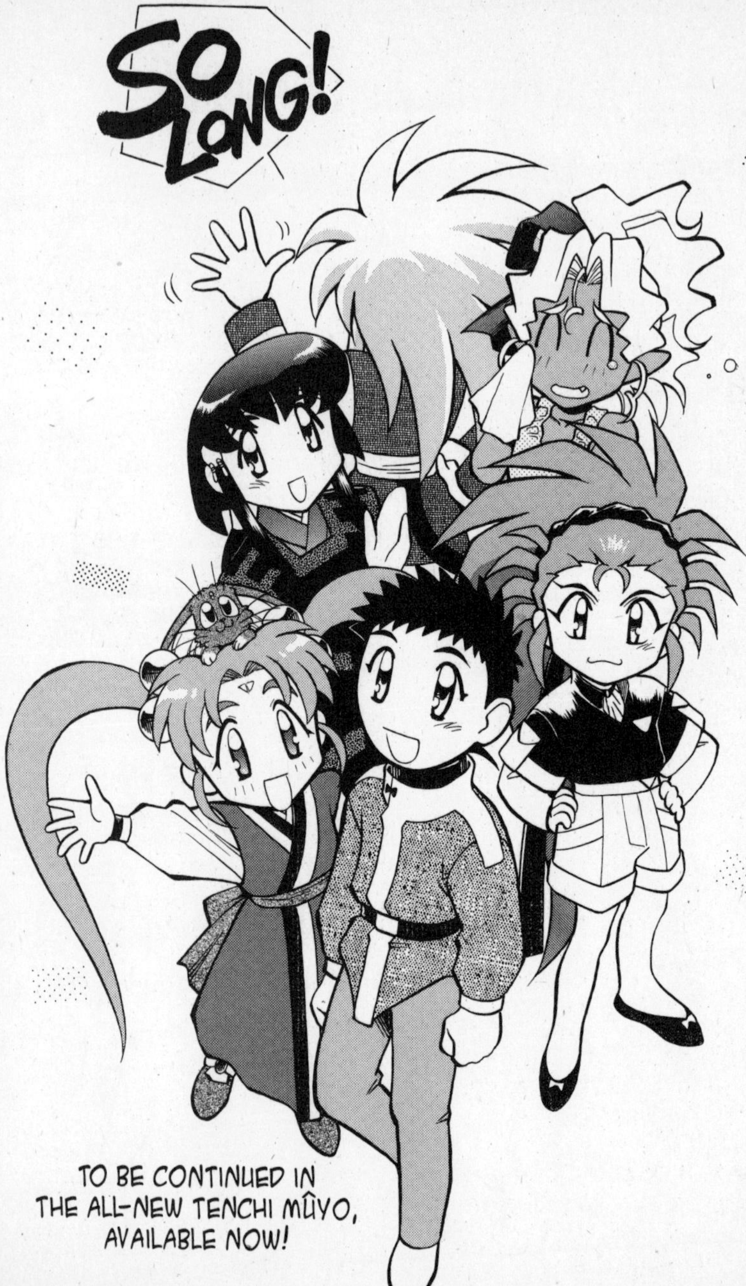
SO LONG!

TO BE CONTINUED IN
THE ALL-NEW TENCHI MÛYO,
AVAILABLE NOW!

INUYASHA

Read the action from the start with the original manga series

Full color adaptation of the popular TV series

Art book with cel art, paintings, character profiles and more

TV SERIES & MOVIES ON DVD!

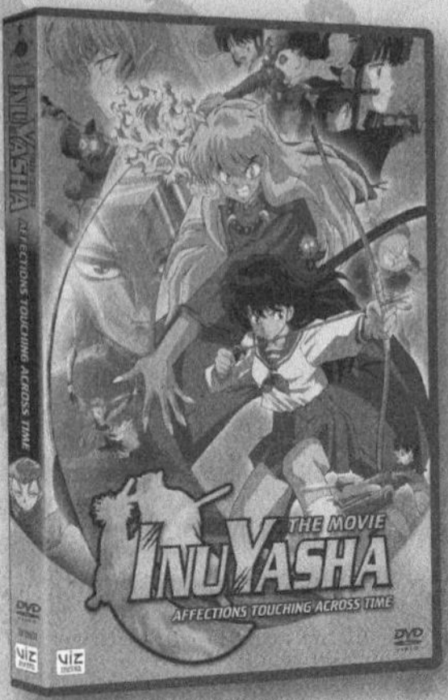
THE MOVIE
INUYASHA
AFFECTIONS TOUCHING ACROSS TIME

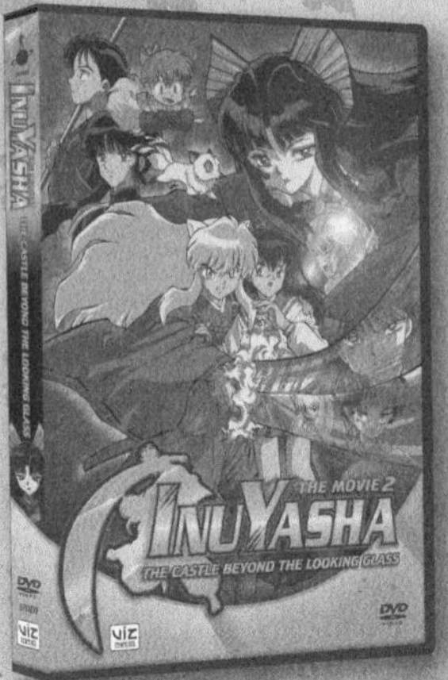
THE MOVIE 2
INUYASHA
THE CASTLE BEYOND THE LOOKING GLASS

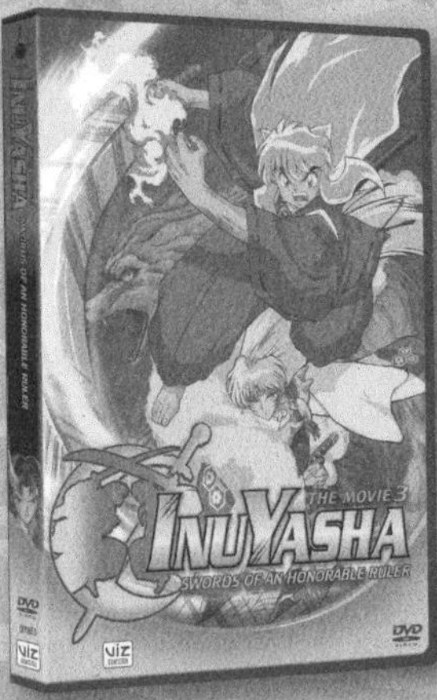
THE MOVIE 3
INUYASHA
SWORDS OF AN HONORABLE RULER

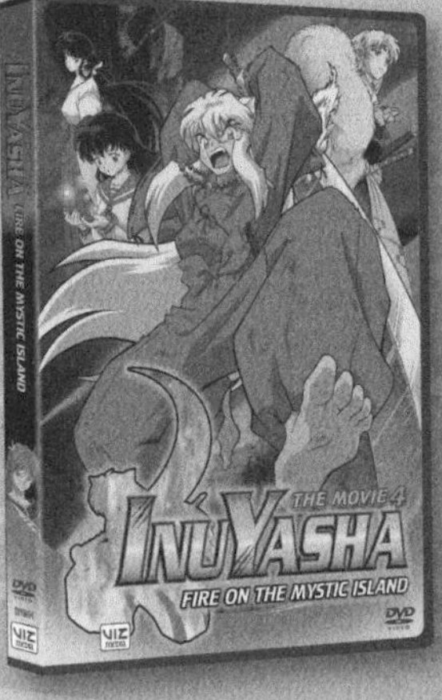
THE MOVIE 4
INUYASHA
FIRE ON THE MYSTIC ISLAND

See more of the action in *Inuyasha* full-length movies

viz media

www.viz.com
inuyasha.viz.com

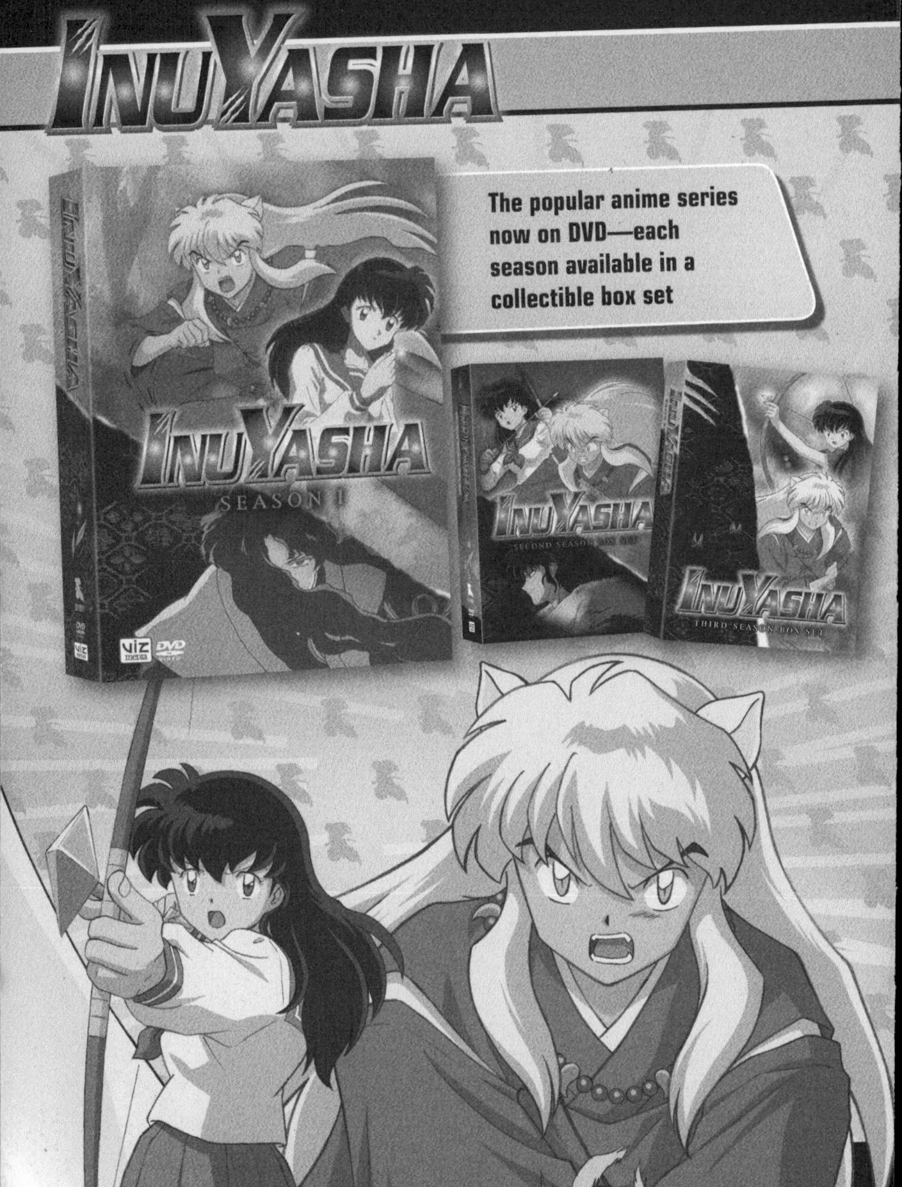
INUYASHA
The popular anime series now on DVD—each season available in a collectible box set
INUYASHA
SEASON 1
viz media
DVD
INUYASHA
SECOND SEASON BOX SET
INUYASHA
THIRD SEASON BOX SET